3

CONSUMERS
IN
TROUBLE

DAVID CAPLOVITZ

*Graduate School and University Center
of The City University of New York*

With the assistance of
Eric Single

CONSUMERS
IN
TROUBLE
A Study of Debtors in Default

THE FREE PRESS
A Division of Macmillan Publishing Co., Inc.
NEW YORK

Collier Macmillan Publishers
LONDON

The Free Press
A Division of Macmillan Publishing Co., Inc.
866 Third Avenue, New York, N.Y. 10022

Collier–Macmillan Canada Ltd.

Library of Congress Catalog Card Number: 73–14747

Printed in the United States of America

printing number
1   2   3   4   5   6   7   8   9   10

Library of Congress Cataloging in Publication Data

Caplovitz, David.
    Consumers in trouble.

    (Banking and finance)
    Includes bibliographical references.
    1. Consumer credit—United States. 2. Debtor
and creditor—United States. I. Title.
HG3755.C35   332.7'43   73-14747
ISBN 0-02-905260-2

To Paulann

CONTENTS

FOREWORD

In the *Rubaiyat* of Omar Khayyam we are advised to "take the cash and let the credit go." Fortunately, or unfortunately (depending upon your point of view), the American consumer has chosen to ignore that advice. Americans have gone into debt in record numbers to the extent that the "buy now, pay later" philosophy has become a permanent addition to the Americay way of life.

One out of every two families has some form of consumer installment debt. The heaviest users of consumer credit are families with children, heads of the household under 45-years old, and annual incomes between $10,000 and $15,000. Two out of every three families with these characteristics are in debt. These are the people often referred to as "middle America" by the press and other social commentators.

For those who have installment debt, the average debt comes to over $4,000. The total amount of debt owed on all forms of consumer debt including noninstallment came to $172 billion in August of 1973.

The growth in consumer credit can also be seen in another way. In 1949, consumers used 8 percent of their take-home income to meet payments on their installment debt. By 1973, the percentage of take-home income used to repay installment debt has more than doubled to 17 percent. Of course, these figures are nationwide averages. Many families use 30 percent, 40 percent or more of their income to repay consumer debt.

Most Americans in debt take consumer credit for granted—as long as they are able to meet their monthly payments. But what happens to those who, for one reason or another, cannot pay? *Consumers in Trouble* answers this question in compelling detail. It is a victim's view of our consumer credit system. It provides convincing evidence that debtors in default do not receive justice through our legal system and, in fact, are often exploited by that system.

The rights and remedies available to creditors on consumer credit transactions are derived from the law governing commercial transaction. Commercial law, however, assumes an equal bargaining position for both parties to the contract. This model in no way describes the reality of consumer credit transactions. The consumer borrower does not enter the transaction on equal terms with the creditor; nor is the consumer permitted to bargain over the terms of the contract or loan agreement, even if he could understand the legalistic language written in fine print. The terms have already been carefully prepared and standardized by the creditor's attorney and are not subject to negotiation. The borrower is faced with a take-it-or-leave-it proposition. If he wants the credit, he must agree to the terms.

Given the unequal bargaining power between borrowers and creditors, it is little wonder that the typical consumer credit contract is heavily weighted on the side of the lender. The advantage given to the creditor is most evident when the borrower defaults. The creditor is then free to pursue a variety of questionable remedies to enforce his contractual rights. He can demand payment for the entire amount due if the borrower is one day late in making a payment, he can repossess the collateral without a court order and sue for a deficiency judgment to recover any remaining indebtedness, in some states he can obtain a confession of judgment without even notifying the debtor, he can attach the debtor's wages, and in some states he can do this without a court order. In other cases in which the original creditor has sold an installment contract to a bank or other financial institution, the borrower is legally required to continue his payments to the holder of the contract even though he may have a valid defense or claim against the merchant who sold him the goods on credit.

Critics of the consumer credit system have charged that the courts frequently operate as a collection agent for the creditor and that the consumer does not really receive a fair hearing. Professor Caplovitz has provided us with the empirical evidence to support this charge.

Consumers in Trouble seeks to answer two basic questions: (1) why do debtors default on their obligations, and (2) what happens to them after they default. The answers to these questions were obtained from over 1320 interviews with debtors in default in four cities.

Contrary to the conventional wisdom espoused by some spokesmen for the credit industry, the typical debtor in default is not a recalcitrant deadbeat determined to ignore his legitimate obligations. Professor Caplovitz's interviews show that only 16 debtors out of 1,320, or slightly more than one percent of all debtors in default, fit the credit industry stereotype of the classic deadbeat.

While few consumers are deliberately fraudulent or dishonest, the same cannot be said for the credit industry. The data assembled by Professor Caplovitz show that in about 19 percent of the cases examined, fraud or deception by the creditor was cited as a reason for the debtor's default. In another 4 percent of the cases studied, the default was attributed to a billing error on the part of the creditor.

In another 25 percent of the cases, the debtor defaulted because he was overextended. While borrowers have some responsibility to live within their means, the creditor is at least partially responsible for extending credit to borrowers who are already overburdened with debt. In some cases, the creditor may be unaware of the borrower's existing debt through errors in the credit reporting system. Other creditors, however, may be tempted to extend credit to overburdened borrowers in the expectation of recovering through the use of harsh collection practices or unfair contractual remedies.

In a majority of the cases studied, the default was beyond the control of either the creditor or the debtor. Either the borrower lost his job, incurred unexpected medical bills, or experienced some other emergency which impaired his ability to repay his debt. A suit by the creditor generally adds to the borrower's misfortune at a time when he can least afford it. A successful judgment can compel the borrower to repay his entire debt at once plus pay excessive attorney's fees and court costs. In addition, a record of the judgment goes on his credit record and can impede his ability to obtain credit in the future. Instead of spreading the cost of an unforeseen emergency to all participants, as is done by insurance, our consumer credit system centers most of the cost on the victim.

What happens to debtors when they default? Through tables and direct quotations from interviews with debtors, Professor Caplovitz traces the collection process in depressing detail. Almost 60 percent of the debtors surveyed were subjected to one or more varieties of abusive collection practices. These included calling the debtor's employer and threatening garnishment, writing insulting letters, using abusive language, and threatening to notify friends and relatives.

In 25 percent of the cases, the creditor repossessed the collateral often without notice to the borrower or approval from a court. When the creditor did apply to the courts for a judgment, the debtor was not always notified. In New York, for example, where the practice of "sewer service" is prevalent, almost half of all debtors in default claimed they received no formal notification from the court about the creditor's complaint. Notification is essential, however, for unless the borrower answers the charges, a judgment is automatically rendered in favor of the creditor.

Another device available to creditors is the wage garnishment. Although the Federal Truth in Lending Act prohibits wage garnishment in excess of 25 percent of a debtor's take-home pay, this remedy is still a potent weapon in the hands of the creditor. One reason is that many employers have a policy of dismissing employees who incur repeated wage garnishments. Professor Caplovitz shows that those creditors who are most likely to engage in fraudulent or deceptive practices, that is door-to-door sellers or ghetto merchants, make the greatest use of wage garnishments. Compared to other debtors in default, blacks and poor people stand a much greater chance of being garnished—a finding which reinforces the argument that creditors use their remedies to discriminate against the weak and disadvantaged.

Wage garnishments are an effective device for coercing a debtor to resume payment, even when the debtor feels the debt is unjust due to fraud or deception on the part of the creditor. More than one-half of the debtors in this category resumed payments following a wage garnishment, even though they felt their debt was not legitimate.

Consumers in Trouble is an important addition to the literature on consumer credit. It provides convincing evidence that the consumer does not receive justice through our legal system and that the system is unfairly weighted on the side of the creditor. Ironically, those creditors who make the most frequent use of unfair remedies are often guilty of unfair or deceptive practices themselves. Our legal system benefits the unscrupulous and penalizes the weak.

The need for consumer credit reform has been recognized by legal scholars, consumer advocates, government officials, and responsible leaders within the consumer credit industry. The imbalance between creditor and consumer rights would be at least partially redressed in the proposed Uniform Consumer Credit Code which has been adopted in seven states. A more effective reform measure was drafted by the National Consumer Law Center and adopted in modified form by the state of Wisconsin. The National Commission on Consumer Finance, a bipartisan body appointed by President Nixon, also recommended a thorough restructuring of creditors' remedies.

Consumers in Trouble strengthens the case for reform and provides convincing empirical evidence that our present consumer credit system is sadly out of date. Professor Caplovitz has made a vital contribution to the continuing debate over the legal structure of our consumer credit system. His findings will be of immeasureable help to those interested in reform legislation at both the state and federal level.

Senator William Proxmire

ACKNOWLEDGMENTS

This research on consumers who ran afoul of the credit system was made possible by a generous grant from the Office of Economic Opportunity (Grant No. NY-CAP-66-9702), which shared my conviction that a key problem of low-income persons is their entanglement in an exploitative system of consumer credit. The research task, including the writing of this book as well as the final report, exceeded the limits of the OEO grant, and the completion of this project would not have been possible without an additional grant, gratefully received, from the Center for Studies of Metropolitan Problems of the National Institute of Mental Health (Grant No. 1 RO1 MH17327).

A number of persons participated in this study, and I welcome this opportunity to acknowledge their contributions. I begin by citing key consultants in the sample cities who generously contributed their time and knowledge at various points. My chief consultant in Chicago was Agnes Ryan of the Chicago Legal Aid Bureau, who is the consumer expert of that organization. Among other things, she classified for us the Chicago creditors and plaintiffs that fell into the sample.

In Detroit, my consultant was Michael Domonkos, an attorney with the University of Detroit Law School's Urban Law Program and a professor at the Detroit Law School. He not only assisted us in gaining access to the records in the Detroit court but also classified the Detroit creditors and plaintiffs according to our conceptual scheme. The sampling of the Detroit cases was greatly facilitated by the cooperation of the chief clerk of the Court of Common Pleas of Detroit, Herbert D. Levitt, who was most sympathetic to the purposes of the study.

In Philadelphia, the study benefited from having as its consultant Max Weiner, the founder of a militant consumer action group known as the Consumer Education and Protection Association. The monthly newspaper produced by this organization, *Consumer's Voice* (which has the subtitle, "Let the Seller Beware"), has been a great source of knowledge about consumer fraud in Philadelphia, and its anecdotes confirm those we encountered through our interviews with default debtors in Philadelphia. Mr. Weiner also helped our research effort by classifying the Philadelphia creditors and plaintiffs who showed up in our survey.

Since New York was our home base and we had some familiarity with the system of consumer credit in that state, we were less in need of New York consultants. Even so, I am indebted to James Finney, then a recent graduate of Columbia Law School, who took charge of sampling cases of New York default debtors. He obtained the court's permission to carry out this work and he recruited and supervised a team of clerks who drew the sample.

My chief educator on matters of consumer credit has been Philip Schrag, the first occupant of the position of consumer advocate of the City of New York (a position housed in the Department of Consumer Affairs) and now a faculty member of Columbia Law School. If this report suggests that I have some familiarity with the law of consumer credit, I owe this education mainly to him. In addition to acting as a consultant and critic through the preparation of the various drafts of first the research report and then the manuscript for publication, Professor Schrag carefully read the final draft and made innumerable suggestions relating not only to the substance of the text but also to its style. One of the joys of this research project is that it led to my friendship with this highly talented man.

A former student of Professor Schrag, Howard Rubin, was also of great help. He read an earlier draft to make sure that I was not misinterpreting the law, and he did the bulk of the work on Appendix A, the glossary of terms.

The study owes a great deal to the research organization retained to collect the data, The National Opinion Research Center. Eve Weinberg and Carol Bowman Stocking of the Chicago office of NORC and Pearl Zinner of the New York office made innumerable suggestions on how to reorganize and simplify the questionnaire on the basis of their expertise and the pretests they had carried out.

The last group of persons I take pleasure in acknowledging consists of those with whom I worked closely during this research project. Irma Lorenson was most helpful during the data-processing phase of the study, when raw questionnaires were transformed into IBM punch cards. Chris Camarano did yeoman work during the complicated and arduous task of coding reasons for a default.

My most important acknowledgment is to the person who assisted me during the analysis and report-writing phase of the study, Eric Single. Not only did he know how to communicate with the computer, and thus generate all the tables that appear in this report, but much more important, he served as a sounding board and critic during the difficult process of translating raw data into a coherent and, I hope, enlightening report.

The research was conducted at the Bureau of Applied Social Research of Columbia University, and I am most grateful for the supporting services provided by that organization. In particular, I express my thanks to Madeline Simonson, the head of the Bureau typing pool, and to Nelson Glover and Charlotte Fisher, who shared the typing of the many drafts of this report.

CONSUMERS
IN
TROUBLE

INTRODUCTION

This book deals with a relatively new and increasingly serious social problem: debt entanglement. In the span of a single generation, the acquisition of durable goods shifted from a cash to a credit basis, and the widely heralded affluent society became a credit society as well.[1] This is shown by the growth of outstanding *installment* consumer debt. In 1945, such debt was a negligible $2.5 billion. A decade later, it had climbed to $29 billion. By 1965, it had soared to $66 billion, and by December 1970, five years later, it had reached $100 billion. This figure, which excludes mortgage debt and noninstallment debts such as charge accounts and bills for professional services, represents approximately $1,600 of debt per American household.[2]

The credit explosion has been linked to the country's prosperity, both as cause and as consequence. By stimulating consumer demand, it has greatly aided the growth of the economy, and as more and more Americans obtain discretionary income (income beyond their subsistence needs), their consumer wants increase. But however beneficial installment credit may be to the economy as a whole and to those who use it, it is also the source of a growing social problem: the overextended debtor, or, more accurately, the debtor who, for whatever reasons, fails to continue the payment of his debt. This person is subjected to harsh collection practices, is apt to have his legal rights violated, and often suffers a number of debilitating consequences, ranging from trouble on his job

[1]See David Caplovitz, "Consumer Credit in the Affluent Society," *L. and Contemp. Prob.,* V. 33, No. 4 (Autumn 1968).

[2]By March of 1973, installment credit had climbed to $129 billion, bringing the average per household close to $2,000. When noninstallment debts and mortgage payments are added to this figure it is apparent that relatively steep indebtedness is part of the American way of life.

to trouble in his marriage and trouble with his health. The growth of this negative side of consumer credit is suggested by the statistics on personal (as distinct from business) bankruptcies. Between 1948 and 1967 personal bankruptcies increased from 16,000 a year to more than 191,000 a year.[3] Another indicator of the growing number of consumers with credit problems is the rising number of wage garnishments, the attachment of wages by creditors.[4] Unfortunately, national statistics are not kept on wage garnishments, but in cities where such records are kept, the pattern is clear. In Chicago, for example, wage garnishments increased from 64,000 in 1960 to 78,000 in 1969.[5]

The excesses or dysfunctions in the consumer credit system stem in large part from two related conditions. First, the phenomenal growth of installment credit has been a boon to deceptive and fraudulent marketing practices. Insofar as consumer transactions depended on cash, sellers had little opportunity to employ deception and fraud. The consumer who could afford to pay cash for an expensive commodity was probably more deliberate and sophisticated in his shopping behavior, and there was no point in trying to convince the person without cash to make an expensive purchase. All this changed with the advent of installment credit. Whether the consumer could afford the purchase became much less relevant to the seller. Once the contract was signed, the seller could count on the law to enforce his right to be paid. The second condition that contributes to the dysfunctions of the consumer credit system is the failure of the law to keep abreast of the abrupt changes in the field. The laws regulating consumer credit in most states today are largely borrowed from commercial law, which regulates relationships between buyers and sellers in the business world. The law of contract in commercial transactions is based on the assumption that the parties not only enter the transaction in good faith, but that they fully understand all the rights and duties embodied in the contract's various clauses. This is a reasonable assumption, for business firms routinely enter into contractual relationships with other parties, often the same ones, and they are apt to have at their disposal the services of experts (lawyers, in particular) to help them draft the contract.

[3]In 1968 this trend was reversed for the first time as personal bankruptcies declined to 181,000. Personal bankruptcies have fluctuated around this figure ever since. In 1969 they declined to 169,000, but by 1971 they had climbed to 183,000. The fall-off in personal bankruptcies since 1967 is generally attributed to changes in state laws and the 1968 Consumer Protection Act, which exempt more of the debtor's income from wage attachments and hence lessen the need for bankruptcy.

[4]See the Glossary (Appendix A) for a definition of garnishment.

[5]The 1969 figure actually represents a decrease from the decade's peak, which occurred in 1966. In that year more than 87,000 Chicago residents were garnisheed. The rate fell precipitously in 1967, to 78,000, and has remained at about that figure ever since. One theory links the decline to a sharp increase in the filing fee for confession-of-judgment suits, which went into effect in 1967. This presumably discouraged creditors from trying to collect on small debts by this means.

This model breaks down when the parties to the contract are a business firm and a consumer. The consumer, unlike the business firm, rarely enters into contractual relationships and has little understanding of the document to which he affixes his signature. Moreover, the contract he signs is not one developed specifically for this relationship by expert counsel for both sides. Rather, the contract signed by the consumer is known in law as a contract of *adhesion,* that is, a standard form contract, sometimes drafted and reproduced in large numbers not by the seller but by the finance agency with whom the seller does business. The law assumes that the debtor reads all the clauses of this contract and grasps their meaning *before* he signs the document (or that he is negligent if he does not). But this image of the transaction is more fantasy than reality. As is well known by those close to the consumer credit field, the would-be debtor is in many instances actively discouraged by the seller from reading the contract. Moreover, it is unlikely that most debtors could understand the esoteric language of the contract even if they had the opportunity to read it. In short, the would-be debtor does not have access to a legal expert who would interpret the document for him before he signs it. This fundamental inequality would be less aberrant if legislators recognized the fundamental differences between commercial contracts and consumer credit contracts. Instead of carefully studying these differences and evolving equitable consumer credit laws, most legislatures have simply borrowed the principles of commercial law and applied them to the consumer credit field. Thus, some states honor the principle of "confession of judgment," under which the debtor waives his defenses at the time of the transaction. Although an argument might be made for such a principle in commercial transactions, it comes close to violating the debtor's constitutional right of due process in consumer transactions.[6]

Still another example is provided by the holder-in-due-course doctrine, which, by freeing the third party of the buyer's defenses against the original seller, has the function of making contracts into negotiable instruments in much the same way that money or checks are negotiable. This doctrine has been a boon to commercial transactions, but in the field of consumer credit, this principle all too often operates to encourage unscrupulous sellers to stay in business by shutting off the debtor's defenses against the firm that bought his contract.[7]

Inequities in consumer transactions are exacerbated by the fact that the consumers most likely to run afoul of the system are the very ones least likely to meet the law's assumption that the debtor fully understands the terms of the document he signs. As we shall see, debtors in default

---

[6]The Supreme Court in a 1972 decision did not share this view; it upheld a lower court decision which placed restrictions on confessions of judgment but did not abolish it. See Swarb v. Lennox, 405 U.S. 191 (1972) and 314 F. Sup. 1091 (1970).

[7]The reader not familiar with "confession of judgment" and "holder-in-due-course" should consult the glossary of terms in Appendix A.

are disproportionately recruited from the lower halves of the income and educational scales. They tend to be semiskilled and unskilled working-class persons whose incomes may place them above the poverty line but well below the level considered adequate for urban families. Moreover, a substantial number of debtors in default are located in the poverty class and only a small proportion have relatively high income. Debt troubles of the kind that are the subject of this research thus contribute to the vicious cycle of poverty: they tend to attack those least able to cope with them, and they further undermine the economic position of their victims.

THE CONSUMER MOVEMENT AND EFFORTS TO REFORM CONSUMER CREDIT LAW

The failure of the law to take account of the relatively new phenomenon of consumer credit represents a kind of cultural lag, and in recent years a number of efforts have been made on federal, state, and local levels to redress the balance.

That "slum of a decade," the 1960s, for all its horrors, might well go down in history as the decade in which the consumers of America rose up to protect their interests and managed to obtain some response from government. The sixties saw the phenomenon of Ralph Nader, who single-handedly took on the automobile industry on the issue of auto safety and has evolved into the consumer's crusader on many other issues. But long before Nader there were two senators who labored hard in the consumer's interest. At the beginning of the decade, Senator Kefauver passed legislation regulating the drug industry, but only after the Thalidomide scandal shocked the nation and created a favorable climate of opinion for his bill. During this time, Senator Douglas of Illinois carried out his lonely battle for "truth in lending," the requirement that creditors disclose the cost of loans and credit in terms of a simple annual interest rate. Unfortunately, Senator Douglas was no longer in the Senate when his battle was finally won in 1968 with the passage of the Consumer Protection Act, which had acquired new champions in Senator Proxmire and Congresswoman Sullivan. This law not only requires creditors to state the true cost of credit in terms of a simple annual interest rate but also contains other salutory provisions. For example, it regulates the amount of income exempt from garnishment, thus correcting some excessively harsh state garnishment laws.[8] This victory for the consumer on the issue of truth in lending was delayed for many years by the powerful

[8] Under the 1968 act, a minimum of 75 percent of the debtor's income is exempt from garnishment. Some states, including California and Michigan, had permitted creditors to attach 50 percent of the debtor's income. (On the other hand, some states, New York, for example, exempt an even larger proportion of the debtor's income.)

lobby of the credit industry, which argued that if the public knew how much it was paying for credit it would be so dismayed that it would curtail its consumption and thus provoke a recession (a rather strange twist on the aphorism that the truth shall make you free).[9]

The passage of the Consumer Protection Act has been followed by a flurry of Congressional activity on behalf of the consumer. Bills have been introduced ranging from a "cooling off period" in direct sales and the creation of an independent consumer agency, to the strengthening of the Federal Trade Commission in its consumer protection activities and consumer class action legislation. So far none of these proposals has become law, although the chances are good that at least some of them will be passed in the near future.[10] The last of these proposals, consumer class actions, would be a powerful recourse for consumers in their battle against fraudulent sellers. Under such a law, a class of consumers would be able to join forces and collectively sue a creditor for damages. The problem has been that the sums in dispute are generally small, and the consumer would have to pay more for legal services than he stands to gain if he should win his case. But when a class of consumers collectively brings a suit, each consumer seeking to recover a few hundred dollars, the collective amount is likely to be sufficient to warrant the often long and complicated work of a lawyer.[11]

Not only has Congress made some effort to respond to the consumer's interest, but the sixties saw the executive branch of the federal government respond as well. One of President Kennedy's campaign promises was to provide for consumer representation on the executive level. Unfor-

[9]Given the current need to control inflation, such an outcome would probably be welcomed rather than feared by the Nixon administration. But these dire predictions seem to have been in error. The disclosure provision of the 1968 act went into effect July 1, 1969, and it is rather obvious that in itself it has not curtailed consumption. As far as can be determined, disclosure of interest rates has had no impact on consumption.

[10]Direct selling is notorious for its high pressure and deceptive tactics. Some years ago, England, followed by a number of states in America, passed legislation that gave the buyer a certain length of time, usually three days, to rescind the contract. In 1969 Senator Magnuson introduced such a bill in the Senate, but it has not been enacted. Congressman Rosenthal has worked for a number of years to establish a federal agency to protect the consumer's interest. Initially, he advocated a Department of Consumer Affairs, but his bill evolved into an independent consumer agency with strong powers. Such a bill passed the Senate but was narrowly defeated in the House in 1970. A consumer agency bill passed the House in 1971, but was filibustered to death in the Senate in 1972. Several bills have been introduced to strenghten the power of the Federal Trade Commission. The FTC, even before such laws are enacted, has taken a very aggressive stance against industry on behalf of consumers and is in the process of promulgating a number of regulations, including a "cooling-off" period in direct sales, that have dubious legality until Congress grants it more authority. Consumer class action legislation was introduced by Senator Tydings; since his defeat, the battle on behalf of such a law has been taken over by Congressman Eckhardt.

[11]For a vivid account of the complicated and time-consuming legal work involved in representing consumers, see Philip Schrag, *Bleak House 1968: A Report on Consumer Test Litigation*, 44 N.Y.U. L. Rev. 115 (1969).

:unately, this promise was not kept during his tenure in that office, and :t remained for President Johnson to appoint the first consumer advisor to the President, Esther Peterson, who assumed that office in 1964. Mrs. Peterson took her role as the consumer's advocate seriously, and she soon became so unpopular with the business community that the President replaced her with Betty Furness (who achieved some fame selling refrigerators on TV). To the surprise and delight of the consumer forces, Miss Furness proved to be a rather strong advocate of the consumer's cause.[12] When President Nixon took office, his first response was to slight this office by appointing a weak candidate associated in the public's mind with the interests of industry rather than those of the consumer. But this appointment aroused such indignation that the President quickly rescinded it and appointed instead Virginia Knauer, a woman who had earned her spurs as a consumer advocate in Pennsylvania and commanded the respect of consumer groups. The aforementioned legislation to create an independent consumer agency was designed to strengthen this office by institutionalizing it and making it independent of Presidential control.

Contributions to the consumer movement have been made not only by Congress and the executive branch of the federal government, but also by the judiciary branch. In June 1969, in what is known as the Sniadach case (Sniadach being a debtor in Wisconsin whose cause was taken up by the NAACP's Legal Defense Fund), the Supreme Court declared prejudgment garnishments to be unconstitutional. The prejudgment garnishment, which was recognized in 17 states, was a device that permitted creditors to attach the wages of debtors and have the attached sums held in escrow until the court rendered a decision on the case. The purpose of this practice was to preclude the debtor's absconding without paying anything on his bill. The Supreme Court decided that garnishment prior to judgment was in violation of the debtor's right to due process of law. The implications of this decision are far-reaching. Suits are now being brought by OEO-sponsored legal service programs to have prejudgment attachments of bank accounts, "wage assignments,"[13] and repossessions without notice declared unconstitutional on the same grounds.

[12]In 1969 Miss Furness was appointed by Governor Rockefeller of New York as the chairwoman of a newly created New York State Consumer Protection Board. The rocky road of consumer reform is evidenced by Miss Furness's indignant resignation in July 1971, on the grounds that consumer reform was futile in a state whose legislature was the servant of industry. In the legislative session then completed, Miss Furness noted that only three relatively innocuous bills of the 19 submitted by her agency on behalf of the governor were enacted into law.

[13]A wage assignment is a document signed by the debtor at the time of the transaction granting the creditor the right to attach his wages in case of a default without first getting a court judgment. Wage assignments have been outlawed in transactions for consumer goods (but not loans) in New York and several other states. The wage assignment is quite similar to, although narrower than, a confession of judgment (see Appendix A).

Developments on the State and Local Levels

Senator Douglas's efforts to require "truth in lending" which began in 1959, finally stimulated a highly prestigious body, known as the National Conference of Commissioners on Uniform State Laws (NCCUSL), to look into consumer credit law and draft a model bill for eventual adoption by the states. The Commissioners (three from each state) are appointed by the governors of each state. They tend to be leaders of the bar, men with national reputations, whose mission is to reform and codify the laws of the various states so as to reduce and eventually eliminate the disparities that now exist in state laws. Perhaps their greatest achievement to date was the drafting of a model Uniform Commercial Code, which has been adopted by virtually every state. However laudatory their accomplishments may be, it should be noted that the NCCUSL has a built-in conservative bias, for it sees itself as buttressing the doctrine of states' rights by heading off the need for federal legislation. Although consumer credit laws were in dire need of standardization given the wide variation from one state to another, the various state laws all have in common one major theme: they do a much better job of protecting the creditor's interests than the interests of the debtor. As a result, there was no pressure from the typical clients of the commissioners to take action. But the persistence of Senator Douglas in pushing for truth in lending changed the picture and prodded the NCCUSL to action.

In 1964 the commissioners appointed a committee to work on a model consumer credit code. After much consultation and numerous drafts, the Uniform Consumer Credit Code (UCCC) emerged in 1969. So far, it has been adopted by very few states, and whether it will be widely adopted depends in large part on how willing the commissioners are to amend it to appease certain consumer interests. This bill not only has a truth-in-lending provision much like the federal law, but it covers such things as ceiling rates in credit, and advocates what is known as "free entry" into the lending market by removing the restrictions that now exist on banks, small loan companies, retailers, and the like, to lend money. Under the provisions of the UCCC anyone can become a lender, and the effective rates of interest will be determined by the market mechanism of free competition (provided they do not exceed the generous ceiling). Another distinctive feature of the bill is its attempt to establish enforcement machinery, something notoriously lacking in much of the current legislation.

Still another major development in the consumer movement in the late 1960s was the creation by the Office of Economic Opportunity of the Center of Consumer Law at Boston College School of Law. The Consumer Law Center has taken as its primary mission counteracting what it considers to be the creditor-oriented UCCC. Its staff has drafted a consumer-oriented National Consumer Act which it is presenting to state legislatures as an alternative to the UCCC. The Center of Consumer Law tends to view its activities as a holding action that will force state legislatures to be more responsive to consumer interests when considering the UCCC, although a modified version of the NCA has already been adopted by one state, Wisconsin.

While the Commissioners on Uniform State Laws and the Consumer Law Center have been trying to redress the balance between creditor's and debtor's rights on the state level, even more significant developments seem to be taking place in local government. Perhaps the most progressive consumer legislation enacted to date is the New York City Consumer Protection Act (a bill signed into law by Mayor Lindsay on December 30, 1969). The law empowers the Department of Consumer Affairs to seek mass restitution for all consumers who were victims of a particular fraud (a provision that comes close to the logic of class action). During the first two years of the law's existence, the DCA's division of law enforcement has had considerable success in stamping out fraudulent selling schemes.[14]

As this recapitulation of significant developments in the past decade would indicate, the plight of the consumer–debtor is indeed coming to the attention of legislative bodies, and efforts are being made to redress the balance between debtor and creditor rights. But this battle on behalf of the consumer–debtor is still in its infancy, and even the few remedies that have finally been brought into law over the objections of the credit industry, such as truth in lending, have had much less impact than initially supposed.[15] These reform efforts have taken place primarily in the absence of hard factual data on the nature of the problems and the workings of the consumer credit system. It was to fill this gap that the research reported on here was undertaken. We hope that a careful study of the plight of debtors in default will contribute to a more realistic understanding and solution of the problem of debt entanglement.

THE NATURE OF THE STUDY

This book is based on detailed interviews with 1,331 default-debtors sampled from court records in New York, Chicago, Detroit, and Philadelphia.

---

[14]For an account of these activities, see Philip Schrag, *Counsel for the Deceived* (New York: Pantheon Books, Inc., 1972).

[15]Although it may be too early to evaluate the significance of the federal law that went into effect July 1, 1969, it should be noted that Massachusetts required that the true annual interest rate appear on installment contracts several years before the federal law was enacted. As far as anyone can discern, the Massachusetts law has not cut down on the amount of credit granted in that state, nor has it materially affected the shopping patterns of consumers.

The details of the sampling and the response rates are described in Appendix C. For our purposes it is sufficient to note that the survey was limited to transactions for merchandise and personal loans, thereby excluding contracts for services.[16] The main consequence of this exclusionary principle was to eliminate creditor–plaintiffs in the health fields—hospitals and physicians. The health professions and their institutions turn out to be frequent plaintiffs in consumer suits, largely because overextended debtors are apt to fall behind on these obligations as they try to maintain payments on their homes, automobiles, and appliances, all of which they can lose should they be in arrears.

It is important to note another restriction on the sample, one stemming from the fact that the sample was taken from court docket books, indicating that the debtors had been sued by their creditors. Not all default-debtors are automatically sued. One factor influencing the decision to sue is, of course, the amount of the debt. Creditors are not likely to sue if the amounts are under $40 or so. But another factor is also involved: the type of relationship that exists between the creditor and the debtor and the amount of information the former has about the latter. In small towns merchants are apt to know their customers, and when their customers fall behind on their bills, they are likely to know why. In these circumstances the creditor may well work out an accommodation with the debtor until he is "back on his feet." The small town creditor feels no need to use the impersonal, formal machinery of a law suit to collect his debt. The phenomenon we are studying—the breakdown in credit transactions that result in law suits—is thus very much a product of the anonymity of consumer transactions in urban America. It is this lack of knowledge of each other by the parties to these transactions that contributes to mistrust, misinterpretations of the reasons for the default, and the employment of harsh, bureaucratic procedures to collect debts. In this respect we are dealing for the most part with an urban problem in which trust, based on personal relationships, is absent.[17]

The central theme of this book is the injustice that has evolved in this impersonal world of consumer credit—injustice that stems from the basic inequity between the buyer and the seller, the debtor and the creditor. To write about injustices perpetrated upon consumer–debtors is not to say that persons in this position do not sometimes take advantage of the seller–creditors. (In the view of the credit industry, the creditors are almost invariably the victims of "deadbeat" debtors when the system breaks down.) But, as we shall see, a number of debtors who end in

[16]By excluding debts for services from the sample, we eliminated some of the worst abuses, such as correspondence schools, judo lessons, and dance lessons. Thus the findings on consumer fraud in this book tend to underestimate its frequency.

[17]Some evidence for this theory is provided by a national survey conducted by the author of garnishments relating to manufacturing establishments. That study shows that garnishment rates increase with the size of the community.

default were victimized in the initial transaction because of fraud and error on the part of their creditors. In spite of these extenuating circumstances, few debtor–defendants had their "day in court." On the contrary, the machinery of justice in the consumer field serves almost exclusively the interests of the creditors—the unscrupulous as well as the reputable ones.

In part, the supporting evidence for this theme is based on the realities of consumer transactions, especially door-to-door selling, and the realities of consumer suits, such as the irony that the cost of legal services is often far greater than the amount in dispute. But for the most part the story of this book is based on the testimony of the default-debtors, who were interviewed at length. At no point were their creditors interviewed, which opens the issue of possible bias. On what grounds can we assume that the debtors' accounts were truthful, and in general how much confidence can be placed in the survey's results? The issue of possible bias is dealt with in Appendix B. It is there that the reader will learn of the various checks on bias at our disposal, and that even less-than-truthful responses have their value, especially in a comparative analysis.

THE PARTIES

IN DISPUTE:

THE DEBTORS

AND

THEIR

CREDITORS

2

PORTRAIT

OF THE DEFAULT-DEBTORS

It has been suggested that debtors in default are likely to be members of the disadvantaged segments of society. The major burden of this chapter will be to demonstrate the extent to which this is true. This analysis deals with what might broadly be construed as social or structural determinants of default.

SOCIAL CHARACTERISTICS OF DEFAULT-DEBTORS

To show that default-debtors come disproportionately from certain segments of society, we shall compare some of their characteristics with those of the general population and with those of credit users. Information on the latter was obtained specifically for this study. The National Opinion Research Center (NORC) of the University of Chicago was retained to include questions about consumer credit on a national survey it conducted in January 1967, about the same time that we sampled default-debtors.[1] Of the 1,504 persons interviewed in that survey, 903, 60 percent, were making payments on installment loans or purchases. This group of "current" users will serve as our national sample of debtors (presumably not in default). As for the general population, information on the adult population of the four sample cities would have been most ideal. The 1960 census provides data on major metropolitan areas. We shall make

[1] Information on credit users is also provided by the annual surveys of consumer finances conducted by the Survey Research Center of the University of Michigan.

use of that census for those characteristics that are not likely to change markedly, such as the occupational structure. The 1960 census is too outmoded to be of value in describing income and ethnicity. For this information the Current Population Reports, Series P 60, *Consumer Income,* issued annually by the Bureau of the Census, will be used. This series provides information on nonfarm income by various characteristics. We shall refer to the December 1967 report, which deals with 1966 income. Our information on ethnicity in the sample cities comes from still different sources, to be described later.

Income and Occupation

As noted, the income data in the first column of Table 2.1 refer to nonfarm families in the United States as of 1966. They exclude unrelated individuals, who, in the general population, tend to be the elderly of low income. Fourteen percent of the default-debtors in our survey are unrelated persons, although as credit users they tend to be younger and of higher income than unrelated individuals in the general population. Nevertheless, to make the samples more comparable, unrelated default-debtors are excluded from the third column of Table 2.1.

Table 2.1 / Comparison of Income of Default-Debtors with Income of Current Credit Users and Nonfarm Families in the United States in 1966 (percent)

	nonfarm families	credit users NORC survey[b]	default-debtors (families)[c]
Under $4,000	20	20	24
$4,000–$7,999	34	43	54
$8,000 and over	46	37	22
Total percent	100	100	100
N		(882)	(1,081)

[a]From Table 1 of *Current Population Report on Consumer Income, 1966.*

[b]Current Credit Users in NORC survey are those who were making payments on installment debts at the time of the interview.

[c]Omitted are unrelated persons and those who did not provide information on income.

From the first two columns of Table 2.1 we learn something about the people who use installment credit. Although the Michigan surveys of consumer finances have shown that the very poor are not likely to use credit, this finding is due to the inclusion of unrelated persons who, because they are usually elderly, have both low income and limited consumer needs. On the other hand, low-income *families,* those with incomes below $4,000, are present among credit users in the same proportion as they are in the general population, 20 percent. If income below $4,000 is considered the mark of poverty in the nonfarm population of families, then the poor use credit to the extent that would be expected from their numbers in the population. Reliance on credit increases among the near poor—those above the poverty line but with incomes less than adequate for urban living. Thirty-four percent of the nonfarm families (but 43 percent of credit users) had incomes between $4,000 and $8,000. Those earning over $8,000 are less likely to use credit than would be expected from their numbers alone. They constitute 46 percent of the population but only 37 percent of the credit users. In short, those in the lower middle range of the income scale are most likely to rely on consumer credit and only the well-off, those who presumably can afford to pay cash, use credit less than would be expected by chance.

More relevant for our present purposes is a comparison of the second and third columns, which describe the role of income in consumer defaults. Surprisingly, the poor (income below $4,000) default only slightly more often than their use of credit would suggest. But those with incomes between $4,000 and $8,000, the group that has been identified as the marginal poor in major urban centers, are much more likely to be found among default-debtors than in the population of credit users, 54 compared with 43 percent. Marginal income is thus a major factor in consumer defaults. Debtors with incomes above $8,000 show quite a different pattern, one that testifies to their ability to handle installment credit. Forty-six percent of the nonfarm population in 1966 earned over $8,000, and these relatively well-off families accounted for only 37 percent of the credit users. But those in this group accounted for only 22 percent of the default-debtors.

It should be remembered that the various populations represented in Table 2.1 are not strictly comparable. "Nonfarm" includes rural nonfarm and small town residents as well as city dwellers. From the 1960 census we know that the income of urban families is higher than that of rural nonfarm families and that the residents of very large urban centers tend to have still higher income. In short, the income gap between default-debtors in the four sample cities and the population of these four cities is undoubtedly greater than comparison of the first and third columns of Table 2.1 would indicate. The NORC sample of credit users is also somewhat out of line. As a national sample, it may even include some farm families. This lack of strict comparability has the effect of reducing the income differences between default-debtors and the comparison groups. That these differences are nonetheless quite marked makes it evident that debtors who default come from the lower half of the income scale in numbers much greater than would be expected by chance. Compounding this relationship are the many merchants who extend credit to those who can least afford it, because of either their low income or their other credit obligations. Were credit given only to those who could afford it, the relationship between defaults and marginal income, shown in Table 2.1, would not necessarily pertain.

Table 2.1 actually exaggerates the income of the default-debtors in our sample, for it reports family income. Although 21 percent of the default-debtors had family incomes in excess of $8,000, a substantial number in this group had multiple sources of wages with either both spouses working or the chief wage earner holding more than one job. The data on income refer to 1966, whereas the data on employment refer to the time of the interview, the summer of 1967. As a result of this discrepancy, a few debtors reported high income in 1966 and yet had no wage earners in the family at the time of the interview. Table 2.2 classifies the default-debtors according to the number of sources of wages.

The connection between income and employment is shown by the third column in Table 2.2. As family income decreases, the proportion with no wage earners steadily increases to the point where fully 40 percent of those with income below $3,000 had no wage earners in the family. For present purposes, however, the pattern shown in the first column is more revealing. Among the default-debtors who report family income in excess of $10,000, more than one half had multiple sources of wages, as did more than one third of the debtors with family income between $8,000 and $10,000.

The import of Table 2.2 is that fewer of these default-debtors have middle-class occupations than their family income would suggest. Unfortunately, there is no information on the occupations of the credit users from the NORC survey, but two sources of data on the occupational structure of the general population are available. The first column of Table 2.3 shows, in very broad categories, the occupational distribution of nonfarm families in 1967. The second column shows the aggregate

Table 2.2 / Number of Wage Sources by Family Income (percent)

family income	multiple wage sources	single wage source	no wage source	total percent	N
Over $10,000	53	44	3	100	(116)
$8,000–$9,999	35	60	5	100	(146)
$6,000–$7,999	31	63	6	100	(274)
$5,000–$5,999	26	69	5	100	(188)
$4,000–$4,999	16	72	13	100	(189)
$3,000–$3,999	17	61	22	100	(156)
Under $3,000	10	50	40	100	(173)

Table 2.3 / Comparison of the Occupational Distribution of
Default-Debtors and the General Population (percent)

occupational group	nonfarm families (March 1967)[a]	four-city average (1960 census: males)[b]	four-city default-debtors[c]
Higher white collar: professionals, technical, managerial, officials, proprietors	30	25	8
Lower white collar: clerical and sales	14	19	11
Higher blue collar: craftsmen, foremen	22	21	13
Lower blue collar: operatives; private household, service, and nonfarm laborers	34	36	69
Total percent	100	101	101

[a] Taken from raw data provided in Table 9 of *Current Population Report on Consumer Income, 1966*. Farm owners, farm managers, and farm laborers and the unemployed have been omitted.

[b] These figures represent the average for the four sample cities. Detroit, the most industrialized of these cities, have 62 percent of its male labor force in blue collar occupations and New York, the least industrialized, has 52 percent. These figures refer to the SMSA, statistical units that include the suburbs as well as the city proper.

[c] The data on the default-debtors refer to males only, to make them more comparable to the second column.

distribution of the male population of wage earners in the four sample cities according to the 1960 census, and the third column shows the occupational distribution of the male default-debtors in our four-city sample.

Whether we compare the default-debtors with nonfarm families in the country for the same year (1967) or with the aggregate male population of the four sample cities according to the 1960 census, the same finding emerges: lower blue collar workers are heavily overrepresented among the default-debtors. Thirty-four percent of the nonfarm population in 1967 belonged to the lower blue collar group, as did 36 percent of the male labor force of the four cities. In contrast 69 percent of the default-debtors had lower blue collar occupations.[2]

[2] This pattern is quite pronounced in each sample city. For example, in Detroit, where 39 percent of the labor force had lower blue collar occupations, fully 77 percent of the default-debtors did; in New York, where 34 percent of the labor force was in the lower blue collar class, 66 percent of the default-debtors were.

Employment Status

Table 2.3 dealt only with those who were employed. But as we shall see later, a major reason for the default was the debtor's loss of employment. We know whether the debtors were employed at the time they defaulted and at the time of the interview. Twenty-five percent of the debtors told us that they were not working at the time of the default, a figure that is more than six times the average unemployment rate during the first half of the sixties. Even when interviewed in 1967, these default-debtors had a higher unemployment rate than the country at large. At that time, 84 percent of the debtors were employed, 7 percent had left the labor force, and 10 percent were in the labor force but unemployed. This compares with an unemployment rate of about 2.3 percent among the nonfarm population in 1966. Clearly, unemployment, low occupational status, and low income are related to and contribute to defaults in consumer credit transactions. Apart from the debtor's attitudes, the seller's dubious sales practices, or whatever, a critical factor in the breakdown of credit transactions is the debtor's inability to pay as measured by his income and employment status. But this simple economic model of defaults fails to do justice to the complexities of the debtor–creditor relationship. The reasons for the breakdown are far more complex than these findings would suggest, as many debtors end in default for reasons that have little to do with their economic position.

Education

Since default-debtors tend to come from the lower halves of the income and occupational scales, it is to be expected that they are also low on the third dimension of socioeconomic status, education. One confounding factor is that default-debtors tend to be relatively young, and the young tend to be better educated than the old. This contradiction is confirmed by the data. Default-debtors are somewhat less likely than all U.S. family heads in 1967 to be very poorly educated, having only an elementary school education or less (23 and 29 percent, respectively). (Credit users according to the NORC survey are even slightly less likely to be poorly educated—21 percent.[3] But the default-debtors are much less likely than the general population or the sample of credit users to be high school graduates or to have attended college. Fifty-two percent of the general

---

[3]In part, this apparent difference may be an artifact of the failure of the *Current Population Report* to separate farm from nonfarm household heads in its tabulation of education. It is quite possible that if farm households were eliminated, there would be little difference in the rates of poorly educated persons in the national sample and in the four-city sample of default-debtors.

population, 58 percent of the NORC sample of credit users, but only 39 percent of the default-debtors had graduated from high school. Among those with at least some college education, the figures are 22 percent for all family heads, 26 percent for the credit users (who tend to be younger), and only 11 percent for the default-debtors (who also tend to be young).

The low educational attainment of the default-debtors is no doubt a reason for their low income and occupational status, factors that contribute to defaults. But it is also possible that poor education is a direct cause of defaults. The poorly educated may have more difficulty budgeting their incomes and may be more vulnerable to the pressures of unscrupulous salesmen urging heavy debt burdens upon them.

Age

The work of Katona and his associates has shown that credit usage is related to stage in the family life cycle.[4] Young families, especially those with young children, have great consumer needs and are particularly likely to use credit. One might expect then, that default-debtors are not only younger than the general population, but also younger than the users of consumer credit, since the young are likely to be more financially insecure than their elders. The data confirm this expectation. Among nonfarm family heads in 1966, 25 percent were under 35 years of age; among credit users, this group rises to 38 percent; and among those in default, those under 35 total 45 percent. In the 35- to 44-year age group a similar but less pronounced pattern is found: 20 percent of the general population, 23 percent of the credit users, and 30 percent of the default-debtors in the four-city sample are in this age group. Conversely, 35 percent of the general population is 55 years of age or older, compared with 21 percent of the credit users and only 9 percent of the default-debtors. Clearly, default-debtors are recruited from the younger segments of the population. Various processes might account for this fact. Young debtors are generally in the early stages of the family life cycle when consumer needs are greatest. At the same time they are likely to be in the early stages of occupational careers when income is relatively low. The combination of excessive need and limited resources might well lead the young to be overextended more often than their elders. But it is also possible that youthfulness is the mark of inexperience and vulnerability to the "easy credit" pitches of unscrupulous salesmen, with naivete more than excessive need being the critical factor. Perhaps both processes are at work. At any rate, the data make clear that default-debtors tend to be younger than both the general population and the users of credit.

[4] See John B. Lansing and James N. Morgan, "Consumer Finances Over the Life Cycle," in Lincoln Clark, ed., *Consumer Behavior,* Vol. II (New York: New York University Press, 1955).

Ethnicity

Perhaps the most striking finding about these default-debtors is that a substantial majority of them are members of minority groups (blacks mainly, but Puerto Ricans as well, when they are found in large numbers, as in New York). To demonstrate the overselection of these minorities, neither the 1960 census nor the 1967 nonfarm population of the entire country can be relied on, for they underestimate the number of blacks in these major cities. Estimates based on the year 1967 indicate that blacks comprised 18 percent of the New York City population, 28 percent of that of Chicago, 31 percent of that of Philadelphia, and 34 percent of Detroit's population.[5] In New York, an additional 10 percent of the population was Puerto Rican. (In the other three cities, Puerto Ricans were less than 2 percent of the population.[6]) Although these cities had higher proportions of blacks than is true for the country as a whole, in each city a substantial majority of the population was white. Yet a majority of the default-debtors in each city were blacks (or in New York, blacks and Puerto Ricans), as can be seen from Table 2.4.

Table 2.4 / Ethnicity of Default-Debtors Compared with Population of the Four Sample Cities and Credit Users in General (percent)

ethnicity	range in four-city sample in 1965	credit users NORC survey	four-city default-debtors
Whites	64–72	85	28
Blacks	18–34	15	65
Puerto Ricans	2–10	*a*	7
Total percent	100 (av.)	100	100
N		(903)	(1,331)

*a*Less than ½ of 1 percent.

The reasons for the heavy overrepresentation of minority-group members among these default-debtors unfortunately cannot be satisfactorily analyzed, for we do not have a control group of nondefaulting debtors. Without such a control group drawn from the sampled cities, it is difficult to prove that characteristics more common among blacks, such as unemployment, low income, less education, and lower occupational status provide a reason for the higher rate of default among blacks. Greater economic

[5]The estimates are from the National Advisory Commission on Civil Disorders, *Report* (New York: Bantam Books, Inc., 1968).
[6]Population figures on Puerto Ricans in these cities were provided by the Department of Labor of the Commonwealth of Puerto Rico.

deprivation and insecurity constitute one possible explanation for the overrepresentation of blacks and Puerto Ricans. Another reason might be that minority-group members, confronted with obstacles to social mobility and yet eager to have the symbols of success, are more ready to overextend themselves or are more vulnerable to the blandishments of exploitative salesmen.[7] Still another possibility is that creditors are more ready to sue their monority-group customers than their white customers in arrears, perhaps because of a heightened communication barrier or because of prejudice. We have no way of checking upon the validity of the second and third hypotheses, but by using the census data and the NORC survey we can make at least some inference about the validity of the economic insecurity hypothesis.

If income is a factor in defaults, we should find that the income differential between blacks and whites narrows as we move from the general population to the sample of default-debtors. That there is much merit to this hypothesis can be seen from the figures on median income for blacks and whites in the general population (nonfarm family heads), the credit users (NORC survey), and the sample of default-debtors. These data appear in Table 2.5.

Table 2.5 / Median Income in 1966 of Nonfarm Family Heads, Credit Users, and Default-Debtors by Ethnicity

Sample	whites	blacks	discrepancy
Nonfarm family heads	$7,810	$4,428	$3,382
Credit users (NORC)	$7,200	$4,300	$2,900
Default-debtors[a]	$6,600	$5,560	$1,040

[a]Excludes unrelated individuals.

In each sample the whites clearly earn more on the average than do the blacks. But in keeping with an income theory of the overrepresentation of blacks, the gap in income between whites and blacks steadily narrows as we move from the general population to credit users to default-debtors (see the third column). But the columns of Table 2.5 also contain a surprising finding. Whereas the income of whites steadily declines from the sample of all nonfarm family heads to the sample of credit users to the sample of debtors in default, the same is not true among the blacks. It is true that black credit users earn less than black heads of families in the United States, but the most affluent blacks turn out to be those in the four-city sample of default-debtors. This odd pattern is probably

[7]See the discussion of "Compensatory Consumption" in David Caplovitz, *The Poor Pay More* (New York: The Free Press, 1963), p. 13.

explained by urbanization, especially residence in these four metropolises, which has a greater impact on black income than on white income.[8]

Although the income gap between whites and blacks narrows in the sample of default-debtors, it is still quite substantial. There is reason to believe that the blacks in default are even worse off financially in relation to the whites than the figures suggest. We have seen that a substantial proportion of the relatively high income debtors depend on multiple sources of wages. This is particularly true of the blacks. As Table 2.6 shows, on each level of income blacks are more likely than whites to depend either on multiple earners or multiple jobs. (We limit this analysis to those earning $5,000 or more partly because there are relatively few multiple wage earners below that figure and partly because the base figures decline noticeably because of the large numbers of unemployed among those earning less than $5,000.) Although the sample of Table 2.6 contains more than twice as many blacks as whites, the base figures show that there are actually more whites than blacks earning over $10,000. Most significantly, whereas most whites in this income group (about two thirds) realize their earnings through only one job, the great majority of blacks in this high income category (73 percent) depend on multiple jobs. As income declines, the proportion of multiple wage sources in each ethnic group also declines, but the blacks are more dependent on multiple jobs than are the whites, whatever the level of income.

Having seen that income is a factor related to the overselection of

Table 2.6 / Percentage with Multiple Sources of Wages by Ethnicity and Family Income[a]

income	whites	blacks
Over $10,000	37 (59)	73 (52)
$8,000–$9,999	29 (51)	38 (87)
$6,000–$7,999	20 (85)	36 (180)
$5,000–$5,999	15 (45)	27 (132)

[a] The format of this table should be carefully noted, for we shall make frequent use of it in the subsequent analysis. Unlike the previous tables, this one deals with three variables simultaneously: (1) ethnicity, (2) income, and (3) number of sources of income. The percentages report the proportion of multiple wage sources in each income–ethnicity group. The base figures on which the percentages were computed appear in parentheses. The percentages here, of course, do not add to 100. The variable "number of wage sources" has been dichotomized, the two classes being "one" and "more than one." The percentage of household units with one source of wages can be computed by subtracting the percentages from 100.

[8] According to the 1960 census, the whites in these four cities had incomes averaging 16 percent higher than the white nonfarm population. Among blacks in these cities, the average was about 35 percent higher.

blacks, we turn now to its close correlate, occupation. In the previous section we found that default-debtors came disproportionately from the lower levels of blue collar occupations. If occupation is relevant to the overselection of blacks, we should find that substantially more blacks than whites in the general population are employed in the lower reaches of the occupational scale and that this difference is reduced among the default-debtors. Since occupational structures of cities, unlike income or ethnicity, do not change rapidly, we again use the 1960 census data for the metropolitan area of the four cities as the basis for comparison. (As already noted, occupational data are not available from the NORC survey.) Table 2.7 shows the aggregate occupational structure of the four cities for white and black males according to the 1960 census and the comparable data on white and black males in our sample of default-debtors.

Table 2.7 / Occupations of Whites and Blacks in the
Four Sample Cities (Aggregated) and in
the Sample of Default-Debtors (percent)

| | aggregate of four cities (1960 census) | | debtors in default | |
occupational group [a]	whites	blacks	whites	blacks
Higher white collar	27	8	13	6
Lower white collar	19	15	16	8
Higher blue collar	22	13	17	11
Lower blue collar	32	64	54	75
Total percent	100	100	100	100
N			(345)	(786)

[a] See Table 2.3 for the more specific occupational categories grouped under these headings.

Both within the aggregate population of these four cities and in the sample of default-debtors drawn from them, we find that whites have substantially higher occupational status than the blacks. But, as expected, the relationship between occupation and ethnicity is much stronger in the general population than it is among those in default. Twenty-seven percent of the whites in these four cities have higher white collar jobs compared with only 8 percent of the blacks, a difference of 19 percentage points. The comparable difference among the default-debtors is only 7 percentage points. In the general population blacks exceed whites in the lower reaches of the occupational structure (lower blue collar) by 32 percentage points; among the default-debtors this discrepancy is reduced to 21 points. And the reason for this is quite clear and follows the pattern for income. The whites who default tend to have much lower occupational status than whites in general, whereas blacks who default are not too different from the blacks in these communities. Table 2.7 buttresses the picture emerging from the income data. The blacks who default are not too different from blacks in general, for most blacks live in a world of little economic security, with relatively low income and semiskilled or unskilled jobs—the types of jobs least likely to be protected by tenure principles. Although the majority of whites in these communities are much better off, the minority who are not also run the risk of defaulting on their debts.

The economic data presented in Tables 2.5 and 2.6, although not conclusive, lend some credibility to the economic insecurity–deprivation hypothesis for the overselection of blacks among default-debtors. But other hypotheses (for example, "compensatory consumption" and "discrimination" by the creditor) might also apply, although data are lacking to test them. In sum, the default-debtors tend to be from lower levels of the income scale, to have lower occupational status, to be more poorly educated, and to be relatively younger than the general population or the users of consumer credit. And, as we have seen, they are members of minority groups, blacks or Puerto Ricans, to a far larger extent than would be expected on the basis of their numbers in the population, a finding that would seem to be caused in part by the greater economic insecurity of these minority groups.[9]

In sum, we have tried to locate the default-debtors in the social structure by showing the social groupings from which they are recruited. In so doing we have learned something about the social forces predisposing debtors to default. We found that the great majority of these debtors were living on incomes below those considered adequate for families in major urban centers. The default-debtors were much more likely than the nonfarm population of the country to have incomes ranging from $3,000 to $6,000. It was also seen that the default-debtors were dispropor- tionately recruited from the lower blue collar occupations, that they were much more likely to be out of work, and that their educational attainment was lower than that of both the general population and the sample of credit users. In short, in terms of income, occupation, and education (the traditional measures of socioeconomic status), the default-debtors clearly tend to be in the lower classes. It was also seen that those in

[9]A more recent analysis of still older data, however, casts some doubt on the value of the economic hypothesis as the prime explanation for the overselection of blacks. Eric Single, as part of his dissertation, has done a secondary analysis of NORC data collected in a 1963 panel study of feeling states. [See Norman Bradburn, *The Structure of Psychological Well-Being* (Chicago: Aldine-Atherton, Inc., 1969).] In that survey the respondents, drawn from selected communities, including the inner city of Detroit, a largely black community, were asked if they had installment debts other than mortgages and, if so, whether they had sufficient funds to pay off these debts or would have to borrow to do so. Blacks were disproportionately represented among those who would have to borrow to pay off their debts, a finding that could not be explained by income or occupation. See Eric Single, "Some Sociological Aspects of Debt Entanglement," unpublished Ph.D. dissertation, Columbia University, 1973.

default were apt to be much younger than both the general population and those who use credit, a finding that focuses attention on the importance of the stage in the family life cycle as a reason for default. Those in the early stages, with young children, have many consumer needs, even though they have not as yet reached their peak earnings. An important function of consumer credit is to permit those starting out to meet their consumer needs by mortgaging their future income. The fact that those in default are disproportionately young calls attention to the precarious aspects of these arrangements. Perhaps the most significant finding concerning the social characteristics of those in default was the discovery that the great majority are members of minority groups (blacks and Puerto Ricans)—much more so than the proportion of these ethnic groups in the populations of these cities would have predicted. Although the absence of a sample of non-default-debtors severely limited our efforts to explain the overselection of minority groups, comparison of debtors with the general population suggested that blacks and Puerto Ricans were more vulnerable to credit problems because of their more precarious economic position. Whites and blacks in default were more similar in terms of income and occupation (toward the lower end of the scales) than whites and blacks in the general population.

3

PORTRAIT
OF THE CREDITORS:
THE INITIAL
TRANSACTION

In examining the initial transaction that led to the default-debtors' difficulties, we shall be concerned with two themes. First, what types of transactions with what types of creditors were involved in these defaults? Second, to what extent did the initial transaction conform to the laws regulating consumer credit? These laws make assumptions about the nature of the transaction and prescribe conditions that must be met if the installment contract is to be valid. For example, the contract must contain both the cash price (or amount of the loan) and the total time sales price, and the debtor must be given a copy of the contract at the time of the transaction.[1] In pursuing these themes, we shall also pay attention to the differential experiences of different types of debtors. For example, were certain types of debtors more likely than others to deal with certain types of creditors, and were deviations from consumer credit law more likely to be inflicted upon one rather than another kind of debtor?

[1] The penalties for violating these provisions are virtually nonexistent. For example, if the debtor is not given a copy of the contract at the time of the sale, he may rescind the transaction until the goods are delivered. But once the goods are delivered, the contract is binding upon him even though he may not have received it until some weeks after the sale!

THE NATURE OF THE CREDIT TRANSACTION

The default-debtor could have gotten into his predicament by one of four routes: signing a conditional sales contract for consumer goods, establishing revolving credit at a store, obtaining an installment loan, or cosigning for someone who defaulted on an installment purchase or loan. The distinction between an installment purchase and an installment loan is not as clear as might first appear, because some loans are arranged by dealers. In these instances it is the dealer who decides that the transaction is a loan rather than an installment purchase. Such dealer-arranged loans are likely to occur in automobile transactions, especially when the dealer arranges a loan for the down payment. (In fact, many automobile transactions involve multiple financing arrangements, a small loan for the down payment, and the sale of the contract to a finance company.) Dealer-arranged loans also show up in other areas, such as home repairs, and in Philadelphia we even came across several dealer-arranged loans for cemetery lots. The law does not yet distinguish between dealer-arranged loans and personal loans initiated by the borrower; and were we to follow the legal distinction, we would have to classify dealer-arranged loans as personal loans.[2] There were many questions that we wanted to ask of those who made installment purchases that would have been lost had we treated dealer-arranged loans in the same fashion as personal loans. For example, we wanted to know the circumstances of an automobile purchase, such as whether there was a trade-in, what the cash price was, and the debtor's satisfaction with the purchase. That the debtor was now being sued by a small loan company that advanced the money for the down payment seemed much less relevant than the fact that the debtor had approached a dealer to buy a car. Unfortunately, we were not always successful in screening dealer-arranged loans, and long after the data were processed it was found that some of the debts that were treated as personal loans were actually credit purchases financed by dealer-arranged loans. With these caveats in mind, examine the frequencies of the various types of transactions in each sample city shown in Table 3.1.

The last column of the table shows that 71 percent of these debtors had made installment purchases under conditional sales contracts; an additional 5 percent were being sued for defaulting on their revolving credit accounts; 20 percent had defaulted on personal loans; and 4 percent were in trouble because they had cosigned for someone else. The table also shows some variations among the cities. The Chicago sample did not include debtors with revolving credit accounts, an artifact of the

[2]Massachusetts is the one exception; it recently passed a law that does differentiate dealer-arranged loans from loans initiated by the borrower.

Table 3.1 / Type of Transaction by City (percent)

type of transaction	Chicago	Detroit	New York	Phila-delphia	total
"Conditional sale"	80	76	63	58	71
Revolving credit	—	5	12	2	5
"Loan"	17	16	18	36	20
"Cosigner"	3	3	7	4	4
Total percent	100	100	100	100	100
N	(312)	(438)	(332)	(249)	(1331)

sampling procedure in that city. As explained in Appendix C, the Chicago sample was drawn entirely from the confession-of-judgment book, and the Chicago department stores that offer revolving credit almost invariably bring open suits against their debtors. In contrast, revolving credit accounts are most prevalent in New York, where more than 10 percent of the debtors were involved in such transactions. The frequency of installment loans is quite similar in Chicago, Detroit, and New York, varying between 16 and 18 percent, but increases sharply in Philadelphia, to 36 percent. But this is largely an artifact of how the Philadelphia sample had to be drawn; it was taken from the sheriff's execution books, and the sheriff's office deals only with debts of $100 or more. Although installment purchases, particularly for soft goods, are often for less than $100, almost all loans are for amounts over $100. Hence loans had a much greater chance of falling into the Philadelphia sample.

Remaining to be explained are the quotation marks setting off three of the four categories in Table 3.1. These indicate loose definitions. Although most dealer-arranged loans have been treated as conditional sales, some inadvertently remained in the "loan" category. The "cosigner" category also lacks a precise definition. We found that some debtors were cosigners not merely for friends or relatives but for their own children, who were under the age at which they could sign for themselves. Since these parent–cosigners knew a good deal about the initial transaction, we treated them as if they themselves were the original debtor. There were approximately 17 such debtors (now located in the first category of Table 3.1) who could have been added to the cosigner group. These debtors were asked about the initial transaction, whereas the cosigners for persons outside the immediate family were not; the cosigner category in Table 3.1 refers to the latter group only.

Why Debtors Borrowed Money

The 20 percent or so who got into trouble because they had taken out personal loans were asked to explain the purpose of the loan. The most frequently cited reason, offered by 40 percent of the borrowers in the total sample, was to make a consumer purchase, including home repairs. This reason was most prevalent among the Philadelphia borrowers (48 percent) and least so among the Chicago borrowers (28 percent). The next most frequent reason, offered by 32 percent of all debtors, was to consolidate multiple debts in a single loan. The consolidation loan, featured in the advertisements of small loan companies, offers overextended debtors an opportunity to make smaller monthly payments at the cost of a much longer period of indebtedness. Approximately 12 percent of the borrowers took out loans to pay off medical and hospital bills. This, too, is a type of loan initiated because of overextension, but we differentiate it from the previous category because in this instance the overextension stems from an unanticipated factor—illness. Nine percent took out personal loans to aid their business enterprises or to make mortgage payments. Finally, 7 percent of those who defaulted on their loans offered a variety of other reasons for the loan, ranging from the need to finance a vacation or pay taxes to help a needy friend.

Items Purchased on Credit

As Table 3.1 showed, 71 percent of the debtors bought merchandise under a conditional sales contract and an additional 5 percent bought merchandise on time under a revolving credit arrangement. What was the nature of these installment purchases? Not surprisingly, since almost anything in America can be bought on credit, the goods covered in these transactions covered a wide range. The most frequent purchase was an automobile, accounting for 26 percent of the cases. Automobile transactions were much more common in Chicago, Detroit, and Philadelphia than in New York since Manhattan is so inhospitable to automobile ownership.[3] Furniture accounted for 20 percent of the installment purchases; household appliances, such as refrigerators, stoves, and dishwashers, were in third place, with 13 percent of the instances of defaults over merchandise, closely followed by entertainment appliances, for example, television sets, phonographs, and radios (11 percent). Together these two categories of household appliances account for 24 percent of defaults involving merchandise. In 16 percent of these cases, the default stemmed from purchases of clothing and other soft goods, such as curtains, drapes, and carpeting. Jewelry, watches, and wigs were grouped together in a broad accessory category and accounted for 10 percent of the defaults involving merchandise. In 1 percent of the cases, the item purchased was an encyclopedia, although in Philadelphia this category was much more prevalent, accounting for 6 percent of the suits involving merchan-

[3]The New York City sample is based only on the Manhattan branch of the New York Civil Court.

dise. Finally, 3 percent of these defaults were classified as miscellaneous. including such things as a furnace, cemetery lots, and purchases of paint.

TYPE OF CREDITOR

Having established the type of transaction that resulted in the default, we now confront more directly the main cast of characters of this chapter, the types of creditors with whom these debtors dealt.

Types of Lenders

The minority who got into trouble because of consumer loans could have borrowed from one of three types of agencies: banks, small loan companies, or credit unions. Table 3.2 shows the distribution of loans among these sources within each city.

Table 3.2 / Type of Lender by City (percent)

lending institution	Chicago	Detroit	New York	Phila-delphia	total
Bank	22	14	86	16	32
Small loan company	72	67	14	78	60
Credit union	6	19	—	6	8
Total percent	100	100	100	100	100
N^a	(46))	(74)	(59)	(87)	(266)

[a] Excluded are six loans for which the source of loan could not be determined.

In Chicago, Detroit, and Philadelphia, the great majority of the loans were obtained from small loan companies. In Detroit, where most of the debtors belonged to unions and many were employed in the automobile industry, credit unions are a prevalent source of loans, and almost one of every five Detroit borrowers defaulted on loans from credit unions. The startling deviation in Table 3.2 is the pattern in New York, where 86 percent of the loans were obtained from banks. This is due mainly to a single New York bank, the powerful Citybank, which apparently has a much more lenient loan policy than other banks. Of the 51 default bank loans in New York, 24 were obtained at this bank. Its nearest competitor appeared in only nine cases.[4] In sum, Table 3.2 shows that the

[4] Citybank is the most frequent plaintiff in the Manhattan branch of the New York Civil Court. A recent report by Nader's Raiders points out that its default rate on personal loans (as measured by law suits) is substantially higher than that of other New York banks. Evaluating this record is somewhat difficult. Should Citybank be congratulated for making loans to the near poor who are more likely to default, or should it be reprimanded for being more careless than other banks?

majority of borrowers defaulted on loans from small loan companies rather than banks, presumably because their relatively low income and job insecurity made them ineligible for bank loans. But at least one New York bank is apparently ready to compete with the small loan companies by extending loans to "marginal" persons.

Types of Sellers

Classifying lenders is a much easier task than classifying sellers. A fundamental distinction in this regard is between direct selling and sales made at the dealer's place of business. The institution of installment credit has been a major boon to the direct selling industry. Numerous companies today employ door-to-door salesmen to peddle on credit relatively expensive merchandise such as deep freezers, television sets, and encyclopedias. These salesmen are notorious for their high-pressure tactics, their misleading come-ons, such as promises of free merchandise and referral sales schemes. They often peddle their wares through catalogues, and the prospective customer never sees the merchandise until after the installment contract is signed. Another tactic is for the company to advertise its wares through mass media, and encourage the prospective customer to contact the company. A salesman is then sent to the customer's home.[5] Public concern over the abuses associated with direct sales has steadily mounted and some states have taken action to control such sales. Recently the Federal Trade Commission passed a regulation providing for a cooling-off period of 72 hours in direct sales, in which the buyer has the right to rescind the contract. But this regulation has yet to be tested in court and now has few teeth in it. England adopted such a law some years ago, and several states, including New York and Massachusetts, have recently adopted similar legislation. Behind the cooling-off remedy is the recognition that direct selling departs from the classic model of consumer transactions in which the consumer arrives at a decision to make a purchase and then enters the marketplace to satisfy his want. The techniques of direct selling maximize consumer exploitation since the consumer typically has not made a decision to buy before he answers the knock on his door. He is, therefore, apt to engage in impulse buying in response to the blandishments of the salesman. It is for these reasons that direct sales are distinguished from those made at the dealer's place of business. But the latter group also requires further refinement. We have seen that about one fourth of the consumer purchases that led to defaults involved automobile purchases, most being used rather than new cars. There is substantial folklore about the chicanery of used-car dealers, and to test

---

[5]The phenomenon of direct sales covers both unsolicited and solicited sales that take place outside the seller's place of business.

the validity of this lore we have put automobile dealers in a separate category. Still another distinction among dealers seems appropriate—that between the low-income retailer and the general retailer.[6] This distinction is borrowed from a well-known study conducted by the Federal Trade Commission, which showed that low-income retailers have substantially higher mark-ups on their merchandise than general retailers selling the same items even though the low-income merchants' profits, because of their greater costs, were not much higher.[7] Thus four types of credit merchants have been distinguished: direct sellers, automobile dealers, low-income retailers, and general retailers. Table 3.3 shows the frequency of these types of dealers in each sample city.

Table 3.3 / Type of Seller by City (percent)

type of seller	Chicago	Detroit	New York	Phila-delphia	total
Direct seller	27	30	29	37	30
Auto dealer	38	29	11	31	27
Low-income retailer	24	17	36	20	25
General retailer	11	24	24	12	18
Total percent	100	100	100	100	100
N^a	(230)	(341)	(237)	(144)	(952)

[a] Excluded are some 50 cases in which type of dealer could not be determined.

In the aggregate, 30 percent of these default-debtors had made purchases from direct sellers, 27 percent had dealt with automobile dealers, 25 percent with low-income retailers, and 18 percent with general retailers. General retailers, usually large department stores, were not nearly as frequent in the Chicago and Philadelphia samples as in Detroit and New York because large department stores tend to bring open suits rather than relying on confession-of-judgment contracts, the type we sampled in Chicago and Philadelphia.[8] The most significant finding in Table 3.3 is the relatively high proportion of these defaults that stemmed from direct sales. In every city, more than one fourth of the defaults were initiated by direct sales and in Philadelphia, fully 37 percent were. The aggregate figure of 30 percent is a startling statistic, for direct sales account for not more than 3 percent of all retail sales in America. The most

[6]The distinction between low-income retailers who deal primarily with the poor and general retailers who sell to broad sectors of the community was made on the basis of the judgments of consumer experts and Legal Aid attorneys in each of the cities in the sample.

[7]Federal Trade Commission, *Economic Report on Installment Credit and Retail Sales Practices of District of Columbia Retailers, 1968.*

[8]See Appendix C for a description of the sampling procedures in each city.

conservative estimate would be that direct sales result in 10 times as many defaults as would be expected by chance! This obviously points to the deception and chicanery associated with this mode of selling. Of the many areas in which consumers are in need of protection, direct selling certainly ranks high.

The Age of the Transaction

One aspect of the transaction deserving note is the length of time that elapsed between the original transaction and the law suit. The debtors were interviewed some four to eight months after their case was filed in the court docket book (in Philadelphia, in the sheriff's execution books). Ideally we would want to know the length of time between the consumer's default and the subsequent law suit, but the debtors were asked only when the initial transaction took place. Most installment contracts, whether for loans or for merchandise, do not extend beyond two years, although in automobile transactions it is not uncommon for the debtor to have up to three years to pay, and some consolidation loans cover a similarly long period of time. We might assume then that all these transactions took place within three years of the interview. But as can be seen from Table 3.4, this is by no means the case.

Table 3.4 / Time of Transaction (percent)

how long ago did you buy, borrow?	Chicago	Detroit	New York	Phila-delphia	total
Within the year	15	25	20	12	9
1–2 years ago	50	50	56	44	50
3–4 years ago	22	19	19	25	21
5 or more years	13	6	5	19	10
Total percent	100	100	100	100	100
N^a	(301)	(423)	(306)	(236)	(1,266)

[a] Excluded are the 58 debtors classified as cosigners who were not asked this question and 9 debtors who could not recall when the transaction took place or did not answer the question.

In the aggregate, some 68 percent of the transactions did take place within two years of the interview, but in 31 percent of the cases, the debt was incurred three or more years prior to the interview. In 10 percent of the cases, the transaction was fully five or more years old when the suit was filed. In Detroit and New York, the cases tend to stem from relatively recent transactions. The Chicago cases tend to be older, 35 percent being at least three years old; the deviant city is Philadelphia, where fully 44 percent of the cases refer to transactions that took place three or more years prior to the interview. In fact, almost 20 percent of the Philadelphia cases stemmed from debts that were five or more years old. The absence of garnishment might account for this pattern in Philadelphia. The creditors in that city might well rely on extensive harassment before turning to the limited legal remedies at their disposal, executions against real and personal property.[9]

These data indicate that the collection process is often a rather long and tortuous one. Type of seller is not at all related to the age of the transaction, presumably because many dealers sell their contracts and are thus not the final creditor in the transaction. Among lenders there is some connection between type and age of debt. Banks appear to be the quickest to sue, as only 31 percent of the bank loans were three or more years old. Among small loan companies, these old debts rise to 46 percent, and among credit unions they climb to 59 percent. To some extent, this ordering of lenders corresponds to both the risk level tolerated and the degree of what might be called a personal relationship between lender and borrower. Banks tend to be most impersonal or bureaucratic; small loan companies are more likely than banks to adjust to the special needs of their debtors and make greater allowances for delinquencies; and credit unions, organizations of the debtor's peers, are most likely to hesitate before bringing formal action against delinquent accounts.

DIFFERENTIATION IN TRANSACTIONS BY
TYPE OF DEBTOR

In chapter 2 we reviewed various social characteristics of default-debtors. To what extent are these attributes related to aspects of the transaction? For purposes of this analysis, the two most distinguishing traits of the default-debtors will be considered, income and ethnicity.

Although income is related to many facets of the transaction, it is not related to the *type* of transaction that resulted in default. The poor were as likely as the more well-to-do (22 and 23 percent, respectively) to default on loans, and those of higher income were about as likely as those of lower income to have defaulted on an installment sale. Even the frequency of revolving credit accounts and instances of cosigning varied little from one income group to the next.

In contrast with income, ethnicity is strongly related to type of transaction. Blacks and Puerto Ricans were much more likely to have gotten into trouble because of installment purchases (73 and 72 percent respec-

---

[9]Many Philadelphia creditors eventually sell their bad paper to collection agencies. Philadelphia is the only city in the sample in which collection agencies appear as plaintiffs. This two-step process in Philadelphia defaults might also contribute to the greater average age of the cases in that city.

tively) than were whites (57 percent), whereas whites were much more likely to have been borrowers (30 percent compared with 18 percent of the blacks and 11 percent of the Puerto Ricans). To the extent that loans are taken out to consolidate debts, they represent a second stage in the indebtedness cycle, a stage at which whites, more than blacks and Puerto Ricans, are apt to drop out. In contrast, blacks and Puerto Ricans become ensnared in the first stage of the debt cycle. This would help explain why blacks and Puerto Ricans are so heavily overrepresented among default-debtors. They may be less able than whites to stave off defaults by borrowing to pay other creditors. It is not known whether this is because they do not think of this remedy or because they are less able to than whites to get loans.[10]

Even though banks presumably have higher standards than small loan companies, the income of default-debtors is *not* related to type of lender. Among those who borrowed, those of high income were no more likely than those of low income to have had a bank loan. If anything, the reverse is true, as 35 percent of the borrowers earning under $4,000 borrowed from banks compared with 28 percent of those earning over $8,000. Ethnicity, unlike income, is strongly related to source of the loan. Whites were much more likely than the blacks to get the more favorable bank loans (45 percent compared with 18 percent), and blacks were much more likely than whites to have borrowed from small loan companies (74 percent compared with 47 percent). In both ethnic groups, 8 percent had defaulted on credit union loans.

As noted, the majority got into trouble because of credit purchases. Is the debtor's income and ethnicity related to the type of seller with whom he dealt? The answer in both instances is yes. Although income did not differentiate default-buyers from default-borrowers, it has a strong connection with type of seller among the buyers (Table 3.5).

Table 3.5 / Type of Seller by Income of Debtor (percent)

type of seller	under $4,000	$4,000–$7,999	$8,000 and over
Direct seller	40	28	25
Automobile dealer	20	29	29
Low-Income retailer	28	23	20
General retailer	12	20	26
Total percent	100	100	100
N	(231)	(482)	(188)

[10]In keeping with this speculation is the finding that among the borrowers, the whites were much likely than the blacks to have borrowed to pay off a debt, whereas the relatively few blacks who defaulted on loans were apt to have borrowed to make a consumer purchase.

The poor were much more likely than the others to have dealt with direct sellers and low-income retailers (the first and third rows) and, conversely, those of higher income more often defaulted on purchases from automobile dealers and general retailers. These findings help explain how the poor are able to enter the credit marketplace. They do so by dealing largely with direct sellers and low-income retailers.

The ethnicity pattern follows closely upon that of income. Blacks and Puerto Ricans were much more likely than whites to deal with direct sellers and low-income retailers, whereas whites in default dealt more often with automobile dealers and general retailers.

THE TRANSACTION AS EVALUATED BY THE
DEFAULT-DEBTOR AND BY THE LAW

As noted at the outset, a major theme of this chapter is the extent to which the transaction conformed to the laws regulating consumer credit and whether the debtor considered the transaction to be fair,[11] a matter to which we now turn.

Deception at the Time of the Sale

All the debtors who had made installment purchases were asked whether they were misinformed or deceived at the time of the transaction or whether the wrong merchandise was delivered.[12] The law assumes that both parties entered the transaction in good faith and had full knowledge of the terms of the transaction. Yet more than one third of the debtors (36 percent) answered this question in the affirmative. There is little variation between cities in this respect, but the debtor's judgment of the fairness of the transaction is strongly related to type of seller. Among default-debtors who had dealt with automobile dealers, fully 47 percent reported that they had been misinformed; among those dealing with direct sellers, 42 percent gave this response. In contrast, 31 percent of the debtors who had dealt with low-income retailers and only 18 percent of those who were sued by general retailers gave this response. This finding is significant on at least two counts. First, it indicates that debtors in default

[11]This analysis is limited to transactions for merchandise, as the borrowers were not asked the battery of questions that dealt with the circumstances of the transaction. In developing the questionnaire we may well have been the unwitting victims of the lending industry's propaganda, for our assumption was that licensed lenders were not apt to violate the law. In retrospect, it would have been wise to ask the borrowers such question as whether they were given all the money they were told they could borrow, whether they were told the cost of the loan, and so on.

[12]These possibilities were included in a single question. See Appendix D, question 13.

differentiate between types of dealers, blaming some types more frequently than others for their troubles. Second, the pattern conforms with folk wisdom, for direct sellers and used-car dealers (who account for most of the automobile transactions) are considered in the popular culture to be the more unscrupulous sellers.

Price Disclosure

The law in the four states represented in the survey requires that both the cash price and the total time sales price be recorded on the contract and that the debtor be given a copy of the contract at the time of the sale. In the light of these legal requirements it is quite striking that only 35 percent of the debtor-buyers claimed that they were told the *cash* price at the time of the sale. Direct sellers were least likely to provide this information (23 percent), and, oddly enough, automobile dealers were most likely to have done so (48 percent). Perhaps this merely indicates that an inflated cash price is frequently marked on used cars as a starting point for bargaining.

When asked whether they were told the total time sales price, that is, the total cost of their purchase (regardless of whether they were told the truth), some 79 percent answered affirmatively. (Eleven percent insisted that they were not told the total cost, and 10 percent were not sure whether they had been given this information.)

Of critical importance is whether the quoted total time sales price was the same as the time sales price indicated on the contract when the debtor received his copy. By relating the price quoted at the time of the sale to the true time sales price as the debtor later came to learn it, we can measure price deception. (Some 16 percent of the buyers told us that they never did learn the total time sales price. This might seem odd, but as we shall soon see, a number of debtors insisted that they never received a copy of the contract. An additional 4 percent did not answer this question, and thus information on the true cost of the obligation was provided by 80 percent of the debtor-buyers.) That many dealers engage in deception about the true time sales price is indicated by the finding that fully 46 percent of the buyers who had knowledge of both the quoted and actual cost reported that the actual cost was higher. Apparently, it is common for the dealer to quote only the cash price and give the buyer the impression that this is all he has to pay. Some 21 percent of these debtors gave figures indicating that the true time sales price was up to 25 percent higher than the quoted price, and 24 percent gave figures showing a discrepancy of 25 percent or more. Table 3.6 shows how these price discrepancies are related to type of dealer.

Less than one half of those who dealt with direct sellers and

Table 3.6 / Actual Cost Relative to Quoted Price by Type of Seller (percent)

actual cost relative to quoted price	direct seller	auto dealer	low-income retailer	general retailer	total
Same	44	49	62	69	54
Up to 25% greater	25	20	20	19	22
25% or more greater	31	31	18	12	24
Total percent	100	100	100	100	100
N	(204)	(167)	(180)	(94)	(678)

automobile dealers were told the true cost of their purchase at the time of the sale, in contrast with 62 percent of those who bought from low-income dealers and 69 percent of those dealing with general retailers. Moreover, the price discrepancies in transactions with direct sellers and automobile dealers are quite substantial, for in almost one third of these cases the true cost was more than 25 percent higher than the quoted price. That almost half the debtors who could provide the information (about two thirds of all the debtor-buyers) were not told the true cost of their purchase at the time of the sale is another important clue to the causes of breakdowns in credit transactions. It is one thing for consumers to take on responsibilities they cannot afford; it is quite another if they are being misled by sellers into believing that their obligation is less costly than it really is. Even the prudent consumer may have difficulty maintaining payments under such circumstances.

Receipt of the Installment Contract

Lawsuits brought against debtors in default are predicated upon the violation of a legally binding contract. We might assume, then, that all these debtors did indeed sign a contract specifying their obligations to the creditor. Although this may be true, it is important to note that not all the debtors *thought* that they had signed a contract. The debtors who made purchases presumably governed by conditional sales contracts (excluding the borrowers and those who had revolving credit accounts at stores) were asked whether they had signed a contract at the time of the sale. Ninety-four percent readily agreed that they had. We made a special study of the 6 percent who denied signing a contract. Twelve of the 58 people in this group claimed that they had signed a wage assignment form but not an installment contract, and these cases might well be thought of as part of the group that did sign contracts.[13] Most of

---

[13] If these were truly wage assignments, it is puzzling that the creditor bothered to obtain a court judgment. See the Glossary (Appendix A) for a definition of "wage assignment."

the remaining debtors in this group were tricked into signing contracts when they thought they were signing something else. Twenty-eight had made purchases from door-to-door salesmen and 20 of them claimed that they had signed only the "payment book"; the other 8 were told by the salesman that they were signing an order blank or a bill of sale for receipt of delivered goods. In four cases, the purchase was added on to a previous contract, and a few of these debtors were led to believe that they were signing only a character reference for some one they knew; no explanation could be found for the 10 remaining cases among those who insisted that they had not signed an installment contract.

When the debtor received his copy of the contract is a critical issue. The law is quite clear on this matter. The debtor must be given a copy of the contract at the time of the sale with all the blank spaces filled in. Of the 911 debtors who reported signing a conditional sales contract, 816 gave a definitive answer to the question of when they received their copy of the contract. Their answers are most revealing. The law in these states notwithstanding, 46 percent reported receiving a copy of the contract at the time of the sale. Some 13 percent claimed that the contract came a few days later, and 14 percent reported that the contract came a week or two later. Nine percent said that at least a month passed before they received their copy of the contract. But the astonishing statistic is that *fully 18 percent claimed that they never received a copy of the contract.* Even if some of the 155 debtors who gave this response were mistaken, it is evident that there is widespread violation of the law requiring the debtor to be given a copy of the contract at the time of the sale. Although many of the creditors in these transactions did not abide by the law, every one of them turned to the law to collect their debts. True, many of those who used the law for collection purposes were not the original sellers but rather the finance companies which bought the original contracts. Yet it would seem a mockery of the legal system to permit these finance companies to collect from the debtor when the original seller has violated the law with impunity. If and when the debtor receives the contract depends in part on the type of seller, as can be seen from Table 3.7.

The proportion who did receive their contracts at the time of the sale increases as we move from direct sellers to automobile dealers to low-income retailers and finally to general retailers. The worst offenders are the direct sellers; only 38 percent of their customers were given a copy of the contract at the time of the sale and fully 25 percent of the debtors who dealt with them claimed that they never got a contract. The automobile dealers were almost as derelict as the direct sellers in not providing the buyers with a contract at the time of the sale. But as can be seen from the last row, they were more likely than any other type of seller to eventually give the buyer his copy of the contract. This

Table 3.7 / When Contract Received by Type of Seller (percent)

when contract received	direct seller	auto dealer	low-income retailer	general retailer	total
At time of sale	38	42	54	59	46
Within a few days	13	20	9	6	13
A week or two later	14	19	13	6	14
A month or more	10	9	8	6	9
Never received	25	10	16	23	18
Total percent	100	100	100	100	100
N	(241)	(262)	(202)	(111)[a]	(816)

[a] The number of cases under "general retailer" is substantially smaller in this table, owing to the omission of known revolving credit accounts.

finding calls attention to the fact that automobile dealers typically delay the consummation of the transaction until they have sold the contract to a third party. Although the contract for an expensive item such as a car is binding on the debtor at the time he signs it, the seller is not similarly bound until a finance company has been found that will buy the contract from him. All too often it is the finance company rather than the dealer that sends the debtor his copy of the contract.[14] The odd finding in Table 3.6 is that the general retailers were, in keeping with our expectations, most likely to give the debtor his copy of the contract at the time of the sale, but that they also have a record almost as poor as the direct sellers in never giving the buyer his copy of the contract. That some debtors failed to receive contracts in transactions with general retailers may stem from the seller (unbeknownst to the buyer) treating the purchase as the initiation of revolving credit rather than as a conditional sale.

SELLER DECEPTION AND ITS CORRELATES

Having reviewed some of the ways in which sellers deviated from the laws regulating consumer credit, we now develop a measure of such deviation in order to show how it is related to both type of seller and type of debtor. An index of the seller's deception has been devised by combining three of the items dealt with in the previous section (each of which is empirically related to the others): whether the debtor felt he was misinformed or sold the wrong merchandise, whether the true

[14]Even if the dual standard that binds the debtor to the transaction at the time of the sale and yet gives the creditor the right to back out is considered fair, there is no reason why the debtor should not be given his copy of the contract at the time of the sale.

cost was greater than the total price quoted at the time of the sale, and whether the debtor received a copy of the contract at the time of the sale. A score of 1 was assigned to each indicator of deception and the resulting index ranges from 0 to 3.[15] A deliberately conservative definition of deception is used in this analysis, one based on a score of 2 or 3. In other words, dealers who were deceptive in one of three respects are grouped with those who had a clean slate in all respects to constitute the nondeceptive or "honest" group.[16] On this basis, 51 percent of the debtors are classified as having dealt with honest dealers.

When the items comprising the deception index were considered separately, it was found that each was strongly related to type of seller, with direct sellers and automobile dealers having poorer records for honesty than general retailers. It thus comes as no surprise that these differences appear when the aggregate index of deception is related to type of seller. Among direct sellers, the rate of deception is 61 percent, and among automobile dealers it is 58 percent. This figure drops to 41 percent for the low-income retailers and to 25 percent among the general retailers. Given this strong connection between type of seller and deception, it will be necessary to take type of seller into account when examining the types of debtors who were vulnerable to deception.

Type of Debtor and Seller Deception

We have seen that the poor were more likely than the well-to-do to have dealt with door-to-door salesmen. It is not surprising then, that debtor's income is negatively related to deception. Among those earning less than $4,000, 53 percent scored high on deception; among those in the $4,000–$7,999 group, the deception rate was 49 percent; and among those earning over $8,000, it declined to 42 percent. These differences are not great and perhaps of more significance is the fact that even among the more well-to-do, a substantial minority were deceived by the seller. One might expect that these income differences will tend to disappear when type of seller is taken into account. Table 3.8 shows this to be the case.

An examination of the columns and rows reveals that there is much more variation according to type of seller than according to level of debtor's income. As the columns show, within each income group, those who dealt with direct sellers and automobile dealers were much more likely to have been deceived than those who dealt with low-income

---

[15]Unfortunately, many debtors did not provide information on all these items, and it was necessary to weight their responses according to the number they did answer.

[16]This applies in instances in which all three items of information were available. Where information existed on only one or two of the three indicators, then a score of 1 was sufficient to place the respondent in the high-deception category.

Table 3.8 / Percentage High on Deception by Type of Seller and
Income of Debtor

type of seller	debtor's income		
	under $4,000	$4,000–$7,999	$8,000 and over
Direct seller	69 (91)	61 (133)	46 (46)
Automobile dealer	50 (46)	59 (137)	60 (52)
Low-income retailer	43 (65)	43 (112)	34 (38)
General retailer	30 (27)	25 (95)	23 (47)

retailers; conversely, those who purchased from general retailers were
least often deceived. The oddity in the table is that the more well-to-do
who dealt with automobile dealers were more often deceived than their
peers who made purchases from direct sellers. On balance, it is evident
that type of seller is more significant than the debtor's income in affecting
the degree of deception in the transaction.

Since debtor's ethnicity was related to type of seller, one would
expect that it is also related to seller deception, but the data lend only
slight support for this expectation. Forty-five percent of the whites score
high on deception compared with 51 percent of the blacks and only 41
percent of the Puerto Ricans. These ethnic differences virtually disappear
when type of seller is taken into account (Table 3.9).

Table 3.9 / Percentage High on Deception by Type
of Seller and by Ethnicity of Debtor[a]

type of seller	whites	blacks
Direct seller	50 (40)	64 (225)
Automobile dealer	58 (90)	56 (163)
Low-income retailer	45 (29)	41 (168)
General retailer	23 (70)	27 (100)

[a] Puerto Ricans are omitted because of their small number.

The aggregate difference between blacks and whites in vulnerability
to dealer deception holds only for purchases made from door-to-door
salesmen. Whites do better than the blacks in the aggregate because they
are more likely to get their credit from general retailers and avoid the
direct sellers who seem to plague the blacks.

Education, especially "consumer education," is widely heralded as
an antidote to exploitation in the marketplace. The better educated are
presumably more sophisticated shoppers, less vulnerable to high-pressure
tactics, and hence to deception by the seller. The data on hand lend
some validity to this view. Forty-one percent of those who attended
college and 44 percent of the high school graduates were highly deceived

compared with 52 percent of the high school dropouts and 55 percent of those who proceeded no further than elementary school. But again, it should be noted that even among those in the most favorable educational position, those who attended college, a substantial proportion were in the high-deception category.

The connection between education and vulnerability to deception could result from one or both of two processes. It could be that the better educated, as more sophisticated shoppers, are more likely to demand and receive full disclosure, regardless of the type of seller with whom they deal. Or the better education may avoid the more unscrupulous sellers, the ones more prone to evade the law. The data suggest that the latter view has much merit. Only 20 percent with at least some college and 24 percent of the high school graduates dealt with direct sellers compared with 32 percent of the high school dropouts and 42 percent of those who never proceeded beyond elementary school. Conversely, the percentage dealing with general retailers steadily increases with education, from a low of 11 percent to a high of 33 percent. The role of education, then, would seem to be that it helps determine the type of dealer the debtor turns to, with the well educated avoiding the more unscrupulous dealers. But does it serve the second function of resulting in more disclosure, whatever the type of seller? To answer this question we must examine the simultaneous affect of education and type of seller on deception, as is done in Table 3.10.

Table 3.10 / Percentage Deceived in Transaction by Type of Seller and Education of Debtor

type of seller	elementary or less	some high school	high school graduate	some college
Direct seller	63 (76)	63 (112)	54 (65)	60 (20)
Automobile dealer	70 (43)	62 (90)	51 (89)	48 (25)
Low-income retailer	40 (43)	42 (84)	40 (47)	33 (21)
General retailer	24 (21)	33 (66)	23 (66)	22 (32)

By reading the rows of Table 3.10, we learn that education is an antidote to deception only among those debtors who dealt with automobile dealers. As the second row of the table shows, the consumer's deception in such dealings steadily declines as his education increases. But even this pattern might reflect some variation in type of dealer, for it is possible that the better educated were more likely to deal with new- rather than used-car dealers (about 25 percent of the cars bought were new). When the well-educated occasionally buy from direct sellers, they are just as likely to be deceived as the poorly educated. And the same is true of those who defaulted on purchases made from general retailers (although those who dealt with general retailers were unlikely to be deceived whatever their education). Education also has little impact on deception among those who dealt with low-income retailers; through the first three educational levels, there is hardly any difference, and the college-educated who had bought from low-income retailers were only slightly less likely than the others to be deceived.

The findings of Table 3.10 reinforce what was learned earlier. Type of seller is the critical determinant of the amount of deception that takes place in the transaction. Whether the debtor is rich or poor, black or white, of high or low education is important primarily because such characteristics channel debtors to particular types of sellers. But when the financially better off debtor, or the well-educated one, makes a purchase from a direct seller or a low-income retailer, he is just as vulnerable to deception as the poor and uneducated debtor.

The import of these findings would seem to be that more emphasis should be placed on changing the seller than on changing the debtor. In the long run, of course, more education and more income for the consumer will broaden his choices and make him less dependent upon direct sellers and low-income retailers. But meanwhile consumers should be protected from deceptive sellers by greater enforcement of the laws regulating consumer credit.

In sum, the nature of the transaction that brought debtors into default has been examined. The great majority of debtors had made installment purchases governed by conditional sales contracts, although a sizable minority had defaulted on installment loans. That rapidly growing new form of credit, the revolving credit account, showed up in 5 percent of these defaults, and 4 percent of the debtors were in trouble because they had cosigned for someone else. Most loans were obtained from small loan companies, with the notable exception of the New York borrowers, who tended to default on bank loans, a finding that reflected in part the liberal credit standards of one New York bank.

Direct sellers were heavily overrepresented among all sellers, far in excess of their proportion of retail sales in the country. Blacks and debtors of low income were particularly likely to have gotten into trouble because of purchases from direct sellers.

Data were examined bearing on the seller's conformity with consumer credit laws. We found that many sellers evaded the law by not revealing the cash price or the true time sales price to the buyer at the time of the transaction and by not giving the buyer his copy of the contract with all the blanks filled in at the time of the sale. Direct sellers were most likely to engage in deception, closely followed by automobile dealers, with general retailers being least likely to employ deception. Substantial numbers of sellers of all types failed to abide by the legal requirements of consumer transactions and yet all these creditors resorted to the courts to collect their debts. This finding calls attention to a fundamental inequity in the legal system, one that makes the courts appear to be more the servants of the creditors than the arbiters of justice. This theme, central to the book, is elaborated in the subsequent analysis.

REASONS

FOR

DEFAULT

II

CLASSIFYING

THE REASONS

FOR DEFAULT

A central issue in this study is the question of why the debtors defaulted. The effort to assess the reasons for the default has the major defect of being based entirely on the testimony of only one of the parties to the relationship—the debtor.[1] Nonetheless, we are convinced that the aggregate patterns, based on the stories of all the debtors, are significant and provide a reasonably accurate picture of the multitude and relative frequency of reasons underlying the default.

The question of why the consumer defaulted on his debt obligation is extremely complex and belongs to a tradition of social research known as "reason analysis." Reason analysis attempts to reconstruct the process through which some action occurred or decision was made, such as the decision to vote for a particular candidate, choose a particular occupation, or buy a particular product. The analysis of such decisions often discloses that they are the resultants of many influences. It would have been possible to devote the entire interview with these default-debtors to the single topic of how the default happened and perhaps only such a detailed inquiry would have yielded a definitive portrait of the reasons for the breakdown in the credit transaction. Given the varied purposes of the study, however, the respondents were simply asked:

> What were the main reasons why you stopped making payments on
> the [merchandise/loan]?

[1]See Appendix B for a discussion of the issue of possible bias.

The interviewers were instructed to record the responses verbatim and to probe carefully for possible additional reasons. Uncovering the reasons for the default was aided also by a question that appeared somewhat later in the interview. The debtors were asked whether there was a good reason why they should not have to pay the court judgment against them. Their responses to this question frequently provided additional information on the default. Also of great help were the detailed notes explaining the case that the interviewers often appended to the questionnaires. In short, the diagnosis of the breakdown was carried out by reading various parts of the questionnaire, although we relied mainly on the above open-ended question.

THE CLASSIFICATION SCHEME

In analyzing reasons, social scientists have found it convenient to develop what Lazarsfeld has called an "accounting scheme," a framework or model in which the various types of reasons for an action might be located.[2] The ideal accounting scheme anticipates the variety of reasons that may have affected the act and the researcher makes certain to inquire whether any of these potential reasons were operative in the given instance. Unfortunately, we were not able to follow this procedure in the current study. If a debtor told us that he had stopped paying because he had lost his job, we did not routinely ask him if he would have continued to pay had he kept his job or whether his possible displeasure with the purchase in any way contributed to the default. Similarly, if a debtor told us he stopped paying because he felt the merchant had cheated him, we assumed that he could have paid had he wanted to and did not ask about this specifically. Of course, this additional information was frequently volunteered by the debtor and the careful probing by the interviewers often elicited more than one reason for the default. In fact, almost half the debtors mentioned more than one reason and quite a number offered three reasons.

In classifying multiple reasons, we tried to distinguish the primary one from the secondary ones. (In a few cases, four or more reasons seemed to be involved but we did not identify more than three.) For example, many debtors had assumed a number of credit obligations that they were apparently able to manage until some crisis occurred that impaired their income. A typical response would be, "I got sick and didn't work for a while and there were too many bills to keep up." Since we inquired about other debts at the time of the default, the payment

---

[2]P. F. Lazarsfeld, "The Art of Asking Why," in P. F. Lazarsfeld, ed., *Qualitative Analysis* (Boston: Allyn & Bacon, 1972); Hans Zeisel, *Say it with Figures,* 5th ed., chaps. 10 and 11 (New York: Harper & Row, 1968); and Charles Kadushin, "Reason Analysis," in *Encyclopedia of the Social Sciences* (New York: The Macmillan Company, 1968).

schedule of the debtors who gave such a response often indicated that they were heavily committed. Given such a reply, we classified the curtailment of income due to illness as the primary reason and the heavy debt burden as the secondary one.[3]

To develop a scheme for classifying the reasons for the default, we took as our starting point the underlying premise of the institution of consumer credit, the consumer's ability and willingness to pay. Most of the reasons for the default can be classified into categories that reflect either ability or willingness to pay. The debtor's ability to pay can be undermined either by an unexpected curtailment of income or by increases in his expenditures that are beyond his ability to meet. This component of the credit formula thus branches into at least two main categories, unanticipated loss of income and rival demands on income. The notion of competing demands on income can, in turn, be divided into two sub-categories, those demands that the debtor voluntarily assumed and those which were unexpected. In this fashion the debtor who voluntarily assumes more debts than he can handle can be differentiated from the debtor who is victimized by circumstances beyond his control, a distinction that we refer to as voluntary and involuntary overextension.

Just as ability to pay gives rise to several major categories, so, too, does willingness to pay. According to the credit industry, the person who is not willing to pay lacks character and is therefore a "deadbeat," the term of denegration that the industry so glibly applies to those who default. "Deadbeat" implies bad faith on the part of the debtor, but the debtor's willingness to pay can also be undermined by bad faith on the part of the creditor. Consumers may default not because they cannot pay or are irresponsible but because they feel that the creditor has been irresponsible by cheating them in some fashion.

The components of ability and willingness to pay thus generate but do not exhaust a number of categories for classifying reasons for default. One fairly common category embodies in varying degrees both ability and willingness to pay—a change in the debtor's marital status. As a result of divorce, separation, marital difficulties, or the death of a spouse, ability and/or willingness to pay can be undermined. Other types of reasons are further removed from this scheme or fall outside it altogether. For example, the question formulated to tap the reasons for the breakdown was biased in a most unanticipated way: it assumed that the debtor had indeed stopped paying. But some debtors insisted that they were paying regularly or had even paid in full and blamed their trouble on the creditor's faulty bookkeeping. In some cases the debtor was both willing and able to pay but did not know *how* to pay. These debtors claimed that they

[3]Such distinctions were sometimes difficult to make and our decisions were to some extent arbitrary. We tried to reduce the arbitrariness by checking and double checking the coding. The study director himself was closely involved in the process and did much of the coding.

did not receive payment books or were not told where to send the payments. Thus errors, misunderstandings, and confusion regarding the method of payment constitute another range of reasons. Another group insisted that they had not stopped paying altogether, but were making partial or late payments. Some of these debtors insisted that their creditor had approved of the arrangement of less than full payments, and these accounts of partial and delayed payments have been grouped into a separate general category.

✓In many cases the debtor's problem stemmed from misplaced trust in a friend or relative; that is, the debtor's own "third parties" were the cause of the breakdown. In most of these cases the debtor was a cosigner for someone who defaulted, but this category includes other subtypes as well, such as the debtor who was betrayed by someone he entrusted to make the payments for him. Another type of reason for the default is related to the debtor's no longer having the merchandise that he had bought on credit. Included here are debtors who returned defective merchandise to the dealer and mistakenly thought that the deal was terminated, as well as debtors who assumed that they were no longer obligated to pay after their merchandise had been repossessed. (The latter, of course, could only be a secondary reason for the default.) A handful of debtors mentioned harassment by the creditor as an additional reason for their not paying (again a secondary reason), and six debtors gave accounts that were so unusual that they are grouped into a miscellaneous category.

Including "harassment" and the miscellaneous group, 12 general categories of reasons have been distinguished, and within these categories a large number of subtypes have been identified, about 60 in all. The number of subtypes is quite arbitrary. As we shall see in subsequent chapters, even within the more specific categories there are variations that could have been distinguished. For example, one of the more specific subcategories, the one containing the largest number of cases, is loss of income resulting from a negative change in employment status. We have not bothered to identify what the change in employment was. For many it meant the loss of a job, for some it meant shifting to a shorter work week, and for others it meant being unemployed during a strike.

The categories of reasons can be thought of as comprising a continuum, at one end of which are those reasons that reflect the misfortunes and shortcomings of the debtor, and at the other, reasons that implicate the creditor. Table 4.1 shows the frequency of the general categories of reasons, with the categories grouped roughly according to locus of blame. The table shows the distribution of primary, secondary, and tertiary reasons as well as the distribution of all reasons (regardless of order) and of the debtors among these various categories.

Before examining the distributions in Table 4.1, notice should be taken of the base figures shown in the last row of the table. Five of

Table 4.1 / Major Categories of Reasons for Default (percent)

	first reason	second reason	third reason	total reasons	total individuals
Debtor's mishaps and shortcomings					
Loss of income	43	18	10	24	48
Voluntary overextension	13	23	32	17	25
Involuntary overextension	5	12	7	7	11
Marital instability	6	4	5	5	8
Debtor's third parties	8	4	6	6	9
Debtor irresponsibility	4	2	—	4	5
Creditor may be implicated					
Fraud, deception	14	13	15	14	19
Payment misunderstandings	7	3	—	6	8
Partial late payments	—	15	6	5	7
Item returned to creditor	a	6	14	2	4
Harassment by creditor	—	1	5	1	1
All other (miscellaneous)	1	—	—	a	a
Total percent	101	101	100	101	145
N	(1,320)	(570)	(110)	(2,000)	(1,326)

a Signifies less than ½ of 1 percent.

the debtors in the sample gave no reason at all for their default and hence the total for this analysis is 1,326, as shown at the right. An additional six debtors gave explanations for the default that seemed to be secondary rather than primary reasons (for example, "I stopped paying when they repossessed the car"), and these cases are excluded from the primary-reason column (bringing that total to 1,320). Approximately 570 debtors gave second reasons for their default, and 110 volunteered a third reason, bringing the total number of reasons to 2,000.

A word of explanation is also in order concerning the percentages in the various columns, particularly the last one. The percentages in the first four columns add to 100 (or 101 due to rounding) and are calculated on the base figures shown in parentheses. The percentages in the last column are not quite so obvious. They refer to the number of individuals who gave *at least one* reason in the various categories over the total number of individuals offering reasons (1,326). Since many persons have reasons that refer to more than one of these general categories, the total is 145 percent.[4]

[4]Actually the total of 2,000 reasons amounts to 151 percent of 1,326. The reason the last column adds to 145 rather than 151 percent is that some debtors gave more than one reason in the same general category. For example, some mentioned both illness and unemployment as reasons for loss of income, and some mentioned more than one type of fraud. The percentages in the last column thus refer to the number of individuals in each category regardless of the number of reasons they supplied appropriate to that category.

The table shows that the single most important reason for the default is some reversal in the debtor's flow of income. This is the primary reason in 43 percent of the cases and at least a contributing factor in 48 percent. In the aggregate, voluntary overextension is the second most frequent reason, affecting the default of 25 percent of the debtors. This is more often a secondary than a primary reason, for when income diminishes, many people suddenly discover that they are overcommitted. The third most frequent reason, one that is as frequent as overextension as a primary reason, is the allegation of fraud or deception on the part of the creditor. In almost one of every five cases, fraud plays some role in the default, and it is the primary reason in 14 percent of the cases. These figures actually underestimate the role of fraud in the breakdown of the transaction, for many of the cases classified as "payment misunderstandings" also suggest fraud and deception. Moreover, as we saw in chapter 3, the proportion of debtors who were deceived by unscrupulous sellers is actually much higher, indicating that many debtors were ready to pay even though they felt that they had been cheated.

Debtors who were confronted with unanticipated demands on their income—the involuntarily overextended—constitute the fourth most frequent category, with approximately 11 percent of the debtors mentioning such a reason. But this was more likely to be a secondary than a primary reason. Close behind are those reasons relating to the debtor's third parties, marital instability and payment misunderstandings, with each of these categories containing slightly under 10 percent of the debtors. Of some interest is the frequency of the category we have labeled "debtor irresponsibility." This group is rather heterogeneous, including those who never intended to pay as well as those who forgot to pay, those who missed payments while they were temporarily out of town, and some who no longer felt obligated to pay after the item they had bought was stolen or destroyed in an accident. This category, with all its variations, comes closest to the credit industry's image of the deadbeat; as can be seen from the table, it contains only 5 percent of the debtors. To use the term "deadbeat" to refer generally to those who default, as the credit industry is prone to do, is certainly a misnomer.

The frequency of reasons for default according to locus of blame is revealing. Table 4.2 presents a collapsed version of the previous table, which shows the distribution of cases in the first six categories (the debtor's mishaps) and in the last six, in which the creditor may also be implicated.

In almost four of five cases the primary reason for the default reflects upon the debtor; the creditor is implicated in more than 20 percent of the primary reasons. Almost all the primary reasons involving the creditor refer to either fraud or payment misunderstandings. The more dubious categories, such as accounts of partial payments and merchandise that reverted to the seller, rarely show up as primary reasons. Table 4.2 also

Table 4.2 / Summary: Classification of Reasons by Locus of Blame (percent)

locus of blame	first reason	second reason	third reason	total reasons	total individuals
Debtor's mishaps and shortcomings	79	63	60	74	80
Creditors may be implicated	22	38	40	27	35
Total percent	101	101	100	101	115
N	(1,320)	(570)	(110)	(2,000)	(1,326)[a]

[a] These percentages are computed in the same way as in Table 4.1. Regardless of the number of debtor's mishaps categories that apply to a given person, the debtor is counted only once. The same is true for the creditor-related categories. As a result, these percentages total 115 percent rather than 145 percent as in Table 4.1.

shows that creditors are more likely to be implicated in secondary reasons than in primary ones. Many debtors admitted that they fell behind because of loss of income, but then added that they were also reluctant to pay because they felt that they had been cheated. Of all the reasons offered, about 27 percent fall into the categories in which the creditor is likely to be at least partly to blame. Finally, from the last column we learn that although four of every five debtors gave at least one reason for their default that reflects their own shortcomings, more than a third gave at least one reason that implicated the creditor as well.

DEBTORS' MISHAPS

AND

SHORTCOMINGS

As we have seen, causes of the default which reflect the debtor's misfortunes and shortcomings constitute the great majority of reasons offered. About 8 of every 10 debtors mentioned at least one reason of this type. In this chapter we examine these categories of reasons with illustrations provided by the debtors. We begin by considering the ways in which the debtor's ability to pay was undermined by loss of income.

LOSS-OF-INCOME REASONS

Fully half the debtors mentioned loss of income as a reason for their default, and in most instances this was the primary reason. Closer examination shows that in a majority of these cases the vicissitudes of the job market were to blame. More than one fourth of all the debtors ended in default because they lost their jobs, were laid off temporarily, were shifted to a shorter work week, or were victims of strikes. Illness of the chief wage earner is the next largest subcategory. Sixteen percent of the debtors fell behind on their payments because illness impaired their earning power. Although these subcategories account for most of the loss-of-income cases, other factors were encountered as well (Table 5.1).

Table 5.1 / Sources of Income Loss as Reasons for the Default

loss-of-income categories	first reason (no. cases)	second reason (no. cases)	third reason (no. cases)	total reasons (no. cases)	total reasons (percent)	total individuals (percent)
Adverse employment change	310	34	1	345	17	26
Illness to chief wage earner	193	23	1	218	11	16
Loss of secondary wage earner's income	28	30	1	59	3	4.5
Debtor on welfare	10	5	4	19	2	1.5
Adverse job change because of debt problem	—	10	4	14	1	1
Business failure	10	—	—	10	[a]	1
Debtor goes to jail	4	1	—	5	[a]	[a]
Loss of supplementary income	3	1	—	4	[a]	[a]
All other	2	—	—	2	[a]	[a]
Subtotal cases	560	104	11	676		
Percent of total cases	42	18	10		34	51
Total cases	1,320	570	110	2,000		1,326

[a] Percentages of less than ½ of 1 percent.

Considerable strides have been made in America to reduce the hardships resulting from unemployment. Most wage earners when unemployed can count on unemployment benefits, on sick leave benefits, and, as a last resort, on welfare. But these programs are geared to assisting the wage earner to meet his minimal needs for survival; they do not protect him from his creditors. These findings call attention to a pressing need in a society in which installment credit is increasingly becoming the pillar of the economy. Most creditors now insist that consumers buy credit life insurance policies to protect them in the event of the debtor's death, and some also make the debtor buy health and accident insurance. As we shall see, these health and accident policies often do not perform the function for which they are intended. What is clearly needed is a system of insurance, perhaps one financed by government, that protects both creditors and debtors from the hardships imposed by unemployment and illness. The defaults of more than two of every five debtors result from these unexpected setbacks, and it makes little sense to subject such debtors, already suffering financial strains, to the harsh collection practices that follow upon law suits. The debt grows substantially during the collection process as a result of interest, legal fees, and court charges. Such debtors suffer not only a loss of income, but by defaulting they have their debts compounded. (The additions to the debt would more than pay for the requisite insurance policy.) Under the current system, the only relief available to such debtors is bankruptcy, a limited remedy at best, for the debtor's credit rating, an increasingly precious commodity in modern society, is jeopardized by a bankruptcy proceeding. In addition, the debtor can take advantage of this remedy only once every seven years, and there are many unscrupulous dealers who take advantage of this rule by offering credit on shabby merchandise to bankrupts, knowing that this remedy has been cut off.[1]

There is little need to exemplify the two most frequent categories shown in Table 5.1, an adverse change in employment status and illness to the chief wage earner. These accounts are quite similar and familiar. It may be noted that of the two, illness to the chief wage earner is generally the more severe hardship, for it means not only loss of income, but also an increase in expenditures to pay for medical bills. The failure of society to provide adequate low-cost health plans for its citizens is a major institutional failing that contributes substantially to breakdowns in the system of consumer credit. This theme will become more evident

---

[1]Perhaps the greatest obstacle to the bankruptcy remedy is the stigma attached to it. Several years ago, the OEO-sponsored legal services program in Washington, D.C., made a concerted effort to assist overextended debtors declare bankruptcy. Of those eligible, less than one fourth of those approached opted for this remedy.

when cases of "involuntary overextension" are considered. Although less frequent, the other categories shown in Table 5.1 are less obvious sources of income loss and therefore will be discussed in more detail.

Loss of Secondary Wage Earner's Income

Almost 5 percent of the debtors (59 cases) suffered an economic reversal because a secondary wage earner, almost invariably the wife, lost her job either because of illness or pregnancy. These cases are divided almost equally between accounts of illness to the wife and pregnancies which forced the wife to leave the labor force. Typical of the former is this story of a young black Detroit woman, whose husband was a factory worker, earning $6,000–$8,000 a year.

> I became ill and was hospitalized for 43 days, and I wasn't able to work. My husband doesn't make too much money and we needed my income. So we just didn't have the money. We were trying to spread it out as far as we could, but we just couldn't make it.

Typical of cases involving the wife leaving the labor force because of pregnancy is this account of a black Chicago woman, whose husband earned $6,000–$8,000 a year as a factory worker and who defaulted on some clothes that she had bought.

> I was pregnant and had to stop working just before the baby was born and we just didn't have the money to pay right then.

One of the few cases in this category that did not involve illness or pregnancy to the secondary wage earner is that of a New York Puerto Rican woman who had to leave the job market because her child became ill.

> I had to stop working because the baby was sick and I had to take care of her. After that we just didn't have the money to pay.

Such cases are a reminder that the income of these debtors often rests on multiple wage earners, particularly, as we saw in chapter 2, in families with incomes over $8,000 a year. Some of the functional connections between installment credit and other institutional spheres of society have been noted. The accounts of pregnancy call attention to yet another: the relationship between installment credit and family planning. A special count was made of mentions of pregnancies in the accounts of defaults. Such references occurred in 52 cases, about 4 percent of the sample. We have no way of knowing how many of these pregnancies were unplanned, but the educational level of our respondents tends to be quite low and family planning is known to be related to education. Family planning is thus another dimension of the credit problems of consumers.

Debtor on Welfare

Included under the heading "loss of income" are 19 debtors who link their default to their being on welfare. Some of these debtors were on welfare when they made the credit purchase; others went on welfare because of illness or job loss after incurring the debt obligation. Although this category is not necessarily independent of the others shown in Table 5.1, in all these cases the fact of welfare somehow influenced the default.

A middle-aged New York white woman, the head of a broken family, had borrowed $300 from a bank to pay off other debts when she lost her job and had to go on welfare.

> When I first went on welfare, I called the bank and told them I'm going on welfare but they would be paid eventually. They weren't interested in my problems. I had a checking account in the bank and they took two payments from the checking account. I told them it was welfare money and was meant for food, but they weren't interested. I closed out my checking account. The man I spoke to said that people on welfare never pay off their debts. I told him I would pay it off but they had to give me time. He was nasty about it and not at all willing to cooperate. So I got a summons telling me that they were suing me. If they want to be like that, I'm not bothering to pay them. Let them sue me. They can't get any money that way.

This case is similar to some that will be presented in chapter 8 dealing with debtors who unsuccessfully attempted to work out arrangements for partial payments with their creditors.

In some of these cases the debtors stopped paying because of welfare regulations. A New York black couple with seven children bought several sets of furniture and eventually became eligible for supplementary welfare since the husband's earnings were quite low. At the time of the interview, their annual income, including welfare, was slightly above $4,000. The wife explained the default this way:

> I was not on welfare when we bought the furniture. My husband works and he still does but his salary is small and we have a large family and so we applied for supplementary welfare and eventually got on. They [the welfare department] stopped me from making the payments on the furniture because they said it was not worth it and to let them come and take it out. But I did not want that. It's too

> embarrassing for the family. So the store and I came to an agreement.
> I'll make payments when I can.

From other information she provided, it appears that this agreement evolved only after the store had sued her.

As noted, some of these debtors were already on welfare when the purchase was made. They assumed that they could pay irregularly or in smaller amounts and were surprised that they were being sued. A Philadelphia black woman, the head of a broken family, illustrates this pattern. She had purchased a $135 wig even though she was on welfare. Her attitude was that she would pay as much as she could when she could, a viewpoint that did not please her creditor.

> I never stopped paying. I just paid what I could. I didn't have the money to pay the way he wanted, because I'm on assistance.

Loss of Income Because of Debt Problem

Of particular interest are the 14 debtors who pointed out that their debt problems contributed to their loss of income. They had either lost jobs because of garnishments or had quit jobs for fear of garnishment, by either previous or current creditors. This type of reason understandably shows up only as a secondary one, with overextension as the primary reason.

A young Detroit black with only an elementary school education who had been an assembly line worker in the automobile industry and had earned less than $4,000 a year was currently being sued by Elroy Jewelers, a firm that we shall encounter frequently, which sells suits as well as jewelry. (This man had bought a suit.)

> I got sick and broke my arm. I was off sick in the hospital for two weeks with an infection. I had three garnishees on my job and I had everything taken away. They took my car away and didn't even let me know about the auction. I worked at   Corp. and they started to give me five days off because of these garnishees. I quit the job because of these garnishees as they told me to pay it all up and I couldn't. They were going to fire me anyway. So I claimed job dissatisfaction. If they fire me, they would never hire me again, so I quit yesterday. The garnishees were coming in so fast and more to come. I didn't know I could get into so much trouble by buying. I didn't figure it all out. I am 22 years old and married two and a half years and my wife is only 19. We didn't know that these things could happen. I have two children and I pay alimony for another child. I can't pay anything. I have to declare bankruptcy. . . .

The youthfulness and low education of this debtor undoubtedly contributed to his debt problems, as he himself admits. His account also illustrates the self-defeating aspects of the garnishment sanction. He knew that he stood a good chance of being fired because of the garnishments and would then have a black mark against his record. Rather than risk that possibility, he simply quit his job.

The self-defeating aspects of garnishment are evident in the next account, provided by a middle-aged Chicago black woman whose family income amounted to $6,000–$8,000 a year. She and her husband were being sued by a small loan company.

> My husband wasn't working at the time and he stopped paying. Then they sent a wage garnishment to my job and got me fired so I couldn't keep up the payments.

A final example of this category of reasons illustrates the devastating consequences of garnishment for the earning power of debtors. This account is provided by a 28-year-old Detroit white, currently employed in the construction industry and earning $6,000–$8,000 a year at the time of the interview, although his job status was precarious because of the debts hounding him. His troubles started because he was being sued by a department store over a series of purchases intended as Christmas presents for his children.

> We had too many bills and too many kids, and I was laid off on and off. We just had no money and they were all hounding us. . . . I lost a job at _____ that I had for eight years because of a garnishment. So I lost eight years' seniority. . . . That was one year ago. Because of this, I had a bad reputation and I haven't been able to get a good job since. . . . I just get a job and then they [the creditors] find out about it and they garnish me again. . . . Now we are losing our house and everything.

Other Forms of Loss of Income

The four remaining categories shown in Table 5.1 refer to extremely rare phenomena. Some 10 debtors who had been self-employed experienced a financial setback because their businesses had failed. These men had both consumer and business debts. Five of the debtors admitted that they had gotten into some trouble which resulted in their going to jail. No sooner were they released from jail than their creditors brought law suits to collect on their unpaid debts. One of these five was put in jail by his ex-wife because he had failed to maintain support payments. Four default-debtors blamed their debt problems on the failure of their ex-husbands to maintain child support payments and the residual category of income loss contains but two cases: in one a middle-aged Chicago white who owned a three-family house said his income was impaired because he could not rent one of his apartments and in the other, the debtor became delinquent because he had been drafted.

VOLUNTARY OVEREXTENSION

As seen in Table 4.1, overextension as the result of excessive voluntary debts is the second most frequent reason for default, affecting approximately a quarter of the debtors. Of the 338 debtors who were so classified, approximately half mentioned their excessive bills as a secondary reason. These people were apparently able to manage their heavy debt burden until some crisis occurred that lowered their income. In almost all these cases the overextension resulted from consumer debts, but there were 11 debtors who defaulted on personal loans taken out in order to meet business debts.

Overextension, of course, refers not to the absolute amount of debt but to the ratio of debt to income. Although many of the overextended debtors had large debt obligations, some found themselves unable to keep up with even modest payments. For example, a 49-year-old white New Yorker with six children earned only $3,000–$4,000 a year as a night-time cab driver. He defaulted on a used car for which the payments were $55 a month. He also was obligated to pay $25 a month for a small loan. Although his total payments were only $80 a month, relative to his income and large family, this debt was too much for him to handle.

> I wasn't making enough money to cover my big family. . . . That's all. I have six children. . . .

Perhaps more typical is the story of a 32-year-old white Detroiter who at the time of the interview had a good job as a steam-hammer repair man, earning over $10,000. But at the time of his debt troubles he was a truck driver. He defaulted on an automobile for which the payments were $65 a month and in addition he was making payments to various small loan companies which came to $160, bringing his monthly payment schedule to well over $200.

> We were paying on so many things. I don't remember them all. Every time I borrowed, they just added it on to the bill. . . . At that time, I started driving a truck and it didn't pan out like I thought it would.

His wife, in an aside to the interviewer, observed:

I don't think he really wanted to make it work. He was always spending more than he was making.

Undoubtedly, many overextended debtors are unable to discipline themselves by keeping their debts within the range of their income.

A young white Detroiter, employed as an iron worker and earning $5,000–$6,000 annually had multiple debts and monthly payments totaling $175. He tried to find relief by going to a debt-pooling agency.

> That debt-pooling company really messed us up good, because they didn't pay our bills. We kept getting calls from the people we owed money to and we told them that this company was paying our bills, but they weren't. They just kept the money we gave them. And so we had to file bankruptcy. That was our only way out. It got so that we couldn't even feed the kids.

This overextended debtor's reference to a debt-pooling agency that disappointed him foreshadows a reason for the default that will be encountered when debtor's "third parties" are considered.

The notion of voluntary overextension is somewhat misleading, for it places the burden entirely on the debtor who presumably has been imprudent. But it must be remembered that even the most imprudent debtor, the one with many debt obligations, was still able to get credit at a time when he was heavily in debt. Because many merchants and lenders do not carry out careful investigations before extending credit, they encourage debtors to overextend themselves. Moreover, in a number of instances, debtors were overextended because they had been victimized by a creditor other than the one who had brought the suit. Their overextension stemmed not from imprudence but from their being the victims of error and fraud by other creditors. For example, a white Chicago gas station attendant, earning $4,000–$5,000 a year, defaulted on a $1,000 loan because he suddenly found himself too deeply in debt. The straw that broke his back was a mix-up on the part of a major store that sent him a more expensive furnace for his home than the one he had ordered.

> We were so far in debt we couldn't even get out. When our account with Noble's jumped from $11 a month to $42 a month, we just couldn't make it any more. We only owed them $300 when we ordered a furnace for $249. There was a mix-up and they sent the wrong one, but the guy said we could keep it for the same price. Then they sent us a bill for over $400 and later they sent us a bill for over $1,000 for *two* furnaces.

By the time this debtor unraveled his problems with this store he was in default with the small loan company.

Another case that illustrates the dynamics of credit-determined over-extension is that of a white Detroit couple who lost their home because of their debt problems. The husband was a truck driver earning $8,000–$10,000 a year. They were being sued for defaulting on a sewing machine purchase, the result of a bait ad. (The wife had seen a TV ad for a $25 sewing machine, responded, and ended up buying one for $300.) This couple is typical of the overextended debtors in that they were paying some six creditors (mainly small loan companies) at the time of their default. But how did they get so overcommitted? The wife, who was the respondent, gave this account.

> ✓ In 1963 we applied for a home modernization loan and we got a letter that we were refused. A few months later, Manufacturers National Bank sent us a letter and said we had been accepted. But meanwhile we realized that we couldn't afford to get into this debt. We called the modernization company and told them that we couldn't afford this kind of money and that we had changed our minds. They said it was too late, the loan had already gone through. It was about $3,000 or $4,000 and we are still paying on it. They are threatening a garnishment now. I feel that this contributed to our eventually losing our home.

Since the home improvement loan was not the basis for the law suit, many of the details surrounding it are missing. But judging from other cases in our study, it is quite possible that this couple was approached by a door-to-door salesman for the home improvement company who persuaded them to sign a contract for the repairs. The salesman's firm then tried to sell the contract to a bank and apparently the first bank refused the loan, much to the relief of the couple. It was only some months later that the home improvement firm found a bank ready to accept the contract, by which time the couple had changed its mind. Nonetheless, they were still held responsible for the note that they had signed previously. Certainly a law instituting a cooling-off period in such sales would be of help. A basic question remains: on what grounds is a contract that the dealer is not prepared to guarantee binding on the debtor? Certainly the home improvement firm treated the contract as conditional at the time of the transaction. Why then should debtors be forever bound by such contracts? Had this episode not occurred, it is conceivable that this couple would not have defaulted on the expensive sewing machine.

Several other debtors volunteered stories about their other credit problems which contributed to their overextension. A middle-aged black couple in Detroit fell into our sample because they were being sued as the cosigners on a car bought by their son, who had fallen behind in his payments because of illness. The couple made some payments on the car, but they too fell behind and were sued. (With both spouses working, their combined family income was over $10,000.) Among the payments that this couple was making at the time of the suit was a debt to the wife's credit union, which required payments of $75 a month. This loan in turn was taken out to pay off a small loan company.

> We had borrowed $1,700 from a place called the Downtown Mortgage Co. They sold the loan to a place called Super Credit Corp. The payments were $55 a month for 60 months. This came to $3,300 for borrowing $1,700. This is a horrible rate of interest. After paying $55 a month for 24 months, I borrowed from the credit union to pay them off. They said I still owed them $2,895. I paid this $2,895 in cash plus the twenty-four months of payments at $55 per month.

This is an astonishing story in that the couple had already paid in the course of two years $1,320 on what was to be a five-year debt of $3,300. And yet when they tried to settle the debt three years in advance of the final installment they were required to pay an additional $2,895, an amount that brought the cost of their $1,700 loan to $4,215. Even if this woman was not fully correct about the regularity of her payments, it would seem that the cost of this loan was exorbitant. And with such financial burdens, small wonder they were unable to maintain payments on their son's car.

Although the stories presented illustrate the imprudence of many debtors, they also show how debtors are victimized by unscrupulous lenders and sellers and find themselves overextended through no fault of their own.

INVOLUNTARY OVEREXTENSION

In Table 4.1 we saw that 11 percent of the debtors got into trouble in part because of some unanticipated financial obligation; for 5 percent, this was the primary reason for their default. These cases fall into several subtypes (Table 5.2).

The majority involve unexpected medical bills because of illness in the immediate family or the pregnancy of the debtor's wife. Almost 8 percent of the debtors had such medical expenses, and in 2 percent of the cases these bills were related to the wife's pregnancy. It should be noted that these figures seriously underestimate the strains placed on these debtors because of illness, for they refer primarily to family members other than the chief wage earner. As seen in Table 5.1, fully 16 percent of the debtors suffered losses of income because of illness to themselves, and in many of these cases medical bills stemming from the debtor's illness probably presented added strains on the family's financial

Table 5.2 / Involuntary Debts as Causes of Default

involuntary debts	first reason (no. cases)	second reason (no. cases)	third reason (no. cases)	total reasons (no. cases)	total reasons (percent)	total individuals (percent)
Medical and hospital bills for immediate family member	39	48	6	93	5	7.5
Added bills due to illness—death of a relative	19	9	2	30	2	2
Added expenses due to liability for an accident	4	—	—	4	[a]	0.5
Expenses related to repairs of purchased item	4	5	—	9	[a]	1
All other types of involuntary expenses	2	4	—	6	[a]	0.5
Subtotal cases	68	66	8	142	7	11.5
Percent of total cases	5.2	12	8			
Total cases	1,320	570	110	2,000		1,326

[a] Percentages of less than ½ of 1 percent.

resources. The need for programs of medical insurance has long been recognized in America, and in recent years some effort has been made by the government to meet this need in the form of medicare and medicaid. But these programs do not meet the needs of the public in the face of rising costs of medical care. The United States lags far behind other advanced countries in meeting the health needs of its people. Although the credit industry might not at first consider government-sponsored health insurance as compatible with its own free enterprise ideology, these data suggest that such a program might well be in its interest.

Medical–Hospital Bills of Immediate Family Members

The process through which unexpected medical expenses can push other-wise prudent consumers over the brink is well exemplifed by this report of a 26-year-old Philadelphian, employed as a machinist and earning $5,000–$6,000 a year, who defaulted on a used-car purchase.

> My wife had to go to the hospital to have a tumor removed and I got behind because of the doctor bills. I had no hospitalization and I was robbing Peter to pay Paul. . . .

In 20 of these 93 cases of unanticipated medical bills for immediate family members, the problem was related to the wife's pregnancy. Illustrative of these cases is the account of a middle-aged Detroit black earning $5,000–$6,000 annually as a parking attendant. He defaulted on a TV purchase.

> My wife was pregnant and having a lot of trouble. We were paying the doctor $15 every visit and for a while she had to go every week. Then when the baby was born he had to stay in the hospital for a long time because he was premature. So we had all that to pay and then by the time the baby was born we had to pay another doctor, a specialist.

Expenses due to Illness–Death of a Relative

The second category of Table 5.2 also touches upon an unmet social need. Some 30 debtors, 2 percent of the entire sample, explained that they got into financial difficulty in large part because of illnesses or dealths in their extended family. Typically, a parent or sibling would become ill or die, and the debtor would have to cope not only with medical and funeral expenses but also with the relative's bills and, in some instances, provide for the relative's survivors.

An unmarried 46-year-old black Detroiter, employed in the auto industry, earning $5,000–$6,000 a year, defaulted on some home repairs.

> The reason [for the default] was that I had to have a girl in the house to take care of my mother. This cost me $35 a week. My mother was sick and there were doctor visits and expenses were high and I couldn't work overtime because my mother needed me.

A black Chicago steel worker, earning $5,000–$6,000 annually, gave this reason for falling behind on his automobile payments:

> I got behind because my father died and I had to leave town and assume all the funeral expenses. I was going to make a payment the day they picked up the car.

And a middle-aged Chicago woman, the head of a broken family, earning $6,000–$8,000 a year as an office worker, defaulted on an automobile. The interviewer recorded her story in the third person.

> She had brought her parents to live with her in Chicago. Four days after they came, her father died, leaving her with her sick and senile mother to care for—in addition to her two children. Her mother's medical bills were over $100 a month, just for drugs, and she saw that she could not possibly pay for the car. She called the auto agency and asked them to take it back and they refused. Then she called the bank and asked them to take it back. Finally, after two weeks—it was during this period that she finally got her copy of the contract—the car agency came and repossessed the car. They told her she would have to pay the difference between the amount on the contract and what they would get for re-selling the car and she agreed since she had no choice.

These cases, too, call attention to unmet social needs, from burial costs to the costs of caring for aged and disabled parents. The trend in modern society has been to shift the burden of caring for the aged from the family to public institutions, but often it still falls upon the adult children.

Accident Liability, Repairs, and Miscellaneous Cases

The remaining three categories of involuntary expenses shown in Table 5.2 are extremely rare, affecting only 19 debtors, less than 2 percent of the sample. In four of these cases, the debtor was involved in an automobile accident and did not have sufficient insurance to cover the damages involved. The account of a 28-year-old Detroit black employed as an assembly line worker and earning $6,000–$7,000 a year is typical.

I had an accident and after the accident I fell into a whole lot of debt because of it. I ran into another car and the man was hurt. . . . All the insurance was, was $100 deductible. It covered the damages on my car but it didn't cover the other car or the other driver. This was the insurance they sold me with the car. I know now that I'm supposed to have insurance for the other car and driver, but when they said I was paying insurance I thought that's what I had. I never bought a car before.

This story points up the gross inadequacies of the insurance arrangements made by dealers for their customers. Many consumers have little understanding of the insurance that is automatically added to their contracts, nor are they given any choice in the matter. The abuses of this system have come to the attention of Congress and, as this man's experience shows, the need for reform is great.

Nine debtors, all of whom had purchased automobiles, pointed out that they had difficulty maintaining payments on their cars because they had to invest so much money in unexpected repairs on these automobiles. These cases, unlike the others in this general category, would appear to implicate the dealer, who may deliberately pass off shoddy merchandise to the unsuspecting debtor under the principle of caveat emptor. Typical is the following account provided by a middle-aged white New Yorker employed as a landscape gardener and earning $5,000–$6,000 a year.

I had it at the garage all the time getting it fixed. It was costing me more to get it fixed than the payments were. I had to take out a small loan just for the car repairs. The dealer wouldn't do anything about it. He wouldn't take it back. The bank wouldn't do anything about it. They had sent the money to the dealer. I called the bank's loan department and the man said he had gotten complaints about that dealer before.

Of interest here is that the bank, the holder-in-due-course, acknowledged hearing a number of complaints against the original seller; yet in spite of these signs that the dealer might be less than honest, the bank did not hesitate to buy his paper. We shall come across a number of similar examples which question whether the holder-in-due-course is as innocent of the original transaction as the doctrine implies. Certainly, if the financing agencies were liable for the debtor's defenses against the original seller, they would be more careful about the kinds of paper they buy. These cases call attention to a kind of double jeopardy in installment buying. To cope with the defects in the merchandise purchased, the debtor is forced to make expenditures which in turn interfere with his ability to maintain payments. This type of reason for the default is closely related to some we shall consider in chapter 6, where we will encounter debtors who refused to pay on defective merchandise.

Finally, six debtors were classified in a category where miscellaneous unanticipated expenses contributed to the default. In two cases, fires broke out in the debtor's home, and the repair bills caused the debtors to default. In another case a heater burst and the debtor was confronted with a major repair bill. One debtor was involved in a law suit unrelated to his debt and fell behind because of his legal expenses. Another debtor was ordered by the court to pay alimony; and one husband and wife who worked found themselves with an enormous transportation bill when their car underwent repairs for several weeks, and they frequently had to take taxis to work.

The various types of unanticipated expenses reviewed here, ranging from illness of family members to expenses stemming from accidents —including such rare occurrences as fires—are a reminder of the many problems that can upset the daily rhythm of life, bringing well-intentioned and even prudent debtors to a position where they are unable to pay.

FAMILY PROBLEMS

The defaults of about 9 percent of the debtors could be traced to family problems; in about 6 percent of the cases this was the primary reason for the default. In the great majority of these cases, the dissolution of the marriage through separation or divorce was the critical factor underlying the default, but marital strains short of separation were also a factor in some cases, and family problems other than marital strain were occasionally relevant. Table 5.3 shows the distribution of cases among the various subtypes in this general category.

Broken Marriages

As can be seen from the table, the majority of the cases refer to broken marriages (the first two categories). The distinction that we have made between the husband leaving the wife and the wife leaving the husband is quite arbitrary and refers simply to whether the husband or the wife was the person interviewed at the address found in the court records. Yet this distinction corresponds to somewhat different reasons for the default. In the 45 cases in which the husband left and the wife was the person interviewed, the wife almost invariably explained that she lacked the financial resources to maintain payments on the debt. In some instances she felt that the debt was solely her husband's responsibility. It must be remembered that in many instances both the husband and wife are the defendants in the court action, and a number of the wives in these marital split-ups were also being sued by the creditor. Illustrative of this

Table 5.3 / Family Problems as Causes of Default

type of family problem	first reason (no. cases)	second reason (no. cases)	third reason (no. cases)	total reasons (no. cases)	total reasons (percent)	total individuals (percent)
Broken marriages						
Husband leaves wife	41	2	2	45	2	3.5
Wife leaves husband	19	6	1	26	1	2
Marital tensions compounding debt problem—pathology of breadwinner	16	11	3	30	2	2.3
Other family problems	4	4	—	8	[a]	0.7
Subtotal cases	80	23	6	109		
Subtotal percent	6	4	6		5	8.5
Total cases	1,320	570	110	2,000		1,326

[a]Percentages of less than ½ of 1 percent.

73

category of reasons is the story of a 22-year-old white Philadelphia woman separated from her husband.

> I don't know why he stopped. I was separated from him and I don't know why he stopped paying on the car. When I asked him about it later he said he just never got around to it.

This account suggests an attitude of irresponsibility on the part of the husband, an attitude that appears often in these cases.

Equally interesting are the cases of the 26 husbands who blamed the default on their separations. In most of these cases the husband assumed that he had an understanding with his wife that she would continue to pay for the item that she took with her at the time of the separation. Typical of these cases is the following.

A 42-year-old black Detroit tool and die maker, earning $8,000–$10,000 a year, was sued for a TV set bought on time.

> I thought my wife would continue to make the payments as we had separated and she had the TV. I asked her to finish paying for it as I had so many bills to pay and I felt it was only fair for her to pay for it when she took it with her.

As this case suggests, the default is often a consequence of the confusion and strains accompanying the marital separation. These husbands assumed that their wives would continue the payments, but the wives may have been unable to pay perhaps because the husband was not providing the funds agreed upon in the separation.

Not all these cases follow this pattern. In some instances the husband found that he could not keep up his payments because of the added financial burdens stemming from the marital separation.

A 32-year-old Detroit black production worker in the auto industry with an income of $8,000–$10,000 a year gave this account.

> I couldn't pay because I didn't have that much income for the outgoing bills. Because of the divorce, I had to pay child support. If we didn't get divorced, I probably would have been able to make the payments because we were both working.

Marital Tensions and Pathology of the Breadwinner

Thirty debtors, about 2 percent of the sample, were placed in a subcategory called "marital tensions and pathology of the breadwinner." In about half the cases, the debtor reported that his payment schedule was upset by strains in his marriage, strains that often led to subsequent separation or divorce, making these cases close to those in the two preceding categories. In the other half, the breadwinner had a drinking problem that interfered with his earning power or led him to squander his earnings on liquor. Typical of the first variant of these cases is the account of a 25-year-old Detroit black earning $6,000–$8,000 a year in the auto industry.

> We had domestic problems at this time and were temporarily separated. I just didn't keep up the payments. . . . I didn't care.

This account is very much like others that we will consider under the heading of debtor irresponsibility and indeed has been classified there as well, for it indicates the process through which martial difficulties undermine the debtor's willingness to pay.

Illustrative of the second theme in this category, pathology stemming from a drinking problem, is this account of a 35-year-old New York white woman, now living on welfare, who defaulted on a small loan.

> I borrowed the money to pay household bills. My husband would just drink up his pay. He has a bad drinking problem. He drinks until there is no money left in his pockets. We just didn't have any money to make the payments. As I said, he would drink and drink until he ran out of money, no matter what the money was for.

Miscellaneous Family Problems

Eight debtors fall into a miscellaneous category under family problems. In six of these cases, the default was linked to a death in the family which either so upset the debtor that he failed to maintain payments or left the surviving spouse with insufficient funds to maintain payments.

Typical of these is the account of a middle-aged white Philadelphia woman who defaulted on carpet payments after her husband died.

> My husband passed away and I didn't have any money. I offered to pay him a couple of dollars a week but he wouldn't take it from me. I explained at that time that I couldn't possibly pay $27 a month.

Not all of these residual cases involved deaths in the family. A middle-aged black Detroit automobile worker mentioned as a secondary reason for his default being distracted by worry over his son, who was having school problems.

> The main reason was that I got sick and couldn't work. But also at that time I was having a hard time with my kid, and this knocked

me for a loop. I was more concerned with my boy who was having
school problems than I was with the car. He wasn't in school when
he was supposed to be.

These examples indicate the ways in which family crises, breakups
in marriages (through divorce, separation, and death), and instability on
the part of the breadwinner undermine the debtor's ability and/or willingness to pay. We now turn to another general category of debtor's mishaps,
the various ways in which the debtor's own "third parties" undermined
the credit relationship.

DEFAULTS RELATED TO DEBTOR'S THIRD PARTIES

For 10 percent (127) of the debtors the default was linked to persons
(or in a few instances, agencies) whom they involved in their debts or,
more frequently, persons who involved them (the debtors in our sample)
in their debts. The majority in this category were cosigners for friends
or relatives who had defaulted. These cosigners posed problems both
for the design of the study and for the classification of reasons for the
default. We assumed that any debtor who cosigned for a friend or relative
outside his immediate family would know very little about the initial
transaction, and thus all questions dealing with the transaction (price,
satisfaction, and so on) were not asked of these cosigners, nor were
they asked about the reasons for the default. (Some volunteered this
information when asked whether there was a good reason for not paying
the judgment.) There were 59 cosigners of this type in the sample. Where
the cosigner was a parent of the original debtor, we assumed that he
would have this information and the parent-cosigners were treated as
if they were the debtors themselves. There were 18 such cosigners. In
these cases the reason for the default often refers to one or both of
the parties involved; we sometimes learned why the original debtor
defaulted (a father might explain that his son lost his job) and also why
the cosigner did not assume the obligation. More often we were told
only why the initial debtor defaulted. All these instances of cosigners
have been put into a separate "reason" category, which, of course, is
not really a reason for the default at all since we often do not know
why the original debtor defaulted or why the cosigner did not take over
the payments. As we shall see, in many instances the cosigner apparently
was not presented with a choice and was immediately sued when the
original debtor defaulted. In short, the category of "cosigner" covers
a multitude of reasons that we know little about.

The various subcategories under the more general heading of debtor's
third parties and the distribution of cases among them is shown in Table
5.4.

Table 5.4 / Debtor's Third Parties as Reasons for the Default

reasons linked to debtor's third parties	first reason (no. cases)	second reason (no. cases)	third reason (no. cases)	total reasons (no. cases)	total reasons (percent)	total individuals (percent)
Debtor sued as cosigner	64	10	2	76	4	5.8
Debtor sells merchandise—new owner defaults	7	1	—	8	[a]	0.6
Debt run up by someone else using debtor's credit cards or forging debtor's name	15	2	—	17	1	1.3
Debtor entrusts payments to someone who fails to make them	10	3	—	13	1	1.0
Complaints regarding debt-pooling and debt-counseling agencies	—	4	4	8	[a]	0.6
Miscellaneous third-party stories	4	1	—	5	[a]	0.4
Subtotal cases	100	21	6	127		
Subtotal percent	8	4	6		6	9.7
Total cases	1,320	570	110	2,000		1,326

[a] Percentages of less than ½ of 1 percent.

It will be noted that "cosigner" appears most often as a primary reason (64 of the 76 cases were classified this way), signifying that we do not know the reason for the default in these cases. In the 12 cases where "cosigner" is a secondary reason, the respondent was able to explain why the original debtor defaulted and that reason was coded as the primary one. We have included cosigners in our tabulations for two reasons: to show the number of debtors who got into trouble by being cosigners, and to give these cosigners an opportunity to express their grievances.

Debtors Who Were Cosigners

The 76 debtors who were sued because they were cosigners for defaulters frequently had stories which implicated not only the person who left them "holding the bag" but the creditor as well. A white Detroit housewife, whose husband earned $6,000–$8,000 annually as an assembly line worker in the automobile industry, was indignant about a transaction in which her husband had cosigned for his younger brother, who had purchased an automobile.

> My husband was under the impression that he was cosigning for his brother and his name would also be on the contract. When we got the papers I was flabbergasted. Only my husband's name was on it. . . . My husband doesn't take anything seriously and his brother told us not to worry, he'd make the payments. But we ended up having to make the payments. I called the bank and told them that it was wrong to put our credit through without really checking. We were already paying on a car of our own and we didn't have credit for more.

Of interest in this account is the woman's surprise that the bank accepted her husband as a cosigner when "we were already paying on a car." Judging from some other accounts this is not an uncommon attitude on the part of cosigners. They apparently agree to cosign in order to assist some friend or relative but never fully grasp the idea that in so doing they may be liable for the debt. As in the case of this couple, some cosigners do not believe that their signatures will be accepted by the creditor, but go through the motions in order to appease the friend or relative who is pressuring them. Their mistake is to trust the creditor to carry out a careful credit check. This process is made even clearer by the account of another cosigner, a 59-year-old black Detroiter, earning $3,000–$4,000 in the automobile industry, who also did not think it was fair that he be made to pay the judgment.

> I was surprised that the company accepted me as a cosigner because
> I had gone bankrupt a few years before.

What this man failed to realize is that some creditors find recent bankrupts to be desirable credit customers since the bankruptcy law prohibits them from declaring bankruptcy again for a period of seven years. It is that logic that lies behind the frequent advertisements by used-car dealers addressed specifically to bankrupts.

A number of cosigners told us they would have maintained the payments if given the chance before the creditor repossessed the merchandise and initiated the law suit. A Chicago couple, the husband now employed as an actuary, earning $8,000–$10,000 a year, told this story, which the interviewer recorded in the third person.

> Mr. H. had been a teacher in a school for handicapped children and had cosigned for a car bought by the janitor of the school, Mr. S., who was a rather unstable, hard-luck person. Not too long ago Mrs. H. received a phone call from a person representing himself as a State traffic officer who said an unidentified man (presumably Mr. S. who had disappeared last August with the car for which Mr. H. had cosigned) had been injured in an accident and had Mr. H.'s name in his pocket and wanted to know where Mr. H. could be reached. Mrs. H. told him. The same person had previously called Mr. S.'s mother and Mr. H.'s mother with the same story but had not been able to get Mr. H's office or home address. Within minutes of this conversation, Mr. H. received a call at his office from a loan officer at the Main Street National Bank berating Mr. H. because S.'s loan was delinquent and threatening to talk to Mr. H.'s boss. Mr. H. explained that he knew nothing of the matter and that the bank could at any time have reached him since he has his own car financed at the same bank, and that they had not at any time attempted to contact him with regard to Mr. S.'s failure to pay. Mr. H. told them that he recognized it as his obligation and would work something out. In spite of this conversation, two days later he was served with a summons. The bank was apparently waiting only for an address to serve the summons.

This cosigner convinced the bank to drop the court action and agreed to settle the debt by paying $600, but he was incensed both by the bank's suing him *after* he had told the loan officer that he was ready to pay, and by the bank official impersonating an officer of the law in the bank's effort to find his address. That creditors bring suits against cosigners before alerting them of the situation and giving them a chance to pay would seem to be a serious infringement on the rights of cosigners. Credit bureaus routinely file information on law suits, and cosigners who are sued without having the opportunity to demonstrate their good faith have unjustified black marks entered on their credit records.

Even more common among the cosigners than complaints against the creditor were feelings of indignation toward their friends and relatives whom they felt had betrayed them. Typical of this attitude is the account of a 38-year-old white Chicago woman, the head of a broken family earning $8,000–$10,000 a year doing general office work.

> I cosigned for this friend who bought a car. He told me they were charging him a lot and he wasn't going to pay. When he was single he kept his payments up but then he got married and said he wasn't going to pay any more because even though he was making payments, it was never going down.

Included among the debtor–cosigners are a few people who were victimized by a credit practice that has been outlawed in only some states—the "add-on" contract. Under the add-on conditional sales contract, subsequent purchases by the debtor at the same store are added to the same contract that governed his initial purchase. Should the debtor default on a later purchase, the creditor has the right to repossess all the merchandise bought by the debtor under the contract, even though the debtor may have made sufficient payments to cover the cost of the earlier purchases. From the perspective of the creditor, these subsequent payments are allocated among all the items purchased under the contract, and therefore the earlier items are not fully paid for when the debtor defaults. In short, while the debtor assumes that all the subsequent payments are applied to the first item purchased on a "first-come-first-served" principle, the creditor parcels out the payments among all the items purchased under some perversion of the "spreading-the-wealth" principle. If the add-on contract is unjust to the original debtor, it is doubly so to the cosigner. Even those cosigners who know that they are liable if the original debtor defaults do not understand that by signing the initial contract they can be held liable for all subsequent purchases by the person for whom they have cosigned. This is yet another instance of the disparity between consumer credit law and the commonsense view of justice held by the debtor–cosigner. A good illustration of this injustice is provided by a black Detroit woman, earning $4,000–$5,000, who cosigned for a purchase made by the son of a friend.

> I cosigned for a young man I know. I'm a friend of his family. He wanted to buy his mother a kitchen set for Christmas and he didn't have established credit. He had to have a cosigner and asked me and I said yes. He paid $50 down and made some more payments. I thought he had paid enough so that it should have been paid off. Then they let him charge some more stuff without letting me know. If his credit wasn't good without a cosigner, why did they let him add to this bill without letting the cosigner know? . . . I told them

that if my name was on the second add-on, it must be a forgery because I didn't know about it. They said I didn't read the fine print. They said I didn't have to sign again and I was still responsible no matter how much the bill was.

The logic of this woman's question seems impeccable. Under what system of justice should she be responsible for purchases that she knows nothing about? The fine print of installment contracts, which consumers rarely read, and often cannot understand when they do read, records principles that are legally binding on the consumer but as this case demonstrates, what is legal and what is just are not always the same.

The State of Illinois in 1968, more than a year after our interviews with Chicago debtors, passed legislation that explicitly exonerates cosigners from liability for subsequent purchases. One of our Chicago debtors apparently was the victim of the old law. A 25-year-old Puerto Rican factory worker in Chicago, whose annual income was below $3,000, had cosigned for a friend.

I thought it had been paid a long time ago. But then I got a letter saying that I owed $89. They claimed something else was purchased, but I didn't buy anything. I was just the cosigner.

As these anecdotes indicate, cosigners are victimized not only by their untrustworthy friends and relatives but also by creditors and the laws regulating credit transactions. Their being sued before being notified of the original debtor's default, their being denied the right to maintain payments and obtain the merchandise before repossession, and their being held responsible for subsequent purchases made by the original debtor under the add-on contract all indicate the pressing need for a cosigner's bill of rights.

Original Debtor Sued
after Debt Transferred to Third Party

Eight debtors arranged for their debt to be taken over by someone else and yet ended up being sued when the new debtor failed to maintain payments. These cases are almost the reverse of the cosigner cases in that the original debtor rather than the person who took over the debt obligation was sued. This process is well illustrated by the account of a black Detroit auto worker, earning $5,000–$6,000 a year.

What happened is that I sold this car to another person, and let him take over the car payments. I went to the bank with him and they checked out his credit and gave him the payments. This man took

> over everything but he isn't paying for it. The bank says that because my name is still on the original contract as the car purchaser, they are holding me to the original contract. This other guy signed with the bank and had the payment book from the bank. They turned the car over to him as I was going through bankruptcy and now they can't find him and they are holding me responsible. This all happened over three years ago. I never heard from them until a week before I lost my job. Then they laid on this garnishee and took my last paycheck.

This debtor was given every assurance that he was absolved of any further liability when he brought his potential customer to the bank and the bank agreed to accept the new party as the debtor. And yet the bank still held him liable and, given all the nuances of the fine print of installment contracts, this may well have been a legal law suit. The bank may simply have treated the original debtor as a cosigner, totally without his knowledge.

Debt Incurred by Others
Using Debtor's Credit Card or Name

Seventeen debtors were betrayed by relatives and friends who ran up bills on their charge accounts and credit cards or even forged their names and then failed to pay.

One such episode was reported by a New York black man who had been victimized by his wife's nephew.

> This is what happened. My wife's nephew came here from Maryland and stayed at our house for a while. Once he asked if he could use my Merit Credit Card. I said O.K. Then some time later he asked me again for the credit card and I gave it to him. So he went and bought all the clothes he wanted on my card and then left New York. I thought he was taking care of the payments right along and had taken care of it. I don't know what he bought, when he bought them, or anything about the transaction. All I know is that when I went to deposit $100 in my account—the bank teller says a Marshal's letter was received by the bank, freezing my assets, including the $100 I just deposited! [The interviewer asked him if he had been contacted by the store.] If any mail came here about this, for all I know, he may have been opening them himself.

The interviewer was astute to ask this man if he had received any notice, for a garnishment against a bank account can occur in New York only after a court judgment, and the debtor is supposed to be notified at several prior points in the legal process as well as of the judgment against him.

In chapter 11, we shall see that legal procedures are frequently violated, with the result that such an event could easily happen even if the nephew in this case did not intercept his mail.

A black Chicago woman, employed as a domestic and whose husband worked as a carpenter (family income, $6,000–$8,000 a year), had a similar experience.

> I had allowed this friend to use my charge account at the store. She was to give me a certain amount every month, but she didn't take care of the bills herself. Then when I got the bills from the store, I realized she hadn't paid. I didn't have the money to pay. She finally moved away and she didn't give me any of the money she owed me.

Debtor Betrayed
by Person Entrusted To Make Payments

Thirteen debtors ran into trouble when the person entrusted to make the payments failed to do so. A middle-aged white Philadelphia woman, whose husband earned $8,000–$10,000 a year from his own automobile repair shop, told this story.

> My sister was sick and I was helping with her expenses. I was using the loan payment money to help her out. My husband didn't know this. He thought I was paying off the loan.

A 27-year-old black Detroiter, earning $6,000–$7,000 a year in a chemical factory, had bought a $125 suit from a door-to-door salesman.

> I was working two jobs at the time and I had no time to make the payments, so I gave the money to a friend of mine and he never made the payments. I did not know about this until I heard from the court. It was a mix-up. I thought I was all paid up and I told the people I had sent the money in, but apparently they never got it. Then I started to make double payments until I got caught up.

Complaints about
Debt-Pooling and Debt-Counseling Agencies

From Table 5.4 it can be seen that eight debtors blame part of their trouble on the agencies they turned to for help when they found themselves overextended, debt-pooling and debt-counseling firms. This type of reason is, of course, a secondary one, for the debtor was already in trouble when he contacted the agency for help. Although we have grouped debt-pooling and debt-counseling agencies, these are different types of organizations. Debt-pooling firms promise to help debtors allocate payments among their creditors. These firms make no investment themselves (nor do they make consolidation loans) but rather charge a fee for managing the debtor's accounts. They presumably count on their goodwill to get creditors to accept more lenient payment schedules. Debt-counseling agencies, in contrast, are nonprofit firms, often sponsored by the local credit bureau. They advise debtors on ways to cope with their delinquent accounts, but they do not assume responsibility for making the debtor's payments. The debt-pooling industry has been fraught with scandal, and some states, including New York, have outlawed it on the grounds that it preys upon debtors rather than helps them. But these firms are not illegal in two of our sample states, Illinois and Michigan.

Two Detroit debtors had turned to the same debt-pooling company for help. One, a 32-year-old black automobile worker, earning $6,000–$8,000 a year, told this story.

> I didn't stop really. I was paying through Debt Aid for about three months. They were supposed to be paying on the car, too, but they didn't, and I didn't know about it until the bank came to repossess the car.

A 35-year-old black assembly line worker in Detroit earning $6,000–$8,000 a year turned to a different debt-pooling firm.

> From June to August of 1966 I was unemployed, and fell behind with all my creditors. I decided to turn it all over to the Credit Budgeting Service. But then I got two summonses and found out they weren't keeping up all the payments. They were just paying the largest creditors.

Miscellaneous Debtor's Third-Party Reasons

A tiny fraction of debtors, five in all, were classified in a miscellaneous category under the general heading "third parties." In two of these cases, the debtor had taken out a loan on behalf of someone else who presumably could not get credit and ended in default when the friend failed to repay the debt. A 31-year-old white Philadelphian earning $8,000–$10,000 a year as a salesman said:

> I borrowed the money for a friend of mine. He had already reached his limit and couldn't get a loan. I did this to help him out. I didn't stop paying, my friend did because he was in financial difficulties and couldn't afford the payments at that time.

Although it is not clear from this account, it would seem that the friend for whom the money was borrowed had agreed to make the payments to the bank and the debtor was sued only when the friend stopped the payments.

The other three cases in this miscellaneous category involved some form of confusion, misunderstanding, or treachery between the debtor and some other person implicated in his debt. A white divorced Chicago woman earning under $3,000 annually as a waitress had bought a ring for which a male friend had cosigned. She had to go into the hospital and the cosigner insisted that he keep custody of the ring while she was away. He never returned the ring and so she stopped paying. She felt that she should not have been the party sued since he had possession of the ring. In another instance, the former boy friend of a black New York woman had bought her a phonograph as a gift, only he had charged it in her name. When she learned this, she returned the phonograph to him with instructions that he return it to the store.

DEBTOR IRRESPONSIBILITY

The last major group of reasons reflecting upon the debtor rather than the creditor is debtor irresponsibility. This is perhaps the most arbitrary category. It could be argued that the 172 debtors who defaulted primarily because of voluntary overextension behaved irresponsibly and that many debtors who failed to live up to their obligation after they became separated or divorced were also irresponsible. But in both of these types, the default stemmed primarily from inability to pay rather than unwillingness to pay. The more narrow category of debtor irresponsibility applies to 66 debtors, about 5 percent of the entire sample, and in almost all these cases this was the primary reason for the default. These cases fall into four distinct subtypes, bad faith, forgetfulness (the debtor admits that he simply forgot to pay), failure to pay while the debtor was out of town for a period of time, and refusal to pay on merchandise that was stolen or destroyed in an accident.

The largest of these categories, containing 21 of the 66 cases, is the one that fits least well under the notion of irresponsibility, for it consists of debtors who left town temporarily and failed to arrange for payments in their absence. As we shall see, in a number of these cases the debtor was called out of town suddenly because of some family crisis.

Bad Faith—Debtor Lost Interest in Paying

Some 16 debtors gave accounts of their defaults that reflect bad faith on their part. They come closest to the credit industry's image of the deadbeat; as a group they comprise only 1 percent of the entire sample. Illustrative of this pure form of irresponsibility is the story of a 26-year-old Chicago black, now married, whose family income is above $10,000 (his wife works as well). Some four years previously, he had bought a watch for a girl friend.

> I didn't particularly care. During that phase of my life I was a drifter. I didn't have any responsibilities. I wasn't married. When I bought the watch, I didn't have any intention of paying for it. They never garnisheed my wages when I did have a job. . . . They would send me letters, but that's all . . . until my wife got this summons.

A classic case of debtor irresponsibility is that provided by a 26-year-old white Detroit woman now separated from her husband.

> My husband went into this store to exchange a camera for his dad. While he was there, this high-pressure salesman sold him some engagement rings, a wedding ring, and a radio. The merchandise came to $389.60 and he paid $1 down. He had no intention of paying for this stuff. It was a Saturday when he was at the store and they made up the sale. They told him he could pick up the merchandise on Monday. He told them if they couldn't trust him they could keep their stuff. They let him have it right away and he came out to the car and bragged that he knew how to handle people like them. I was horrified to think that they would give him all this credit with so little proof when we were so deeply in debt. He took all of this stuff directly to a pawn shop and hocked it, he didn't even unwrap it. . . . Later he went back to the pawn shop, got some of the things back and returned to the store. But he didn't get the wedding ring or the radio. Later we were sued for $389. . . .

When asked if this was fair, she replied:

> I think if you buy something, you should pay for it or don't buy it. My husband isn't a bad person, he's just irresponsible. He needs help from a psychiatrist.

Certainly this man was irresponsible to the point of being dishonest, but it should be noted that the store was so eager to make the sale that it failed to carry out a credit check, much to the horror of the wife.

An example in which the attitude of irresponsibility was generated by excessive indebtedness is provided by a young New York black couple (the husband earned $6,000–$8,000 yearly as a machinist).

> My husband started getting disgusted because we had too many bills and he just stopped paying them. He started just throwing the money away on foolish things.

We have already noted that marital break-ups can undermine the debtor's willingness to pay. A good example of this process is provided by a 28-year-old black factory worker in Detroit, earning $5,000–$6,000 a year.

> After my wife and I separated, I started to lose interest in things like that. I figured I didn't need any credit any more. I now realize how stupid that was. I can't even buy a car now.

In most of these examples of irresponsibility, the debtor's marriage either broke up or was in jeopardy. The causal connection seems to work in both directions. Some debtors apparently become irresponsible after their marriages break up, whereas others behave irresponsibly, contributing to the dissolution of their marriages.

Debtor Claims That He Forgot To Pay

The second type of irresponsibility consists of a rather homogeneous grouping of some 13 debtors who admit that they had been careless and had simply forgotten to make their payments. The following are typical cases.

A 37-year-old Detroit black earning $6,000–$8,000 a year defaulted on a watch.

> I could have made the payments. I just didn't. It was my fault. Neglect on my part.

A 48-year-old Chicago black earning over $10,000 annually defaulted on a credit union loan.

> I stopped working for that company and apparently I still owed a balance on the loan from the credit union. I just didn't think about it until they sent the summons.

The other cases in this category are much the same. In every instance the debtor blames himself for being negligent by forgetting his obligation. What is odd about these cases is that their creditors apparently made no effort to remind them of their debt. Certainly such reminders are considered good credit management practice. It is possible, of course, that these debtors are not reporting all the facts.

Debtor out of Town and Missed Payments

The largest of the "irresponsibility" subcategories, consisting of 21 debtors, is the one in which the default was linked to the debtor temporarily leaving town. In almost all these cases the debtor was confronted with a family crisis that required his leaving. A New York Puerto Rican couple, with annual income between $3,000 and $4,000, defaulted on a sewing machine they had bought from a door-to-door salesman when they were called to Puerto Rico.

> My husband's grandfather died and we had to go to Puerto Rico. It was very important that we go there.

A 26-year-old black Chicagoan, employed as a welder (he refused to report his income), gave this account of his default on an automobile:

> The main reason was, when I had to go to Florida, I couldn't make the payments. My brother got hurt and I had to go. I wasn't working when I was down there and I had to quit my job here in order to go to Florida.

Not all debtors who left town did so because of crises in their families. A young Chicago black earning $4,000–$5,000 a year as a factory worker was in arrears on a TV set (with which he was most dissatisfied) when he left town to report to his draft board.

> I left town to report to my draft board. When I got back the finance company had a wage assignment on my job. The job started to take out payments for the finance company. But then I got behind on my rent and I was only making $58 a week then. You can't do much with that kind of money! I had to go to court about the rent and that's when I found out that the judges don't care about the little man. All they listen to is the company lawyer! So I said the hell with them all.

It is doubtful that his trip out of town was the only cause of his being in arrears, for garnishment proceedings against him were already under way. More likely, he had skipped payments because, as he explained elsewhere, "the TV set was no good." The attitude that this debtor developed toward the court is of some interest. All too frequently debtors see courts as the agents of their oppressors rather than institutions committed to justice.[2]

Debtor Refuses To Pay for Stolen
or Destroyed Item

Some 16 debtors stopped paying after the item they had bought was stolen or destroyed in an accident. In most of these cases this was the

---

[2] In chapter 11 we explore debtors' experiences with courts in more detail.

primary reason for the default. Unlike debtors we shall encounter in chapter 6, who felt that their insurance should have covered their loss, these debtors made no mention of insurance and presumably were not covered. We have classified them under the heading "irresponsibility" because they assumed that the accident or theft exonerated them from having to make further payments, and thus by implication they felt that the creditor should assume the responsibility for their misfortune. As we shall see, some of these debtors had theories about their transaction that further buttressed their belief.

In several of these cases, a TV set bought on time was stolen. Typical of these accounts is the case of a middle-aged black New York woman whose husband had left her and whose annual income at the time of the interview was under $3,000.

> The TV was stolen. Since it was stolen, I felt I shouldn't have to pay for it, and they never gave me a guarantee. I can't see paying for something I don't have.

Apparently this woman expected some kind of guarantee from the company against theft.

Most of these cases involve automobiles that were either stolen or destroyed in accidents. The case of a 30-year-old black Chicagoan employed as a truck driver and earning $4,000–$5,000 a year is typical.

> Well, the car was in an accident. It burned up in front of the house. I was at work at the time. I asked them for another car, but they refused to do it.

This debtor believed that the creditor had an obligation to share his risk and replace the destroyed car. He did not provide much information about the transaction and we do not know whether he had bought insurance to cover this type of accident.

Several debtors assumed that the creditor was insured against the possibility of theft and therefore were not responsible for the untoward event. For example, a 30-year-old New York black truck driver had purchased some rings, which were stolen.

> I spoke to the credit manager after the rings were stolen. You see, these people are insured and they are going to get their money regardless and so I can't see paying for it.

These cases of debtor irresponsibility are of particular interest, for they place the blame for the default squarely upon the debtor. As noted, this analysis of the reasons for the default suffers from the fact that it relies entirely on the testimony of the debtor. There is always the danger that the debtor will distort the facts so as to present himself in the most favorable light. But the very fact that some debtors were willing to admit their irresponsibility lends considerable validity to our system of classification. Had we not encountered such cases, we might have had reason to suspect the veracity of our debtors. It would seem that the debtors did try to be honest and that considerable weight can be given to their accounts of what went wrong. In later chapters we shall find other evidence of the respondents' veracity.

6

ALLEGATIONS
OF WRONGDOING
BY THE SELLER

We have seen that 35 percent of the debtors gave reasons for their default that implicated the creditor in varying degrees. By far the largest category of creditor-related reasons consists of allegations of fraud and deception. Nineteen percent mentioned such wrongdoing by the seller as part of the reason for their default, and for 14 percent of all debtors it was the primary reason. The broad category of fraud covers a multitude of sins. The more specific subtypes under this heading and their frequencies are shown in Table 6.1.

The captions in Table 6.1 provide some idea of the frauds claimed by these debtors. They range from complaints about defective merchandise, wrong merchandise, price and insurance deception, to allegations of being tricked into signing contracts. The largest proportion of these complaints, almost half the total, deal with defective merchandise, represented by the first three categories. Approximately 1 of every 10 debtors mentioned defective merchandise as contributing to his default; for 6 percent this was the primary reason. (These figures refer to the sum of the first three categories.) The distinction between the first two categories of defective merchandise corresponds to the legal distinction between an express and an implied warranty. If the merchandise does not perform its presumed function (for example, the automobile does not move or the toaster does not work), then the implied warranty has been violated even if no written guarantee of performance was provided (the first category). The third category differs from the first two in that

Table 6.1 / Claims of Fraud and Deception as Reasons for Not Paying

fraud–deception reasons	first reason (no. cases)	second reason (no. cases)	third reason (no. cases)	total reasons (no. cases)	total reasons (percent)	total individuals (percent)
Defective merchandise						
Warranty complaints	17	4	1	22	1	2
No mention of warranty	59	18	3	80	4	6
Merchandise wears out prematurely	19	9	0	28	2	2
Wrong or used merchandise	19	10	3	32	2	2
Failure to deliver all merchandise ordered	10	1	2	13	1	1
Complaints about price deception	19	19	3	41	2	3
Complaints about insurance	15	5	1	21	1	2
False promises in initial transaction	10	5	3	18	1	1
Debtor duped into signing contract	11	2	0	13	1	1
Miscellaneous—complicated frauds	3	2	0	5	a	a
Subtotal cases	182	75	16	273		21
Percent of total cases	14	13	14	14		
Total cases	1,320	570	110	2,000		1,326

a Percentages of less than ½ of 1 percent.

the defect was not immediately apparent. The debtor in these cas
the merchandise for a short period of time only to discover that
of such poor quality that he felt betrayed by the creditor. We shall illu
these types, beginning with the 22 debtors who were led to believe that
the defective merchandise was protected by an express warranty. (In
17 of these 22 cases, this was the primary reason for the default.)

Violations of Express Warranties

The abuses associated with warranties have recently attracted national
attention. Both Congress and the Federal Trade Commission have investigated the deception employed by manufacturers and dealers, particularly
automobile firms, with respect to warranties. Most of the 22 cases in
this category involved automobiles and, since it was frequently a used
car, it is doubtful that the warranty was in fact written into the contract.
Rather, the salesman probably promised that the car was protected by
a warranty when in fact it was not.

This form of deception is well illustrated by the account of a white
Detroiter who thought he was buying a new car until he received his
contract.

> I showed him the paper that was sent to me saying that it was a
> used car. He said it wasn't his responsibility what the salesman said
> to sell the car. In other words, no holds barred. They could say
> what they want. The salesman told us it was a demonstrator. We
> had already signed the papers. It was sold to us as a new car and
> everything was filled in. When the papers came back it was stamped
> a used car and the warranty didn't cover anything. The old guy who
> was the manager jumped on me like I was out of my skull and he
> was really quite nasty about it.

Another example of verbal deception by the salesman is the story
of an elderly Detroit black, recently retired, with an annual income of
$3,000–$4,000.

> He guaranteed the car in case something went wrong, but he didn't
> give it to me in writing. That's the reason why he backed out. After
> I made some repairs, it still didn't work. I took it back to him [the
> used-car dealer], parked it, and gave him back the keys. He gave
> me back the $10 check I gave him and he told me he would give
> the bank their money back, but he didn't give the money back and
> the bank kept after me until they garnisheed me.

It should be noted this debtor was given every reason to believe
that the transaction was nullified when he returned the car and got back

his down payment. Clearly he was the victim of fraud. This case falls outside the usual criticism of the holder-in-due-course doctrine in that the dealer apparently agreed to rescind the transaction, and the critics of the doctrine rarely contemplate such deception by the dealer.

A story of a defective TV set is provided by a 41-year-old black Philadelphian, employed as a meat cutter, earning $5,000–$6,000 annually.

> We had a warranty on it but the television set stopped working soon after we got it and we couldn't get them to do anything about it. So I just said I wasn't gonna pay any more.

The logic of this debtor shows up time and again in these cases. Since the creditor did not live up to his end of the bargain, the debtor concludes that he is no longer bound by the agreement. But, of course, this "folk logic" is far removed from the world of consumer credit law, and this debtor, like so many others of like mind, became a defendant in a law suit. In fact, he was forced to pay the creditor in order to forestall the sale of his home.

The hardships imposed on debtors when dealers fail to honor warranties are well illustrated by the next account, that of a well-educated 39-year-old Chicago black who lost his job because of the debt problem (arising from a used-car purchase some five years prior to the interview). At the time of the interview he was earning over $10,000 a year as a free-lance writer.

> The warranty was written into the agreement with the dealer and myself and not with me and the acceptance company, although I didn't find this out until later. The head gasket was blown and the motor needed an overhaul. . . . I called the dealer and when I told him what was wrong, he didn't keep his agreement. I took the car to the dealer and I should have complained to XYZ Acceptance [the finance company]. The dealer promised to fix it but he did not and I finally took the car back to the dealer after they gave me the runaround for three months. Being ignorant of legal matters, I felt that I was finished with them as I had given up my $400 down payment.

Of course this was not the end of the matter, as the finance company kept pressuring him for payments. In response to this pressure he decided to borrow $1,500 from his credit union and settle the complete debt. Since he was prepared to pay in full, he believed that he should not have to pay all the carrying charges, but the finance company was of a different mind.

> I went to my credit union and got a check to pay off the amount without the carrying charges and they said they would accept the check but not reduce the carrying charges. . . . The way the guy talked in the office, like "You people have a very nasty habit of

> not paying your bills.' and "the job that you are on—you can forget
> it" . . . . When this happens, you can't believe it. It's like hearing
> someone say that he can take away your livelihood and I was even
> willing to forget everything, if he would have taken off the interest—but
> he said, "No, sonny, you are going to pay everything."

His vivid quote of the creditor's employee, "You people have a
very nasty habit of not paying your bills" suggests that racial slurs are
also part of the harassment techniques of creditors. In spite of this debtor's
legitimate claim to a reduction of the finance charges for paying in advance,
the company carried out its threat and sent several garnishment orders
to his job, with the result that he was fired.

> He made good on his threat of taking my job from me by sending
> in the wage assignments.

Four years later, the finance company took him to court again for
what they considered to be the balance of the debt. He reported that
he hired an attorney and the debt was settled for $500 plus a $75 lawyer's
fee. The financial data he provided do not make it clear whether the
creditor accepted the $1,500 check that he offered, but they raise questions
as to why this would not have been adequate even from the finance
company's point of view. He claimed that the car cost $2,200 and that
he had made a $400 down payment and three monthly payments of $68
each. He also reported that the car was sold at auction for a mere $200,
which would further reduce the balance. Regardless of the arithmetic
of this case, note should be taken of the discrepancy between the initial
cost of the car and the amount that was realized in the auction three
months later. The planned obsolescence of our economy notwithstanding,
it seems quite remarkable that an automobile priced at $2,200 could lose
90 percent of its value in three months' time.[1] We shall encounter other
cases that sharply question the legitimacy of deficiency judgments.

Violations of Implied Warranties

Almost four times as many debtors, 80 in all, complained about defective
merchandise as a factor in their default without mentioning warranties
or guarantees. More often than not, this complaint was a secondary reason
for the default. A young New York black who was on welfare at the
time of the interview, with annual income under $3,000, gave this explana-
tion for his default on a used-car purchase:

[1] See Philip Shuchman, *Profit on Default: An Archival Study of Automobile Repossession
and Resale*, 22 Stanford L. Rev. 20 (Nov. 1969), for an explanation of the marked loss
in value of the repossessed car.

> Because the day we got the car it broke down. They came and picked
> it up. They told me to call when it would be ready and I kept calling. . . .
> We finally picked it up and when we brought it home it just broke
> down again. After that I just stopped making payments because they
> kept deceiving us on the condition of the car.

A number of other cases in this category involved complaints about defective used cars.

Complaints about defective merchandise were almost as common in connection with furniture as with used cars. A middle-aged white carpenter who earned over $10,000 a year bought a living room set in a Harlem furniture store and gave this reason for his default.

> The furniture wasn't constructed right. I called them and they were
> supposed to pick it up and repair it. They said they would but they
> kept putting it off. So I stopped paying. They never came to pick
> it up. We didn't hear from them and we tried calling them. Finally,
> we were told that they were bankrupt. When we heard from this
> other company [Grand Furnishings], I went down to complain. The
> furniture wore out one month after we bought it. They told me they
> couldn't fix it and I said why must I pay? I made a few payments
> and he said he'd see what he can do for me.

Needless to say, this man was sued by the company that took over his contract. His experience calls attention to yet another flaw of the holder-in-due-course theory. The original seller in this instance went bankrupt, so that even if the buyer had the resources to sue the seller, it would be to no avail. And yet the third party is given the legal right to sue the debtor, who is totally without recourse.

Included among those who refused to pay because they were sold defective merchandise is a middle-aged black couple in Detroit who owned their own home. Both the husband and wife worked (he as a laborer in the auto industry) and their combined annual income was over $10,000. They were victimized by a fraudulent direct-selling firm that soon went out of business. Two salesmen came to their door and got them to sign a contract for wall-to-wall carpeting and patio awnings, the total price coming to $1,269. This episode, as related by the husband, is particularly valuable because it illustrates both the ineffectiveness of community agencies in combating fraud and the evils of the holder-in-due-course doctrine.

> The salesman made all kinds of promises, like free drapes for the
> front room with the purchase of the carpeting and free formica tiles
> for the kitchen with the purchase of the patio awnings. The carpeting
> was left on the front porch. My son and I had to lug it in. They
> never came back to put it down. I finally put it down myself. They
> left the kitchen tiles and drapery material also on the front porch. . . .

I found that the carpeting was short. Not enough material. The drape material was never made up and the tiles for the kitchen are still down in the basement along with the cement. No workers ever showed up to complete the job. One of the salesmen came over once and tried to snatch the contract from my wife but she snatched it back. I have it here and I wish you [the interviewer] would look at it. They really took us. I will never make that mistake again. We were gypped, defrauded, and left holding the bag. We called the Better Business Bureau and they later told my wife that one of these salesmen would be out to see us to make an adjustment. He came out and told us he would fix everything, but we never saw him again. I made two payments and stopped because the job never was completed. I went to the bank [the holder-in-due-course] and told them my story. They were real nice and their lawyers contacted the police Bunko squad, which checks on people who cheat and defraud other people. They said they would look into the company's records. They finally told the bank that this company was in trouble and had declared bankruptcy. . . . In the end, we found out that we'd been swindled by a bunch of crooks.

It may be noted that this debtor was appreciative of the solicitous attitude of the bank and its help in investigating the firm. This debtor goes on about his obligation to the bank:

> I am still responsible to the bank for the loan so I am paying it . . . even though we were gypped. . . . The bank was nice to us. Their lawyers tried to help us every way they could. They called the police and the Better Business Bureau. . . .

In view of the help that this debtor received from the bank in trying to trace the firm that had swindled him, the question might well be raised as to who brought the suit against him. Those familiar with the workings of the credit industry will not be surprised to learn that it was this very bank that sued him.

> We had been to the bank and they were trying to help us find out what had happened to this construction company and then the summons came. That's when I found out I was first being sued for the money. . . . But the bank was nice about it. . . . They even took off the lawyer's fee and the court costs and the summons cost.

The "benevolence" of the bank shines through further when the respondent was asked how much he had to pay to settle the debt. Reverting to the third person, the interviewer recorded:

> The summons showed that he owed $1,177.60 to the bank. . . . The respondent told me that because the bank felt sorry for him and because he had such a good record and was never involved in a credit problem

before, they were going to take off $200 [presumably the court costs and lawyer's fee] and that his balance would be $977.60. They made his payments higher to catch up with the back payments.

But even this debtor, in spite of his gratitude to the bank, developed some suspicions that the bank may not have fulfilled its responsibilities. When asked whether he felt that there was a good reason why he should not pay the court judgment, he replied:

> Not now. I know that we are liable as long as we signed the contract. I just wanted to find those crooks and see if our installation could be made. That's all except that I think the bank who gave the loan to the construction company should have the responsibility of correcting things. I signed with the construction company. I did not go to the bank for a personal loan. The construction company got the loan to cover my credit. I know now that I signed and am legally responsible. I thought I was responsible only to the construction company. I know the law better now. The hard way.

It is extremely difficult for laymen to grasp the idea that the law, which presumably evolves according to the ideal of justice, can be unjust. Who can question the reasoning of this poorly educated man when he hesitatingly suggests that the bank, with whom he had no direct dealings, should assume some responsibility for correcting the abuse? And it never even occurs to him to ask how such a presumably responsible institution as a bank could have dealings with a fraudulent firm. The law that this debtor sadly acknowledges that he now knows better is, of course, the doctrine of holder-in-due-course.

Merchandise Wore Out Prematurely

The third category under defective merchandise contains 28 debtors, most of whom show up in the primary-reason column. These debtors felt that they had been deceived when the merchandise they had bought wore out well in advance of expectations. Two of them, a middle-aged white Philadelphian (a mechanic, earning $6,000–$8,000) and a 30-year-old New York Puerto Rican (a craftsman earning $6,000–$8,000 a year) had identical complaints about plastic furniture covers they had bought for $140.

> They tore—they ripped at the seams. I called up and they were supposed to send someone out. They never did. So I just told them I wasn't going to pay for it.

> Because after I had them a month, they were all torn up. I called the credit department [the finance company] and they told me that that wasn't their business.

Again we see the finance company evading any responsibility for the transaction.

Included in this category are some automobile purchases in which the defect was not immediately apparent. A typical example is the story of a 30-year-old Detroit truck driver, earning $4,000–$5,000 annually.

> They didn't tell me that the car had been damaged at one time and most of the parts and the engine had been replaced by rebuilt parts. They weren't good parts. They took paint and sprayed them to look new. I took it to a bump shop and they said it must have been totally wrecked in the front end. . . . The first 30 days it ran perfect. From then on it was one thing after another going out. . . . Every day it was something else. Then the brakes went out entirely and I couldn't drive it. I told them [the finance company] to come and tow it away because I couldn't drive it.

The numerous used-car episodes in these categories of defective merchandise point up a fundamental inequity in the current marketplace. The used-car buyer typically makes a substantial financial commitment, generally well over $1,000. And yet with no effective warranty, he runs the risk of having to make additional expenditures to repair his defective automobile. As we saw in chapter 5, such unexpected expenditures can push the debtor over the economic brink. Certainly a more equitable system could and should be devised. The buyer obviously enters the transaction on the assumption that he is buying a reasonably good product and will not soon have substantial repair bills. Warranties should be required in used- as well as new-car sales.

COMPLAINTS ABOUT WRONG OR USED MERCHANDISE

In 32 cases, almost 3 percent of the entire sample, the reason for the default was linked to the dealer's failure to deliver the merchandise for which the debtor thought he had contracted. In most of these cases, this was the primary reason for the default. Included here are debtors who were led to believe that they were buying one model or brand of merchandise but received another, and debtors who contracted for new merchandise but were sent used goods. Most of these cases involved purchases of furniture and appliances but a few dealt with automobiles. A middle-aged white Detroiter in the trucking business with an income over $10,000 reported on his effort to buy a truck.

> When I bought the truck, I wanted a sleeper. I just got a few miles from the lot when the truck broke down. I called them and they came and towed me in. They got me to take another truck while they were fixing it. This was not a sleeper. They gave me the runaround.

> I couldn't get the first truck back and the second one was no good.
> It broke down and was a real lemon. I also found out that they had
> switched serial numbers from the first truck to the second. I told
> them to take it back, it was no good to me.

This debtor's experience points up the inadequacies of deficiency
judgments. He made only one payment of $150 on the truck that was
priced at $2,500. He was informed that the truck (whether the first or
the second is not clear) was sold at auction for $1,200 and he was sued
for a deficiency judgment of $1,200. By his own account, this man had
the original for only a few hours and the substitute truck was so unsatisfac-
tory that he soon returned it. Yet in the brief span of time that he had
the truck, it managed to depreciate in value by $1,300.[2]

This debtor's case has another point of interest. When presented
with the deficiency judgment on the truck, this man consulted a lawyer,
who advised him to settle out of court for $500.

> The lawyer said that they had more money than I did and that it
> was better to settle out of court and get out from under and so I
> wrote them a check for $500.

The lawyer's advice is a reminder of the basic inequity of the creditor–
debtor relationship. However valid the debtor's defenses, his pressing
them through the legal process involves substantial attorney's fees and
often these expenses come to more than the amount in dispute. Such
is the exploited debtor's paradox. If he is to obtain justice through the
legal system, he may well have to spend more than he stands to gain.
It is small wonder that so few debtors, even the knowledgeable ones
who have access to lawyers, bother to assert their defenses.

As noted, most of the complaints about wrong or used merchandise
dealt with appliances and furniture. The wife of a middle-aged black
Detroit truck driver earning $3,000–$4,000 a year was victimized by a
bait ad for a sewing machine. She had seen an ad on TV for an inexpensive
machine, called the company, and they sent out a salesman who convinced
her to buy a more expensive model. She refused to pay when the higher-
priced machine failed to perform as the salesman said it would.

> I had the cash for the one I wanted. But he told us that the more
> expensive one would be better. The machine didn't do what he said
> it would. We called to tell him that it wasn't the proper merchandise.
> But he wouldn't take it back. After the third week, we were informed
> that the company had sold out.

[2] As Shuchman explains, debtors are given only the value of the "wholesale resale,"
usually the sale from the financing agency to the original dealer. The repossessed car
is then sold at retail, a price very close to the amount owed, but this "retail resale"
price is never credited to the debtor. See Shuchman, *ibid*.

It should be noted that this debtor had every intention of being a cash customer and became a credit buyer only because of the "bait and switch" tactics of the salesman. This company, too, apparently went out of business, but as we have seen, this in no way relieves the pressure on the debtor who is in the clutches of a holder-in-due-course.

One Chicago debtor, a middle-aged black earning $3,000–$4,000 a year in a cleaning plant, had bought a phonograph from a door-to-door salesman on the basis of the salesman's catalogue.

> The set was not the same as the one I had ordered from the pictures. It was longer and lower. . . . I told them I wouldn't pay for it and they said they would pick it up but instead they turned it over to a lawyer. . . . He said it would be a new set, but I'm pretty sure it was a used set. . . . He said it would cost $356, but when I received the book it was $456. . . . I made a couple of payments, but then I stopped because I didn't want that phonograph and they were supposed to come by and pick it up.

Another debtor who defaulted because the merchandise was not what he had ordered is a 59-year-old Chicago black, earning under $3,000 annually, who agreed to buy stainless steel cooking utensils from a door-to-door salesman.

> I picked it out of a catalogue. It was supposed to be stainless steel. When I opened the box and looked at the pieces, they weren't stainless steel as they were supposed to be. They were really made of aluminum. When they sent an agent to the house, I asked him to take them back but he wouldn't. So I wouldn't pay for them.

This case, like the previous one, calls attention to some of the defects of direct sales. The buyer frequently orders from a catalogue and does not see the merchandise until after he has signed the contract, at which time he is without recourse should he be dissatisfied. For this reason alone, a cooling-off period during which the buyer can rescind the contract is very much in order in direct selling. But if the merchandise is not delivered until some days after the transaction, even a two- or three-day cooling-off period would provide little relief for the debtor.

FAILURE OF DEALER TO DELIVER
ALL MERCHANDISE ORDERED

Some 13 debtors, about 1 percent of the entire sample, traced their default in part to the dealer's failure to deliver all the merchandise entered on the contract, or in a few cases to their being billed for merchandise that they had not ordered. This was typically given as the primary reason for the default. A middle-aged New York black, employed as a cook in a hospital, with an annual income of $6,000–$8,000, contracted for three rooms of furniture.

> We didn't get exactly what we had contracted for. The dresser was broken and the delivery man said to keep it until they sent us a new one. And the chair wasn't there. On display we saw a matching chair for the sofa and that was in our contract. But they only delivered the sofa. Then they said that the chair would be $45 more. I simply said that I would not pay until they sent us what we had asked for.

Certainly the dealer's breach of contract in not delivering all the goods contracted for would seem to be a valid defense. Nonetheless, this debtor was pressured into resuming payments with the store. At the time of the interview, he was making payments and was not even aware that he had been sued.

Other debtors also refused to pay when they discovered that not all the furniture ordered was delivered. Furniture dealers in the low-income marketplace employ as their standard come-on advertisements for three rooms of furniture at unusually low prices. The would-be buyers are soon switched to more expensive merchandise, but to sweeten the transaction, the dealer often promises to throw in extras at unusually low prices, such as end tables. For example, a Philadelphia black woman complained that the end tables were not delivered and she refused to pay for this reason.

> They charged us for two end tables that they never delivered. They said they had been sold and they would bring what we wanted when they had it, but they didn't deliver what they promised. I don't have all the merchandise that they charged me for and I still don't. When I asked about it, they just stalled me from one month to the next.

A few debtors in this category claim they were sued for merchandise they never received. The tale of a 33-year-old Detroit black machinist, earning between $8,000 and $10,000 a year, who tried to buy a used car is typical.

> The car I decided to buy needed some fixing. They said they would fix it and I could call for it the next day. The salesman brought me home after a test drive. I signed some papers before the test drive. . . . The next day I went back to get the car and they said it had been stolen. I didn't have any papers of ownership. They never gave me any. The dealer said to wait and see what the insurance company would do. The insurance company wanted me to sign saying that I had taken delivery of the car. I wouldn't do it because it was something I never had. I never had the car. . . .

When asked whether he had signed a contract, he replied:

> It was a contract to buy all right. But I didn't know I was signing to buy then. I thought I would sign for it when it was delivered to me. I just thought I was signing to test drive it.

This debtor had made a down payment of $186 on the car, which was priced at $1,481. His contract was sold to the same benevolent Detroit bank that we encountered earlier, and the bank sued him. The outcome of this case was still uncertain at the time of the interview. Unlike most debtors, this man contacted a lawyer and his case was soon to come to trial.

DEFAULTS RELATED TO PRICE DECEPTION

In chapter 3 we saw that 45 percent of the debtors who were told a price at the time of the sale were misled about the true cost of their purchase. In about 25 percent of these cases the discrepancy was substantial, in that the total time sales price was greater by 25 percent or more than the quoted price. In spite of this widespread abuse, only 2 percent of the debtors (41 cases) mentioned price deception as a *reason* for their default, and in only a little more than 1 percent of the cases was this the primary reason. The disparity between the actual amount of deception regarding price and the role such deception played in the default is yet further evidence that many debtors were willing to meet their obligation even though they felt they had been cheated.

These complaints about price fall into two classes. The larger group consists of debtors who claimed that the price on the contract which they received some time after the transaction was substantially higher than the price the salesman originally quoted. The smaller group consists of some debtors who discovered soon after the transaction that they could buy the same merchandise at a much cheaper price. That these debtors refused to pay after their belated discovery would seem to place the onus for the default on them rather than on the dealer, in accordance with the principle of caveat emptor. Nonetheless, we have included these cases as well in the category of price complaints. Some justification for doing so is provided by recent court decisions, which have ruled that excessive prices fall within the meaning of "unconscionable contracts," a doctrine developed in the Uniform Commercial Code.[3]

---

[3]For a critique of the unconscionability doctrine, see A. Leff, *The Emperor's New Clause,* 115 Univ. Pa. L. Rev. 485–559 (Feb. 1967). For cases supporting this theory of unconscionable contracts, see American Home Improvement Corp. v. MacIver, 201 A.2d 886 (N.H. Sup. 1964) and Jones v. Star Credit Corp., 298 N.Y.S.2d 264 (Nassau Co. S. 1969).

A naive victim of price deception by a door-to-door salesman was a 65-year-old poorly educated black in Detroit employed as a construction worker but with annual income under $3,000. He was seduced into buying a TV set from a direct seller and was resentful not only of the price deception but of the failure of the salesman to deliver a promised prize.

> A door-to-door salesman came around selling a portable TB [sic]. He said it would cost $150 and that's all I agreed to pay. He said we would also get a special turkey or cake because it was around Christmas and we could get a special bargain. . . . But I never got no turkey or cake. So I called and the man said I was too late, the offer was over. He told me it would cost $150 but it turned out to cost $263.23. I didn't agree to pay no $263.23. They didn't say nothing about carrying charges or insurance or nothing like that. . . . And when I bought the TB set I didn't know about no loan company. I just thought I was buying it from the Moon TB Company. [The respondent showed the interviewer the contract on which was stated that payments were to be made to the Likable Loan Co.]

Still another victim of a direct seller's price deception was a 26-year-old New York black woman whose annual income was under $3,000. She had been told that her TV set would cost $360, but this was clearly the cash price, for she showed the interviewer an installment contract with the following entries:

Unpaid cash balance	$360.00
Credit life insurance	3.83
Accident and health life insurance	11.05
Property insurance	8.84
	$383.72
Credit service charge	76.60
Time balance	460.32
Time sales price	480.32

The discrepancy between the last two entries obviously refers to a $20 down payment that this woman must have made at the time of the sale. A number of points of interest are contained in these figures. The price quoted to the woman at the time of the sale, $360, refers only to the unpaid cash balance and not to the total time sales price, which was $100 more. This woman was sold, without her knowledge, three different types of insurance in connection with this transaction. Credit life insurance is quite common and many creditors insist that their customers pay for such a policy in connection with their purchase. Such a policy, of course, protects the dealer in the event of the debtor's death. There has been much criticism from many quarters that the rates for such insurance are scandalously high, but this need not concern us now. In addition to life insurance, this debtor was also charged $11.05 for accident and health life insurance. This can refer only to a policy which protects the creditor in the event of the debtor's illness, a type of insurance which, if offered at reasonable rates, has much merit in light of the many debtors who default because of illness. Finally, this debtor was charged $8.84 for insurance on property, the property being the television set. Should the television break or be stolen, the debtor and the creditor are presumably both protected by such insurance.

In addition to not being told about the interest on her credit purchase, which came to $76.60, this woman had no idea that she had to buy three different types of insurance for a total of $23.73. Ironically, the law in New York (and in the other states studied) requires that the debtor be provided with a copy of the contract with all the blank spaces filled in at the time of the sale. In short, the law assumes that all debtors know the true time sales price before they sign the contract. But this creditor, according to the woman, did not give her a copy of the contract until a full month after the sale, in clear violation of the law, and yet it was she who was confronted with legal sanctions. Her uncle, who had cosigned, was garnisheed because of this debt.

Another form of price deception is almost endemic in the used-car business, only this time the deception applies to the size of the monthly payments, a factor even more critical to many debtors than total cost. A widespread deceptive practice in automobile sales is to advertise that the would-be customer need make no down payment and can walk off the lot with an automobile. These deceptive ads invariably involve two financial obligations for the debtor: one to the small loan company that quickly materializes at the dealer's bidding (regardless of the hour of night) to provide the funds for the down payment, and the other to the finance company or bank that is prepared to buy the contract in light of the down payment, which serves to reduce the finance company's risk in the value of the car.[4] Typical of these cases is the account of a middle-aged white laborer in Detroit, who is earning less than $3,000 annually.

> I saw an ad in the paper. It said they would give credit to anyone who had never had credit before. . . . I went out there to buy a car. . . . . He took me to Benevolent Finance. . . . I thought I was signing for a car loan, not a personal loan. It turned out I signed

[4]We shall come across a number of these dealer-arranged down-payment loans. Their function is to lessen the gap between the value of the car and the amount that the finance company has advanced to make the purchase possible.

> two papers, one for a car loan and one for a personal loan. I
> told them I couldn't pay over $50 a month, but it was $49.67 to the
> Retailer's Bank and $38.24 to Benevolent.

This debtor told the creditor that he could not pay more than $50 a
month and yet the dealer foisted upon him a system of multiple debt
payments that came to $88 a month.

An example of the cases in which debtors stopped paying when
they discovered that they had been overcharged is provided by a middle-
aged Chicago black, employed as an X-ray technician, earning
$4,000–$5,000 annually. He had bought a ring for $380 and had paid
all but $46 of this amount. He eventually needed money and decided
to pawn the ring. The pawn shop would not give him more than $10
for the ring, and so he had it appraised and learned that it was not worth
$50.

> When I found out it wasn't worth $50, I just got so angry I did not
> pay them any more.

Of course, this debtor was sued and the judgment against him came
to $70.

DEFAULTS RELATED TO INSURANCE COMPLAINTS

Table 6.1 showed that 21 debtors, almost 2 percent of the sample, blamed
their default in part on their being misled about the insurance they had
bought in connection with their purchase. Almost all these cases involved
automobiles; the debtors claimed that they were led to believe that they
were covered when in fact they were not, or that they were misinformed
about the extent of coverage that they had. It is debatable whether all
these cases belong under "fraud and deception"; it is possible that the
debtor may have misunderstood the terms of his insurance. Nor do these
insurance complaints necessarily reflect upon the creditor who sold the
merchandise and the accompanying policy. The insurance company itself
may be at fault, as is exemplified by this account of a middle-aged white
Philadelphian who worked for the city santitation department.

> The car was stolen and was never found. We stopped making payments
> and filed an insurance claim. We turned the car title over to the insur-
> ance company and they were supposed to pay Transcendental Credit.
> We didn't know they hadn't paid until we couldn't get credit to buy
> a color T.V. about six months ago. We were told that the insurance
> company had gone out of business.

The automobile insurance industry has been subjected to much criticism and has been investigated by Congress many times. A number of states, including Pennsylvania and Illinois, have very weak controls over insurance companies, with the result that fly-by-night companies come into being which specialize in selling automobile insurance at high rates to persons of relatively low income. Those who buy such insurance think they are fully protected, only to discover after an accident that the firm is bankrupt and that they must pay the damages themselves.

Although automobile insurance is required by law in most states and car dealers will not sell on credit unless the car is insured, there is no law requiring the buyer to obtain the insurance from the dealer as part of the sale. But the sale of insurance is profitable for the dealers, and they routinely include insurance as part of the sale without giving the debtor the option of getting his own insurance. Stemming from this practice was the default of one New York debtor, a 23-year-old white machine operator, earning between $6,000 and $8,000 a year, who contracted for a new car.

> I tried to figure out how much the cost was. The salesman figured it at $90 a month, but when the car was ready it was $105 a month. They were charging me for insurance. I had gone to my regular insurance place, and bought insurance. So I was being charged for two insurances. I sent the payment book back and told them to adjust it. They sent it back and said they wouldn't fix it. I stopped paying because they charged me for insurance I didn't want and then they wouldn't change it. That's the reason.

When he found out he was being sued, he contacted a lawyer who called the dealer's lawyers. "He told me that they had me since I'd already signed the papers." His case, too, illustrates the inequities of deficiency judgments. When asked whether there was a good reason why he should not have to pay the judgment, he replied:

> They sold the car for way less than I paid for it. It's costing me $2,000 for four months' use of the car. That's the difference between what they sold it for and what they said I owed plus court fees and marshal fees.

Included among the six cases in which an insurance complaint was a secondary reason are two debtors who defaulted because of illness. They claimed that they were forced to buy health insurance as part of their installment purchase and could not understand why this policy did not protect them. Recall the case of the New York woman who was charged $11 for accident and health insurance in connection with her

TV purchase. A 63-year-old Chicago security guard, earning $4,000–$5,000 a year, fell behind on a small loan when he missed two months of work because of illness.

> I was off sick for about two months and I called them and I also wrote them a letter telling them that I would be late in making my payments. What I don't understand is that in the first place they take out insurance in case of death or sickness or disability and I was paying for this insurance too.

It would seem that even the debtors who do pay for health and accident insurance derive little benefit from such policies and end up being sued anyway.

FALSE PROMISES
BY THE SELLER AS REASONS FOR DEFAULT

Virtually all the cases of fraud involve false promises of one kind or another, whether about warranties, quality, price, insurance, or whatever; hence the label "false promises" as a specific category of fraud is somewhat misleading. What we are concerned with here are deceptive selling schemes that are used as come-ons.

In chapter 3 we saw that 35 percent of those who made purchases said that they had been misinformed in some way about the transaction. Quite a number of these debtors pointed out that the dealer made false promises. Although such reports were fairly common among these debtors, only 18 of them, about 1 percent of the sample, specifically cited such false promises as a reason for their default (in most of these cases, it was the primary reason). The most common pattern here is the chain-referral scheme, under which the buyer is promised price reductions or even free merchandise in return for finding more customers. A second pattern in these cases is the "tie-in" sale, in which the buyer is supposedly given something free and need pay only for some service or supplies.

Illustrative of the phony tie-in sale is the account of a middle-aged Detroit black working in an automobile factory, who was taken in by a door-to-door salesman's pitch for a movie camera-film offer.

> The salesman said I wouldn't have to pay for the camera at all. Only for the film. The film was to cost $2.60 each time I ordered it. He said they give you the camera free if you contract to buy the film from his company. He said the movie camera would have a voice to it. It was to be talking pictures but the one I got had no voice

to it, just the camera and the projector. . . . When I got the contract
a week or two later, it looked like the same contract except different
figures and words were in it that I had never seen before. It was
for $16.50 a month for a period of five years, and the cost was $500.
A payment was due right there and then. I tried to call the salesman
but he was never there.

Not only did the salesman lie about the camera, but he violated the
law by filling out sections of the contract after it was signed and by
giving the debtor his copy of the contract some time after the sale. In
spite of being victimized in this fashion, this man kept up the payments
while trying to negotiate with the company.

I paid for a while—twelve payments in all—and in the meantime I
was trying to get the company to take the camera back but they
wouldn't take it back and so finally I stopped paying.

A popular racket that emerged in the 1960s was the deep freezer–food
plan. High-pressure salesmen would explain that the family's entire food
needs would be met if they subscribed to the plan. Sometimes the customer
understood that he was to buy the freezer, but more often than not the
salesman would claim that the freezer was free and that the family would
have to pay only for the food. Subscribers to this plan would soon learn
that the freezer was not free and that the food delivered did *not* meet
the family's need.

A 35-year-old white New Yorker, employed as a garage attendant
and earning $5,000–$6,000 yearly, was told by the salesman that the freezer
would be free if he subscribed to the food plan.

He gave us a list of food. We thought we were buying the food plan,
not the freezer. The freezer was supposed to come as part of the
deal. We simply picked out on the list the food we wanted. We told
him at the beginning that we would like to replace the fish on the
list with meat and he said that's all right. "We'll send you that."
We never received the meat and when we called, they said, "You'll
have to pay extra for that. We are not responsible for what the salesman
told you." All the pork chops were rotten. . . . We were told $79
a month for the freezer and $30 a month for the food. . . . The food
was bad and the price of the freezer came to $1,400 and you can
buy the same freezer for $300. . . . [What were your reasons for not
paying?] They had me strapped for money and when I was late once
they threatened to garnishee my salary. I really got disgusted. By
this time I was very fed up with this fraud—the inferior bad food—and
I saw that I was being overcharged. They kept changing their story
every minute and then they got nasty and tried to get at my salary.
So I decided to stop paying and look into the whole mess.

Although sued, this debtor at the time of the interview was still waiting for his case to be scheduled on the court calendar.[5]

It should be noted that the food-freezer racket forces the victims to become overextended through no fault of their own. Given assurance from the salesman that their needs will be met by the plan, the debtors become overextended when they find that they must make additional food purchases at stores.

The majority of false promises involve chain-referral schemes. Such schemes are the stock-in-trade of the salesmen employed by Detroit jewelry–clothing stores. These salesmen tell their customers that they will get $10 or $20 reductions for each customer they refer. But when the customer tries to claim this reduction, he is met with a blank stare from the store official. The story of a 28-year-old Detroit black who earned $4,000–$5,000 annually is typical. He had made a purchase from a salesman for Elroy Jewelers.

> I purchased the ring from the salesman on the street. I returned the ring for full credit at the store and they told me that the salesman wasn't there. They weren't going to give me no credit on the ring. So I said I would take a suit instead. I picked out a suit which was too big. They didn't have my size. He told me if I had it altered, he would take the price off my last payment. So I left the store and then I received my book for $125, same price as the ring. I contacted them back and said I wanted credit for the customers I gave them for suits. The first salesman had said that if I had found them some customers I could have the suit free. I told the man in the store what the man in the car had said, but he told me I would have to get the guy who sold me the ring, because he didn't know what kind of agreement I had made with him. I stopped paying because he wouldn't give me credit for the suits I had sold for him.

[5]This case arose in late 1966 and the debtor was eager to have his day in court. As of June 1967, the time of the inteview, the case had not yet been scheduled. There were at least three other food–freezer cases in our sample, in which the debtor was led to believe by the salesman that the freezer was free and he need pay only for the food. The very fact that there were several cases of this type in different cities would indicate that this is a pattern of fraud rather than the isolated experience of a single debtor. And yet it is dubious whether this debtor and the others similarly victimized would find relief if their cases did come to trial. In 1961 such a trial took place in New York. The debtor–defendant claimed that the seller had told him he would have to pay only for his food needs, which they judged would come to $100 a month. This debtor defaulted when he discovered that the food plan did not meet his needs. The creditor sued him for defaulting on a contract for the deep freezer, a contract that made no mention of the food plan. After studying the contract and ascertaining that the debtor was literate and therefore capable of reading the contract, the judge ruled in favor of the seller, and the debtor had to pay $1,342.80 for the freezer. See Thor Food Service Corp. v. Makofske, 28 Misc. 872, 218 N.Y.S.2nd 93 (1961). What appears to be a reasonable decision based on the facts of a single case (the debtor can read, the contract refers only to a freezer) takes on a different cast in the light of observations on a number of similar cases. This calls attention to the role empirical research can play in the judicial process.

Perhaps the most artful practitioners of the chain-referral scheme are vacuum cleaner companies, which learned long ago to sell their wares through door-to-door salesmen. Their typical sales pitch is that the buyer can earn commissions for finding other customers, commissions that are deducted from the cost of the cleaner. Sometimes the salesman convinces the customer that he can actually earn money and is really taking on a job rather than buying something.[6] A white New Yorker employed by a wholesale food distributor and earning $6,000–$8,000 a year was approached by a salesman selling central vacuum cleaning systems.

> The salesman came to the door and he had a business proposition. He said for every interview he got through me, I would get money off on my vacuum and for every vacuum he sold through me I would get money. The vacuum was to cost $800. When the guy interviewed us he told us that there was a $300 bond that they guaranteed us. . . . If they got 20 interviews through me I was supposed to get $300 back from them. As far as I know they got the interviews but I never got my $300.

This debtor had made 18 payments and owed only the money he had been promised as a refund when he stopped paying. His contract had been sold to a large New York bank, which later sued him for $338.[7]

A final example of false promises is provided by a middle-aged black couple in Philadelphia. The husband was a laborer earning $4,000–$5,000 annually. Their case involves not only the chain-referral idea, but trickery in signing the contract and price deception as well. But all of these are

---

[6]For a classic description of the deception employed in the sales of vacuum cleaners, see Philip Schrag, *Counsel for the Deceived* (New York: Pantheon Books, Inc., 1972), chap. 4.

[7]It is quite possible that this particular variant of the chain-referral scheme has come to an end in the New York area, for in 1968, in a precedent-establishing case, the U.S. Attorney of New York successfully prosecuted the owner of a series of firms which sold central vacuum cleaners, quartz broilers, and color TV sets under the ruse that the customers would earn money simply by providing the salesman with the names of additional customers. The customers were told that 6 or 7 of every 10 persons would agree to buy and that given this ratio, they would actually make money as well as receive the merchandise free. The federal government obtained standing in the court on the grounds of mail fraud in that the mails were used for transmitting contracts and payments. Richard Givens, who then headed the consumer fraud division of the U.S. Attorney's office in New York, was the prosecutor and he pointed out in his brief the mathematical impossibility of any significant proportion of the customers earning anything in commissions approaching the price of the items they bought. Whereas the first customer need contribute to only 8 sales to break even, his customers would have to make 64 sales and their customers would have to make 512. By the tenth step in this progression, over 1 billion sales are required, and of course there are not enough people on earth to permit the progression to reach the eleventh step. The conviction in this case was upheld by the United States Court of Appeal for the Second District, and the defendant is now serving a jail term. This is an unusual case only because it is one of the few in which an unscrupulous dealer has met criminal sanctions. For more details see U.S. v. Sterngass. Docket no. 32704 (Second Cir. 12/18/68. See also U.S. v. Armantrout, 411 F. 2d 60 (Second Cir. 1969).

secondary reasons for the default, the main reason being that the husband became ill. Their trouble started when they were approached by a door-to-door seller of garbage disposals.

> He said if we got two or three customers, we could have it free. We didn't know that we were signing a judgment note. We thought we were signing a receipt for the installation of the disposal. And he didn't say anything about price. A week or two later we got a payment book from the First Quaker Bank. Each coupon was for $10 and there were 36 of them.

Again we find a bank as the holder-in-due-course in a shady transaction. This couple, in spite of their deception, tried to maintain payments and fell behind only when the husband became sick. The wife called the bank to explain that she would have to miss some payments and also to complain about the price because she had since learned that the same disposal could be bought at a department store for $79. Since she was angry about the deception and the price and never heard again from the bank, she decided to stop payments. A year later she received a payment book from a collection agency claiming that she owed $600 for the disposal and must pay $20 a month. She claimed that several such payments were actually made but that she could not keep them up. She then learned that because of this debt, her house was to be put up for sale at a Sheriff's auction. At the time of the interview she was hoping that a lawyer she had retained could forestall the sale.

This account is remarkable not only for the initial deception but because it illustrates so well the mushrooming costs of these debts as they are passed from one creditor to another. We also find here an example of the harsh collection procedures permitted in Pennsylvania under confession-of-judgment notes, a theme to be taken up later.[8] Meanwhile, as this case demonstrates, the villain of the nineteenth-century melodrama, the wicked mortgager who forecloses on the family farm, has a counterpart in the last third of the twentieth century in the more complicated guise of door-to-door salesmen, banks, and collection agencies all taking advantage of consumer credit laws.

DEBTORS WHO WERE TRICKED
INTO SIGNING CONTRACTS

We have examined cases in which debtors were deceived about the quality and the price of the merchandise they bought as well as various terms

---

[8]Under the Consumer Protection Act passed in 1968, creditors who wish to attach real property must give the debtor the right to rescind the contract within 24 hours of the sale. Some experts think that this will discourage the creditors from using such contracts, but the effectiveness of this new law remains to be seen.

of the transaction. Perhaps the ultimate form of deception occurred in those cases in which the debtor was unaware that he was signing an installment contract at all. The Philadelphia garbage disposal case just presented falls into this category and in all, some 13 debtors, not quite 1 percent of the sample, had this complaint.

Most of these debtors had been tricked by direct sellers, but at least one New York debtor, a 26-year-old Puerto Rican earning $4,000–$5,000 a year, got into trouble because of the duplicity of a furniture store's salesman. The interviewer recorded his story in the third person.

> A friend of his invited him to go to a furniture store while the friend bought a living room set. He went to Puerto Rico after that and when he came back and went to work, someone from the furniture store came to visit him at the factory where he was working at the time. The man from the store asked him to sign several papers because the only way his friend could get the furniture was if he signed. The man guaranteed him that there was no obligation and that he wasn't going to get into any kind of trouble. Mr. _____ did not want to sign, but his boss (who, according to Mr. _____, knew less English than he did) asked him to sign and he did without reading the papers. Now he appears as the customer who bought the furniture. His friend disappeared. The lawyer of the furniture store told him that he has to pay $347 . . . . The lawyer threatened him that he was going to notify his employer and later he did.

This defendant was sued because he was deceived into being a cosigner. In spite of the salesman's assurance that he had no obligation, he was held responsible for the debt and was eventually garnisheed because of this deception.

The story of a 31-year-old Chicago black is even more strange in that he insisted that he had never cosigned for the person who had defaulted.

> I bought furniture at the Loop Department Store three days before my friend bought his furniture. We didn't go together. I signed a contract for my purchase. I did not cosign for him. He got me into this. I was making my payments and didn't know anything about this until my boss told me my wages were being garnisheed. I told my boss that I had nothing to do with this but the store said that the bills should be together. My friend was working at the same place I was. He has since quit. Since I'm being forced to pay his bill, I'm going to keep the furniture he bought.

It is not clear how this debtor became the cosigner for his friend. Perhaps the friend forged his name, or perhaps the dealer, knowing of the friendship, held him responsible. In any case, it was this man who was sued for his friend's default even though he never signed the friend's contract.

A middle-aged Philadelphia black also did not understand the nature of the transaction when he was approached by a door-to-door salesman selling cemetery lots. The salesman told him that he could arrange a loan for such a lot, but this debtor did not understand the salesman's pitch.

> The way he explained it, I didn't know I was taking out a loan. I didn't know I was buying a lot. He just asked me to come out and look at it. I didn't know that I was borrowing money.

This debtor later received a payment book from a small loan company for a $603 loan. When asked why he had not paid, he replied:

> Because I did not have the deed to show that I owned the lot. I hate for someone to take advantage of me. I didn't know I was buying anything from that salesman.

This man lost his home because of his entanglement with the salesman of cemetery lots.

The home repair business has been identified in the President's Crime Commission report as a major source of white collar crime. The report estimates that American consumers lose from ½ to 1 billion dollars a year because of home repair frauds alone.[9] Some of the debtors in our sample were victimized by fraudulent home repair firms. The modus operandi of these firms is well illustrated by the account of a 39-year-old Detroit black, earning $6,000–$8,000 a year in the automobile industry. He is placed in this category of reasons for the default because he did not know that he was signing an installment contract. The following story is reconstructed from various parts of the interview:

> The company told me to sign a paper so I could get an estimate and see if I could get a loan. It turns out I was really signing a contract and didn't know it. . . . The company contacted the bank. . . . I even called the bank and told them not to O.K. the loan when I could see that they wanted to do more work than I wanted done. . . . I wanted to get some estimates and talk to the insurance company before I had my roof repaired. . . . I never even worked anything out with them. They checked the damage, and took my name. The next thing I knew the men were here with materials for the roof. I sent them back with the stuff and called the bank and told them not to O.K. the loan. They said they wouldn't but they did anyway, and the Monarch Co. came back with materials and put the roof on. . . . They took a judgment against me. I was supposed to be covered by the insurance company. I only had the house five months.

[9] *Task Force Report: Crime and Its Impact–An Assessment* (Washington, D.C.: U.S. Government Printing Office, 1967), p. 104.

> I wrote to the insurance company and to FHA and nobody would do anything. They said I'd have to get a lawyer and sue them. One lawyer said it would be $100 down and $50 every day he went to court. I couldn't afford that kind of money. Now even after the job is done, it still leaks. The plaster is falling and I have to put new ceilings on.

This debtor thought that his insurance company would pay for the repairs, but he was not given the opportunity to check on this before the contract that he was tricked into signing became effective. When he did reach the insurance company, he was told that since the damage was done by a leaking drain pipe rather than by the wind, his policy did not apply.

This case is of interest not only for the description of the contract signing, but also because it illustrates so well the multitude of institutions which, acting in terms of their narrow interests, fail to prevent the exploitation of consumers. This man was deceived by the home repair firm; when he learned that a bank would accept the contract, he urged it to disapprove the loan. Although he was promised that the loan would not be approved, it was. The debtor then contacted the company that had insured his house only to learn that his insurance did not cover this type of damage. He even appealed to the FHA, which had the mortgage on his house, but this governmental agency could only advise him to consult an attorney. And when he contacted a lawyer, he found he could not afford his services. Many of the debtors we have encountered were too passive or too intimidated to seek help with their problems, and many of them hastily made purchases under the pressure of fast-talking salesmen. But this man had every intention of collecting various repair estimates *before* signing a contract, that is, of acting like a rational consumer, and when he learned that he had been deceived, he contacted the relevant parties and did his best to rescind the deal only to find his efforts of no avail.

MISCELLANEOUS (COMPLICATED) FRAUDS

During the early phases of classifying the reasons for default, we developed a category that would signify unusual, complicated, or multiple types of fraud. As the classification process proceeded, many of the cases initially placed in this residual category were reallocated to other categories, but five of the debtors' stories remained in this group because their stories were unusual.

One involves the money-making schemes that unscrupulous dealers employ to sell their wares, in this instance the infamous vacuum cleaner. It is distinguished from the chain-referral scheme encountered earlier in that the dealer enticed the debtor by giving him the false impression that he was being hired for a job. (The case could easily have been classified under the heading of false promises.) In this respect it is quite close to a fairly common fraud employed by many firms, the various "earn-money-in-your-spare-time" schemes that are advertised in the mass media. But it is the only case of its type in our sample. The victims were a young white Detroit couple with annual income of $4,000–$5,000.

> It all started when my husband answered an ad for part-time work on an electronics job, but it was really for selling Kays vacuum cleaners. He didn't really want to buy one. They asked him to sign a paper so they could start checking on his credit. He wanted to wait so he could talk to me but they said to sign so they could start checking our credit. He signed. They said if he would work for them, they would give him names of people to call on and they would make payments on the demonstrator for each call he made. He had classes to attend to learn about the machine and he went to all of them. When he finished they wouldn't give him any names. They said they gave them only to full-time men and that he would have to go to his friends. But we didn't know anybody. We'd only been in town a few months. On the day after he first went to Kays, a lady came here. I guess she was from Gray Finance Co. but at the time I thought she was from Kays and came to get me to agree to his working for them. I agreed and then we got another vacuum cleaner besides the demonstrator. We were able to send one back. My husband could have sold this one to himself and made the $70 commission or at least have saved that much, but they didn't tell him that until another man got the commission. We didn't pay because we didn't like the circumstances in which we ended up buying the machine. Kays didn't come through with the working conditions they promised in the verbal agreements.

When this couple was served with court papers, they called the finance company that had their contract and were told that the court action would be stopped only if they started to make payments. They explained that the vacuum cleaner firm had not lived up to its agreement. The finance company checked with the firm and according to the wife:

> The finance company said that Kays said my husband hadn't attended all the classes, but he went to them all.

Certainly a finance company that knows about this deceptive selling scheme of the dealer whose paper it buys cannot be innocent of the transaction.

A further example of the violation of all ethics governing consumer transactions is provided by a 31-year-old black Chicagoan, employed as a skilled worker, earning $6,000–$8,000 annually, who had this unhappy experience when he went to buy a used car:

> I put a down payment on a Buick and took it home and drove it for five or six days. When I returned to the lot to get something or other (I forgot what) they wanted to take the Buick away and give me an older Cadillac instead. I didn't want it. We had a long, long argument, it lasted almost the whole day, and we called each other a lot of names. They said they couldn't finance the Buick and the only way I wouldn't lose my down payment was to take the Cadillac. . . . That's all they said, but that Cadillac was in terrible shape and they wouldn't fix it like they said they would. It's been sitting out in the back of the house for three years.
>
> I stopped paying mainly because I got disgusted. I felt that I had been cheated. I kept trying to make them live up to their promises to fix the car. I don't think they wanted the car themselves. I kept calling them to come and pick it up. I was putting in so much money trying to fix it up so that it would run, I just got disgusted and stopped paying. It hasn't run in at least three years. It would take at least $1,000 to get it to run. That's the only reason I stopped paying. . . .
> I got disgusted.

This firm not only rescinded on the deal, but it forced the debtor to accept an inferior automobile on the threat that he would lose his down payment. Such coercion must certainly be illegal. One rule of thumb for distinguishing unscrupulous dealers from more legitimate ones is provided by this account. The legitimate dealer tries to find a finance company to accept the contract before he considers the deal final. If he cannot find one, he will return the down payment and call the deal off. The less scrupulous dealer, as in this case, will rewrite the terms of the contract and force the debtor into a transaction for inferior merchandise.

Two cases in this miscellaneous category of fraud involve reports in which automobile dealers absconded with money. Both of these are Detroit cases, but the automobile firms were different. A middle-aged Detroit black, employed as an assembly line worker in an automobile factory, was attracted by a newspaper ad announcing that an auto firm would consolidate the would-be buyer's debts at the same time that it sold him a new car.

> The ad read: "Cars for all. Come in and let us consolidate your bills and we will be able to get you a loan to pay them all off with one bank and have a new car too." I liked that idea so I went to Harry's [the dealer] and saw this man who is mainly a consolidator. He told me that if I bought a new car, they would consolidate all my bills and finance a loan to pay everything off. They said they

would pay off the Retailer Bank where I had a loan for the car I had. I bought a car from them but they kept stalling me and telling me they couldn't get a loan from a bank to pay off the other bank. I kept running from one place to another. The Retailer Bank wanted their money. The car dealer's consolidator had taken my other car and was supposed to sell it and give me the money. I gave him $800 to pay off the Retailer Bank but he kept the money and never paid them off. The Retailer Bank finally came to the lot and took my old car and auctioned it off. Meanwhile, I'm stuck with the new car for which they got me a loan, but they never consolidated my debts like they said they would and then this man disappears—the money consolidator. He disappeared with my money and the Retailer Bank never got paid off.

The final case of an unusual and complicated fraud also involves an automobile purchase and the allegation by the debtor that the salesman absconded with funds. This case is of particular interest because the interviewer, on the urging of the debtor, actually called the creditor involved and obtained his version of the event. Because of its complexities and the wealth of information provided, we shall spend more time on it than on any other case. Three voices are to be heard in this episode, those of the debtor, the small loan company, and the interviewer. The debtors are a middle-aged black Detroit couple. The husband was employed by the city as a maintenance man, the wife worked as a domestic and their combined income was $4,000–$5,000. The wife, who provided the details, was, according to the interviewer, quite agitated.

We decided to buy a car over three years ago. This car dealer told us he would give us $500 for a trade-in on the old car, but we needed more money for a down payment. So he contacted Benevolent Finance Company at 11:30 at night and made arrangements for a personal loan in the amount of $840. They were supposed to have turned the money over to the car dealer, but they never did and we have never seen the money either. Benevolent knows this. Why else is it that they have never taken us to court to get the money? The one time they talked about going to court, about a year ago, we were getting ready to appear gladly. We had even taken off work to go to court when someone called us early in the morning and told us the court appearance was cancelled and the judge would give us a new date. But we're still waiting. I never paid a dime for that so-called "loan" and to my dying day I vow I never will. We are paying, and willingly too, to Happy Discount Corp. for a loan in the amount of $2,977.56, which is the total amount the car cost us, and I'm not sure how they got into the act. I tell you, lady, we got a fast shuffle. The night we signed papers for that car, the car dealer skipped town. I know he took the loan from Benevolent with him. He probably got Happy Discount to finance the car.

So far this excited woman's account contains at least one contradiction. At first she claimed that the small loan company never turned the money over to the dealer, but then later she said that the salesman skipped town that very night with the loan. Since the arrangement of loans by dealers for down payments is quite common in used-car transactions, it might seem that this woman is mistaken about the loan in question and it is indeed part of her liability for the car. But the financial data on the transaction which she provided casts serious doubts on this hypothesis. They were told that the car would cost $2,800. The amount owed to the finance company, which she knew precisely, was $2,977.56, a figure close enough to the quoted price that the couple accepted it as fair. It is unclear what role the $500 trade-in played in the transaction. Perhaps without the trade-in the used car would have cost $3,500. But if the alleged loan was indeed for the down payment, then the car would have cost $3,820, almost $1,000 more than the quoted price. These data would seem to confirm her view that the alleged loan had nothing to do with the transaction.

One additional observation is in order. The wife claims that she received a summons almost a year prior to the interview and that before she could appear in court, the case was unexpectedly postponed and they have not heard any more about the lawsuit. This seems strange because her case was sampled from the docket book only about six months prior to the interview. Thus, either this woman was mistaken about the time of the court action, or the creditor reinstituted action at a later point. From further details on this case, it would seem that the latter interpretation is correct.

At this point in the interview, the woman insisted that the interviewer call the Benevolent Finance Co. to find out the name of the car dealer and the exact amount of the alleged loan. The interviewer then recorded this account of her call, which further complicates the story:

> The man at Benevolent told me that Harry Auto Sales was the name of the dealer and that $843.11 was the amount borrowed. I asked what the loan was for and what proof they had that the money was ever paid. The man said that the loan was a personal loan, that the cosigner had died, and that a cancelled check, endorsed by Mr. B. [the husband], was their proof. After I hung up, Mr. and Mrs. B. told me that they never saw the check [the one for $843.11] and they never endorsed it.

Before continuing the story, it may be noted that the finance company was able to identify the used-car dealer and obviously understood that the money was to be used as a down payment on a car. Only in a legal sense was the alleged loan a personal one, which implies that the debtor came in to borrow money on his own. The woman then proceeded to explain to the interviewer what the agent for Benevolent Finance was really referring to.

> The cosigner he is talking about is José H. I'll tell you about that. During the time they were pestering and pestering us, our house was robbed of everything. The only one home was poor old 81-year-old Dad. They broke in with a crowbar and took all our furniture. They just pushed Dad aside and took everything. Benevolent must've heard of the robbery because soon after, they called us and said they were going to help us out as we probably needed money. They were going to give or lend us $200 which we did need at the time. They told us to bring a cosigner. We brought José. After both signed, they told us we could only have $101. I told him no thanks and the next day José died.

This was the explanation offered by the woman of the interviewer's conversation with the man at Benevolent. In short, she insisted that the finance company was referring to a much later loan, one which she did not accept after the papers were signed because its cash value was only one half of the stated amount. Almost two years after this interview, the interviewer was asked to revisit the couple to find out if this mysterious account could be unraveled. The subsequent information provided by this woman helps somewhat in straightening out the case.

> José wasn't with us the time we bought the car. He cosigned for only one loan, the one for $200. You see, what Benevolent wanted was our signature. Fred here [her husband] and old José were too dumb and gullible to see that. They kept begging me and begging me and so did the Benevolent man, to sign this loan, so I finally broke down and signed, but I wish to God I hadn't because I just signed my life away when I signed for that loan and they got our signatures. Even though we didn't take the $101, they could start legal proceedings now, garnishments and court orders. They garnisheed Fred's salary five or six times and Fred about lost his job. We finally agreed to pay and we're still paying.

The interviewer pressed the woman and asked her why she thought they wanted her signature so badly.

> Look, did you ever hear of a finance company pestering anyone for three years without a court order or garnishments or any legal action? They didn't have nothing to prove they ever loaned anyone $843! That's what I kept telling them for three years when they kept calling me. I'd say, "If you think I'm paying you $843 that some fly-by-night car dealer left town with, you're barking up the wrong tree." So finally they got us when we were freshly burglarized and in bad shape

financially and like fools we put our signatures on something that made everything legal for them to start collecting. All three of us signed for that $200 loan.

This woman's theory is not only eminently plausible but it provides an explanation for the apparent discrepancy about when legal action was instituted. The first court action, which was dropped, was apparently initiated before the second loan, whereas the second court action, the one that we sampled, took place after the loan and resulted in a series of garnishments *after* the first interview.

This case concludes our review of the various types of fraud that play a role in the breakdown of the credit transaction. But it also highlights a theme that should be made more explicit: the procedures through which automobile sales are financed. It must be remembered that this debtor was not sued by the company that financed the car, but by the firm that had been approached by the dealer to finance the down payment. Dealer-arranged loans for down payments are quite common in automobile transactions, and they deserve to be examined more closely, especially in connection with the controversy that has developed over the holder-in-due-course doctrine.

A NOTE ON THE FINANCING OF AUTOMOBILES

It will be remembered that the plaintiff in the case we have just reviewed was a small loan company with whom the automobile dealer had presumably arranged a loan for the debtor to cover the down payment. The dealer then sold the contract to a finance company, thus saddling the debtor with two debt obligations in connection with the same purchase. Dealer-arranged down-payment loans are in violation of the doctrine of holder-in-due-course because of the collusion between the dealer and the lender. Nonetheless, they are quite common in the used-car (and even new-car) business. Their function is to reduce the gap between the value of the car as collateral and the amount that the finance company must put up to finance the transaction. If the car is being sold for $1,500, it probably does not have a resale value of more than $1,100 or so, and hence the finance company demands a down payment of $400 to reduce its risk. In such a fashion, debtors who are enticed by such advertisements as "no money down" find themselves saddled with two debt obligations, one to the small loan company that put up the down payment and the other to the finance company that purchased the contract from the dealer.

A number of such dealer-arranged down-payment loans were encountered in the interviews. For example, the wife of a 30-year-old Detroit assembly line worker earning $4,000–$5,000 a year gave this account:

> We saw an ad in the paper for a car. We called and the man came
> and picked us up and took us to the lot. We didn't have the down
> payment, so he took us to a place in Dearborn called the Consumer
> Finance Co. to borrow $450, I felt this was too much for a 1960
> Chevy. (Is that how much the car cost?) No, the car cost $1,000
> and the $450 was for the down payment. We had to make payments
> to the First National Bank as well. We had to pay $27 a month to
> the loan company and $45 a month to the bank.

Earlier, to illustrate deception regarding price, we cited the case
of a Detroit man who was saddled with such a loan and found that the
payments on his multiple debts exceeded the amount he could afford
to pay. We now cite further details of this debtor's case (a white laborer
earning under $3,000).

> I saw an ad in the paper. It said they would give credit to anyone
> who had never had credit before. It was the Harry Auto Sales on
> Fort Street in Hyandette. I went there to buy a car. I told the man
> I had never established credit before. He said, "Never mind, we're
> credit specialists." He took me over to Benevolent Finance but they
> turned me down because I never had credit before. We went back
> to the car lot. He said not to worry. He would get me credit. After
> 8 o'clock that night the manager of Benevolent Finance came over
> to the lot and said he was establishing my credit. He didn't say he
> was from Benevolent at that time. I thought I was signing for a car
> loan, not a personal loan. It turned out I signed two papers, one
> for a car loan and one for a personal loan.

It is of some interest that this debtor's story dovetails with the account
of the "agitated" Detroit black woman that we examined in some detail.
He, too, dealt with the Harry Auto Sales Co. and he, too, was taken
to the Benevolent Finance Co. by the salesman to arrange for a loan
for the down payment. Furthermore, in his case too, the loan was arranged
in the late evening hours.

As noted, these dealer-arranged loans would appear to violate the
doctrine of holder-in-due-course. But it would be difficult to establish
this point in court. The problem is that the small loan company is not
the holder-in-due-course (this status belongs to the finance company) but
rather an agency that has made a "personal loan" to the debtor. That
the debtor did not apply for the loan and never had the money in his
possession does not detract from the lending agency's defining this as
a personal loan. The salutory efforts to do away with the holder-
in-due-course doctrine are in danger of being undermined by a shift from
finance companies to small loan companies as the agencies financing consumer purchases. True, the small loan company would not have access
to the merchandise as collateral, but it would receive a higher rate of

interest than the finance company (the law permits higher rates on small loans than on conditional sales contracts), and it would still be able to attach the debtor's personal and real property (including his salary) after obtaining a court judgment. The reformers of consumer credit law have become aware of the loophole posed by the involvement of direct lenders in consumer transactions. A clear need exists for a set of rules that would define such lenders as parties to the transaction and thus liable to the debtor's defenses against the original seller. Such rules might be based on the dealer having arranged the loan, the loan taking place outside the lender's normal place of business (for example, the used-car lot) and the debtor never having the money in his possession (the lender usually just writes a check to the dealer after obtaining the debtor's signature to a contract).

7

PAYMENT

MISUNDERSTANDINGS

This chapter takes up another class of reasons for the default in which the creditor is implicated: breakdowns in the system of payments. In chapter 4 we saw that misunderstandings, errors, and fraud regarding payments were present in 9 percent of the cases and that in 7 percent, such reasons constituted the primary cause of the default. The critical point about these reasons is that in almost every instance the debtor was both able and willing to pay.

Under the general heading of misunderstandings about payment arrangements we have distinguished seven categories of more specific reasons. The categories and their frequencies are shown in Table 7.1.

From the last row of Table 7.1 we learn that payment misunderstandings are most often primary reasons for the default, occasionally secondary reasons, but never tertiary reasons. In more than one third of these cases, the debtor claimed that he had either paid off the debt or was paying regularly. He blames his trouble on the faulty bookkeeping of the creditor. The other categories of reasons shown in Table 7.1 are of interest, for they call attention to the variety of ways in which debtors run afoul of the system of consumer credit through no fault of their own.

DEBTORS WHO CLAIM TO HAVE PAID IN FULL

From Table 7.1 we learn that 18 debtors felt that the court action against them was unjustified because, in their view, they had paid off their debt

Table 7.1 / Reasons for Default Linked to Payment Arrangements

flaws in payment arrangements	first reason (no. cases)	second reason (no. cases)	third reason (no. cases)	total reasons (no. cases)	total reasons (percent)	total individuals (percent)
Debtor claims to have paid in full; blames creditor's faulty bookkeeping	17	1	—	18	1	1.4
Debtor was paying regularly; blames faulty bookkeeping or dishonest collector	20	2	†	22	1	1.7
Debtor does not know how to make the payments	16	3	—	19	1	1.4
Creditor fails to respond to debtor's inquiries—debtor unable to learn how much he owes	9	2	—	11	1	0.8
Creditor changes payment schedule, payments higher or more frequent than debtor led to believe	6	5	—	11	1	0.8
Mishaps between creditors and their third parties—debt-consolidation confusion	9	2	—	11	1	0.8
All other misunderstandings regarding payments	14	3	—	17	1	1.3
Subtotal cases	91	18	—	109		8.5
Percent of total cases	7.0	3.1	—	5.5		
Total cases	1,320	570	110	2,000		1,326

obligation. Most of these cases involved some error on the part of the creditor in recording payments, but a few of them were sufficiently ambiguous to make the assignment of fault a difficult task. An example of these ambiguous cases is provided by an unmarried New York black woman, employed as a secretary and earning under $3,000 a year, who had bought a TV set and made 22 payments on it.

> I left a deposit that was to be subtracted from my final payment, which would have been equal to the amount I owed. Then I went out of town for a while and when I got back there were these letters. Since I thought it was paid for with the deposit, I forgot about it.

This woman clearly thought she had paid off her debt, but from her story, it is not certain that she had. The "deposit" may have been no more than a down payment, which would not have exonerated her from the final payment. The finance company's attorney insisted that she owed $35, and at the time of the interview she was trying to arrange some kind of settlement.

The likelihood of error on the part of the creditor is suggested in the next incident as well, that of a 37-year-old Chicago white truck driver whose annual family income, including the earnings of his wife, exceeded $10,000. Two years prior to the interview he had bought a bed and some lamps at a furniture store.

> We did not stop paying. We paid in full! We had sent them our check—it was the last payment and our account was paid in full. Then recently I received a notice that *we still owed the full amount*. I have the cancelled checks to show that the account was closed. They wouldn't believe me. I got sick and tired hearing from them, so now our case is in the hands of a lawyer.

In a number of these incidents, the creditor eventually came to agree with the debtor that a mistake had been made. For example, a 26-year-old New York black, earning under $3,000 a year as a salesman, bought furniture and his contract was sold to Big City Credit Corporation. His story is typical of these cases.

> I was a little behind in payments a few times but the company kept sending me different late notices. As I said, I may have been behind a few times but I wasn't so constantly late or anything. . . . At one point I was as much as a month behind. . . . I finally called the company and told them that my records showed that I was up to date. I spoke to a lady there and I asked her to send me a photostatic copy of the company's record of my payments, so I could compare it with my own record. That was in March and I never received it. Then I called again in April and said that I never received their record, and this lady checked my account and said it was paid in full. After

the summons came, I checked with their lawyer and he agreed I
was paid up and only owed $3.00 in late payment charges.

These cases are disproportionately reported by the New York debtors
and they tend to involve the same finance company, Big City Credit
Corporation. Another New York debtor, a middle-aged black bus driver,
earning $6,000–$8,000 a year, had borrowed money from a small loan
company and his account was also sold to Big City Credit. When asked
why he had stopped paying, he claimed that he had settled his debt.

> The company changed hands, and the new people, which is Big City
> Credit, sent me a letter threatening to garnishee my wages and so
> I paid them off. Two or three weeks after I paid them off they put
> a garnishee on my salary. I called them up and told them that the
> company I worked for was threatening to lay me off because of the
> garnishee. They said it must have been a mistake and that they would
> see the marshal, but it took three or four weeks before I got
> released. . . . I certainly shouldn't have to pay any more because
> I paid it already.

Another New York debtor, a 30-year-old black woman whose husband is a truck driver, earning $8,000–$10,000 a year, had a revolving
credit account at one of New York's major department stores.

> My account was down to $36.80 and we decided to pay it off. I
> sent a check to them for $36.80, closing our account. They kept billing
> us and we called and told them we had sent the check. They finally
> wrote a letter saying they got the check but it didn't look like my
> husband's handwriting and wanted us to send another check. We
> wrote and told them to send the other check back, but they never
> sent it. . . . The $36.80 we were supposed to owe was in May, 1965.
> We finally sent a money order without them returning the check we
> sent. They sent another letter saying we owed another dollar. We
> sent that. . . . But again the monthly bills kept coming for $36.80
> each month plus service charges which they added on each month.
> I called after each bill and told them we didn't owe them anything.
> Then they began to send letters, and calls from their lawyer. Then
> we sent a money order for the amount. The case is closed now and
> we paid $84.00.

The $84.00 that this couple paid to this store covered not only the disputed
payment but lawyer's fees and court costs as well. By this woman's
account, she paid not only $84 to close the case but a $36.80 money
order as well, or a total of $120 over a disputed $36.80 debt.

As a final example of the cases in which the debtor claimed to be
unfairly sued because he had paid in full, we cite the story of an articulate
28-year-old New York white, employed in the publishing business and

earning over $10,000 a year. This man had a revolving credit account at a reputable New York department store. The multiple errors in his account so outraged him that he wrote a letter to the president of the company, a carbon of which he provided to the interviewer. He explained that in June 1964, he made a cash payment of $50. Because this amount did not appear on his statement, he asked the credit department to check its records. They were unable to locate the difficulty and recommended that he continue making payments. After making two more payments, he again contacted the credit department. They again suggested that he continue his payments while they checked their records. When his next monthly statement failed to show his $50 payment, he decided to stop paying. The balance was then $112.85. The debtor received many harassing letters from the credit department. He decided to pay off the balance, which he thought was $102.85. Realizing his error, he paid the remaining $10.00. Some time later he received a letter from the store's attorney stating that he owed the store $155.60, had been served with a summons, and was about to be served with a judgment. His letter to the store's president concluded:

> Well, Sir, I don't owe your store the money and I never received
> the summons and you must stop that judgment. I will call your office
> and hope that you have cleared up this mess.

One further facet of this man's problem should be noted. In spite of his letter, he was indeed sued by the store and as a result of the suit he had to pay an additional $50. That he was sued only for this amount rather than the $155 indicated in the lawyer's letter to him would suggest that the creditor acknowledged that the debt had been paid. The additional $50 may have been the amount of the attorney's fee and court costs.

Given the broad range of reasons for the debt problem, the relatively few cases in which the debtor's problem stemmed from the creditor's faulty bookkeeping may not seem significant, but the very fact that such cases do exist calls attention to the imperfections of the system of consumer credit, imperfections that result in unjustified black marks against debtors who have fulfilled their obligations. As noted, credit bureaus routinely collect information on law suits but do not generally check the outcomes of such suits. Thus debtors who fall victim to the creditor's faulty bookkeeping are just as stigmatized as those who do not pay their debts.

DEBTORS WHO CLAIM
TO HAVE MADE REGULAR PAYMENTS

In addition to those who insist they paid in full, some 22 debtors claimed that they were paying regularly and that the creditor's faulty bookkeeping was the cause of the difficulty. For example, a Chicagoan, a 40-year-old white, a self-employed insurance broker earning over $10,000, had bought carpeting and his contract was sold to the Electric Credit Company. He blames his trouble on the company's failure to credit him with two payments that he insisted he had made.

> The Electric Credit Company had no record of the two payments that I had made to them. I would have made more payments, but I requested a statement of how much was owed and they never sent me one. Therefore, I stopped paying. Then I received a bill for $600 or $700 and I didn't know what it was for. Their office had probably mislaid the payment record and never recorded the two payments I made. The bill was higher because of lawyer fees and interest.

This debtor, like others we shall encounter, claimed that some of his payments were not acknowledged.

In some of the cases classified in this category the confusion seems to have resulted from the contract being sold to a finance company. A middle-aged New York Puerto Rican whose annual income was below $4,000 had bought a TV set from a furniture store and his contract was subsequently sold to that ubiquitous firm, Big City Credit.

> It was all a mistake. I was never late or stopped making payments at any time. But as I said, I was paying Central Furniture Store and not the company that sued me. I made no deal with them.

This debtor's account suggests the possibility that the furniture store continued to collect from the debtor and did not turn the payments over to the finance company.

Included in this category of payment foul-ups are a few cases in which the debtor claimed to have made payments to a collector who absconded with the funds. A middle-aged New York black earning under $3,000 arranged to buy a bed through a door-to-door salesman.

> They never gave me a payment book. I had nothing to show that I was making the payments. They must think I'm a fool. The man that was coming by every week to collect the money was stealing it. I had no receipts to show I was making the payments. They told me they had locked the man up for stealing the money, and they would not send anyone else out to collect. But when I bought it they said they would come around to collect.

This debtor apparently counted on a collector's coming by. Although the store admitted that their collector was a thief and had him arrested, the man was sued by the store for not paying his debt.

DEBTORS WHO DO NOT KNOW HOW TO PAY:
COLLECTOR STOPS COMING

The next category under the general heading of payment misunderstanding represents a major breakdown in communication between the creditor and the debtor. Nineteen debtors reported not knowing where or how to make the payments on their debt. Significantly, all but four of these debtors had made purchases from door-to-door salesmen. That these were likely to be direct sales is related to the most frequent pattern among them: a collector stopped coming or shifted his visits to a time when the debtor was never home. Almost half of these cases are of this type. Illustrative of these collector mishaps is the account of a 37-year-old Puerto Rican New Yorker, employed in a factory and earning $4,000–$5,000 a year. This man purchased a set of "unbreakable" china from a door-to-door salesman for $122 and told the interviewer that most of the pieces were broken when the set arrived. He had paid $25 in $2, $3, and $4 payments to a collector who suddenly stopped coming.

> They did not come to get the payments. They were supposed to come
> and get payments here but then they stopped coming.

The man was garnisheed because of this debt.

A 64-year-old Chicago black, employed as a laborer and earning under $3,000 a year, had a long-standing relationship with a canvasser employed by a store.

> We would pay him $5 a week and buy what we want. We paid from
> 1956 to 1965 until he stopped coming by. He used to come every
> week to collect and we had been buying from him for years. I got
> behind because he stopped coming. . . . They said we owed them
> $255 but over the years we paid them over a thousand dollars. We
> probably overpaid them. . . . I lost my job after my employer received
> the garnishment.

This case is a good example of the more traditionalistic economic relationships that many low-income families have with peddlers who make weekly visits to deliver the goods that the family needs and to collect payments.[1] This debtor had become accustomed to the system over the years and blames his default on the collector who stopped coming by. The store for whom the peddler worked did not send a different collector nor did

---

[1]For a more detailed discussion of these peddlers, see David Caplovitz, *The Poor Pay More* (New York: The Free Press, 1963), chap. 5.

it instruct him on how to make the payments. As a result of this breakdown, the debtor was garnisheed and lost his job.

Apart from breakdowns in the relationship with collectors, a few debtors who did not know where to make payments were in this position because the company that they had been dealing with had moved and they no longer knew how to contact it. A 24-year-old Chicago black, employed as an inspector by an automobile firm and earning between $8,000 and $10,000 a year, gave this account.

> Because I didn't know where to send the payments. They moved. Then about three or four months later I got a notice from this lawyer saying I was being sued. He asked why I didn't make the payments and I told him I didn't know where to make the payments to.

Perhaps the strangest pattern within this category consists of six debtors who claim that they did not make payments because they never received payment books and consequently did not know where to send payments. Five of these debtors were from New York and four of them had made purchases from the same creditor.

A New York Puerto Rican employed as an unskilled worker in a nursing home, earning $3,000–$4,000 annually, had bought a bedroom set and waited for his payment book to arrive. Although he did not know it, his contract was sold to Big City Credit, but the payment book did not arrive until five months after the purchase.

> I did not pay because I didn't have the payment book. And when it finally came some five months later, I was already five months past due. And by then I had lost my job. . . . I shouldn't have to pay because it was their fault. I did not get the payment book and I did not get everything I was supposed to get in the merchandise either.

The remaining four New York debtors in this category had all bought watches from the same notorious direct-selling firm, Trademark Jewelers. The canvassers for this firm sell not only door to door but they frequently approach debtors at their place of work, as in these four cases. Thus when asked where they had made the purchase, they gave these answers:

> He came to the factory where I work.
> A man came to the job; he gave no name but was about 50 years old.
> A man came to the job; they come around at lunch time with this stuff.
> A man came to my husband's job, selling watches out of a suitcase.

Their reasons for not paying appear to be variations on the same theme.

A 25-year-old black employed as a silk-screener and earning $8,000–$10,000 a year:

> We lived at—————and then we moved to our present address and we never got the payment book. The man didn't come back to the job so we didn't know how to contact him in any way. They sent a garnishee notice to my husband's job. The amount was more now, because they added interest and court costs, $107 and change. I don't think we should pay this extra because we didn't know where to pay.

A middle-aged black earning under $3,000 annually:

> I don't think he took down the right address and before I could get the book, they had put a garnishee on my salary.

A 28-year-old black porter earning $3,000–$4,000 a year:

> This guy told me he would send me a book and I would know where the payments would go and how much, but he never did.

The salesman for this firm did not always get the address wrong. A young Puerto Rican earning under $3,000 yearly did receive some payment envelopes:

> I did not have any more payment envelopes and so I let it go.

He too was garnisheed.

The modus operandi of this firm is of some interest. By having its salesmen approach the would-be customers at their place of work, the firm is well aware of where the debtor works and where to send the garnishment order. It is almost as if this firm prefers to rely on garnishment rather than to make the effort to instruct its customers on payment arrangements. Some of these debtors were never sent payment books, although the firm obviously did know where the debtors lived for we were able to interview them at the address entered on the summons, a document drawn up by the firm's lawyer. Nor did the salesmen ever make an effort to contact the presumably delinquent debtor at his place of work. This firm is one of the most frequent plaintiffs in New York City, filing approximately 7,000 suits each year, for amounts ranging from $80 to $110. When it is kept in mind that the watches that this firm sells are highly overpriced, it would seem that even if it collects only a portion of the judgments it obtains, it is making a substantial profit. Like the Detroit jewelry firms that also rely on garnishment, this firm's contracts call for weekly rather than monthly payments, with the result that the debtor who is only a week or two in arrears is subject to a law suit.[2]

That these debtors did not know where to send the payments might seem puzzling in the light of the law, which requires that the debtor be given a copy of the contract at the time of the transaction on which the name and address of the seller must appear. But as we saw in chapter 3, some debtors claimed that they never signed contracts, and fully 19 percent of those who made credit purchases claimed that they never received a copy of the contract. Among the four Trademark Jewelers' cases reviewed here, in only two of them did the debtor claim to have signed anything, but all four of these debtors insisted that they never received a copy of the contract. It is evident, then, that these transactions were carried out in an illegal fashion. Yet the law was invoked by the firm to collect, and three of these four debtors found themselves being garnisheed!

CREDITOR FAILS TO RETURN PAYMENT BOOK
OR TO PROVIDE INFORMATION REQUESTED BY DEBTOR

Related to the previous category in that it implies breakdowns in communication between debtor and creditor is a group of 11 cases in which the debtor's default was linked to the creditor's failure to return the payment book or to respond to the debtor's inquiries about the amount owed or the nature of the obligation. In seven of these cases, the debtor's complaint was that the creditor had not returned his payment book or had not provided him with receipts for his payments.

A middle-aged Chicago black, living on welfare and social security with an income under $3,000, had purchased furniture that was added onto a contract for a TV set that the debtor claims was almost paid for at the time he bought the furniture. He had several reasons for not paying.

> Because the couch was broken by the delivery men when they delivered
> it. I went to the store and asked them to send someone to fix it
> and I did this three times but no one ever came to fix it. Also I
> had a payment book but they have that book and won't give it back

[2]Craig Karpel, who published two articles on consumer fraud in the May 26 and June 2, 1969, issues of *New York Magazine,* noted in a sampling of the New York docket books that Trademark Jewelers brought an inordinate number of suits for the identical amount, $107.50. We now know the reason for this strange pattern. The debtors probably never made payments because they did not know where to send them. In 1970 Trademark Jewelers was sued by the U.S. Attorney's office for flagrant violation of due process, that is, for widespread "sewer service." In 1972 Trademark entered a consent judgment drafted by the U.S. Attorney's office that would ensure proper service of process.

to me, making it necessary for me to keep track of payments by saving my receipts. Since they have the payment book, I haven't any idea how much I owe the company. Also the garnishment made me lose my job.

This debtor's case well illustrates the destructive and, from the creditor's point of view, sometimes self-defeating, aspects of garnishment. Because of the garnishment, this debtor lost his job and is now on welfare.

A 22-year-old Detroit black, working in a meat-packing firm and earning $5,000–$6,000 annually, had bought a suit of clothes from a door-to-door salesman for that standard Detroit price in these transactions of $125.

I stopped paying because they wouldn't send me a receipt and I didn't know how much I owed. I missed two payments waiting for them to send me a receipt and when on the third week I sent in two payments, they sent them back saying that they had garnisheed me.

This debtor's payments were $10 a week. He had made four previous payments and had received receipts for the first three. It was during the two-week period in which he was waiting for his fourth receipt to arrive that the store instituted garnishment proceedings. This is clearly an example of the "trigger-happy" creditor, a type we have already come across and will examine in more detail in chapter 8.

The accounts of these debtors point up the importance to them of their payment books and receipts as bookkeeping devices for keeping track of their debts and regulating their payments. Should these familiar guidelines fail to appear because of error or deception on the part of the creditor, the debtor becomes confused.

The debtor's bewilderment about the payment arrangements and his uncertainty about how much he owes is vividly portrayed in the account of a middle-aged Detroit black with a working wife and a combined family income in excess of $10,000. He had purchased a used car and his contract was financed by the Retailers Bank of Detroit. His complaint was that the bank would never give him a payment book and would not answer his queries about the amount he owed.

I used to make two or three payments at a time. I never had a payment book with the bank. I asked for one but they told me they don't do it that way. They said they would send me a letter each month. I would go out sometimes to the bank and pay them in person, or I would mail in a money order. I quit paying because each time I asked them how much I owed, they would give me the run-around. They sent me a letter, finally, as to my balance. I know I owed five more payments at $56.66 each, which would come to $283.30 but when they finally straightened out their records, they told me

> I owed $600. I took all my receipts out there to prove to them that
> I had only five more payments to go. I was told to leave them there
> so they could check them out. I left them in a large envelope with
> the manager. The next day, when I came back as I was told to,
> they said I never left the receipts there. They argued with me and
> it had already been going on for a year since I first stopped paying
> them. I feel I was defrauded and cheated out of my money. This
> bank should be investigated. Every time I went there the place would
> be full of people claiming they were cheated. I talked to a number
> of people there who were in the same circumstances.

We have already come across cases that raise questions about whether banks deserve the reputation they have as conservative, trustworthy institutions. This man's account further damages that image.

The remaining cases in this category refer to instances in which the debtor sought information from the creditor concerning his debt obligation and failed to maintain payments when the information was not forthcoming. For example, a white New Yorker earning over $10,000 annually had difficulty getting the information he sought from a well-known department store where his wife had a revolving credit account. Each time his bill came, his name was spelled somewhat differently. This led him to be concerned whether the charges were really being made by his wife. He tried many times to straighten the matter out, to no avail.

> I was exhausted after so many calls imploring them to bill me for
> my wife's bills under one name, instead of three or four varieties
> of names, but they ignored my letters and calls. In one month I got
> three different billings with totally different items of purchase and
> different versions of my name. I just got fed up and wouldn't pay
> them further. That's all.

The inflexibility of large bureaucracies in meeting the requests of their clients is well illustrated by this account and this, too, turns out to be a factor in defaults.

CHANGES IN PAYMENT SCHEDULE—DISAGREEMENTS
ABOUT AMOUNT OF DEBT

Some 11 debtors, less than 1 percent of the sample, linked their default to misunderstandings regarding the frequency or amount of payments and in a few instances to disagreements about the amount owed. And again we find more specific patterns among these cases. In five instances the debtor claimed that he was misled about the amount or the frequency of payments. Further instances of changes in payment schedules appear in chapter 9, where accounts of partial or irregular payments are considered, and a few of the cases classified in the current category might, with more detailed information, belong in the partial payment group.

One of the debtors who felt he was misled about the size of his payments was a middle-aged Philadelphian, a black taxi driver who earned $3,000–$4,000 a year. He had contracted to buy an oil heater, but the home repair company installed a gas heater at almost three times the cost.

> I stopped paying because I found out that I was paying $31 a month
> when I was supposed to be paying $23 a month. When I found out,
> I stopped paying it until they would come here and make an adjustment
> on their mistake.

This debtor not only resented the higher payments but felt that he should not have to pay for the wrong merchandise. He had made five payments at the lower rate and stopped when he discovered that the company expected him to pay at the higher one. He believed that this was a mistake and waited for the company to correct it only to find himself being sued.

An automobile buyer, a 37-year-old Philadelphia black, employed as a press operator at $6,000–$8,000 a year, told the following story:

> The payments were too high. I was supposed to have payments for
> 18 months, but they gave me only 12.

That these debtors were misled about the true amount of their payments can mean only that the law requiring full disclosure of the credit terms at the time of the transaction was violated.

MISHAPS INVOLVING THIRD PARTIES AND CONFUSION OVER DEBT CONSOLIDATION

As we saw in Table 7.1, 11 debtors, again less than 1 percent of the total sample, ended in default for reasons that have more to do with mishaps between the creditor and his third parties than with any shortcoming of the debtor. These cases, too, fall into several subpatterns. In three instances, the problem had to do with the title of an automobile. The first of these reflects the inflexibility of the financing agency in transferring the title from one state to another. A 31-year-old Detroit black, employed in a factory and earning $8,000–$10,000 a year, had this story to tell:

> I worked in construction in Tennessee and came here to get into
> the plants. After I came here, I tried to get the title of the car transferred
> so I could get license plates for the car. But the finance company
> [one of the largest auto financing companies in the country] refused.

> The branch here said the note couldn't be transferred. I never heard of that. I agreed to pay him $20 a month until the car was paid off. But I wasn't driving the car. I didn't have plates on it. . . . I paid three months. . . . It finally got to a collection agency and they told us we could settle with them. I made some payments and then got a summons and we are now paying $15 every two weeks.

This case involved only one firm and its various branch offices. It seems odd that some arrangement could not have been worked out that would have allowed this man to get a license in his new state. If this is indeed a general policy of creditors, then credit buying would appear to interfere unwittingly with the constitutional right of freedom of movement.

A 39-year-old Chicago black, self-employed as a handyman, whose wife also worked and whose annual family income was between $8,000 and $10,000, had purchased a used car for $600 in another instance of a night-time loan arranged by the dealer.

> The car dealer called this man at his office [The Happy Finance Co. of Illinois] around 9 P.M. and told him to come down, he had a deal for him. We had never heard of this company. He came down and wrote a check for the balance to the car dealer.

Even though this debtor's car broke down frequently, the reason for his default stemmed not from his resentment of the poor merchandise, but from confusion over who had the title to the car. As his wife told the interviewer:

> The car stopped running that night before my husband got home. He called them and they told him to bring it back. Later that same week it broke down again and again he took it in to them. Later on they fixed it but it never gave good service. It stopped finally on the boulevard. The police towed it away to the pounds and they would not release it until we brought in the title. We went to the finance company but they did not have the title. They told us to go to the State Attorney's office. He filed a suit and advised us not to pay any more until the title was produced. After the suit was filed, the dealer disappeared. No one knew anything about him. The finance company kept calling us for payments and we told them that we were willing to pay when they produced a title so that we could get the car. They never did and we never paid.

This is yet another case in which a car dealer disappeared. It is not clear whether this transaction involved a dealer-arranged loan to the debtor or whether the loan company was acting as a holder-in-due-course, having bought the contract from the dealer. Since the check was made out to the dealer, the latter might well have been the case. But if so, then the title to the car should have been transferred to the loan company. It should be noted that this debtor received professional help with his problem from the State Attorney's office and was advised not to pay until the title was produced. And yet the loan company sued him, although he insisted that he had never received a summons, or any court papers telling him how much he owed. In short, as far as he knew, he was not being sued and had made no payments.

Other cases in this category refer to instances of confusion resulting from debt consolidations with the same creditor. A 29-year-old Detroit black factory worker earning $6,000–$8,000 a year had purchased an automobile and then some time later purchased a bar from a different dealer for $600. His primary reason for defaulting was that he became sick and fell behind on his payments. But when he went back to work he discovered that the same company that was financing his automobile had also bought the contract for the bar and had consolidated the debts, raising both the payments and the interest. His state of confusion is suggested by his comment concerning why he should not have to pay:

> For one thing, they told me I had to pay $218 for the car. I don't know how they figured it, but I figured I had paid it up. But when I thought I was through, I discovered I was paying a lot more because they combined it with the bar. . . .

Big City Credit figures prominently in the next case, that of a young New York black couple. Although the husband was employed in factory work, the family also received supplementary welfare, and their total income was below $3,000. This couple became entangled with two Brooklyn furniture stores in a credit transaction involving furniture and a TV set. The wife, who was the respondent, had many complaints about the furniture and the TV set, but the excessive indebtedness that contributed to their default was in large part due to the finance company. They went initially to a furniture store after hearing a radio advertisement for furniture that could be bought with no down payment. Their complicated story, as told by the wife, is as follows:

> We went to Jacksons for the furniture and the man there sent us to the second store, Kaseys, for the TV set. The furniture was no good. The sectional bottom fell out one month after we bought it. The TV combination never really worked and the man came and tried to fix it but he never did. The repairman said not to call him any more because the wires were all rotten in it and it should be sent back to the warehouse. I told the man at the store and he said the repairman didn't know what he was talking about. He sent out about five different repairmen but none of them ever really fixed it. Now they say that our guarantee has expired and we'll have to fix it ourselves.

After making ten payments to the finance company, we got these coupons in the mail from them. I called Big City to find out what this was all about. They said that because our payments were up to date, we were able to use the coupons to add to our accounts. They sent us $170 worth of coupons for the first store and $140 worth for the second. We went back to Jacksons and bought the dinette and two lamps. One lamp was delivered broken and they never replaced it. The salesman said that the purchase wouldn't add any more to our monthly payments. We went to Kaseys (the second store) and got a portable TV to use until they fixed our combination. The people there said our payments would be $2 more a month, and they would have both payments combined. Big City said they would combine both payments. We received the book one month later calling for $25.33 a month. I called Big City and asked was this both bills combined, and the lady said yes. The next month we received another payment book for $20.90 a month. I called Big City and they said there wasn't anything they could do about it. The stores made out the payments. After looking at the books, it seems that they are charging us all over again for the bill that we paid for ten payments. I called the stores and they said they had nothing to do with it and they would call Big City and get it straight. Nobody seems to be able to do anything.

Numerous emissaries from Big City Credit came to visit this family. One said they would settle the $1,600 account for $800. Another came and mentioned $500 and the family consulted the welfare department, which promised to assist them in making such a settlement.

It has been observed that many low-income families remain perpetually in debt to low-income retailers in a pattern reminiscent of the share-cropper's relationship to the company store.[3] This debtor's account provides a new insight into the pattern. Apparently finance companies, such as Big City Credit, encourage the pattern of perpetual indebtedness by giving their customers unsolicited coupons for extending their credit with the initial seller. By sending coupons that could be redeemed at the two stores that had already saddled this family with shoddy merchandise, Big City set in motion the sequence of events that led to this family's overextension. This couple had checked carefully with the finance company about whether the new payment book covered both obligations and they were assured that it did, only to find the company sending them an additional payment book. Until recently, Big City Credit was one of the largest holders-in-due-course in the New York metropolitan area. A few years ago, Big City found itself losing money, and its stock declined precipitously in value. It then decided to go out of the consumer finance business and shift instead to the small loan business, for which it had a license.

[3]See Caplovitz, op. cit.

MISCELLANEOUS PAYMENT MISUNDERSTANDINGS

The final group of cases to be considered under the general theme of payment misunderstandings is a residual, miscellaneous category consisting of 17 debtors, almost 2 percent of the sample. Several patterns are noticeable in these cases. In a few instances, there was a misunderstanding about when the payments were due. For example, a 24-year-old Detroit black employed in a foundry at the time of his debt had been hoodwinked by one of Elroy Jewelers' canvassers into buying a $125 suit. As his wife reported:

> The man told him he wouldn't have to make a payment for one month and then he was supposed to pay $7 every two weeks. But before the month was out, they stopped his paycheck at the plant. . . . He figured he had a month before the payments would start. He bought the suit in November and in December he got garnisheed for it. . . .

This debtor was obviously misled by the salesman as to when the payments were to start. We have come across other instances in which this creditor was quick to resort to garnishment, presumably without any notification to the debtor that he was in arrears. Elroy Jewelers in Detroit, like Trademark Jewelers in New York, would seem to be in the garnishment business.

Another debtor who insists that she was not in arrears and blames her trouble on a misunderstanding about when the payment was due is a 36-year-old New York black woman employed as a saleswoman, whose husband worked for the Transit Authority (their combined annual income was $8,000–$10,000). She had borrowed $400 from a bank and was given two years to pay off the loan. She had made 23 of the 24 payments when she discovered that the bank had obtained a garnishment order against her.

> I didn't stop paying. The payment was due on the 28th of January and I got the garnishment on the 26th of January. I was behind a couple of times earlier but I was caught up to January, and I got the garnishee two days before the payment was due.

A young white Chicago couple defaulted because they were misled by the creditor as to when the next payment on their automobile purchase was due. At the time of the interview this couple was separated because, according to the wife, of the strains that resulted from their debt problems. They were misled initially by the used-car dealer, who convinced them that rather than trade in their old car, they should let him try to sell it and he would deduct the proceeds of the sale from the cost of the "new" used car. After several weeks the dealer called and said he could not sell the old car and they were stuck with two cars on which they were making payments. After making payments for almost a year to a bank that presumably held both contracts, they called the bank to find out when the next payment was due.

> We called and asked when the November payment was due. The girl who answered said we were O.K. until the next month. Then a short time later the cars were gone. Both cars were parked by the house and they just took them. I thought they were stolen and I called the police but they said no. They had something saying the bank took the cars. It was not a full month since we had made a payment and we would not have missed a payment except their girl said it was not due. Then we wanted to make the payment and they refused. They said they wanted the full amount in cash. I've heard from other people that this bank is known for this. If you fall one month behind, they will not take that payment. They use it as an excuse to demand the full amount or take your car. . . . And it was a foul-up in their bookkeeping. We asked the girl when the payment was due and she said not until the next month. So the whole thing is really their fault. We were willing to pay.

This debtor's ability and willingness to pay notwithstanding, legal action was instituted by the creditor. This woman was particularly bitter because of what she considered to be the bank's underhanded tactics.

> The repossession was so underhanded. They came and took the cars without our knowing it. We did not have any notice either. Not even an overdue notice. The first we knew was when the cars were gone.

A second theme among the cases in this miscellaneous category concerns disagreements about the interest on the installment purchase. In previous chapters we came across a few debtors who wanted to pay off their debt in advance only to discover that the creditor held them liable for the full interest. (These cases were also classified in this miscellaneous category to indicate a secondary reason for their default.) Another debtor mentioned such a reason. A middle-aged white Philadelphian, earning $8,000–$10,000 yearly as an office worker, had cosigned for an automobile bought by his son. The experience was actually his son's.

> He [the son] first got into trouble when, after five payments, he was only 15 days late and they came in the middle of the night and took the car and left a note under his door. He got in touch with the bank and they told him that General Acceptance now had the contract. The next two days they sent him on a runaround for the car. They said he had to pay the late payment and the next payment ahead.

They sent him to a couple of places for the car and it wasn't there. Finally, they delivered the car to him on the third day. Then he kept making payments until the 30th month. Then he wanted to pay off in full but they wouldn't take off any of the interest. After 30 months they said he still owed $700. He stopped paying because he was mad. He hoped they would come and get the car. It had been just sitting in the garage, it wasn't working. Then I got a notice that our house would be taken. He [the son] had a house but they didn't want that, just our house. . . .

As in the previous cases of this kind, this debtor assumed that part of the interest charge would be returned if he paid in advance and when the finance company refused to abide by this legitimate principle, he refused to maintain payments.

In two other instances, the confusion concerning payments seems to stem from the practice of creditors allocating the bulk of the early payments to the interest charges rather than to the principal. Although this is apparently a time-honored practice of the credit industry, one that applies to mortgage loans especially, some debtors failed to understand it and became discouraged when they found that the principal hardly diminished at all. An example of this is provided by a 34-year-old Detroit black, earning $4,000–$5,000 yearly in an automobile factory. He had bought a used car and defaulted after 11 payments because it seemed to him that his debt was barely diminishing:

The money I was paying wasn't going on the car. Only about $5 a month was going to the principal. My bill wasn't lowered hardly at all. So I told them to come and get the car and they finally did but they still wanted me to make the payments. They were putting most of the $30 payments on the interest. I figured it would take me 10 years to pay for the car.

Even though the credit industry's practice of applying much of the early payments to interest rather than to principal might be defensible, it would seem that creditors have an obligation to explain this practice to the debtor so as to avoid the discouragement that might ensue.

In this chapter we have examined reasons for default in which something went awry in the method of payments. In most cases, the debtor met the creditor's basic requirements of being *able* and *willing* to pay and yet something went wrong in the recording of payments, in the system of collection, in the communication between debtor and creditor, or in the creditor's relations with the finance companies. It was seen that creditors sometimes make errors when recording payments, fail to instruct debtors in how to make payments, fail to inform debtors of the nature of the obligation or the amount owed, consolidate debts without explaining their actions to the debtor, misinform debtors as to when payments are due, and fail to instruct debtors as to how the payments are to be allocated between interest and principal. Moreover, collectors sometimes stop coming or, without notice, change the time when they call; and finance companies sometimes fail to obtain title to the merchandise. In all of these respects the creditor must take some, most, or all of the blame for the default. But as so many of these cases make clear, it is the debtor rather than the creditor who suffers because of these mishaps. Some of these debtors were subjected to garnishments and some even lost their jobs because of the garnishment. And all of them suffered from being sued because of the debt problem.

8

PARTIAL PAYMENTS

AND

OTHER REASONS

FOR DEFAULT

We have examined reasons for defaults that account for the great majority of the breakdowns in credit transactions. Still to be considered are some relatively infrequent types, most of which are secondary reasons, which affect about 13 percent of the debtors. Most of these residual cases fall into two major categories, misunderstandings about partial or irregular payments and reasons related to the debtor no longer having the merchandise. We have made a separate category of the handful of debtors who mentioned harassment by the creditor as an additional reason for their default. Finally, there are a few debtors whose stories could not easily be classified, cases which constitute an "all other" category. Table 8.1 shows the distribution of cases among these groups. These categories account for more than one fifth of the secondary and one fourth of the tertiary reasons, and eight percent of all the reasons offered.

PARTIAL AND IRREGULAR PAYMENTS

The largest number of these cases, 94, about 5 percent of the sample, involve misunderstandings about partial or irregular payments, mentioned

Table 8.1 / Additional Reasons for the Default

type of reason	first reason (no. cases)	second reason (no. cases)	third reason (no. cases)	total reasons (no. cases)	total reasons (percent)	total individuals (percent)
Partial or irregular payment	1	86	7	94	5	7
Refusal to pay linked to no longer having merchandise	4	30	15	49	2	4
Harassment by creditor as an additional reason	—	7	6	13	1	1
All other reasons	6	—	—	6	a	a
Subtotal cases	11	123	28	162		
Percent of total cases	1	21	25	8		12
Total cases	1,320	570	110	2,000		1,326

[a] Percentage of less than ½ of 1 percent.

almost always as a secondary reason. Actually, this category is underestimated, for we include here only those debtors who specifically referred to partial payments in the account of their default. Had we asked all debtors whether they had attempted to make partial payments, we might have found substantially more answering in the affirmative. At first glance it seems odd that partial or irregular payments could in any way be a reason for default. Presumably the critical factor in such cases is the reason for the debtor's inability to make regular payments according to the terms of the contract. But it must be remembered that this analysis is based on the debtor's point of view, and in most of these cases the debtor *assumed* that it was all right to pay irregularly or in small amounts. As we shall see, they were sometimes given this impression by the creditor. Most of these debtors protested that they had *not* stopped paying and were resentful of the lawsuit against them. As was also the case with the other major categories of reasons, this one is comprised of more specific subtypes. Table 8.2 identifies them and shows their frequency.

The more specific categories under partial and irregular payments are variations on the same theme. The critical distinction between the first two is that debtors in the first group claim their creditors agreed to delayed or smaller payments, whereas those in the second were accustomed to smaller or irregular payments and *assumed* that their creditors acquiesced to this arrangement. The third category, comprising 14 debtors, is, strictly speaking, not a reason for the default at all. Like those in the first category, these debtors approached their creditors when some problem arose and tried to work out a system of partial payments. But, unlike the others, they were rebuffed. We have counted these experiences as additional reasons for the default partly because these debtors were prepared to honor their obligation if suitable arrangements could be worked out, and partly because these cases question the claim often made by the credit industry that it is ready to accommodate debtors who, because of some emergency, are unable to maintain full payments. Had these creditors been willing to cooperate with the debtors, the relationship need not have broken down.

The fourth category consists of debtors who claimed that they were only slightly behind and were catching up when the creditor sued them. They, too, insisted that they had not stopped paying and were resentful of their creditors quickness to sue. The fifth category consists of those who objected to late payment fees, a few who resented the frequent turnover of their contracts from one third party to another accompanied by a rise in their debt obligations, and a few who objected to their contract being sold to a finance company.

A close examination of these subtypes will provide some clues to the operation of credit-granting agencies, particularly the dubious principles regulating interest charges on late payments.

Table 8.2 / Reasons for Default Linked to Partial and Irregular Payments

reasons for partial or irregular payment	first reason (no. cases)	second reason (no. cases)	third reason (no. cases)	total reasons (no. cases)	total reasons (percent)	total individuals (percent)
Creditor agrees to partial or delayed payment	—	22	1	23	1	2
Debtor accustomed to partial or irregular payment	1	21	2	24	1	2
Debtor seeks arrangement with creditor and is rebuffed	—	12	2	14	1	1
Debtor slightly behind—the trigger-happy creditor	—	18	—	18	1	1
Debtor resents late payment fees or sale of contract	—	13	2	15	1	1
Subtotal cases	1	86	7	94		
Percent of total cases		15	6	5		7
Total cases	1,320	570	110	2,000		1,326

Creditor Agrees to Delayed or Partial Payments

The 22 debtors in this category all experienced problems that prevented them from maintaining regular payments. They explained their situation to the creditor and were given assurance that suitable arrangements could be made. Yet in spite of the creditor's agreement to partial or delayed payments, the debtors were sued. These debtors were particularly bitter, for they felt that their creditors had reneged on an agreement. Typical of these cases is the account of a middle-aged New York black woman, employed as a nurse's aide and earning $4,000–$5,000 annually. She had bought some furniture and her contract was sold to Big City Credit.

> I wanted to stretch my payments so I could maintain my daughter's apartment because she was ill at the time. So I notified the furniture company and they told me not to make any more payments until they told me to. Then I received a summons at the hospital. That was the first I knew about it. I called the company and they said that my application to extend payments had been turned down and they hadn't notified me.

It should be noted that this woman turned to the original creditor, the furniture store, and was advised not to make further payments even though the contract had been bought by a finance company. Whether the furniture store had tried to work out more equitable terms with the finance company is not known, but this woman was led to believe that some relief would be provided or that she would at least be notified before legal action was taken against her.

In the cases now under consideration the debtor felt that the creditor had reneged on his promise by taking him to court. This comes through quite clearly in the account of a young Detroit black, with an income of $4,000–$5,000 a year, who had dealt with a street canvasser for that infamous seller of $125 suits, Elroy Jewelers.

> I was in the hospital in October. When I called them in November I told them I would have a payment for them in a few weeks. They said, "All right and thank you for calling." Then I got a letter from them saying that if they didn't receive a payment in five days they would garnishee my check. It took me two weeks to get my check and when I did they had already taken the money out of it, even though I called them and told them what had happened.

The patterns of particular creditors become evident from the testimony of different witnesses. This is at least the third case we have presented in which Elroy Jewelers was quick to garnishee wages.

Another Detroit debtor, a middle-aged black, had a similar experience. His family had bought a TV, stereo, and refrigerator from a furniture store.

> My husband works for————————and he had a heart attack a little over a year ago, and he had to quit work. He had unemployment compensation and some other small check and we made payments as often as we could. We had explained that to them and they had said that it was all right and so that is what we were doing. And then after six months they came and repossessed the TV, stereo, and refrigerator. . . . We didn't expect that.

This woman felt betrayed by the repossession but was particularly annoyed that the company still expected to be paid in spite of the repossession of the merchandise.

> I don't see why we have to pay for something we don't have. We had almost paid for it anyhow and we were still paying when it was repossessed.

In some of these cases it would seem that one department of the creditor's firm was unaware of what another department was doing. Such bureaucratic confusion is strongly suggested by the account of a 39-year-old black in Detroit, earning $8,000–$10,000 a year in the automobile industry, who had bought a used car.

> We were swamped with doctor bills. My wife is a rare blood hemophiliac. She bleeds. We had all kinds of specialists. We were just starting to see our way clear and we called the bank and told them we would send them $50 on two weekends and we would be caught up on our back payments. They of course agreed to take the money and we sent the two payments of $50 each to them. After sending the second payment, I received a telegram telling me that legal action was started against us. I called the bank and reminded them about the arrangements we had made. I told them about the two payments I had made. So he said to ignore the letter about the suit. The next day I sent them a third payment of $50. A few days later my car disappeared and I called the police to report it stolen. The next day the police told me that the car had been pulled [repossessed]. A neighbor told me he thought the car was being stolen and he chased the car. He said the hood, door, and fenders were damaged when the repossessors broke into it. They broke the glass to get into it.

Still another reason repossessed automobiles realize so little in public auctions is provided by his account. Damage connected with the act of repossession may well lower the value of the car. It should be noted that this debtor's car was repossessed shortly after he was assured by a bank official that the court action would be suspended and that his system of payments was satisfactory. Is it possible that one credit manager is unaware of what another is doing, or do credit managers behave this inconsistently?

There were two cases in this category of reasons for the default in which the creditor reassured the debtor who became unemployed that he would wait for payments until the debtor was reemployed. The creditor then promptly garnisheed the debtor as soon as he was back at work. One reason creditors are prepared to accept offers of partial payments is suggested by these cases. Knowing they cannot use the harsh collection device of garnishment until the debtor is reemployed, they may wish to avoid alarming unemployed debtors with fruitless pressure.

Debtors in this category of reasons believed that the creditor was prepared to accommodate to their problem and thus felt betrayed by the lawsuit. Had the creditors respected these informal agreements, presumably the relationship would have remained intact. Our examples help to explain why creditors failed to abide by the agreements. Credit managers may well be forced to behave inconsistently because of pressures from their superiors; the bureaucratic organization of credit agencies under which multiple officials deal with the same case at different times is also likely to be a factor, and, as we have just seen, the benevolent response may mean only that the creditor does not wish to discourage the debtor from returning to work so that his wages can then be garnisheed.

Debtor Accustomed to Partial or Irregular Payments

In addition to the debtors who felt that they had worked out an agreement with their creditor regarding partial or delayed payments, there were 24 others who, because of some emergency, maintained partial payments for some period of time and assumed that this was acceptable to the creditor, only to discover subsequently that they were being sued.

A pure case of this type is that of a middle-aged New York white couple in which both spouses worked and collectively earned over $10,000 annually. The wife had a revolving credit account at one of New York's major department stores and ran into difficulty when her husband became unemployed. When asked why she had stopped paying, she replied:

> I never stopped any payments. I always paid every month without fail but I'd pay between one-half and three-quarters of my payment every month. I stopped charging anything for the longest time and they let this go on for months and months, and never said boo. And then they turn around and sue me without notice. I definitely never

> received a summons because I would have gone to court myself.
> I feel my case was good since I always showed good faith. I made
> sizable payments every month and I didn't run up the bill. The judge
> would never have taken a judgment against me if I'd given him the
> facts but I wasn't notified.

It should be noted that this woman was conscientious about her debt
and felt that she was paying it off, although in partial installments. The
store seemed to accept the arrangement by permitting it to continue for
many months, never informing her that she was failing to live up to
its expectations.

A young Detroit black couple (the husband earned $6,000–$8,000
a year as an assembly line worker in an automobile plant) fell into arrears
on a furniture purchase when the husband was laid off, and they thought
that partial payments would appease the creditor.

> My husband was laid off. We were making partial payments. After
> the first couple of payments to the furniture store, we paid to a loan
> company that had bought our contract. We didn't know anything about
> being in trouble until we got a notice in the mail.

This woman too felt that the suit was unjustified.

> We weren't delinquent in this bill at all. I think they should have
> been more understanding after they found out my husband wasn't
> working.

The psychology of so many of these debtors shines through this
woman's account. In her mind, as well as that of many other of these
debtors, regular partial payments is not the same as being delinquent.
But of course to the creditor this is a mark of delinquency. Perhaps
better communication between the creditor and debtor would ease this
strain, and perhaps some system is needed whereby debtors with good
intentions, those willing to pay what they can, are permitted to extend
their indebtedness under a system of smaller payments. Chapter 13 of
the bankruptcy law in effect operates this way. Could not creditors on
their own arrange such a system without the debtor first having to declare
bankruptcy?

Debtor Fails in Effort
To Work Out Accommodation with the Creditor

Fourteen debtors who fell behind in their payments because of an emergency told us that they had tried to work out some arrangement with
their creditors but were rebuffed. Two points are of interest here: first,

like those in the previous categories, these debtors demonstrated their awareness of their obligation and their willingness to pay; second, these cases call attention to the harshness of some creditors, who do not make even a pretense of trying to accommodate the debtor of good faith who has come upon hard times.

Typical of this category is the story of a middle-aged black Detroiter, earning $3,000–$4,000 yearly as an assembly line worker in the automobile industry. He had purchased a vacuum cleaner from a door-to-door salesman.

> Actually, I never stopped. I was put on part time at _____ , like two days a week. I found that I could not keep up with my payments, so I went to XYZ and tried to tell them that I could only pay a few dollars a month, until I got back on full-time. They said they couldn't help me and that they had already turned it over to their lawyer. I tried to work something out with them so that the payments would be less than $20 a month until I got back on more time at work. They said it was too late. I went to all the other people I owed money to and was able to work something out with them but not with this company. The next thing I know, I had a summons from XYZ.

From this man's testimony it would appear that some creditors are more ready than others to accommodate the debtor.

A young black couple in Detroit with annual family income of $4,000–$5,000 was in arrears on an automobile purchase after the husband became ill.

> The man came to the house and my husband explained to him that he was on sick leave. He (the husband) wanted to make a half payment then and a full payment the following week but the man wouldn't accept the payment because my husband was two months behind. After the man refused the money, my husband said he would be better off going down to the Common Pleas court, because they would accept the money.

The logic of this debtor was manifested by a few others. In their view they were better off working out some system of partial payments with the court than submitting to the terms of the creditor.

Debtor Slightly Behind, Was Catching Up

As we saw in Table 8.2, 18 debtors, almost 2 percent of the sample, insisted they were only slightly behind on their payments and had every intention of maintaining their payments when they were sued. We have commented earlier on instances of the trigger-happy creditor who was quick to sue, a term applicable to the creditors in these cases.

A New York debtor who was only one month delinquent on an automobile purchase had this story to tell:

> My car was picked up. I reported it stolen and called the bank but they said, no, it was not stolen. They had the car picked up. I said, "Why, I only owe you for the month of October and I have the money for this month in my pocket." He said, "I don't want the money, I have the car."

Of course, the bank was within its legal rights to repossess the car but it is debatable whether such inflexibility is more likely to serve the creditor's interests than a more flexible approach.

Detroit's Elroy Jewelers, already identified as a trigger-happy creditor, shows up in this account provided by a 31-year-old black hospital attendant, earning $3,000–$4,000 a year.

> I was out sick and only got insurance money which they were late in paying, so I got behind on my rent and my other bills. But I never did get behind more than three weeks with Elroy. That was all and they garnisheed me, with no warning at all.

From this and the previous accounts of debtors who had dealt with this firm it would seem that Elroy Jewelers well deserves the label "trigger-happy"; they seem all too eager to rely on garnishment as their collection procedure.

Resentment of Late Payment Fees and Interest Charges

Under the general heading "partial and late payments" are 15 debtors who complained about late payment fees and interest charges when describing the reasons for their default. These cases are of particular interest because they deal with an aspect of the credit industry unfamiliar to most consumers, the method used by creditors in computing late payment charges. (This will be described shortly.)

Even among these 15 cases, subthemes occur. In two instances the resentment against late payment fees is implicit, the explicit complaint concerning the rising amount of the debt as the contract is sold from one creditor to another. A 49-year-old Chicago black, employed as a laborer in the trucking industry and earning $6,000–$8,000 a year, had contracted for $700 worth of furniture. He claimed to have paid more than $1,400 on this bill and apparently had not yet finished paying it. He admitted to having gotten behind as bills piled up, but he still felt that he had made sufficient payments through the years to settle the debt.

> Well, I figured I had done paid for it as I had made payments for four or five years, but then they would move the account to someone else for collection and the price would rise again.

This man sought relief from his debt problems by filing for bankruptcy.

A 43-year-old black Detroit assembly line worker in the automobile industry (earning $6,000–$8,000 a year) had contracted for a deep freezer–food plan.

> I called them and told them I couldn't make full payments. They agreed to take $5 a week. After a couple of payments I found that they were applying only $1 toward the bill, and the $4 they said was for late payments. I thought I'd never get it paid off that way. I wanted it to go to court. I'd rather do it that way. I was being cheated and I wanted the courts to get at it.

Although this debtor felt that the creditor's policy of applying most of his partial payments to interest rather than to the principal was so unfair that it must indicate cheating, the fact is that this practice of creditors is not illegal.

The next example of a debtor resentful of late payment fees is a man we encountered before. We cited his case in chapter 5 to illustrate the practice of dealer-arranged loans for down payments in automobile transactions—a dual set of loans that resulted in his being overextended. His case is of particular interest in the current context, because he insisted that the interviewer copy the figures from his payment book with the small loan company that provided the money for the down payment, the Benevolent Finance Co. This man insisted that he had never really stopped paying Benevolent Finance, but the data indicate that he missed many payments. The payment record, as copied by the interviewer, is as follows:

date	total amount paid	charges	principal	unpaid balance
Aug. 9, 1965	$38.24	$29.79	$ 8.45	$991.55
Aug. 30, 1965	$38.24	$11.30	$26.94	$964.61
Nov. 15, 1965	$38.24	$34.53	$ 3.71	$960.00
Jan. 10, 1966	$38.24	$29.42	$ 8.82	$952.08
June 30, 1966	$38.24	$38.24	—	$952.08
March 27, 1967	$12.00	court cost		
	$26.24	$26.24	—	$952.08

Contrary to the debtor's claim that he had missed only a few payments, the record shows that he was two months in arrears in the fall of 1965, that after the November payment he missed the December payment, and that after the January 1966 payment he missed payments for the next four months. In short, he missed seven payments during the first year of his obligation. It is also clear that after the June 1966 payment, he stopped paying altogether and it was not until after the law suit that he made another payment, part of which was allocated to court costs. According to the record, this man made five payments during the first 11 months of his obligation. Initially, he had a debt obligation of $1,000. The five payments that he made during this 11 month period totaled $191.20. And yet this amount reduced the principal by only $48.92. In short, only a little more than one fourth of his payments over this period was applied to the principal. As the payment schedule indicates, the two-month gap between August and November meant that only $3.71 of his $38.24 payment was being applied to principal; the one-month gap between November and January resulted in the principal being reduced by only $8.82, and the four-month gap between the January and June payments resulted in the entire payment of $38.24 being allocated to interest.

According to the figures in his payment book, this debtor was clearly delinquent, missing more payments than he made during the first year of his loan. But the data also show that after some delinquency most or even all of the payment was applied to interest rather than to the principal. This example calls attention to a little-understood procedure employed by the credit industry in calculating late payment charges. Should a debtor be late with a payment (even 10 or 15 days late), the credit industry taxes him a late payment fee. Should he then be on time with all the subsequent payments, the creditor deducts from the subsequent payments the late payment fee, thus automatically making the subsequent payments only partial ones, subject again to late payment fees. Home Kripke, a consultant to the committee that drafted the UCCC, prevailed upon that body to outlaw this practice in their model code. The credit industry objected to this reform on the grounds that it would present them with untold hardships because their computers would have to be reprogrammed. This anecdote is perhaps a portent of things to come: the appeal to the omniscient computer as a rationalization for perpetuating social injustices. The debtor who is slightly in arrears on one payment is still being taxed 12 times for his one lapse.[1]

Still another theme among the cases classified in this category of resentment of late payment fees is one that applies in particular to low-income consumers accustomed to informal payment arrangements with local merchants—the sale of their contracts to third parties. Ghetto

[1]For example, a debtor who did not pay the late payment fee for a single delinquency, say $5.00, with his next payment, would find himself at the end of the year in arrears in the amount of $60 rather than $5.00. Since few states have adopted the controversial UCCC, this practice is still legal in most states.

merchants anticipate that their customers will miss at least one out of every four payments and take this into account when computing markups. These merchants think of themselves as operating on a "13-month" year.[2]

But the relationship between the understanding local merchant and his low-income customer breaks down when the merchant sells the contract to a third party. The finance agency, unlike the local merchant, is not prepared to have the customer miss payments, and it does not hesitate to penalize the debtor with late payment fees. Several of our debtors, mainly people on welfare, were deeply resentful of the sale of their contract and blame their default on this practice. For example, a Detroit black woman whose family income was under $3,000 gave this account of the reasons for her default on a purchase of furniture from a neighborhood dealer who sold her contract to a finance company:

> I felt that every time I sent a payment it was one day late because of my mailing it on a weekend or because of mail delay and they would charge me $1.00 extra. I felt they were cheating me out of an extra $12.00 a year. I talked to them on the phone and they told me that my payment should come in on time. I told them that I didn't make no damn agreement with them at all. I had made my agreement and contract with Crown's [the furniture company]. I already had plenty of charges from them [the furniture company] and I was not going to pay the finance company extra money.

This woman entered a relationship with a local merchant with whom she had dealt in the past and her assumption was that irregular payments would be tolerated. She obviously did not count on her contract being sold to an impersonal, bureaucratic finance company.

REASONS FOR NOT PAYING
LINKED TO REVERSION OF MERCHANDISE TO CREDITOR

We now consider the second largest group of these residual reasons—defaults related to the merchandise reverting to the creditor. Some 49 debtors, about 4 percent of the entire sample, gave such a reason. These cases fall into several subtypes, some of which implicate the creditor, while others are indictments of the debtor, indicating his ignorance of his contractual obligation. The subdivisions under this general heading and the distribution of cases among them is shown in Table 8.3.

In almost all these cases, the matter of not having the merchandise is a secondary reason for the default. In the first group, it was the debtor himself who returned the merchandise, mainly because he was dissatisfied

[2]See David Caplovitz, *The Poor Pay More* (New York: The Free Press, 1963), chap. 2.

Table 8.3 / Reasons for Not Paying Linked to Merchandise Being in the Possession of the Creditor

merchandise reverts to creditor	first reason (no. cases)	second reason (no. cases)	third reason (no. cases)	total reasons (no. cases)	total reasons (percent)	total individuals (percent)
Debtor initiates repossession, assumes debt settled	1	10	5	16	1	1
Company repossesses, debtor assumes debt settled	1	18	8	27	1	2
All other reasons linked to not having merchandise	2	2	2	6	[a]	[a]
Subtotal	4	30	15	49		
Percent of total cases	[a]	5	14	2.4		3.6
Total cases	1,320	570	110	2,000	1,326	

[a]Less than 1 percent.

with it, but also because sometimes he could not afford the payments. In the second group it was the creditor who initiated the return by repossessing the merchandise. The debtors in this group failed to understand the principle of deficiency judgment. In fact, more debtors than indicated by the table did not understand this principle, although they did not mention it in connection with their defaults.[3]

Finally, there are six debtors who fall into a residual category in this more general group of debtors who stopped paying because they no longer had the merchandise. Following our usual procedure, we shall illustrate each of these subcategories in turn.

Debtor Encourages Repossession, Assumes Debt Is Settled

Even the subcategories presented in Table 8.3 are not precise enough to capture the nuances of the default. The 16 debtors who defaulted after they encouraged a repossession fall into several subtypes. Some of them returned the merchandise because they were unable to pay and were given some assurance by the creditor that the debt was settled. Some, also unable to pay, returned the merchandise and assumed that they were in the clear. But the majority in this category were debtors who returned the merchandise because it was defective, thus assuming that they were exonerated from further obligation.

Among those who could not pay and were led to believe that the debt was settled after they returned the product was a 38-year-old Puerto Rican living in Chicago who earned $4,000–$5,000 yearly as a machine operator. He had purchased wedding rings on time.

> I couldn't pay because I don't make enough money. When I bought the rings, my wife was working. . . . We have six kids and we spend a lot of money. . . . My wife called them and told them to take the rings back and they said O.K. So I took the rings back and they said they would accept them and they gave me a receipt. [The respondent showed the interviewer the receipt, which recorded that one set of rings had been received by the company.] They told me they would mail me my contract back but they never did.

[3]About 72 percent of the debtors we interviewed got into trouble because of some installment purchase as distinct from a loan or being a cosigner. In almost one fourth of these cases a repossession occurred. Those who experienced repossession were asked whether they thought the debt had been settled because of the repossession, and 54 percent or some 107 debtors answered affirmatively. In short, a majority of those who had goods repossessed assumed that they no longer owed anything to the creditor. But in spite of the widespread ignorance of the principle of deficiency judgment, only a tiny fraction of the debtors mentioned the repossession as a reason for not paying.

Illustrative of the few debtors unable to pay who *assumed* that by returning the purchase they would be free of further obligation is a 24-year-old Detroit black woman, the head of a broken family with annual income under $3,000. She had defaulted on a purchase of an automobile.

> I got sick and I quit my job. I called the company and told them
> to come and get the car. . . . I thought that by giving them the car,
> they could get enough out of it to pay the balance.

This debtor apparently understood that the company would sell the repossessed car and apply the proceeds to her debt but she failed to understand the dynamics of the resale of repossessed merchandise that result in proceeds far below the value of the goods, the process exposed by Shuchman.[4]

Another debtor who assumed that the value of his purchase would more than cover his debt obligation is a 28-year-old white Philadelphian employed as an insurance adjuster at the time of the interview. His wife worked and his family income was over $10,000 a year. He had purchased a new car and at the time of the default was failing in a business venture of his own.

> I was in financial trouble because of this business and I wrote all
> my creditors and said I would be late. They all responded except
> the Central National Bank, which I was paying for the car. . . . When
> I turned in the car to them I assumed the debt was cleared because
> the market value of the car was greater than my indebtedness. So
> the bank should have come out ahead of the game. But they said
> I still owed them $586, which shows that they sold the car for only
> $1,100 or $1,200, which is $800 under the market value at that time.
> To me, what this shows is that somebody at Central National picked
> up a cream puff of a car for only $1,100 and I'm getting hit for the
> difference.

This man had a good idea of the market value of his car, but he too failed to understand that the system of disposing of repossessed merchandise almost never results in the realization of the market value.

The third subgroup consists of those debtors who returned defective merchandise feeling that the seller had not lived up to his end of the bargain and that, by returning the defective merchandise, they would be in the clear. We have already come across such cases, most of which dealt with automobile purchases. The one nonautomobile episode in this group involved a TV purchase from a door-to-door salesman. A 36-year-old black Chicagoan, employed as a cook and earning $8,000–$10,000 a year, had this story to tell.

[4]Philip Shuchman, *Profit on Default: An Archival Study of Automobile Repossession and Resale,* 22 Stanford L. Rev. 20 (Nov. 1969).

> The TV wouldn't work properly. I bought it from Moon and they sold the contract to Retail Finance Co. and the TV kept going on and off. I called Moon and told them and they sent someone out to pick it up and take it back to the store. They were supposed to have fixed it but it came back and it still didn't work. So I called up Retail and Moon and told them to come and get it because I wasn't going to pay for no set that didn't work. They came and picked it up. A man from Retail told me that he did not blame me for not paying for it.

Of course, Retail Finance, the holder-in-due-course, brought the suit against this debtor.

All the debtors in this category encouraged the creditor to take back their purchase. We now turn to the debtors who assumed that they were no longer liable after the company repossessed the merchandise.

Company Repossesses:
Debtor Assumes Debt Is Settled

In most of the 27 cases in this group the debtor fell behind in payments and stopped them completely after the repossession on the false assumption that he was no longer liable. These debtors apparently assumed that the purchased product was the collateral for the loan and were unaware of the principle of deficiency judgment.

A 41-year-old Detroit black housewife, whose husband was employed as a janitor and earned $6,000–$8,000 annually, had her refrigerator repossessed.

> They came and got it. There was no need for me to pay any more. I was only behind one-half payment. My husband was put on less time at his job and so our payments had to get behind. Then there were unexpected illnesses and money needed for that. I thought if they took my refrigerator back and resold it, I didn't have to pay. . . . I never thought there would be such trouble like we is in now.

A 46-year-old Philadelphia black employed as a laborer in construction work with annual income between $4,000 and $5,000 had a rather complicated experience concerning an automobile debt. The first car he had bought was wrecked in an accident and the finance company urged him to go back to the dealer and pick out another one. They misled him by saying that he would receive a check for the first car. Only after the second purchase did he learn that he now had to pay for both cars and the promised check was never received. In spite of this deception he tried to maintain payments until he became sick and was hospitalized.

Meanwhile, after the repossession, his note had been sold by the acceptance company to a bank.

> When the bank entered the picture, the man from there told me that the finance company had been paid off and that I only owed him about $200. I paid all but $16 and then the bank started sending letters and telegrams and sheriff notices. He said every time he sends a sheriff out to my house it will cost me $100 and that the telegrams cost me $15. . . . He always gives me my balance by word of mouth and never in writing.

This debtor too resented having to make additional payments after the repossession.

> I don't see why I should have to pay after the company took the car back. . . . Actually it was in better shape when they took it back than when I got it. I had the motor overhauled.

Miscellaneous Reasons for Default
Linked to Debtor No Longer Having Merchandise

Six debtors spread evenly among primary, secondary, and tertiary reasons for default had still other reasons for not paying on merchandise that they no longer had. In three cases, the item bought on time was installed in their homes and they subsequently lost their houses. A middle-aged black, earning $5,000–$6,000 a year as a janitor, had bought a gas heater on time.

> I stopped paying because I lost my home. I went "bankrupt." When they sold the house, I figured everything went with the house. Central National was the one I was making payments to at the time I lost my home. Then they turned it over to Commonwealth. I told them it wasn't right for me to be paying for something I wasn't using.

This man was told that he still owed more than $1,800 on this gas heater, which initially was to cost $1,100 (an amount that he claims he had just about paid). It should be noted that this debtor used the word "bankrupt" in a colloquial sense. Apparently he did not actually file for bankruptcy for, when asked directly whether he had, he replied: "I figured that when I lost my home, that was bankruptcy." In short, he felt bankrupt when the mortgage on his house was foreclosed.

Another Philadelphian, a 56-year-old black woman, employed as a factory worker at $75 a week and whose son earned $100 a week, bringing their combined income to $9,000, had been talked into buying a fire alarm system by a door-to-door salesman.

> I lost my home and I didn't see why I should have to pay for something that I don't have. I talked to this attorney and he agreed with me.

Both these debtors concluded that they should not have to pay for something which belonged to property that they no longer owned.

In a few cases in this residual category, the debtor stopped paying initially because the merchandise was defective and the dealer took the merchandise back to make the necessary repairs. These debtors assumed that they did not have to make payments while the repairs were being made, but their creditors apparently defined the situation differently.

A 36-year-old black Chicagoan employed in the automobile industry and earning $6,000–$8,000 a year had bought a color TV set to please his wife at a time when he thought she might be near death.

> My wife was very sick and I bought it for her. That is a poor damn excuse but it's the truth. She was in the hospital having a baby, but the doctor said she might die and she said she always wanted a color TV, so that's why I bought it. I never made a payment because it never worked. They sent a man out to fix it and he couldn't. They took it back saying they would fix it or give me a new one but they never brought it back and they never gave me a new one. I got a notice from them saying the set was faulty and that every TV number under that series was bad.

It should be noted that this debtor thought he was buying a $650 set, the price told to him by the salesman, but when he received the contract from a finance company, the price had doubled, to over $1,200. Moreover, the company officially admitted that the set was defective by sending the debtor a notice to this effect. And yet in spite of this admission by the dealer, the man was sued by the finance company.

HARASSMENT AS AN ADDITIONAL REASON
FOR DEFAULT

Debtors who fall behind on payments are often subjected to many forms of harassment by their creditors. For example, some debtors are called at all hours of the day by their creditors, some find that their relatives and neighbors are called and told that they are deadbeats, occasionally debtors are told that they will be arrested unless they pay, and most commonly they learn that their employers have been contacted and threatened with garnishment unless they persuade the debtor to settle his account. We shall deal with this theme more systematically in a later chapter. For the moment we are concerned with how harassment can become self-defeating by strengthening the debtor's resolve not to pay. Thirteen debtors mentioned harassment as an additional reason for their not paying. This was, of course, never a primary reason, for the harassment developed only after the debtor was in arrears. We have come across a few of these cases in connection with other reasons for the default, for example the black free-lance writer encountered in chapter 6 who was told that he would lose his job and that his kind of people never paid their bills.

A 34-year-old black Philadelphian, employed as a welder and earning $4,000–$5,000 a year, held up payments because he was sold a defective car. He, too, resented the harassment, which took the form of insults to his wife.

> First of all, the car was just a complete mess. He lied to me about it. And then they came around making insults. . . . They insulted my wife and I resent this. . . . I refused to pay them or any other individual until they apologize to her. Then I will try to pay each and every month.

An even more vivid example of harassment is provided by a 32-year-old white Chicagoan who had had his own demolition business that failed. Because of his numerous business debts, he was unable to maintain payments on a ring that he had bought.

> I couldn't pay. I am out of a job. But also I wouldn't pay. Not after the way that lawyer, Mr. S. was his name, talked to me and my wife. He was rude and treated me like an animal. He talked to my wife like she was a tramp. He said if I didn't have the money to pay him, I had better go out and steal it.

When asked if there was a good reason why he should not have to pay this debt, he referred again to the harassment.

> Because of their attitude. I'm not an animal, but that's how he talked to me, the lawyer from the jewelry company. . . . It's a shame that people with money would pick on someone who had nothing. I guess I have to die to be free of them. No one wants to help. They just push you down again.

It should be noted that the insults came not from some employee of the credit firm, but from the creditor's attorney. Collection work has very low status in the bar and may well attract lawyers whose own ethical standards leave much to be desired. Since the bar is often concerned with its public image and the problem of winning the public's trust, one might well wonder why attorneys such as this man who urges a debtor to steal are not disbarred.

These instances of harassment, however infrequent they may be, cast some suspicion on the credit industry's often-voiced claim that it is ready to come to terms with debtors who because of unexpected misfortunes are unable to maintain payments. As we have already noted, the term "deadbeat" is frequently misused by creditors. It would seem that the indiscriminate use of this term serves only to provide the justification for outrageous harassment tactics. In some places in the country, a new branch of law is developing, harassment suits against creditors. If more states instituted such legislation, it might well be that debtors such as these might find some redress through the courts for the indignities to which they have been subjected.

ALL OTHER REASONS FOR NOT PAYING

In this and the previous four chapters we have described and illustrated the rather complicated scheme for classifying reasons for the debtors' default. The various categories reviewed account for all but 6 of the 1,331 cases, and even these residual cases that seem so unusual might on further reflection be fitted into one or another of the categories already presented. They will be briefly summarized, mainly to provide some idea of the complexity of classifying them.

A 34-year-old white Detroit man blames his trouble with a small loan company on a mixup in his checking account. His bank made an error in his balance and as a result some of his checks, including one to the creditor who sued him, bounced. In another instance, a black Detroit couple fell behind on payments on a TV set because both the husband and the wife were hospitalized and their creditor did not know how to reach them. Once released from the hospital, they settled their account and the suit was dropped.

In another unusual case, a middle-aged white Chicago debtor maintained payments on his car until his license was suspended. He asked the company to repossess the car, and like debtors encountered earlier, he mistakenly thought that the repossession ended the matter.

Still another strange case is that of a 32-year-old white Chicagoan who found himself being sued because his former landlady in Pennsylvania had attached his furniture and appliances as part of what he claimed was a false property damage suit. Some of the property the landlady had seized was bought on time from a dealer who mysteriously had not exerted his claim to the chattel mortgage, and it was this dealer who brought suit against the debtor in his new state of Illinois.

The creditor is clearly implicated in the next unusual case. A 25-year-old white Detroit housewife was forbidden by her husband from buying anything on time. She went to a store to buy a rug for cash at $70. The salesman talked her into buying a much more expensive rug on credit. Although the wife said she could not afford it, the salesman took her across the street and arranged a loan to cover the purchase. When her husband learned of the transaction, he refused to pay. According to the wife's account, the husband's approval of the loan had been solicited and he disapproved. Yet the company arranged the loan and sued the couple in spite of the husband's refusal to sanction the loan. The power of the credit industry is shown by the fact that this reluctant man was making payments of $30 every two weeks on this unwanted debt at the time of the interview. This case raises an interesting issue of law. Is the husband liable for his wife's debt if the purchase was for a nonessential item? Perhaps a skilled attorney might have pressed this claim, but like so many of these debtors, this couple did not have legal help with their problem.

The last of these unusual cases is a rather incredible story in which the wife of the debtor established a rotating credit charge with a $300 ceiling at a major New York department store. At the time of the interview, the debtor's wife, who had had a long history of emotional instability, was in a mental hospital. The husband was being sued because his wife had purchased a $1,300 ring on her limited revolving credit account. The husband, who was interviewed, was extremely indignant and blamed the store for extending so much credit to his emotionally unbalanced wife in clear violation of the store's own credit limit.[5]

[5]One might think that once a store establishes a customer's credit limit that the amount set cannot be exceeded. This naive view fails to take into account the pressures operating on the business concern. Although all major retailers set credit limits on their customers, they do not dare disclose them to their customers for fear of insulting them. Rather than risk the anger of a customer denied credit, the typical department store will extend credit beyond the customer's credit limit and hope that the transaction will work out. In short, the company's concern with goodwill is so great that it readily becomes a party to the overextension of the debtor.

A QUANTITATIVE ANALYSIS OF
REASONS FOR DEFAULT

The previous chapters have described the specific reasons for the default offered by the debtors themselves. As seen in chapter 4, virtually all the reasons fall into one of ten major categories, six of which reflect the debtor's misfortunes and shortcomings and four of which implicate the creditor in varying degrees.[1] This chapter examines how these reasons for default relate to various types of debtors and types of creditors. To simplify the analysis, we shall deal only with the primary reason for the default. Two consequences follow from this decision. First, the frequency of reasons in which the creditor is implicated is reduced, for, as Table 4.2 showed, such reasons were offered more often as secondary ones. Second, the number of major categories of reasons is reduced from ten to eight, as "partial and irregular payments" and "item returned to dealer," two categories that partially implicate the dealer, were rarely offered as primary reasons. Our procedure will be to present each of the remaining eight categories of reasons in each table as well as a summary that differentiates reasons reflecting the debtor's mishaps from those in which the creditor is implicated.

Reasons for Default by City

We begin the statistical analysis by considering whether there is any intercity variation in reasons for default (Table 9.1).

[1] Table 4.1 contained two other categories, quite small in size: harassment as an additional reason and a miscellaneous category. Only 19 of the 1,331 debtors gave reasons for not paying that fell into these categories, and they are excluded from this analysis.

Table 9.1 / Primary Reason for Default by City (percent)

	Chicago	Detroit	New York	Phila-delphia
Debtor's mishaps and shortcomings				
Loss of income	42	46	38	46
Voluntary overextension	14	15	14	8
Involuntary overextension	5	5	5	7
Marital instability	5	6	5	10
Debtor's third parties	8	7	10	6
Debtor irresponsibility	3	3	5	2
Creditor implicated				
Allegation of fraud	15	11	14	15
Payment misunderstanding	8	7	10	5
Total percent	100	100	101	99
Summary				
Debtor's mishaps	77	81	76	80
Creditor implicated	23	18	24	20
Total percent	100	99	100	100
N^a	(300)	(432)	(325)	(241)

[a]Excluded are 12 Chicago, 6 Detroit, 7 New York, and 8 Philadelphia debtors who either gave no primary reason for the default or gave a reason classified as miscellaneous. These numbers also apply, of course, to the upper half of the table.

The distribution of reasons in the four cities is quite similar. The patterns in Chicago and Detroit are virtually identical and, with slight deviations, those in New York and Philadelphia are also much the same. In each city, loss of income is by far the most prevalent reason, although in New York it is somewhat less frequent than in the other cities. In each city similar proportions mention fraud, involuntary overextension, and irresponsibility. Marital instability as a reason for the default is somewhat more common in Philadelphia, and Philadelphians mention overcommitment (voluntary overextension) less often than the debtors in the other cities. From the summary table we see that creditors are implicated in the chief reason for the default in about 20 percent of the cases, somewhat more so in Chicago and New York, somewhat less so in Detroit and Philadelphia. Owing to the absence of marked city differences, city will be omitted from subsequent analyses.

Ethnicity

Stereotypes held by many in the credit industry to explain the disproportionate number of minority group members among defaulters include such notions as irresponsibility and overcommitment as being more prevalent among blacks.[2] The reasons offered by the debtors for their troubles fail to support these stereotypes (Table 9.2). The distribution of reasons was rather similar among white and black debtors, with white debtors mentioning overextension more often than the blacks. Blacks were somewhat more likely than whites not to pay because of fraud, and they also were more likely to suffer from income losses, a finding in keeping with their less secure employment.

Table 9.2 / Primary Reason for Default by Ethnicity (percent)

	whites	blacks	Puerto Ricans
Debtor's mishaps and shortcomings			
Loss of income	40	45	39
Voluntary overextension	16	13	7
Involuntary overextension	7	5	7
Marital instability	8	6	5
Debtor's third parties	8	7	15
Debtor irresponsibility	2	3	8
Creditor implicated			
Allegation of fraud	13	15	10
Payment misunderstandings	7	7	10
Total percent	101	101	101
Summary			
Debtor's mishaps	80	78	80
Creditor implicated	20	22	20
Total percent	100	100	100
N	(362)	(841)	(92)

In view of all that has been written about the instability of the Negro family, one might expect that marital problems account for defaults of blacks more often than of whites. But this is not the case. If anything, the reverse is true; 8 percent of the whites compared with 6 percent of the blacks cite marital instability as the reason for their default. In several respects the Puerto Ricans show a pattern different from both whites and blacks. They were less likely to get into trouble because of overcommitment, but they were much more likely than whites and blacks to default because of third parties and reasons classified as irresponsibility. The third-party role in Puerto Rican defaults no doubt reflects the greater importance of the extended family and patterns of

[2]In presenting the findings of this study before various groups, I have more than once heard about blacks getting into trouble because they all want to own expensive cars. "Everyone knows," said one member of an audience of creditors, "that all the Negroes in Harlem own Cadillacs that they can't afford."

mutual aid for these relatively recent immigrants. Their greater presence in the irresponsibility category stems from our classifying here instances in which people forgot to maintain payments while they were out of town for extended periods of time. As several of the anecdotes indicate, Puerto Ricans sometimes returned home for family reasons, visits that often turned into extended stays.

Income

Income turns out to be more closely connected to reasons for default than either city or ethnicity. As might be expected, loss of income was a much greater hardship for the relatively poor and contributed to their defaults more often than those of higher income. Conversely, payment misunderstandings were more common among the more well-to-do than among the poor. These patterns are shown in Table 9.3.

Another notable pattern is that voluntary overextension, the mark of the imprudent debtor, turns out to be a more frequent reason for default among those of middle and high income than among those of low income. (The more well-to-do are twice as likely as the poor to give this reason.) This would suggest that persons of low income are in some respects better money managers than those of higher income. At least they are more likely to resist the temptations that lead to overextension. The poor tend to default not only because they suffer income

Table 9.3 / Primary Reason for Default by Income (percent)

	under $4,000	$4,000–$7,999	$8,000 and over
Debtor's mishaps and shortcomings			
Loss of income	49	43	37
Voluntary overextension	7	16	14
Involuntary overextension	5	5	7
Marital instability	7	6	5
Debtor's third parties	8	7	9
Debtor irresponsibility	3	3	4
Creditor implicated			
Allegations of fraud	15	14	12
Payment misunderstandings	6	5	12
Total percent	100	99	100
Summary			
Debtor's mishaps	79	80	76
Creditor implicated	21	20	24
Total percent	100	100	100
N	(327)	(642)	(257)

reversals, but also because they are slightly more likely to be victims of fraud. These categories together account for 63 percent of the defaults of the poor but for only 47 percent of the defaults of those of high income.

Given the close connection between income and ethnicity, there is some merit to examining the joint impact of these attributes on reasons for default. As can be seen from Table 9.4, ethnic differences occur primarily among those of low income. In this group, whites default much more often than blacks for reasons that reflect their own shortcomings, such as overextension and marital instability. In contrast, poor blacks were much more likely to be victims of fraud and payment misunderstandings.

Table 9.4 / Primary Reason for Default by Income and Ethnicity (percent)

	under $4,000		$4,000–$7,999		$8,000 and over	
	white	black	white	black	white	black
Debtor's mishaps and shortcomings						
Loss of income	48	52	42	44	35	36
Voluntary overextension	10	6	19	17	16	14
Involuntary overextension	10	3	5	5	8	7
Marital instability	13	6	8	5	2	7
Debtor's third parties	8	6	5	7	12	6
Debtor's irresponsibility	2	2	3	3	2	5
Creditor implicated						
Allegations of fraud	10	17	14	15	12	13
Payment misunderstandings	—	7	4	5	12	12
Total percent	101	99	100	101	99	100
Summary						
Debtor's mishaps	90	76	81	80	75	75
Creditor implicated	10	24	19	20	25	25
Total percent	100	100	100	100	100	100
N	(52)	(233)	(188)	(419)	(106)	(138)

Among those of middle income, the reasons for default are strikingly similar for blacks and whites. In the high-income category the similarity across ethnic lines is almost as great, although in this group marital instability is slightly greater among blacks, and being victimized by one's own third parties is more prevalent among whites. But in the aggregate, the frequency of reasons reflecting on the debtor and the creditor are virtually identical among blacks and whites of middle and high income. But, as the summary table makes clear, poor blacks were much more likely to be victimized by their creditors and default for this reason than their white counterparts (24 percent compared with 10 percent). From chapter 3 we know that the poor were more likely to deal with the less scrupulous door-to-door salesmen, and that poor blacks were especially likely to get into trouble because of such transactions. This would suggest that reasons for default might well be related to type of creditor, an issue to which we now turn.

Type of Creditor and Reasons for Default

Of the characteristics examined so far, only income proved to be related to reasons for default.[3] Ethnicity showed some connection with reasons for default only among the poor, a finding that suggested that attributes of creditors may be critical in understanding reasons for default. Table 9.5 relates the various primary reasons to type of creditor.

As the summary table shows, the ordering of the seller–creditors according to the extent to which they play a role in the default is identical with the ordering of sellers according to deception in the original transaction, as shown in chapter 3. The more unethical the seller, the more likely he is to be implicated in the debtor's default, either because of fraud or mishaps in the payment arrangements. Among lenders, in contrast with sellers, the reason for the default is almost always a result of the debtor's shortcomings. But even among these creditors, a tiny fraction of the debtors place the blame for their default on the lending agency. Thus lenders are not completely immune to the debtor's claim to defenses in these law suits. But the critical finding in Table 9.5 is the frequency with which direct selling is associated with reasons for default that place the blame on the creditor's fraud and payment misunderstandings. In chapter 8 we saw that many of these payment misunderstandings involve collectors who fail to come around or payment books that are not returned. In more than one third of these transactions, a figure that far outdistances general retailers, low-income retailers, and even automobile dealers, the creditor is implicated in door-to-door sales. It is also rather significant that "debtor irresponsibility" appears more often among those who bought from direct sellers than among any other type of creditor. Relatively few reasons were so classified, but even so, debtor irresponsibility shows up two to three times as often among those who dealt with door-to-door salesmen. Direct sellers were found earlier to score high on deception at the time of the sale. It is rather ironic, then, that there is a connection between creditor and debtor irresponsibility. It may even be that creditor irresponsibility breeds debtor irresponsibility.[4]

[3] Other characteristics of debtors, such as occupation, age, and education, also failed to show consistent relationships with reasons for default.

[4] Recall the anecdote of the classic case of irresponsibility cited in chapter 5. The husband bought many expensive items and had no intention of paying. The seller was so eager to make the sale that he suspended his usual procedure of checking the debtor's credit and permitted the debtor to take the goods from the store. The debtor's wife, the respondent, blamed the store's irresponsibility for their troubles.

Table 9.5 / Primary Reason for Default by Type of Creditor (percent)

	sellers				lenders	
	direct seller	auto dealer	low-income retailer	general retailer	small loan company	banks
Debtor's mishaps and shortcomings						
Loss of income	37	42	49	48	55	51
Voluntary overextension	10	10	13	14	18	25
Involuntary overextension	4	6	5	7	8	5
Marital instability	4	4	7	7	8	8
Debtor's third parties	2	6	3	6	3	4
Debtor's irresponsibility	6	2	3	3	2	3
Creditor implicated						
Allegations of fraud	24	23	14	7	3	1
Payment misunderstandings	12	7	6	6	4	4
Total percent	99	100	100	98	101	101
Summary						
Debtor's mishaps	64	71	80	86	93	95
Creditor implicated	36	29	20	14	7	5
Total percent	100	100	100	100	100	100
N	(277)	(249)	(225)	(175)	(145)	(77)

NOTE ON THE VERIFICATION OF REASONS

The issue of the validity of survey data of this kind, epecially when only one side of a story is heard, is dealt with in Appendix B. There it is noted that one check on validity consists of tests of internal consistency. The fact that the ordering of creditors in terms of the deception index in chapter 3 corresponds to their ordering with regard to the frequency of creditor-implicated reasons is one such example of internal consistency. This inference is further strengthened when the deception index is directly related to reasons implicating the creditor (fraud and payment misunderstandings). Among transactions that scored low on deception, only 9 percent of the debtors cited fraud as the primary reason for default. This figure climbs to 17 percent in the middle group on deception and to 26 percent in the high-deception group. Although this pattern is in the expected direction, as already noted, even in the high-deception group only a minority cited fraud as a reason for their default. Apparently, many debtors did their best to maintain payments even though they felt that they had been deceived.

CREDITOR'S

REMEDIES

AND

THE ROLE

OF THE COURTS

10

HARASSMENT AND

REPOSSESSION

This chapter begins the analysis of creditor's remedies. If in the previous chapters the people under study have been viewed as debtors in default, they are now to be seen as defendants in court actions. But before creditors take delinquent debtors to court, they are likely to rely on a variety of practices aimed at pressuring debtors to resume payments or, at the very least, at cutting their losses. In this chapter we examine two of these extrajudicial processes. We consider first the pressures applied by creditors in the form of "dunning" letters, phone calls, and efforts to intimidate the debtor by contacting his friends and employer, practices that blur the principles of clever debt management with harassment.[1] We shall then look at the frequency of repossession, a creditor's remedy based on the principle of the conditional sale, under which title to merchandise remains with the creditor until final payment is made. The analysis deals with such questions as the frequency of pressures bordering on harassment, the types of plaintiffs that use these techniques, and the types of debtors that are likely to be subjected to them. Similar questions will be examined with respect to repossession with the addition of a new theme: whether or not debtors understand the meaning of repossession.

[1] For a classic primer on the do's and don't's of debt collection written from an industry point of view, see E. H. Barnes, *Barnes on Credit and Collection* (Englewood Cliffs, N.J.: Prentice-Hall, Inc., 1961). See also "Collection Techniques," an unpublished training manual prepared by The American Collectors Association, Minneapolis.

177

HARASSMENT

In chapter 8 several cases were cited in which the debtor was so offended by the abuse vented upon him by the creditor that he cited this as an *additional* reason for not paying. The anecdotes that were presented by no means exhaust the group of debtors who felt they were being harassed by their creditors. Many others mentioned insults and practices indicative of harassment, although they did not refer to these as reasons for their default.

The distinction between harassment and legitimate collection procedures is by no means clear. To explicate the concept of harassment it is necessary to review the events that ensue when a debtor misses payments. Virtually all creditors send their delinquent debtors a series of dunning letters of increasing harshness. One collection lawyer we interviewed, whose major client was a large New York bank, pointed out that the bank's computer was used to send out the first few letters automatically. The early letters are usually polite reminders of the delinquency; subsequent letters threaten legal action, the ruining of the debtor's credit rating, and the involvement of the debtor's employer. Typical of the latter is the following:

> We are holding you responsible for this debt and unless arrangements are made to pay it, we will notify [name of debtor's employer] concerning this matter. They frown upon employees owing these kinds of debts.[2]

In a number of cities, local credit bureaus offer debt collection services to their members. Debtors then receive dunning letters on the stationery of the credit bureau, letters which indicate that their credit rating will be ruined unless payment is made. The effort to intimidate delinquent debtors via dunning letters has even led to the formation of fraudulent collection firms with Washington, D.C., addresses, whose stationery contains seals that make the letters appear to be official communications from the federal government. The recipients of such letters are given the false impression that the federal government will be after them if they do not settle their debt.

The borderline between the legal and illegal is quite fuzzy in these extrajudicial collection procedures. It has been argued that the creditor's communication with the debtor's employer prior to judgment, or even the threat of such communication as in the above sample letter, denies the debtor his constitutional rights. Since many employers who receive such letters order their employee to settle the debt or face dismissal,

---

[2] This letter is cited in Kenneth M. Block, *Creditor's Pre-judgment Communication to Debtor's Employer:* An Evaluation, 36 *Brooklyn L. Rev.* 95 at 98 (Fall 1969).

the debtor may be forced to pay even though he has valid defenses. In short, such pressures may well deprive the debtor of his day in court. However valid this reasoning may be, the courts have yet to accept it. Debtors who have sued creditors for damages done to them because their employers were contacted have yet to win their suits, and the consensus of the courts seems to be that the creditor has a legitimate right to contact the employer.[3]

Creditors have also been known to contact neighbors and relatives of debtors in an effort to get them to exert pressure on the delinquent debtor. And of course the creditor's representatives have been known to call debtors at all hours of the day and night and be rather insulting in the course of these conversations.

Some indication of the possibilities for harassment involved in collection procedures is provided by the manual on collection techniques produced by American Collectors Association for its members. The primer begins:

> Don't be a "tough guy." This is the one image that seems most inviting to the neophyte collector, and the one image that the collector must strive to avoid. Belligerence begets belligerence. Speak softly but imply that you are carrying a big stick and "get tough" only when it will serve a good purpose. . . . it is fundamentally true that every person has his secret Achilles heel . . . a weak spot in his armor. Once found by the collector and properly pressed, it will almost always produce payment.

The manual then goes on to enumerate some typical weak spots:

> It took you years and years of hard work and sacrifice to build up the good record you own—are you going to jeopardize it all with this one bad bill?

> Your boss pays his bills on time and I think I know how he feels about people who don't.

> Nobody wants to hire a fellow with bills in a collection agency. For one thing he is usually thinking about his bills instead of his job.

> You have to have insurance to drive your car, and insurance companies are checking people's credit ratings pretty closely before renewing policies.

The manual even covers the possibility that the debtor hangs up on the collector.

[3]See Block, *ibid*. It should be noted that legal opinion is not unanimous on this issue. Some dissenting opinions have argued that such letters constitute an invasion of privacy. In 1970 the Department of Consumer Affairs passed a regulation, subsequently upheld by the courts, prohibiting such prejudgment communications with employers. So far, only Wisconsin, by adopting its version of the National Consumer Act, has followed the lead of New York City in this respect.

> Occasionally a debtor will hang up on you. Immediately dial again
> with a firm voice [sic] saying something to the effect, "If you hang
> up on me again, it will cost you plenty."

The manual is filled with advice to cover all sorts of situations. Even
the lame, halt, and infirm are covered. Conceding that many of these
debtors may be unable to pay, those who wrote the manual suggest adopting this tactic:

> There is an old saying that if you knew your neightbor's troubles,
> you would never trade. We all have troubles of some kind. Now
> about this bill. . . .

As these quotations on collection techniques issued by the collectors
trade association suggest, harassment is closely connected with the collection process.

Debtors in all four cities were asked a series of questions designed
to measure harassment. The first of these inquired about insulting letters
from the creditor. This is perhaps the weakest indicator of harassment,
for it is not clear how debtors define insulting letters. But it is clear
that they sharply differentiate between typical dunning letters and insulting
ones, for although almost all the debtors got dunning letters, only 28
percent reported that they received *insulting* letters. An example of an
insulting letter is provided in the April 1970 issue of *Consumer's Voice,*
the newspaper of the Consumer Education and Protective Association
of Philadelphia. Behind in payments on a loan, a nurse received the following note written on the back of a late notice signed by two bank officers:

> I don't want to hear any sob stories, you are working and can afford
> to go to Carolina but you can't pay your bills. I may as well write
> these notes to an animal or some illiterate. They would have the
> same effect on them as they do on you. I don't care how or where
> you get the money but I want it by Friday and no more rubber checks.
> I'll come to your house Friday morning to get the money. I don't
> want to hear any excuses or bull. I've heard it from you for a month
> and I don't believe a word you say.[4]

A second measure of harassment is the question: "Did they call
you names or use bad language in talking with you?" Such crudity on
the part of creditors and collection agencies has already been encountered
in stories presented in chapter 8, and, in all, 15 percent of the debtors

---

[4]*Consumer's Voice,* 5 (Apr. 1970). An earlier insulting letter uncovered by CEPA,
a letter that spoke of the "pig treatment," was cited in Senator Warren Magnuson's book,
The Dark Side of the Marketplace, (Englewood Cliffs, N.J.: Prentice-Hall, 1968).

answered affirmatively. One of these was a middle-aged Philadelphia woman who had cosigned for a loan from a small loan company. Her account was eventually turned over to a collection agency. She elaborated on her affirmative answer to this question as follows:

> Yes, one time he had the nerve to call me a name—a "black nigger."
> That's why I had to get my phone number changed.

Another example is provided by a middle-aged white New York woman who had defaulted on furniture. This woman claimed that she had received insulting letters and had been called names by the creditor:

> I was ill and wasn't working and couldn't make the payments [on furniture] . . . but I kept in touch with them and made a payment when I could. They scare the life out of you with their letters and phone calls. They said they were coming to take everything I had and I almost died. . . . I have so little and I was not trying to run away or anything. Oh my God, I hope I can pay them soon. I am so glad to talk to someone about this. I sit here and worry and worry.

We inquired, too, about yet another form of harassment, the creditor's threats to contact and actually contacting friends and relatives. Sixteen percent of the debtors replied that such threats had been made or carried out. The final harassment question dealt with whether the creditor had contacted the debtor's employer. This query resulted in the largest proportion of positive responses, 36 percent.[5]

Since garnishment is not allowed in Philadelphia, we expected that the debtors in that city would make fewer reports of their employer being contacted and more frequent reports of insulting letters and name calling than the debtors in the other cities. Whether this is so can be seen from Table 10.1, which presents the city patterns for each of the four indicators of harassment.

Although the content of an insulting letter is somewhat ambiguous, it is evident that the Philadelphia creditors, denied the remedy of garnishment, are much more likely than those in other cities to compose harsh letters. The Philadelphia creditors were also somewhat more likely

---

[5]Since garnishment is prohibited in Philadelphia, we assumed that the creditors in that city would be more prone to rely on extrajudicial tactics such as harassment. We asked the Philadelphia debtors about two additional forms of harassment, phone calls late at night and threats of arrest. It is of some interest that 15 percent of the Philadelphia debtors answered "yes" to each question. Arlen Specter, the current District Attorney in Philadelphia, did a survey of the city's Magistrate Courts, which have jurisdiction in debts under $100. The Specter report indicated that the constable attached to these courts frequently used the unwarranted and unenforceable threat of arrest as a tactic in debt collection. See the "Report of the Attorney General on the Investigation of the Magisterial System," Commonwealth of Pennsylvania, Department of Justice, 1965.

Table 10.1 / Affirmative Responses to Harassment Questions by City (percent)

type of harassment	Chicago	Detroit	New York	Phila-delphia	total
Insulting letters	25	27	24	42	29
Name calling, bad language	18	15	10	18	15
Threatening to or actually contacting friends, relatives	16	16	12	20	16
Calling employer	45	26	46	27	36
Maximum base figures [a]	(312)	(438)	(332)	(251)	(1,333)

[a]On any given question the base figure is less than the maximum, owing to exclusion of the "no answer's."

than those in other cities to contact the debtor's friends and relatives. Given their inability to attach wages we might suppose that they would also be more likely to use abusive language, but the Chicago creditors show up as frequently in this category as those in Philadelphia (18 percent, slightly more than the Detroit creditors and almost twice as frequently as the New York creditors). Contacting the employer as a source of pressure on the debtor is quite prevalent in Chicago and New York, and, as expected, this tactic is employed much less frequently in Philadelphia. But the surprising finding is that Detroit creditors also use this procedure infrequently, no more so than the Philadelphia creditors.

These four items have been combined into an index of harassment. In all cities combined, some 41 percent of the debtors escaped all these forms of pressure, 34 percent experienced one form, and 25 percent, two or more. In the aggregate, 59 percent of the debtors experienced some harassment. These rates did not vary much from city to city. Philadelphia debtors were most likely to have been pressured (64 percent) and Detroit debtors least likely (53 percent) with the New York and Chicago rates closer to that of Philadelphia.

TYPE OF PLAINTIFF AND HARASSMENT

We have seen that certain types of firms are more prone than others to employ deception, and it is reasonable to assume that such firms, when they are also plaintiffs, are more likely to use the harsh collection practices that amount to harassment. In the aggregate of all cities combined there is some merit to this expectation for, as can be seen from Table

10.2, direct sellers are close to the top when it comes to harassment and general retailers are close to the bottom. But heading the list are the collection agencies, closely followed by the small loan companies and at the bottom, as might have been expected, are the credit unions. Oddly enough, the few automobile dealers who kept their own contracts were less likely than most other types of plaintiffs to harass debtors.

Table 10.2 / Harassment by Type of Plaintiff

type of plaintiff	percentage harassed	N
Collection agencies	68	(53)
Small loan companies	67	(233)
Direct sellers	61	(155)
Finance companies	59	(302)
Low-income retailers	58	(148)
Banks	57	(208)
Automobile dealers	53	(34)
General retailers	49	(135)
Credit unions	41	(22)

The aggregate pattern is most typical of Detroit and least so of Chicago. In the latter city all types of plaintiffs resort to harassment frequently.

REPOSSESSION

Of the 1,331 default-debtors in the sample, 907, 69 percent, had made purchases governed by conditional sales contracts. The creditors in these transactions could exercise their right to reclaim the merchandise, subtract the value realized in the resale from the balance of the debt, and then seek a deficiency judgment for the remainder.[6] But apart from automobiles, most merchandise bought on time, even TV sets and furniture, quickly loses so much value that it hardly pays for the creditor to repossess it. In an earlier study, some merchants reported that they repossess TV sets and the like primarily to punish a buyer whom they think has been dishonest or to frighten other customers.[7]

Another factor influencing the creditor's decision to repossess is the difficulty of removing objects from the debtor's home. This operation can be dangerous to the creditors and their agents and, although they

[6] See Appendix A for a definition of "deficiency judgment."
[7] See David Caplovitz, *The Poor Pay More* (New York: The Free Press, 1963).

are not required to do so, they may seek a court order known as a "replevin," which permits them to enter the debtor's home without being guilty of breaching the peace.[8]

Given the absence of a reason for repossession in many instances and the other obstacles attending this remedy, it is perhaps not surprising that repossessions occurred in only about one fourth of the cases in which they could have taken place. Our assumption that repossession will occur only when the merchandise is likely to have some value is well borne out by the data. By far the most frequently repossessed item is the automobile. Of the 258 purchases of automobiles in the sample, 58 percent resulted in repossession. For major household appliances, this figure drops to 24 percent; for entertainment appliances such as television sets and for furniture the rate of repossession is only 13 percent, dropping to a mere 1 percent for all other merchandise, such as minor appliances, soft goods, jewelry, wigs, and books.

Repossession varies not only by type of purchase, but also by city. Repossessions were most likely to occur in Detroit, as 33 percent of the items bought on time in that city were taken back; Chicago and Philadelphia have similar rates of repossession, about 25 percent; and New York has by far the lowest rate, only 8 percent. These city differences can, of course, reflect differences in the types of merchandise purchased. For example, there were fewer automobile transactions in New York than in the other cities. Thus whether the four cities do indeed differ in their rates of repossession requires taking into account the type of item purchased (Table 10.3).

Table 10.3 / Percentage Repossession by Type of Purchase and City

type of purchase	Detroit		Chicago		Philadelphia		New York	
Automobile	68	(101)	58	(89)	47	(45)	39	(28)
Major appliance	38	(56)	8	(13)	15	(13)	—	(17)
Entertainment appliance, furniture	26	(53)	9	(71)	23	(47)	4	(89)
Other	2	(114)	2	(64)	—	(37)	1	(72)

[8]Replevin actions require the creditor to post a bond that may be forfeited should the replevin action prove unwarranted. Unlike law suits in which the creditor seeks a judgment against the debtor, replevin actions did not require prior notice to the debtor. But because of law suits brought by OEO legal services programs, the Supreme Court ruled in 1972 that advance notice must be given in replevin actions on the grounds that without such notice people would be deprived of property without due process of the law. This decision has not yet been extended to "self-help" repossessions that take place outside the debtor's home, as when a car parked on the street is repossessed. But a number of OEO-sponsored law suits now in progress might well lead to the extension of the replevin decision to cover "self-help" repossessions as well.

By reading down the columns, we learn that in each city automobiles are most likely to be repossessed. But whether major appliances or furniture and entertainment appliances are next depends on the city. In Detroit, major household appliances are more likely to be repossessed than furniture, whereas the reverse is true in Philadelphia; in both New York and Chicago few repossessions occur in these categories. The city differences persist when type of item is taken into account. The repossession rate in New York lags well behind that in the other cities even for automobiles. In fact, examination of the rows shows that creditors in Detroit are most likely to rely on repossession irrespective of type of item. The overall Chicago rate matches that of Philadelphia only because of the relatively high rate of automobile repossessions in that city; when the other categories are taken into account, it would seem that Philadelphia creditors in general rely more on repossession than do those in Chicago.

Why do New York plaintiffs repossess so infrequently when compared with creditors in other jurisdictions? And why is this remedy so popular in Detroit? Our data do not permit definitive answers to these questions. Perhaps these frequencies are related to the other remedies available to creditors in these different jurisdictions. In New York it is relatively easy to garnish wages, and the garnishment law is such a progressive one that it poses much less of a burden on the debtor than the harsh garnishment law in Michigan at the time of the study. Perhaps, then, Detroit creditors turn to repossession as a chief tool for controlling the credit system in that city, whereas New York creditors rely more on garnishment. In chapter 12 we shall consider the frequency of garnishment in each city and will see that there is some merit to this reasoning. But this is mere speculation; whatever the explanation, the fact remains that the frequency of repossession varies significantly from city to city.

The city differences shown in Table 10.3 persist even when type of plaintiff is taken into account. Whether the goods at stake are automobiles, furniture, or appliances, New York plaintiffs are not nearly as likely to repossess as their counterparts in other cities.[9] All types of Detroit plaintiffs are more likely to repossess than those in other cities, especially the Detroit low-income and general retailers, who far outdistance their counterparts in the other cities in repossessions. Thus repossession is associated more with city than with type of plaintiff. Presumably the variations in credit laws among these cities makes repossession a more reasonable creditor remedy in Detroit than in New York, with Chicago and Philadelphia falling in between.

[9]In only one instance is a type of plaintiff in New York more likely to repossess than one of the same type in another city, and the difference is too small to be significant. Only 3 percent of Chicago low-income retailers repossessed appliances and furniture compared with 7 percent of the New York low-income retailers.

Repossession and Characteristics of Debtors

Just as we did not expect harassment to be related to type of debtor, so there is even less reason to assume such relationships with regard to repossession. Income has virtually no relationship to repossession, as about one fourth of those in each of the three broad income groups experienced repossession. But at first glance ethnicity does appear to be related to repossession, as 35 percent of whites involved in conditional sales had their goods repossessed compared with 22 percent of the blacks and only 9 percent of the Puerto Ricans. But this pattern turns out to be due mainly to the different types of merchandise bought by the various ethnic groups. When type of product is taken into account, the ethnic difference either disappears or is greatly reduced, as can be seen from Table 10.4. (Again we omit the Puerto Ricans because of their small number.)

Table 10.4 / Repossession by Ethnicity and Type of Purchase (Percentage Repossession)

type of purchase	whites		blacks	
Automobile	59	(90)	58	(166)
Major appliance	26	(51)	17	(167)
Furniture and TV–phonograph	14	(36)	10	(120)
All other (e.g., soft goods)	6	(34)	—	(176)

The aggregate difference between blacks and whites, 13 percentage points, is greatly reduced when type of item is taken into account. The ethnic difference completely disappears among the automobile cases, is reduced to nine percentage points in the major appliance category, to only four percentage points in the furniture category, and to six points in the "all other" group. Whites are much more likely than blacks to have fallen into our sample because of automobile transactions; as we already know, automobiles are much more likely than any other type of item to be repossessed. It is this which explains most of the overselection of whites among the "repossessed."

Debtor's Confusion concerning Meaning of Repossession

Several of the incidents presented in earlier chapters suggested that some debtors had no understanding of the terms embodied in their installment contracts. Some apparently thought that their obligation ended when the creditor reclaimed the merchandise. These debtors had no understanding of deficiency judgments and the reasoning underlying them. As we saw in chapter 8, some 27 debtors gave as a secondary reason for no longer paying, the fact that the company had repossessed the merchandise. The number who totally misunderstood the process of repossession is much greater. The 218 debtors who experienced repossession were asked:

> When the [item] was repossessed, did you think that the debt was settled or did you think that you still owed money to the company?

Of those who experienced repossession, more than half (54 percent) thought that the repossession exonerated them from further obligation to the creditor.[10]

If the phenomenon of repossession is to be understood in terms of the value of the item bought on credit, the laws of the various states and the behavior of various types of creditors, then the misperception of this act by the debtor is likely to be understood in terms of his characteristics. One might suppose that the better educated debtors in default would be more likely than the poorly educated to understand the conditions embodied in their contracts and would know that their obligations do not automatically end with the repossession. However, this is not the case. In fact, the better educated seem to be more confused than the poorly educated on this matter. Forty-nine percent of those who never graduated from high school understood that the repossession did not end their obligation, compared with 45 percent of those who did graduate from high school. (Among the relatively small number who attended college, only 45 percent understood the meaning of repossession.) In the aggregate, ethnicity does not differentiate the debtors on this matter either, as identical percentages of blacks and whites (54 percent) were under the impression that the repossession freed them from further obligation. As we shall see, this aggregate pattern disguises some subpatterns of ethnic differences. The one characteristic of debtors that is clearly related to this misunderstanding is income. The lower the income of the debtor, the more likely he was to define the repossession as absolving him of any further obligations. Among those earning under $4,000, fully 67 percent were of this view, compared with 52 percent in the middle-income category and only 42 percent in the high-income group.

In one respect, this rather strong income pattern is puzzling. As noted, in the aggregate there is no difference between whites and blacks in this respect, and yet the black debtors tend to earn much less than the whites. This would suggest that the ethnicity pattern might vary depending on income. The patterns that emerge when income and ethnicity are considered simultaneously are shown in Table 10.5.

---

[10]It is of course conceivable, although most unlikely, that the repossessed merchandise realizes enough in the resale to meet the obligation. But this clearly could not have happened in any of the cases under review, for these debtors were all being sued for deficiency judgments. See Philip Shuchman, *Profiit on Default: An Archival Study of Automobile Repossession and Resale,* 22 Stanford L. Rev. 20 (Nov. 1969).

Table 10.5 / Percentage Who Thought
Repossession Settled Debt
by Income and Ethnicity

income	whites	blacks
Under $4,000	77 (13)	67 (30)
$4,000–$7,999	54 (37)	50 (68)
$8,000 and over	33 (15)	46 (22)

The negative relationship between income and understanding of repossession holds for both whites and blacks, but the pattern is particularly pronounced among the whites. The overall percentage difference among whites is 44 points, while for blacks it is only 21 points. It should also be noted that although there were no ethnic differences in the aggregate, the ethnic groups now show differences and the direction of the difference depends on the level of income. Among the poor, whites are more likely than blacks to think that the repossession ends the debt. Among the more well-to-do, the reverse is true.[11]

The association of income and knowledge of repossession in each ethnic group might be explained by the type of goods repossessed. Debtors who had automobiles taken back were much less likely than those who had other merchandise repossessed to think that the debt was settled (49 percent compared with 65 percent), and those of high income were more likely to have gotten into trouble because of automobile transactions. But as can be seen from Table 10.6, even when type of purchase is taken into account, the income pattern persists.

Table 10.6 / Percentage Who Thought Repossession Settled
Debt by Income Presented Separately for
Automobile Transactions and Other Types

type of purchase	under $4,000	$4,000–$7,999	$8,000 and over
Automobile	63 (27)	51 (77)	38 (32)
Other	72 (21)	54 (28)	(4)[a] (6)

[a]Base too small to percentage.

[11]The more methodologically oriented reader will recognize this as an instance of the specification of a zero correlation. Whereas ethnicity and understanding of repossession are not at all related in the aggregate, they turn out to be related in one direction among the poor and in the opposite direction among the more well-to-do. In short, the overall zero correlation results from a positive correlation in one case canceling out a negative correlation in the other.

Among both those who experienced repossessions of automobiles and other types of goods, income is negatively related to belief that the debt was settled. This pattern is especially marked among the automobile cases, for here we have sufficient cases in the high-income group to see that it is indeed among these debtors that the meaning of an automobile repossession is likely to be understood. There are too few instances of repossession of other merchandise among those in the highest income group to yield reliable statistics, but it may be noted that four of the six debtors in this group had the false impression that the debt was settled. That the concept of deficiency judgment was better understood by the automobile buyers of high income than by any other group may well stem from their greater involvement in the automobile culture.

SEEKING A JUDGMENT:

THE ROLE OF

THE COURTS

IN THE

COLLECTION PROCESS

When extrajudicial methods of collection fail, creditors are likely to enlist the courts in the collection process. Of course, they hope to collect the debt by invoking the power of the court, but even if they do not collect, a judgment against the debtor is still of value for income tax purposes. Bad debts are worth 50 cents in deductions on every tax dollar. Since we sampled default-debtors from court records, each, by definition, had been sued.[1] We now confront the debtors not merely as persons in default

---

[1] It happens that in 4 of the 438 Detroit cases, the process server recorded that he was unable to find the debtor and thus the legal action was stopped. Our interviewers did find these four persons and learned about their debt problem. That such cases of admitted nonservice occurred only in Detroit calls attention to city variations in both the stage at which the case is recorded and the information about the case appearing in the docket book. In Chicago and Detroit, where process serving is an activity of the court, the case is entered in a docket book at the time at which the creditor requests service. In New York, where process serving is a private industry, the case is entered in a docket book only when proof of service is filed. The confirmation-of-judgment book in Chicago records whether service was made. In Detroit, the comparable information appeared only in the file of the case. The two-stage process in Detroit resulted in the four cases of nonservice slipping into the sample.

but as defendants in legal actions. We consider in this chapter the stages of the legal process leading up to judgment. Since most Philadelphia debtors confessed judgment in advance, they are excluded from the subsequent analysis.[2]

SERVICE OF PROCESS

Central to the American judicial system is the concept embodied in the Fourteenth Amendment that prohibits a citizen from being deprived of his rights or property without due process of the law. The doctrine of due process requires that a person be notified of any legal action taken against him in order that he may defend himself in court. In consumer actions, this means that the debtor has to be properly notified of the legal action instituted by the creditor.

The issue of service of process in these three jurisdictions provides an unusual opportunity to study the efficacy of procedural laws, for the rules governing service of process in New York are quite different from those in Chicago and Detroit. One major difference is that process serving in New York is a private industry, responding to the profit motive. Any person 21 years of age or older may serve a summons, and a relatively small number of process-serving firms in New York handle the bulk of the business. In contrast, in Michigan and Illinois, as in most other states, process serving is carried out by an official of the court, the sheriff or a bailiff. The entrepreneurial character of process serving in New York results in a number of illegal shortcuts that we shall soon note.

In all three jurisdictions, the process server is required to attempt personal service; that is, he must try to hand the summons and complaint (which are printed on the same form) to the debtor. But in Chicago and Detroit, the rules regarding substitute service are (or were) much more lenient than in New York. Should the process server in Chicago or Detroit not find the debtor at home, he is permitted to hand the summons to any person 21 years of age or older in the household and then mail a copy to the debtor. Until recently, the process server in New York was required to prove that he had made several attempts at personal service on different days before substitute service was permitted.[3]

[2]As noted, confession of judgment is recognized in Pennsylvania without (unlike Chicago) a process of notification. This doctrine was challenged in 1970 by the OEO legal services program in Philadelphia. A three-judge federal court handed down a decision that permits confession of judgment to be used in mortgage transactions and in consumer transactions only if the debtor earned more than $10,000. The logic of such an income criterion is difficult to follow, but under this decision most of the debtors in the Philadelphia sample would no longer be subjected to confessions of judgment. As noted earlier, the Supreme Court upheld this decision of the lower court. According to one theory, it did so in part because Pennsylvania did not come forth to defend its own law, as the attorney general of the state shared the view of the poverty lawyers that confession of judgment should be abolished.

[3]The New York law was changed in September 1970 to permit substitute service to be made in much the same way as in the other jurisdictions.

The method of service is related to yet another difference between New York law and that in the other jurisdictions—the length of time the debtor has to respond. If personal service is made in New York, the debtor is given only 10 days to answer the summons. If substitute service is employed, the debtor in New York is given up to 30 days to respond before the creditor can claim a default judgment. In Illinois and Michigan the debtor is given about 15 days to respond regardless of method of service.

The fees that can be charged for process serving are quite low in all these jurisdictions, ranging at the time of our study from $1.50 per summons in New York to $4.00 per summons in Detroit, with additional charges for mileage in Chicago. These fees are paid initially by the plaintiff but are passed on to the defendant, being added to the amount sought in the judgment.

One final difference exists between process serving in New York and the other two jurisdictions. The Soldiers and Sailors Relief Act, passed by the federal government years ago, prohibits *default* judgments against members of the armed services on the theory that a member of the military may be unable to appear in court to defend himself because he is off fighting a war or is on assignment in some other jurisdiction. Thus, before a default judgment can be obtained, an affidavit of nonmilitary service must be filed with the court. In Chicago and Detroit the burden of filing this affidavit rests with the plaintiff and his attorney, presumably because they know that at the time of the initial transaction the debtor was not in military service. But in New York the convention is that the process server makes the determination of whether the debtor is a civilian, and it is he who files the affidavit of nonmilitary service. Perhaps one reason for this custom is that process servers are entitled to charge an additional $2.00 for filing the affidavit of nonmilitary service. Because of this fee, they do not hesitate to file such affidavits even when the defendant is an elderly woman. This New York procedure creates an additional strain toward personal service or at least the allegation of personal service, for unless he can see the debtor, the process server is in no position to judge his military or civilian status.[4] Many of these variations in the rules have a significant bearing on the *method* of service, but there is a prior topic to be considered—whether service, regardless of method, is made at all.

City Variations in Rate of Service

The New York system has been widely criticized for stimulating "sewer service," a term that refers to summonses being thrown away (down the sewer) rather than served, and false affidavits of service being signed

---

[4]In many instances, the process server bases his affidavit of nonmilitary service on communications with the debtor's neighbors. But even this procedure involves a visit to the debtor's neighborhood, which some process servers never do.

by unscrupulous process servers and their firms.[5] Regardless of whether service is actually made, the New York system (which at one time or another has been investigated by the State Attorney General's office, the U.S. Attorney's office, and the City of New York's Department of Consumer Affairs) involves other evasions of the law. Various investigations have disclosed that the employees of process-serving firms sign large numbers of summonses in blank. These men come only once a week to collect summonses for their territory and phone in the results of their efforts each day. The central office then fills out the affidavits signed in blank and someone in the central office with the authority to do so notarizes them, thereby committing perjury. This illegal shortcut both speeds up the process of filing suit (no small matter when several creditors may be competing to collect from the same debtor) and saves the process server the expense of making frequent trips to the central office.[6]

As this suggests, the violation of the debtor's right of notification is much more likely to occur in New York than in Chicago or Detroit.[7] The data show this to be so. Service of process was most effective in Detroit, as 84 percent of the sampled debtors in that city reported that they received the summons and complaint. In Chicago, 71 percent said they had been served, but in New York, only a bare majority, 54 percent, reported receiving the summons. Even though some respondents may have wittingly or unwittingly reported incorrectly on this issue, such errors only affect the absolute percentages for each city and would in no way undermine the sharp intercity differences found.[8]

[5]For a detailed account of "sewer service," see Frank M. Tuerkheimer, "Service of Process in New York City: A Proposed End to Unregulated Criminality," 72 Colum. L. Rev. 847 (1972).

[6]The United States Attorney's office in the Southern District of New York successfully prosecuted several process servers for "sewer service" under the Civil Rights Act. See *United States v. Barr*, 295 F. Sup. 889 (N.Y.S.D. 1969). One of the men convicted in these cases admitted that he never served a summons outside Brooklyn, his base of operations, but the U.S. Attorney's office found a number of affidavits of service filed against debtors in other boroughs bearing this man's signature. This provides some indication of the callous attitude of the process-serving firms. They do not even bother to match the signed-in-advance affidavits with debtors who could have been served by the process server. Thus, every debtor outside of Brooklyn who was sued on the basis of a summons signed by this man was denied due process. The U.S. Attorney's office could find many of these cases by going through the files. Yet it would be powerless to take action against the creditors, for each of the innumerable creditors would have to be made the object of a separate legal action. This condition thus differs from a class action in which a large number of persons similarly situated join forces to sue a single defendant.

[7]Forty-two Detroit cases are omitted from this analysis. Thirty-eight are replevin actions in which the plaintiff is seeking to repossess goods, a process that does not involve advance notification. A writ is left with the debtor at the time of repossession informing him that he has 14 days in which to challenge the plaintiff's right to the goods and have them returned to him. The other four are cases in which the process server was unable to make service.

[8]For further elaboration of this point, see Appendix B. To refresh the debtor's memory on this matter of service, the respondent was shown a standard summons and complaint form and asked whether he had ever received such a document.

Note on Debtor's Awareness of the Suit

In all three cities combined, 29 percent of the debtors claimed that they were never served with a summons. How then, if at all, did these debtors find out about the legal action against them? In earlier research we found that some debtors learned about the law suit only when their employers told them about the garnishment order, and then it was often too late to save their jobs, much less defend their legal rights in court.[9] Table 11.1 shows the distribution of debtors in each city according to how they learned that they were being sued.

Table 11.1 / How Debtor First Learned of Suit, by City (percent)

source	Chicago	Detroit	New York	three-city total
Summons	71	84	54	72
Employer	12	5	13	10
Creditor	5	3	11	6
Notice of default judgment	—	—	5	2
Other	2	1	6	2
Unaware of suit	11	7	12	9
Total percent	101	100	101	101
N	(311)	(395)	(332)	(1,038)

When debtors do not learn about the suit from the summons, they are most likely to learn about it from their employer in connection with a garnishment notice. This turns out to be true for 10 percent of the debtors in the aggregate and for a somewhat higher proportion in Chicago and New York. Perhaps the most striking finding in Table 11.1 is that almost 1 in every 10 (9 percent) had no idea that they were being sued until told so by the interviewer, although they were aware of some problem with the creditor designated by the interviewer. Such debtors were most common in New York, 12 percent, but Chicago virtually matched this percentage (11 percent). The Detroit debtors, no doubt because of the more effective system of notification in that city, were most likely to know that they had been sued. (These debtors unaware of the suit may be persons who had worked out settlements with their creditors, or they may be persons removed from the labor market and thus able to escape garnishment proceedings against them.)

Attributes of Debtors and Service of Process

Although service of process is a constitutional right of all Americans, a substantial minority of delinquent debtors are denied this right. To

---

[9]See David Caplovitz, "The Other Side of the Poverty Problem," *Challenge Magazine*, Sept.–Oct. 1965, V. 14, No. 1, pp. 12–15.

what extent is denial of due process linked to characteristics of the debtors?

For various reasons, one might suppose that the ethnic minorities and the poor receive poorer service from the judicial system than the whites and the more well-to-do. But on the matter of service of process, the ethnic and income differences in each city are rather slight, and only in New York, with respect mainly to Puerto Ricans, does a pattern of discrimination seem to be at work. In Chicago, 75 percent of the whites and 70 percent of the blacks were served with the summons and in Detroit an equally small difference is found, 88 percent for the whites and 83 percent for the blacks. But in New York 66 percent of the whites, compared with 56 percent of the blacks and only 37 percent of the Puerto Ricans, said they received a summons. Perhaps this reflects the process server's notion that persons of Spanish surnames, as more recent migrants to New York and handicapped by a language barrier, are ideal targets for sewer service. But it could also be that Puerto Ricans are less familiar with legal documents and more likely to forget that they were served. The debtor's income is also only slightly related to service of process. In Chicago, the gap between those earning less than $4,000 and those earning over $8,000 is only five percentage points: in Detroit, the gap is 9 percentage points (79 percent compared with 88 percent) and in New York, the pattern is curvilinear, with those of moderate income being somewhat more likely to have been served than those of either low or relatively high income. In short, income and ethnicity, characteristics that we have found to be related to many aspects of the case, show only weak relationships to service of process. But even these small differences are provocative. Why should any differences exist between whites and blacks, rich and poor, with regard to service of process? One answer is that the poor and minority groups live in the more squalid sections of the city, areas that process servers are reluctant to enter. The data permit a crude test of this hypothesis. The interviewers were asked to rate the debtor's neighborhood as "good," "fair," or "poor." From the distribution of the cases it would seem that the interviewers equated "fair" with average, "good" with above average, and "poor" with below average, for 28 percent of the debtors were designated as living in "good" neighborhoods, 47 percent were placed in the "fair" category, and 25 percent were listed as living in poor neighborhoods. Table 11.2 shows how quality of neighborhood affects notification within each city.

Table 11.2 / Percentage Receiving Summons
by Quality of Neighborhood

quality of neighborhood	Chicago		Detroit		New York		three-city total	
Good	73	(84)	92	(104)	66	(83)	79	(271)
Fair	72	(130)	86	(189)	53	(157)	75	(456)
Poor	66	(86)	73	(94)	52	(73)	66	(253)

From the last column, showing the aggregate of all three cities, we see that there is some merit to the quality-of-neighborhood hypothesis. As neighborhoods shift from "good" to "fair" to "poor" the proportion of debtors who are served decreases. This pattern is particularly evident in Detroit, somewhat less so in New York, and least clear in Chicago, where the good and poor neighborhoods are separated by only seven percentage points. Moreover, in Chicago, the gap is between the fair and the poor neighborhood, whereas in New York the gap appears between the good and the fair.

Quality of neighborhood is not the only attribute of the physical environment affecting service of process. The debtor's type of dwelling unit is another. Those who lived in a one-family house were more likely to have been served than those living in apartment houses in Chicago and New York, but not in Detroit (Table 11.3). Several factors account no doubt for the pattern in Chicago and New York shown in Table 11.3. In many apartment houses the process server must climb stairs, and in run-down apartment houses it is not always clear who lives in which apartment. The base figures of the table show that the great majority of the Chicago and New York debtors live in apartment houses; the reverse is true in Detroit. This may well explain why dwelling unit is not related to service in Detroit. Since most debtors are of lower income, we can assume that the apartment houses in Chicago and New York tend to be more run-down buildings in lower income areas. But in Detroit the single dwelling unit tends to be typical of the relatively poor, and these buildings may be as uninviting to process servers as the apartment houses in Chicago and New York.

Table 11.3 / Percentage Receiving Summons by Type of Dwelling Unit within Each City

type of dwelling unit	Chicago		Detroit		New York	
Single family house	80	(93)	84	(307)	75	(98)
Apartment house	65	(206)	86	(80)	46	(223)

Type of Plaintiff and Service of Process

To the extent that attributes of debtors influenced service of process, they did so presumably by strengthening or weakening the process server's resolve to carry out proper notification. On what grounds might type of plaintiff be related to service of process? In Chicago and Detroit, where process serving is carried out by the court, it is hard to imagine that any such connection exists. In these cities, the plaintiffs have no control over the service of process and the record of one type of plaintiff in comparison with another should reflect chance factors rather than the policy of particular types of plaintiffs. But type of plaintiff might well be related to process serving in New York, for in that city plaintiffs choose their process servers and sophisticated observers of the scene are convinced that the plaintiffs can control the adequacy of service by hiring one rather than another process-serving firm. The data on hand lend some credence to these expected intercity differences. In Chicago and Detroit, the less reputable plaintiffs, as judged by the measure of transaction deception dealt with in chapter 3, are as likely as the more reputable plaintiffs to score high on service of process. In Chicago, some 71 percent of all defendants receive a summons. General retailers, banks, and finance companies have rates slightly higher than this average, whereas automobile dealer plaintiffs have the highest rate of service (92 percent). Below average in Chicago are small loan companies and low-income retailers, and direct sellers are exactly at the average. A comparable helter-skelter pattern is found in Detroit. In that city 84 percent of the debtors were served with summonses. Credit unions, general retailers, finance companies, and small loan companies all exceed this average, whereas banks and direct sellers fall below it. Thus the types of plaintiffs with good records of service vary from Chicago to Detroit, and whether a type of plaintiff in these cities has a good or bad record is not at all related to the reputation of the type.

In New York, where the plaintiff does have some control over the service of process, the adequacy of service is more closely related to the reputations of the types of plaintiffs. General retailers and banks lead all other types of plaintiffs in getting summonses to their default-debtors, 72 and 64 percent, respectively. Direct sellers, the most unethical type of seller, do much better than expected in New York, as their record for service of process approaches the average (53 percent). Below average in New York are low-income retailers, automobile dealers, small loan companies, and finance companies.

The control that plaintiffs have over service of process in New York becomes evident when we compare the records of the three most frequent plaintiffs in New York, a finance company, a bank, and a direct seller, with those of other firms of their type in New York. These data are shown in Table 11.4. From the first column we learn that different firms

Table 11.4 / Percentage Receiving Summons from Specific Plaintiffs in New York, Compared with Record of Other Plaintiffs of the Same Type

	percentage served by particular New York plaintiff	percentage served by similar plaintiffs in New York
Bank (Citybank)	57 (35)	69 (48)
Direct seller (Trademark Jeweler)	40 (25)	70 (20)
Finance co. (Big City Credit)	32 (50)	52 (27)

in the same city have different performance records. The bank is almost twice as likely to reach its debtors in default as is the finance company. But of greater interest is the comparison of the performance of specific plaintiffs shown in the first column with that of the general class of such plaintiffs shown in the second. In all three instances the frequent plaintiffs have a far worse record of service than other firms of their type. Although the bank's record is better than that of the other two frequent plaintiffs in New York, it is well below that of the other New York banks combined. Trademark Jeweler, the firm that accounts for more than one half of the direct-seller cases in New York, has a far worse record than that of the other New York direct sellers. Big City Credit, a Long Island firm that invariably filed its suits in the Manhattan Civil Court at the time of our survey, has by far the poorest record of service of the three New York plaintiffs, one well below that of other New York finance companies. The patterns in Table 11.4 indicate that the firms that resort to the courts most frequently to collect their debts are also the firms most careless about the constitutional rights of their debtors. They would seem to be the firms employing process servers who are inclined toward sewer service. Such below-average performances regarding notification may well be essential to the mass production of court collections. Or, put another way, firms that have high default rates and rely heavily on the courts to collect their debts are likely to be sufficiently unscrupulous as to encourage sewer service.

METHOD OF SERVICE

Method of service is another aspect of the notification process that bears examination. As noted, the law in all three jurisdictions specifies that the process server must try to make personal service, but in Chicago and Detroit, substitute service can easily be made by giving the summons to any adult in the household and then mailing a copy to the debtor. In New York the law was much more strict regarding personal service. The process server was required to make several attempts at personal service on different dates before substitute service was permitted. Moreover, New York law, unlike that in the other jurisdictions, provides two additional pressures toward personal service: the shorter time span before a default judgment can be claimed, and the requirmement that the process server vouch for the debtor's civilian status. For all these reasons, pressures for personal service have been much greater in New York than in Chicago and Detroit, pressures that might well lead process servers in that city to perjure themselves regarding method of service.

The issue of method of service offers one of the rare opportunities in social research for confronting the response or testimony of one party to an event with that of another. All the debtors in our sample who reported receiving notice were asked about the method of delivery. We also examined the court files in which the sworn affidavit of the process server indicated the method of service he employed. The testimonies of the process servers and the defendants could thus be compared. One might question the veracity of the defendants on the matter of whether they were served at all (since to answer this query in the negative would place those who failed to show up in court in a more favorable light), but there is no reason to suspect the reports of those who admit to being served concerning how they were served. On the other hand, a good case can be made for process servers, especially in New York, having a vested interest in one form of service rather than another—that is, personal service, which was virtually required by state law. If either of these "witnesses" is under pressure to falsify the event, it is much more likely to be the process server than the defendant.

Table 11.5 permits comparison of the responses of the debtors and those of process servers regarding method of service in each city. With the exception of New York, the table is limited to cases in which the debtor admits that he was served, a group that constitutes 84 percent of the Detroit debtors and 71 percent of those in Chicago. In New York, because of the large number who claimed that they were never served, we show two sets of figures for the process servers, one referring to the cases in which the debtor was served and the other to instances in which he was not. The table ignores various forms of substitute service, distinguishing all of them from personal service.[10]

The dramatic finding in Table 11.5 is that based on the sworn affidavits of the New York process servers. Whereas only 20 percent of the New York debtors who were served at all reported personal service (a figure not too different from the Chicago rate), fully 92 percent of these cases were recorded as personal service by the process servers. Among the substantial number of New York debtors who were never served, the rate of purported personal service based on the testimony of the process server is slightly higher (94 percent). Since there is no reason to assume that the New York process servers, who are private citizens operating

[10]For example, substitute service in Chicago can be made at the debtor's place of work as well as at his home. Of the substitute services in that city (72 percent of the total) 29 percent were served on the debtor's employer. Also, the category of substitute service in the debtor columns of Table 11.5 covers a multitude of responses. In Chicago and New York debtors who were not served personally were much more likely to learn of the suit through the summons sent in the mail than from the person to whom substitute service was presumably made. Only in Detroit were debtors more likely to learn of the suit from another household member than from a summons received in the mail (24 compared with 12 percent), indicating that the Detroit process servers made greater efforts at personal service and more frequently visited the debtor's home than did process servers in the other cities. Moreover, in each city, particularly in New York, some of the debtors claimed that the summons had merely been slipped under the door, in clear violation of the rules of substitute service (9 percent of those served in Chicago and Detroit gave this response compared with 16 percent in New York).

Table 11.5 / Method of Service of Process as Reported by
Debtor and Process Server in Each City (percent)

method of service	Chicago		Detroit		New York		
						process server	
	debtor	process server	debtor	process server	debtor	served	not served
Personal service	23	28	54	39	20	92	94
Substitute service	77	72	46	61	80	8	6
Total percent	100	100	100	100	100	100	100
N^a	(214)	(216)	(331)	(332)	(169)	(168)	(145)

[a] That the number of cases in the columns for each city do not precisely match is due to "no answer's," missing files, or missing affidavits of service.

in a profit market, are much more talented at making personal service than their counterparts in the other cities, the safest conclusion is that New York process servers claim personal service when in fact they have either thrown the summons away or have engaged in substitute service. The pressures on them to lie have already been identified. They are, in brief, the stricter rule then in effect regarding personal service, the shorter period of time in which a default judgment can be claimed in instances of personal service, and the need to verify the nonmilitary status of the defendant. Instead of ensuring greater protection to the debtor, these procedural rules have the opposite consequence of pressuring the process server to evade them, thereby undermining the constitutional rights of New York debtors.

RESPONDING TO THE SUMMONS

The debtor who has been served with notice is, of course, free not to respond, in which case he subjects himself to a default judgment. He may not respond because he feels that he has no valid defense or for a host of other reasons soon to be examined. But it is important to note that responding to a summons is by no means the same as having a day in court and, in fact, is no guarantee against a default judgment. Rather it represents but the first stage in a process that may eventuate in a trial before a judge.

The summons informs the debtor that he must appear in court within a specified period of time or on or before a specific date in order to file an answer to the plaintiff's complaint against him. The answer consists of a written document setting forth the debtor's reasons for not paying the debt. The process of filing an answer varied somewhat among the three cities at the time of the survey in 1967. It was perhaps most complicated in Chicago. If the debt was less than $200, the Chicago debtor who appeared on the due date was immediately assigned a trial date and was not required to file a written answer. But if the debt was greater than $200, the debtor who responded was given three copies of a standard answer form. He was told to return one copy to the court within 10 days, to mail another copy to the creditor's attorney, and to keep one copy for himself. He was then assigned a date three weeks hence to appear in the answer call room, at which time he would learn the date that his case was set for trial. If adhered to strictly, the Chicago procedure in debts over $200 could involve three appearances *before* the trial, one on the date specified in the summons to receive the answer form, another within the next 10 days, a third three weeks later to learn about the trial date. Apparently the practice in Chicago, at least in cases where the debtor was represented by a lawyer, was to ignore the 10-day request for the answer and to file the answer on the twenty-first day, thus eliminating one of the three steps.[11]

In both Detroit and New York, the procedure for filing an answer was and is rather simple. When the debtor appears in court with his summons, he is given a standard form to fill out. The clerk will help him fill it out or may even fill it out for him. The answer is thus filed at the time the defendant appears. Moreover, the defendant does not have the responsibility of sending a copy of his answer to the plaintiff's attorney, the theory being that the latter can always come to court and read the answer once he receives the notice of the trial.

In each jurisdiction, filing an answer, whatever its merits, requires the court clerk to schedule a trial (which the plaintiff's attorney can avoid by moving for a summary judgment or by requesting postponements, discovery proceedings, and so on). But, in fact, the clerks in each jurisdiction are likely to exercise some discretion. We know this to be true in New York, where some "answer" clerks were interviewed. They told us that when the debtor does not have a legitimate answer, they advise him not to file and risk the burden of further court costs. The question arises as to how the clerks define a legitimate answer. They apparently have no difficulty with an answer involving violations of express or implied warranties, but it is not clear what advice they give when the debtor claims that he was misled about the price or other terms of the sale. Moreover, the New York clerks told us that they do not regard such reasons for default as "I lost my job" or "I was sick" or "The price was too high" valid defenses, even though under the emerging doctrine of "unconscionability" some merit might be found in such

---

[11]Since 1967, Illinois law has simplified its answer process in two respects. First, the $200 ceiling for a verbal answer and immediate trial date has been raised to $1,000. For cases above this amount, the debtor is now permitted to file an answer within 10 days of the summons and at that time is assigned a trial date. The entire answer call room procedure has been eliminated.

answers. In short, motivated by the desire to save the debtor–defendant additional court costs (and perhaps to avoid crowding the court calendar with frivolous cases), the clerks exceed their authority and usurp some of that of a judge. Such "discretionary justice" has been well documented in the criminal area in studies of the police.[12] We now see that it also exists in civil law, with court clerks as the agents of discretionary justice.

Whatever the procedure for filing an answer, we are not now concerned with the number of answers actually filed but rather with the number of debtors who responded to the summons and presumably tried to file an answer.[13] All the debtors who were served were asked:

> Did you or someone representing you go to court when you got the summons?

The wording of the question allowed for a representative of the debtor, such as a lawyer, to appear in court for him. The direct question of whether the debtor did, in fact, respond to the summons suffers from the same possibilities of respondent error or bias as the question of whether a summons was received. But it is not immediately clear what direction such bias might take. Presumably, if the debtor was ready to admit being served, he might be under pressure to admit that he answered even when he did not. But to falsify a response to the summons would place additional strains on the debtor, for he would then have to explain why the outcome was not more favorable (for, as we shall see, the outcome is almost invariably unfavorable to the debtor). Further room for error is introduced by the fact that the person being interviewed was sometimes the spouse of the debtor, who may have been misled about the debtor's behavior. Moreover, some debtors may have thought that their representatives did appear in court when they did not. In short, there are numerous reasons for questioning the validity of the absolute percentages based on the reports of our respondents.

In one of the three cities, Chicago, it is actually possible to determine the extent of reported error on this question. As noted, any Chicago defendant who answered the summons by the required date was automatically assigned either to a trial at a future date (if his debt was under $200) or to the answer call room (if his debt was above $200), where at a later time he would be assigned a trial date. The clerks manning the confirmation-of-judgment book in Chicago presumably exercised no discretion whatsoever. If the summons was served and the debtor did not appear, his case was stamped "ex parte judgment confirmed," the

---

[12]See, for example, Jerome H. Skolnick, *Justice without Trial: Law Enforcement in a Democratic Society* (New York: John Wiley & Sons, Inc., 1966).

[13]The New York clerks that we spoke to claimed that about one of every three or four persons who respond do not have legitimate answers and are discouraged from filing.

Chicago variant of a default judgment. If he did appear, his case was set down for either the answer call room or for trial. It turns out that 66 Chicago debtors responded to the summons according to the confirmation book, but 79 Chicago debtors told us that either they themselves or some representative of theirs answered the summons. The "true" figure comes to 30 percent of those who received the summons; the reported figure is 36 percent. This discrepancy of six percentage points presumably represents respondent error.[14] But, as in the previous analysis, we are less interested in the absolute percentages (although they have considerable importance as crude estimates of the reality) than we are in the differences among the three cities under study. For this purpose we shall deal with the debtors' reports on whether or not they answered the summons.

We have seen that New York lags far behind Chicago and Detroit when it comes to service of process, but improper service turns out to be only the tip of the iceberg. Upon further examination, the breakdown of the New York judicial system in consumer actions is even more complete than the figures on service imply. Even those New York debtors who are served hardly ever show up in court, only 4 percent, in marked contrast with the substantial minorities in Chicago, 36 percent, and Detroit, 34 percent.[15]

The 4 percent in New York represents a mere 8 persons of the 178 who claimed they received a summons. How is the incredibly poor record for appearances in New York to be explained? Those who said they did not go to court were asked to explain why. Surprisingly, this "reason" question sheds little light on the very low rate of appearances in New York. The kinds of reasons offered were quite varied, but they did not differ substantially from city to city. Table 11.6 shows the categories with the largest frequencies as well as those of particular interest.

By far the most common reason for not appearing in court in each jurisdiction (ranging from one third of the Chicago cases to one fifth of the New York cases) is that the debtor, presumably stimulated by the initiation of the law suit, has arranged for some kind of settlement with the creditor's attorney. These debtors are of the impression, often mistaken, that the court action has been discontinued. The next two categories are closely related to the first in that the debtor was either under the impression that the debt had been settled and that therefore the court action was no longer appropriate, or he did not appear on the advice of either his own attorney or the lawyer for the defendant

---

[14]It is possible that in a few of these cases the debtor successfully had his judgment reopened.

[15]On the basis of the entire sample, including those who claim they were not served, the response rate comes to 25 percent in Chicago, 26 percent in Detroit, and 2 percent in New York.

Table 11.6 / Reasons for Not Appearing in Court in Response to the Summons, by City (percent)

	Chicago	Detroit	New York
Tried to settle and thought court action was discontinued	33	28	21
Advised not to go to court by plaintiff's attorney or own attorney	13	13	9
Thought debt settled and did not owe more money	5	6	10
Unable to go; sick or could not afford loss of day's pay	16	8	12
No particular reason; forgot	10	14	11
Couldn't pay; no defense	7	14	8
Received summons too late to go to court	4	3	3
Did not know that he was supposed to go to court	3 } 4	6 } 7	15 } 19
Afraid to go to court	1 }	1 }	4 }
Total percent [a]	92	93	93

[a] The percentages do not total 100 because we have omitted a miscellaneous category as well as the "no answer" cases.

(more typically the latter). These cases, too, imply that some process of negotiation or settlement was going on outside of court which would make a court appearance unnecessary. These three categories account for 40 to 50 percent of the "no show" cases. The group of debtors who were unable to appear either because of illness or fear of losing a day's work is perhaps not as large as might have been expected, ranging from 8 percent in Detroit to 16 percent in Chicago.[16] Of considerable significance are the figures for the "no defense" category. A number of judges in these courts are well aware of the extraordinarily high proportion of default judgments in consumer actions (a topic discussed later in this chapter), but they are not alarmed, for they reason that this indicates merely that the debtor knows he is at fault and sees no point of risking further court costs by making an appearance and asking for a trial.[17] As these data show, fewer than 10 percent of the Chicago and New

[16]These courts are open from 9 A.M. to 5 P.M., hours when most debtors are at work. Were all debtors represented by lawyers, the assumption underlying the court's hours, this would be appropriate, but as we shall see, most debtors do not have lawyers. The inconvenience factor is probably greater than the figures in Table 11.6 indicate.

[17]See, for example, the testimony of Judge Gittelson, the former administrator of the New York City Court, before the New York State Senate Committee on Codes, hearings on garnishment laws, July 10, 1969.

York debtors who did not appear gave such a reason, and in Detroit the figure is only 14 percent. Obviously, this popular theory is not supported by the reasons offered spontaneously by the debtors to explain their nonappearance. Just as we found that some consumers got into trouble because they forgot to pay their bills, so we find that this brand of irresponsibility explains why some failed to answer the summons. Approximately 10 percent in each jurisdiction (a somewhat higher proportion in Detroit, 14 percent) answered that there was no particular reason or that they simply forgot.

Although the types of reasons reviewed so far show some intercity variation, they do not shed much light on New York's very poor record for appearances. But the last two categories of Table 11.6 provide one clue to that city's poor record. Fifteen percent of the New York debtors, a substantially higher proportion than in the other two cities, told us that they did not know that they were supposed to appear in court, that, in short, they did not understand the meaning of the summons. Moreover, 4 percent of the "no show" New York cases reported that they were afraid to appear in court. This figure takes on significance only when compared with the rate of such fear in the other cities—1 percent. These two categories of reasons conjure up the debtor who is confused by the intricacies of urban life, the new migrant from a more traditionalistic culture. In New York, such persons are apt to be Puerto Ricans who suffer a language barrier. That some New York debtors did not know that they were supposed to appear in court might be explained by their inability to read the summons, which, until very recently, was printed only in English. The last two categories account for about one fifth of the reasons for nonappearance in New York, a rate much higher than in the other cities. But the ignorance–fear–confusion hypothesis explains only part of the "no show" phenomenon in New York. It is most appropriate for the Puerto Rican debtors, but they constitute only one fourth of the sample, and obviously not all of them were unassimilated newcomers.

More significant reasons for the failure of New York debtors to respond are not revealed by their volunteered explanations. Among these is the widespread abuse of the rules of venue. Unlike the other three cities in our sample, New York encompasses five counties, each of which has its own branch of the city's civil court in which these actions are brought. In Chicago and Detroit, the chances are quite high that both the debtor and the creditor reside within the jurisdiction of the court. This is not so in New York. Although we sampled cases only from the New York County Court, the county corresponding to Manhattan, only 25 percent of the New York default-debtors lived in Manhattan. The rest lived in the other boroughs or outside the city. (Some 22 New York debtors, 7 percent of the sample, lived outside the city limits.) The venue rule permits actions to be brought either in the county of the defendant's residence or in that of the plaintiff. This rule is biased against the debtor, for in many instances the sale takes place at the debtor's home, although the creditor is located in a distant borough or outside the city. In such cases, it is permissible for the creditors to bring the suit in the counties where their businesses are located even though the debtors may never have been there.[18] Although all the suits were brought in Manhattan's court, only 55 percent of the plaintiffs were located in Manhattan. Cases in which either the defendant or the plaintiff resided in Manhattan came to 66 percent of the sample, leaving some 34 percent in which the overly generous rule of venue was clearly violated. The callous nature of this system is captured in the reply of Trademark Jeweler's attorney to a reporter who asked him why he files the cases of this Brooklyn firm, whose customers reside for the most part in Brooklyn, in the Manhattan court: "Because that's the court nearest my office."[19] Thus the victims of Trademark Jeweler's confidence game are sued in the Manhattan court because it happens to employ a Manhattan attorney. Perhaps another reason is that the attorney knows that this will make it more difficult for the defendant to respond to the summons.

That fully three fourths of the New York debtors did not live in the same borough in which they were being sued would appear to be a factor in the failure of all but a handful to answer the summons, although virtually none of the debtors offered as a reason for their nonappearance their not knowing where the court was located, how to get to it, or the trip being too difficult.

A comparison of the summonses used in Chicago, Detroit, and New York calls attention to yet another possible reason for the failure of New York debtors to respond. In both language and typeface, the New York summons is much more difficult to understand than those used in Chicago and Detroit. In the latter cities, key parts of the summons appear in large boldface type, set off from other parts, whereas in New York, the essential points are lost in legal verbiage. Moreover, in both Chicago and Detroit, the time for responses is the same whether personal or substitute service was made and therefore there is no ambiguity as to when the debtor should respond. In contrast, the New York summons tries to explain the difference in response time according to method of service.

[18]For example, we once interviewed a Harlem woman who bought a deep freezer from a door-to-door salesman employed by a firm in New Rochelle. She received a summons informing her to appear at the Westchester County Court, a summons that did not even indicate the city in which this court was located.

[19]See Craig Karpel, "Ghetto Fraud on the Installment Plan," in *New York Magazine,* May 26 and June 2, 1969.

These differences are apparent when the actual language that appears on the summonses is examined. In all three cities, the summonses are headed by the name of the court in which they are issued, followed by the names and addresses of the plaintiff, defendant, and plaintiff's attorney, the date at which the summons was issued or served, and, in Chicago and Detroit, the signature of the court clerk. (This does not appear on the New York summons because service of summons is not a court responsibility in New York.) For present purposes, the critical parts of these summonses are their communications addressed to the defendants. In Chicago, the language of the summons differed according to whether the suit was an open one or one based on a confession-of-judgment contract. Since the Chicago sample was based exclusively on the confirmation-of-judgment book, the appropriate summons is the one served on debtors who had signed confession-of-judgment contracts. This document contains the following message for the defendant:

> *to each defendant:*
>
> YOU ARE SUMMONED and required either:
>
> 1. To appear in person in the office of the Clerk of this Court in Room No. 602 in the Chicago Civic Center, Chicago, Illinois, at 2 o'clock P.M., on————, 19—, and file your appearance in writing with the clerk of said Court, *or*
> 2. To cause your appearance in writing to be filed in said action by yourself or attorney.
>
> **If you do not appear or cause your appearance to be filed, the judgment by confession for $———— and costs entered against you on ————, 19—, may be confirmed.**

It should be noted that in this summons for a confirmation of judgment the debtor is provided with a date (and even a particular hour) when he must appear in order to challenge the judgment. The penalty for not appearing is communicated to the debtor in large boldface type set off from the rest of the message. The message to the defendant on the Detroit summons also appears in large boldface type.

> NOTICE TO THE DEFENDANT
>
> **If you care to contest this case, you or an attorney of your choice must appear and file a plea or answer in the clerk's office, Room 1101, City County Building, within fifteen (15) days after date of service of this summons upon you. If you do not, the plaintiff can take judgment against you for the amount claimed in the attached statement.**

Like the Chicago summons, the critical information appears in large boldface type.

In contrast, the messages directed to the defendant in the New York summons read as follows:

YOU ARE HEREBY SUMMONED to appear in the Civil Court of the City of New York, County of New York, at the office of the Clerk of the said court at 111 Centre Street in the County of New York, City and State of New York, within the time period provided by law as noted below to make answer to the complaint which is annexed hereto; upon your failure to answer, judgment will be taken against you for the relief demanded in the complaint, together with the costs of this action.

Dated, New York, N.Y.———196—

Plaintiff's Address   [Name and Address of
                                                                    Plaintiff's Attorney]

Note: The law provides that:
   (a) If this summons is served by its delivery to you personally within the City of New York, you must appear and answer within TEN days after such service; *or*
   (b) If this summons is served by delivery to any person other than you personally, or is served outside the City of New York, *or by publication, or by any means other than personal delivery to you within the City of New York,* you are allowed THIRTY days after the proof of service thereof is filed with the Clerk of this Court within which to appear and answer.

The communications to the debtor–defendant in this summons are contained in but three sentences or parts, the first of which contains 91 words, the second, about personal service, 29 words, and the third, about substitute service, 67 words. (Actually the second and third constitute a single sentence.) The long first sentence contains three messages: first, it tells the debtor that he is being summoned to court; second, it tells him the address of the court; and third it tells him that if he fails to appear, he will be subjected to a default judgment for the "relief demanded in the complaint." Unlike the summonses in Chicago and Detroit, these vital messages all appear in the same lowercase typeface within a single sentence. It talks about "the time period provided by law as noted below," about the complaint "which is annexed hereto," and about "relief demanded in the complaint, together with the costs of this action." A summons so designed is hardly apt to communicate with the typical debtor, who tends to be rather poorly educated; moreover, it falls far short of the clarity of the summonses in the other two cities.

   One additional irony regarding the New York summons should be noted. Its cumbersome language notwithstanding, it does try to tell the debtor who received substitute service that he has up to 30 days in which to respond, whereas those served personally must respond within 10 days.[20] But we know that New York process servers almost always claim

_____

[20]A further aspect of the debtor's confusion stems from the fact that the summonses are usually stamped with the irrelevant date of issuance, not the date of delivery. The discrepancy may be so great that the debtor, when confronted with the date on the summons, may assume that it is too late to respond.

personal service, when, in fact, only about one fifth of those served at all are served personally. Thus, if the typical New York debtor could understand the abstruse language of the summons and made his appearance after the tenth day, he would more than likely find that he was the victim of a default judgment. Without the assistance of an attorney, there is little that the debtor can do to rectify such an injustice, for it is a matter of his word against that of the process server. Although New York law attempts to give greater protection to the debtor not served personally, it actually has the opposite effect. It encourages such a defendant to respond too late to protect his rights in the law suit.

Apart from the reasons the debtors themselves offered for their nonappearance, we have identified two "structural" factors that might account for the poor showing of the New York judicial system: the venue issue, and the complicated, hard-to-understand summons form.[21] To these, we may add a third, the location of the court house. The Chicago summons directs the debtor to a particular room in a particular building, the Chicago Civic Center, in downtown Chicago. This building has become such a landmark and its location is so central to the city that there is hardly a Chicago resident not familiar with it. The Court of Common Pleas in Detroit is also located in the center of the downtown section of the city. But this is not true of the Civil Court of the City of New York, County of New York (Manhattan). The New York summons provides an address: 111 Centre Street. This address is about three miles from the center of New York's downtown section, Times Square. The numerical grid system in Manhattan makes it quite easy for a stranger to get around most sections. But the courthouses of Manhattan as well as City Hall are located in the old section of the city, the very tip of lower Manhattan, where the streets have names rather than numbers. This part of New York is well known to the vast numbers of middle-class persons who work on Wall Street, or in the city's large banks or for local government. But the average Harlem or Bedford-Stuyvesant or East Bronx resident rarely, if ever, has occasion to visit this area. In fact, he is likely to know it only if he has had brushes with the law, for this is where the criminal courts are located. For the typical resident of a low-income neighborhood in New York, 111 Centre Street is not only a mysterious address, but it is far removed from the debtor's residence. Although we have no way of proving it, for we did not ask the New

[21]The contrast between what we have called "structural" reasons and the reasons that the debtors themselves offered for their nonappearance calls attention to a methodological dispute that still remains unresolved. The historians of methodology in the social sciences might well note this discussion, for it bears on the relative merits of "reason analysis," in which the researcher allows the actors to explain their behavior in terms of an exhaustive scheme of possible reasons provided by the researcher, and "correlational analysis," in which the researcher infers causes of social phenomena through his statistical manipulations of the data. For a discussion of this debate and a less than satisfactory resolution, see Harry Kalvin and Hans Zeisel, *The American Jury* (Boston: Little, Brown and Company, 1966), chap. 7.

York debtors if they knew where 111 Centre Street is, it would seem that the remote location of the New York courthouse is another important reason for the low answer rate in that city.

Postscript on New York

In the opening chapter we noted that this study provides a photograph of the consumer credit system and its breakdowns as of 1967. The system has been changing at an ever-increasing rate. Thus the procedural rules in effect in 1967 were modified in certain respects by the fall of 1970. Oddly enough, the findings of this research have played some role in the procedural changes that have been instituted. Some of the findings of this chapter have been presented in public speeches, in testimony before legislative bodies, and in informal gatherings of consumer advocates. The data on the violation of venue reached the ears of the new Administrative Judge of the Civil Court, Edward Thompson. He is concerned about the rights of debtors and in the spring of 1970 he called a meeting of the leading collection lawyers and announced to them that henceforth they must file their suits in the county where either the plaintiff or the defendant resides, a ruling that went into effect in mid-June 1970. During the first week, some 1200 summonses were rejected because of violation of venue.[22] In the second week, about 500 summonses were rejected on this ground, and each succeeding week saw fewer and fewer violations, with the result that by mid-September 1970, only about 50 summonses in all five counties were rejected because of improper venue.

It would be misleading, however, to imply that a system can be so easily changed, in this instance by the edict of an administrative judge. Those who have fought for social reform know that battles are not so readily won. And so may be the case with the venue reform instituted by Judge Thompson. In the fall of 1970, Judge Thompson was sued unsuccessfully by the association of collection lawyers, which claimed that the judge has no right to interpret venue in so strict a fashion and in doing so, he is, in essence, making law, a function of the state legislature.

Another change in New York procedure takes cognizance of the large proportion of Spanish-speaking defendants in these actions. A new state law that went into effect September 1, 1970, requires all summonses in consumer credit suits to be printed in both Spanish and English. Still another recent procedural change requires the plaintiff to send notification of a default judgment to the defendant at least seven days before the default judgment can be claimed.[23] In instances of personal service this

[22]In New York the action commences with the filing of the affidavit of service of process.

[23]This can be done by regular mail. The plaintiff must file some proof that he mailed this notice, usually a certificate of mailing that can be purchased at the post office for a very small sum.

has the effect of raising the time for claiming default judgments from 10 to 17 days, and in instances of substitute service, the minimum period for the default judgment is raised from 30 to 37 days. The purpose of this notification process is to offset the widely publicized scandal of sewer service. The theory is that the debtor with a valid defense who was not served will now have the opportunity to appear in court and challenge the judgment.

Even when those opposed to reforms designed to protect the consumer fail to have them rescinded, it is not clear that the reforms have any real impact on the system. Neither the venue ruling nor the Spanish language summons has led to any appreciable increase in responses to summonses. Finally, the notice of default judgment, which has been law for several years, has not led to any rash of reopened judgments. In the concluding chapter we shall consider the issue of potentially meaningful reforms in the system, but it may be noted now that the modifications that have been made to improve the system have had no impact.[24]

Some Correlates of Answering the Summons

We have considered the debtors' own explanations for their not answering the summons and we have examined "structural" factors that may affect response rates even though the debtors were largely unaware of them. Additional reasons for not responding may emerge by comparing those who did with those who did not respond to the summons. Since only eight New Yorkers responded, there is little reason to include that city in the subsequent analysis. The statistical analysis will be limited to the Chicago and Detroit debtors. Virtually the same proportion in these cities responded to the summons (37 and 34 percent) and therefore they will be treated as a single group.

A number of factors might influence a debtor to respond to a summons. Foremost among these, presumably, is his belief in whether he has a valid defense. Debtors who had not settled their debt once they learned about the law suit (24 percent did but the great majority of 76 percent had not) were asked whether there was "a good reason why they should not have to pay." In all cities combined, about half answered "yes" and half answered "no," but in the two cities that concern us in this analysis, the results were 60 percent affirmative answers in Chicago and 41 percent in Detroit. Since the Detroit sample is larger, the aggregate figures for these cities are 48 percent believing that they should not have

---

[24]One reform suggested by the New York City Bar Association's Committee on Consumer Affairs was not adopted by the administrative judge of the civil court of New York City because he feared that it would be too effective. The idea was to have a tear-off answer attached to the summons on which the defendant could enter his defense and request a trial merely by mailing the answer rather than making a personal appearance. Judge Thompson feared that the resulting demand for trials would wreck havoc with his court.

to pay and 52 percent believing that they should. Our expectation was that the 48 percent who believed they should not have to pay would be much more likely to appear in court than the 52 percent who accepted their liability. But the data fail to support this notion. Among the former, 38 percent responded to the summons, and among the latter, 39 percent responded.[25] Contrary to expectation, then, the debtor's sense of injustice does not play a determinant role in his likelihood of responding to the summons.

With the most obvious hypothesis failing to find support from the data, what other factors might influence the debtor's readiness to respond to the summons? We have noted that only in New York is method of service related to the time period in which the debtor may respond. But even in the jurisdictions where this is not so, it might still be argued that personal service results in both an earlier and more firm type of notification than the various forms of substitute service. On this basis we might assume that personal service—the desired form in each jurisdiction—is more likely to result in the debtor's showing up in court. The data support this expectation. Among those who were served personally in Chicago and Detroit, 40 percent appeared in court; among those who received notice through the mail, 35 percent responded; among those who learned of the suit from a household member who had been served, only 30 percent appeared in court, a figure that drops to 27 percent among those who found the summons under their door.

Still another possibility is that the debtor's readiness to respond to the summons is related to the amount of money for which he is being sued. Debtors who are being sued for relatively small sums, for example, less than $100 or $200, may not treat the summons as seriously as those who are being sued for large sums, say in excess of $500. From our review of the court records, we know the exact amount of money for which the debtors were being sued. There is indeed a relationship between the amount of the debt and the debtor's likelihood of answering. The proportion responding to the summons steadily increases from a low of 23 percent when the debt is under $100 to a high of 44 percent when the debt is in excess of $1,000. But perhaps more surprising than this expected pattern is the fact that even when a considerable amount is at stake—sums in excess of $1,000—a majority of the debtors still do not respond, thereby forfeiting their day in court.

As noted, the question of answering included the idea that a representative of the debtor might have responded for him. This directs our attention to the all-important matter of legal representation for debtors in

---

[25]Both percentages are higher than the percentages of those served who showed up in each of these cities, 36 and 34 percent for Chicago and Detroit, respectively. The reason for this discrepancy is the exclusion of debtors who worked out a settlement with the creditor after they received the summons. Most of these people did not show up in court. In short, we are now dealing with the subgroup that did not settle, and their rate of response is higher than that of the group that settled.

default. In all four cities combined, only one in every five debtors enlisted the aid of an attorney. In New York this figure was substantially below average, only 11 percent, whereas in Chicago it was well above average, 32 percent. Later we shall consider this matter of seeking legal help as a problem in its own right, but for the present we are concerned only with the impact of legal representation on the debtor's response to the summons. The importance of legal representation for consumer– defendants is underscored by the fact that those who were represented by attorneys were twice as likely as the others to answer the summons (55 percent compared with 28 percent).

So far we have considered attributes of the case itself in our efforts to understand which debtors respond to the summons. We have not examined such standard attributes of the debtors as their ethnicity or income. On a priori grounds there is no reason to assume that whites or blacks will be more likely to respond to the summons. (The one ethnic group that might be less prone to respond because of its newness to the urban scene, the Puerto Ricans, is excluded from this analysis because the New York debtors have been eliminated.) The data for the two cities show hardly any ethnic differences on this matter, as 37 percent of the whites and 34 percent of the blacks answered the summons, the difference of three percentage points being of no significance. But the absence of an ethnic difference becomes more puzzling when income is considered, for income is strongly related to responding to the summons. Among the relatively poor, only 23 percent claimed to answer the summons; among the middle-income group, 35 percent presumably responded; and among those of high income, 44 percent answered.

Were the amount of debt to be the key factor explaining the income pattern, we would expect that the more well-to-do were being sued for larger amounts than the poor. But this is not the case to any extent among these Chicago and Detroit debtors who received summonses. We find about one third on each income level being sued for under $100, and from 62 to 64 percent being sued for under $500. Only when we reach the highest debt category, over $1,000, is there some difference between the poor and the more well-to-do. But this difference is slight, as some 13 percent of those earning under $4,000 were sued for $1,000 or more, while among those earning over $8,000 this figure rises to 19 percent. This difference is much too small to explain the income pattern, and when income and amount of debt are simultaneously related to answering the summons, we find that both independently affect likelihood of response.

In a similar fashion, having a lawyer does not explain the income pattern; income and having an attorney affect response independently of each other. Why those of higher income are more likely to respond to the summons is not readily explained. We know that it is not because they are more likely to be sued for large amounts, for they are not. Nor is it due to their greater propensity to seek legal counsel, for even when having a lawyer is taken into account, those of higher income are more likely to answer the summons.

FILING AN ANSWER

To make an appearance by the due date entered on the summons is not in itself sufficient to ensure the debtor his day in court. As the summons states, the debtor is invited to court in order to file his answer. As already noted, filing an answer in Chicago for debt in excess of $200 was a rather complicated procedure, and it is at this stage in the legal process that court clerks exercise discretion by encouraging or discouraging debtors from filing answers. All debtors were asked whether papers were filed with the court telling their side of the dispute.[26] These data, along with those for service of process and court appearances in response to the summons, are shown for each city in Table 11.7. The data are presented in two forms. The first part of the table shows participation in the legal process calculated on the basis of all debtors, whereas the second part shows participation in subsequent phases as a function of participation in the earlier phases.

Table 11.7 / Defendant Participation in the Legal Process Prior to Trial, by City (percent)

	Chicago	Detroit	New York	three-city total
Based on all defendants				
Received summons	71	84	54	70
Appeared in court	25	28	2	19
Filed an answer	8	7	1	5
N	(312)	(396)	(332)	(1,040)
Contingent participation				
Appeared in court of those served	37 (212)	34 (332)	4 (178)	28 (722)
Filed an answer of those who appeared	32 (79)	23 (113)	25 (8)	26 (200)

[26]We have seen that on the basis of the court records in Chicago, there is good reason to believe that some respondents claimed a court appearance in response to the summons, when in fact they did not go to court. So, too, the data on filing an answer may be similarly biased. In each city a few debtors claim that papers were filed with the court, even though they deny that a court appearance was made. These cases have been treated as errors and reclassified as *not* having filed answers. The reasons for these errors are similar to those for the misreporting of trials dealt with in the next section.

By reading down the columns of the top of the table, we see a dramatic decline in participation at each stage. Whereas a majority in each jurisdiction were served with summonses (substantial majorities in Chicago and Detroit), only small minorities made court appearances, and in each city answers were rarely filed. The record for New York is far worse than that of the other cities, but even where service of process is good, as in Detroit, only a tiny fraction of the debtors get to file an answer. The second part of the table shows the proportion of debtors who having passed one stage moved on to another. In every instance, only a minority, no more than one third or so in any jurisdiction, reached the next stage. Of those served, no more than 37 percent (Chicago) appeared in court (in New York, only 4 percent did); perhaps even more striking, of those who made a court appearance, no more than one third got to file an answer. In all three cities combined, only about one fourth of those who made appearances filed answers. This result is quite puzzling, for one might assume that those who took the trouble to appear in court would be sure to file an answer telling their side of the dispute. The complexity of the filing process is not a factor, for the filing rate is greatest in Chicago, where the procedure was most complicated. Perhaps many of those who made appearances had no answer but responded only because the summons instructed them to, but it is also likely that many of them felt that they had an answer but were discouraged by the court clerks from filing it. In short, discretion exercised by court clerks is no doubt a factor in the sharp fall off between appearance and filing an answer.

The income of the debtor, the amount in dispute, and having a lawyer were all found to be related to responding to the summons. But neither income nor amount of the debt show any relationship to filing an answer once an appearance is made. The significance of legal help, however, is well demonstrated by the fact that those who had lawyers were much more likely not only to appear, but to file an answer once an appearance was made (43 percent compared with 14 percent). Of course, debtors with strong defenses may have been more likely to hire a lawyer, but it is even more plausible that having professional assistance contributes to the development of defenses and the filing of answers. At the very least, the attorney is not as likely as the layman to be persuaded by a court clerk that a particular defense is not valid.

THE LEGAL OUTCOME OF THE CASE:
THE RARITY OF TRIALS

We have seen that some 5 percent of the Chicago, Detroit, and New York debtors filed answers with the court (all but two of these debtors being located in Chicago or Detroit). One might assume that at least these people had their "day in court" in the sense that their case was heard by a judge. But those familiar with the legal process know that filing an answer in itself is no guarantee of a trial. Answers filed by debtors, especially by those without legal counsel, tend to be easily challenged by the plaintiff's attorney. He is likely to apply for a summary judgment based on the debtor's faulty answer. (It will be recalled that the plaintiff's attorney is always notified of the defendant's answer and is given an opportunity to study it before the trial date.) Faulty answers are quite common, given the holder-in-due course doctrine. Debtors may file answers based on the breach of express or implied warranties on the part of the seller, but this defense has no bearing on a law suit brought by the holder-in-due course. In short, filing an answer is a much broader concept than "having a day in court" in which a judge makes a determination based on the merits of the case. As we shall see, this meaning of a "day in court" rarely occurs in consumer actions, even though a substantial minority of debtors had valid defenses and a number did file answers.

All debtors, regardless of whether they said they received a summons or responded to one, were asked whether their case "ever came to trial before a judge." The respondents clearly had difficulty with this seemingly straightforward factual question. If there is reason to suspect some exaggeration with respect to the question of answering the summons or filing an answer, there is even more reason to doubt the validity of the debtor's response to the question about a trial. Fourteen percent of all Chicago debtors claimed that their case was tried before a judge. In Detroit, 6 percent of all the debtors made this claim and in New York, only 1 percent (three debtors) did. But closer examination of these cases indicates that the debtors had little understanding of what is meant by a trial, and in fact hardly any of them did have trials.

For example, in Chicago, 44 debtors said that their case had gone to trial, but 26 of these cases were stamped "ex parte judgment confirmed," meaning that the debtor had not shown up on the due date and that he was the victim of a default judgment. Of the remaining 18 cases in which the debtor had made an appearance by the due date, almost all did not come to trial according to the court records. An examination of the questionnaires in these Chicago cases in which the debtor thought his case came to trial uncovered a number of reasons for the debtor's confusion. Thirteen had filed for bankruptcy and they apparently had their bankruptcy proceeding in mind when asked about a trial. Another 20 of these Chicago debtors assumed that a trial must have occurred because they received notice of a judgment against them, incorrectly believing that a judgment can result only from the deliberations of a court. Of the remaining 11 cases in which Chicago debtors claimed that a trial took place, no ready explanation could be found for this belief in nine of them, and in only two cases did the court record confirm that a trial had occurred. The check of the court records revealed that there actually were seven trials in the Chicago sample, although in five of the cases the debtor did not know that a trial had occurred. But all five of these debtors had retained lawyers and it is quite possible that their lawyers represented them in court in their absence. The creditor won in four of these trials and the debtor won in three, suggesting that if more debtors were to have had their cases heard by a judge, the rate of outcomes favorable to them would increase.

The Detroit picture is similar. In that city, 28 of the 438 debtors claimed that a trial had occurred. In five of these cases the debtor confused a bankruptcy proceeding with a trial of the merits of the creditor's suit, and in at least five cases, the debtor assumed that the judgment against him meant that a trial had occurred. A check of the court records indicated that in only a few of these cases did the defendant actually appear before a judge. Twenty of the 28 cases were recorded as default judgments, in three cases the action against the defendant was dismissed because the plaintiff failed to appear at the trial, and two cases were dismissed on other grounds.[27]

In New York, the picture is even more strange. Three debtors claimed that their case had either come to trial or was scheduled for trial. A check of the docket books three years later shows that three New York cases had been scheduled for trial.[28] But in only one instance did these cases overlap, and there is no evidence that the trial actually took place, since no judgment has been entered in the docket book. Such evidence is also lacking for the other two cases, which, according to the docket book, were set for trial. A check of the questionnaires in these two instances shows that these debtors worked out a settlement with the creditor and knew nothing about a trial. Of the two New Yorkers who incorrectly claimed that their case had gone to trial, one was apparently referring to a bankruptcy proceeding and the other was the victim of a default judgment. Perhaps, he, like some of the debtors in the other cities, assumed that a judgment meant that a trial had occurred. In short, after consulting a court clerk who checked a book recording trials, we can report that no trials occurred in the sample of New York debtors, even though three of the New York cases were set for trial.

That these trials never took place is to be explained by yet another practice undermining the system of justice. When the debtor does appear for a trial, he is usually summoned to the bench by the judge, who is

[27]The files were missing in three of these cases and we were unable to determine the outcome.

[28]It will be recalled that only one of the New York debtors who responded to the summons filed an answer. That three New York cases were scheduled for trial suggests that a few debtors managed to file answers even though they did not initially respond to the summons.

anxious to clear his calendar, and is told to go out into the hall and work out a settlement with the plaintiff's lawyer. In this fashion, even debtors with valid defenses are pressured to make some payment. A visitor to the civil court of New York will observe on any given day a score or more of these negotiation conferences taking place in the halls. It is this calendar-clearing practice of judges that no doubt inspired Lenny Bruce, the comedian, to observe that in the Halls of Justice, the only justice is in the halls.[29]

As all this makes amply clear, hardly any debtor–defendants appeared before judges in our three sample cities. As far as we can tell from the court records, none of the 332 New York debtor–defendants had a trial. In Detroit, only a handful, as few as 3 and as many as 11, may have had an appearance before a judge, a group that includes cases in which either the plaintiff did not show up or the action was dismissed "with prejudice," meaning that the defendant could not again be sued on the

[29]The halls-of-justice hypothesis troubled Professor Schrag, for he was not sure that the collection lawyer who first alerted us to the negotiation sessions was correct in asserting that this was routine procedure. At his insistence, we asked several civil court judges whether these judge-initiated hallway bargaining sessions really occurred; each one denied knowledge of them. Schrag, a more determined empiricist than I, recently assigned one of his students to observe events at the court house to determine once and for all whether there is any merit to the Lenny Bruce joke. As soon as he arrived at the court, the student wandered into a courtroom in which the attorney for a basement-waterproofing company was seeking a $200 judgment against a homeowner who was present in court. The defendant told the judge that he was unwilling to pay the debt because his basement still leaked; in fact, he had complained about it to the Department of Consumer Affairs. By some strange quirk, the judge in this case had formerly been an attorney for a fraudulent appliance repair company described in Schrag, *Counsel for the Deceived* (New York: Pantheon Books, 1972). He summoned both parties to the bench and said that this was an extremely complicated case and that a trial would be expensive and time-consuming. He urged the defendant to go into the hall and work out a settlement with the company's lawyer. When they returned the debtor had agreed to pay $100 and to withdraw from government agencies any complaints against the company. The judge praised the settlement.

The basic thesis of this chapter has been that the courts have been corrupted into collection agencies for creditors through the device of default judgments which enable creditors to use harsh collection practices without ever having to persuade judges of the merits of their cases. We have tacitly assumed that debtors would receive justice if they appeared before the bench. But this view must now be corrected in light of the Lenny Bruce theory. Even when debtors do have their day in court, they may not receive justice. Instead of falling victim to the impersonal collection system and the default judgment, the debtor who does show up for a trial may be confronted with a more personal collection system: a judge so intent on avoiding time-consuming trials that he ensures the creditor of at least half a loaf, regardless of the validity of his claim.

After his student reported these observations, Schrag checked with the Department of Consumer Affairs. A few hours before the courtroom incident, the homeowner had discussed his grievance with a Department official. The waterproofing company, a subject of many complaints, had been under investigation by the Department for months, and the Department official had offered to help the defendant by finding a volunteer lawyer to assist him in court. However, recruiting a volunteer could not be accomplished in a few hours, so the official advised, "go to court this afternoon and ask for a postponement of your hearing. Whatever you do, don't settle the case; just insist on a trial later." So great was the pressure of the creditor, reinforced by the prompting of the judge, that the defendant not only failed to obtain the suggested postponement but had to withdraw a complaint that might have helped the agency to prepare its own case against the firm.

same grounds. But even among this handful of Detroit debtors whose cases resulted in favorable outcomes, there is no evidence that a trial actually took place. It is quite possible that of the more than 1,000 Chicago, Detroit, and New York debtors interviewed, only seven, all in Chicago, actually had their cases tried before a judge.

These figures underscore the vast discrepancy between the appearance of judicial outcomes and their reality. Courts render judgments in consumer actions even though a judge is rarely called upon to decide the relative merits of the plaintiff's and defendant's case. The concept of "judgment" is largely a facade for routinized bureaucratic procedures that have nothing to do with the actions of officials known as "judges."[30] The accusation that the courts operate merely as collection agencies for creditors irrespective of the debtor–defendants' defenses finds much merit in these findings.

Remaining to be considered is an examination of the outcomes of these law suits according to the court records. It is widely suspected that the overwhelming majority of these actions result in default judgment. The data on hand bear this out. In each of the three cities, at least nine of every ten cases ended in a default judgment, as can be seen from Table 11.8.[31]

Table 11.8 is divided into three parts. The first, which accounts for at least 90 percent of the outcomes in each city, refers to default judgments, judgments automatically awarded to the plaintiff regardless of the merits of the case because the defendant failed to appear. The second part of the table shows the outcomes that were favorable to the plaintiff even though they did not involve default judgments, and the third part shows the frequency of outcomes favorable to defendants or at least outcomes in which the debtor did not have to pay.

In Chicago and New York almost all the nondefault judgment cases represented settlements favorable to the creditor, whereas in Detroit the

[30]A crude parallel might be found in the criminal law, where the great majority of the cases result in negotiated pleas rather than trials. In the criminal area the presumption has been that virtually all those who "cop a plea" are indeed guilty and are benefiting from the tradeoff. A careful study of the criminal process might well disclose that this presumption is as fallacious as the view that the debtors who never have their day in court are indeed at fault. Our data have shown that this assumption is not valid for a substantial minority of debtors. Were they to have had adequate legal representation and trials, they would have escaped the judgments against them. A comparable study in the criminal field might also disclose that the bargained plea covers up considerable injustices to defendants.

[31]Excluded from this table are the 38 replevin actions in Detroit and the four Detroit cases in which service was not made. It may be noted that in replevin cases the debtor is served with a writ at the time of the repossession informing him that he has up to 14 days in which to challenge the plaintiff's claim to the goods. If he does not exercise this right, a default judgment is entered against him. In only one of the 38 replevin actions in Detroit did the debtor show up in court to challenge the repossession, and his motion to quash the replevin was denied by the judge. Thus had we counted the replevin cases in Detroit, some 37 default judgments of a possible 38 would have been added to the total, bringing default judgments in Detroit to a figure slightly above those in other cities.

Table 11.8 / Legal Outcome of Case according to Court Record
in Each City (percent)

	Chicago	Detroit	New York
Default judgments	91	91	92
Other outcomes, favorable to the plaintiff			
Case dismissed or discontinued because creditor satisfied	4	5	2
Trial: creditor won	1	—	—
No judgment (but questionnaire indicates settlement)	—	—	5
Outcome probably favorable to defendant			
Trial: debtor won	1	—	—
Action dismissed because of debtor's bankruptcy	1		
Action dismissed because:			
Neither party appears			
Plaintiff fails to appear	—	4	—
Dismissed with prejudice			
Answer filed by defendant, no further action	1	—	—
Judgment vacated against one	1	—	—
of the spouses in initial suit	1	—	—
Total percent[a]	101	100	99
N	(308)	(387)	(328)

[a]A few cases in each city are omitted from this tally because the forms containing their court identification numbers were lost in the course of data processing and we were thus unable to check their legal outcome three years later when all the court records were reexamined.

9 percent that were not default judgments were more evenly split between outcomes favorable to the plaintiff and those favorable to the defendant (5 percent versus 4 percent). One sign of the inefficiency of the New York system is that in 18 cases (5 percent) there was no indication in the court record of any outcome. A check of the questionnaires showed that these debtors had worked out settlements with their creditors, and we include them in the second part of the table for this reason. (Apparently, the plaintiff's lawyer in these cases did not notify the court of the outcome nor did the court request this information from him.) When the results in all three cities are combined, the debtor–defendant turns out to be the winner in only 3 percent of the cases. This figure must be judged against the 19 percent who claimed fraud as a reason for not paying and an additional 8 percent who cited payment misunderstandings. As noted, the laws regarding warranty, misrepresentation, typeface on contracts, and other facets of the transaction are such that many more than

the one fourth of these debtors who insisted that they were not at fault would undoubtedly have been successfully defended had they the benefit of legal counsel and a trial. The fact that the legal actions against the debtors in our sample resulted in creditor victories in all but 3 percent of the cases (91 percent being default judgments and another 6 percent cases in which the creditor was sufficiently successful in exacting payments from the debtor that he either moved to dismiss the case or did not claim a judgment) is strong support for the notion that the courts act as collection agencies rather than judicial bodies in the field of consumer credit.

LEGAL REPRESENTATION FOR DEBTORS:
THE DEBTORS WHO HAD LAWYERS

Closely related to the failure of debtors to have their day in court and their legal rights protected is the irony that law suits against consumers generally involve sums of money that are smaller than the amounts the debtor would have to pay a lawyer to protect his rights. It is this dilemma that has led to the movement for consumer class actions, a movement that has led to such legislation in several states and several pending federal bills. We have already noted that about one in every five debtors sought legal assistance with his debt problem.[32] It is to this matter of legal representation, which would appear to be a consumer luxury, that we now turn.

Until now, we have had no reason to consider the Philadelphia debtors, for most of them had confessed binding judgments against themselves at the time of the initial transaction. But since they were then subject to such dire executions as losing their personal property and their homes, the Philadelphia debtors might well have been under strong pressure to seek legal help. As the issue of legal representation clearly applies to them as well as to the debtors in the other cities, they are included in this analysis.

Whether or not the debtor obtained legal assistance varies sharply from city to city. Virtually one third of the Chicago debtors received legal help (31 percent); in Philadelphia the proportion is somewhat less, 26 percent; and it falls off sharply in Detroit and New York where 20 and 11 percent, respectively, had the assistance of a lawyer. The relatively good record of Chicago is in part a reflection of the Legal Aid program in that city. About one fourth of the Chicago debtors who turned to a lawyer for help contacted Legal Aid. Although New York debtors were

[32]Included in this group are about 25 debtors who retained lawyers to assist them in declaring bankruptcy. We have included these cases in the subsequent analysis because it is not clear whether the idea of bankruptcy was initiated by the debtor or his attorney.

least likely to get attorneys, a somewhat larger proportion of those who did went to Legal Aid, 36 percent. In Detroit, only 16 percent of those who turned to lawyers went to Legal Aid, and in Philadelphia, only 11 percent availed themselves of this service. Legal Aid in Chicago might be judged as the most effective in that it served a larger proportion of all debtors than did the Legal Aid bureaus in the other cities.[33]

Remaining to be examined are the types of debtors likely to turn to a lawyer for help with their problem. Since most debtors who contacted lawyers dealt with the private bar rather than Legal Aid, it is reasonable to assume that the debtor's income is related to retaining an attorney. This expectation is borne out to some extent, as only 16 percent of those earning under $4,000 had a lawyer, compared with 23 percent of those of middle income and 26 percent of those earning over $8,000. But this is not a strong difference, and income at best accounts for only a little of the variance in the use of lawyers by debtor–defendants.

We noted that debtors who had not worked out a settlement with the creditor at the time of the interview (70 percent of the sample) were asked whether there was a good reason why they should not have to settle the debt. We saw that the respondents were evenly split, about half saying they should not have to pay and half acknowledging their indebtedness. Not surprisingly, those who believed they should not have to pay were more likely to retain a lawyer, 29 percent, compared with 13 percent among those who accepted the validity of the debt. This finding raises questions. Why did not all the debtors who felt they should not have to pay seek legal help, rather than only one fourth of them, and why did some 13 percent of the debtors who admitted that they did not have a valid defense bother to use a lawyer? These questions call attention to other considerations governing legal representation for debtors. As indicated, one of these is the cost of legal services relative to the amount in dispute. And indeed the likelihood of having a lawyer steadily increases with the amount of the debt. Among those being sued for less than $200, only 11 percent retained a lawyer; among those being sued for $200 to $500, 21 percent hired a lawyer, a figure that climbs to 28 percent for those being sued for $500 to $1,000, and to 36 percent for those being sued for over $1,000. But even these results call attention to flaws in the current system of justice for consumers, for when the debtor has a great deal at stake, most likely more than the cost of an attorney, he is still not likely to get legal assistance. Before accepting this conclusion, account must be taken of the debtor's sense of justice, that is, whether he feels the creditor's suit is justified. Presumably, debtors who feel that they are in the right will be more inclined to enlist the aid of attorneys

---

[33]For many years the Chicago Legal Aid office has had an aggressive consumer advocate who handles only consumer cases, Agnes Ryan, and her reputation has no doubt spread throughout the Chicago low-income community.

whatever the amount of the debt, and especially so if the stakes are high. Table 11.9 shows the joint effect of the size of the debt and the debtor's attitude toward the debt on the likelihood of his having a lawyer.

Table 11.9 / Percentage of Debtors Retaining Lawyer by Amount of Debt and Whether Debtor Thinks He Should Have To Pay

good reason for not paying?	under $100	$100– $199	$200– $499	$500– $999	$1,000 and over
Yes	15 (48)	21 (75)	24 (137)	28 (131)	54 (86)
No	2 (64)	6 (110)	10 (147)	26 (85)	22 (68)

By reading across the rows we see that amount of debt has an impact on seeking legal services regardless of whether the debtor believes he is in the right. Even those who are ready to admit their fault are much more apt to seek legal aid when the stakes are high. But this pattern is much more pronounced when the debtor thinks that he is in the right (the top row) than when he is ready to concede his fault. The columns of the table also show that regardless of the amount, debtors are more likely to retain lawyers when they think they are right. But the conclusion suggested by the effect of the amount of debt can still be found in the results of Table 11.9. Even among those debtors who believe that they are in the right and who are being sued for large amounts (in excess of $1,000), nearly one half (46 percent) are without legal assistance. Clearly, these findings document an area of unmet legal needs, a sector in which the legal profession has failed to perform its function.

12

EXECUTION
UPON JUDGMENT:
THE GARNISHMENT
CITIES

We have seen that the creditor almost always wins a court judgment. When he does not, it is usually because he has exacted a settlement in his favor, making it unnecessary for him to claim the judgment. There is, of course, a major difference between winning a judgment and collecting the debt. The judgment is only a license to use legally sanctioned collection procedures, such as attaching wages and bank accounts or seizing the debtor's personal or real property. This chapter and the next examine the extent to which the remedies at the creditor's disposal actually result in debt collection. The present chapter considers garnishment and its efficacy in the three cities that permitted this remedy. The collection system in Philadelphia, where garnishment is prohibited, is dealt with in the next chapter. But first we briefly consider a legal procedure that sometimes intervenes between judgment and garnishment, what is known as a supplementary proceeding.

SUPPLEMENTARY PROCEEDINGS

Should the plaintiff who has obtained a judgment against a debtor not know where the debtor works or what his assets are, he can file an order demanding that the debtor appear in court on a specific date to give this information. This procedure requires the issuance of a new summons. The sinister implications of supplementary proceedings were unknown to us when the survey was conducted. We have since learned that the debtor who does not respond to a supplementary proceeding can be found in contempt of court and subject to criminal sanctions (that is, a jail sentence). The Chicago, Detroit, and New York debtors were asked whether they had been ordered to appear in court to answer questions about their financial situation and place of employment, but there were no further queries about whether they appeared in court or had been subjected to criminal penalties. Of the 740 debtors asked this question, 96 or 13 percent received such an order. They were located mainly in Detroit and secondarily in Chicago; only a handful were in New York.

The tactic of the supplementary proceeding allows for the resurrection in the latter third of the twentieth century of that seemingly outmoded institution, debtor's prison. It is not known whether any debtor in our sample went to jail because of his failure to appear at a supplementary proceeding, but this contempt of court weapon was widely used against debtors in Maine, and an upstate New York Supreme Court judge has told us in a private communication that such sentences have occurred in his area. One victory for the OEO's legal services program was won in Maine in the summer of 1970, when legal services attorneys successfully argued before a three-judge federal court panel that such jail sentences were unconstitutional.[1]

One might assume that the 99 debtors who were asked to appear at supplementary proceedings were more "marginal" in their economic positions than the others, earning less and of less stable employment. But this was not the case. Those who received notice of a supplementary proceeding (even when New York debtors are excluded) were no more likely to be poor, lower blue collar workers, or black than those who did not receive this notice. It is conceivable, of course, that creditors request supplementary proceedings more often against those debtors who are so hard to find that they escaped our interviewers as well, but the absence of any relationships involving supplementary proceedings within our sample casts doubt upon this. We have gone into this issue of supplementary proceedings because it is sometimes a step in the collection process and because it is the device through which debtor's prison survives in the twentieth century.

---

[1] For an account of the Maine system before this decision, see the testimony of Howard T. Reben before the National Commission on Consumer Finances, June 21, 1970. Reben pointed out in his testimony that in the two Maine counties with which he was familiar, 200 debtors had in the past two years spent 1,754 days in prison because they had been in contempt of court.

VARIATIONS IN STATE GARNISHMENT LAWS

Wage garnishment is the most powerful weapon in the creditor's arsenal in the states that recognize it (officially all but Texas and Pennsylvania).[2] The garnishment order is binding on the employer; should he violate it, he is liable to legal action by the creditor–plaintiff. Because of the nuisance and expense that garnishment represents for employers, many will fire a worker rather than tolerate garnishment. Most employers have garnishment rules that specify the number of ganishments allowed before the employee is dismissed. The Federal Consumer Protection Act of 1968 prohibits the dismissal of an employee for a single garnishment, but such a rule is difficult to enforce, and debtors subjected to multiple garnishments are not protected at all. Thus, apart from its direct role as a collection device, garnishment is a powerful threat forcing debtors to resume payments rather than risk job loss.

At the time of the study, garnishment laws in the three states represented in the sample varied in at least four respects: the amount of salary that could be attached, the duration of a single garnishment order, the agency responsible for executing the order, and the cost of the garnishment proceeding. The Consumer Protection Act of 1968 reduced some of these variations by requiring all states to exempt at least 75 percent of the debtor's income from garnishment. It had a marked effect on some states, including Michigan, which had one of the harshest garnishment laws in the country. The Michigan rule distinguished between a family head and a single person, allowing larger exemptions for the former; it further distinguished between the first and subsequent garnishments, again providing larger exemptions for the former. The most favorable circumstances were extended to the household head who was being garnisheed for the first time and even here the law was quite harsh. The garnishment rule in Michigan exempted 60 percent of the wages of such a debtor but in no case more than $50 and in all cases at least $30. Regardless of size of family or salary, the debtor could not count on keeping more than $50 of his weekly wage. The $30 floor and the 60 percent exemption were rulings that affected only the relatively poor, those earning under $84 per week. For debtors in this income group, the options represented an advantage. Needless to say, the debtor did even more poorly if he was single or had multiple garnishments. Forty percent of the wages of a single person garnisheed for the first time were

---

[2] Although Texas and Pennsylvania are the only states that prohibit garnishment, several others exempt so much of the debtor's wages or make full exemptions so easy as to make the garnishment remedy of little value to the creditor. Among these are North Carolina and Florida.

exempt but never more than $50 and in all cases at least $20. For a multiple-garnishment family head, 60 percent of his wages were exempt but never more than $30 and at least $12. For the multiple-garnishment single person the rule was that 30 percent of his wages were exempt but in no case more than $20 and in all cases at least $10.

There is another aspect of the Michigan law that does much, at least on paper, to mitigate the law's harshness. Upon petition from the debtor, the court is empowered to allow the debtor to pay off the debt in installments to the court in amounts that the debtor can afford. In Wayne County, this aspect of the law has led the chief clerk of the court, Herbert Levitt, to send a letter to all judgment debtors inviting them to take advantage of the partial-payment procedure. But this relief exists more in theory than in fact. In the Detroit sample, about one third of the debtors accepted this invitation, and a number of them failed to maintain payments. At the time of the interview only one fifth of the Detroit debtors had paid in full or were still making payments to the court under this arrangement.[3]

In contrast, the garnishment rules in Illinois and New York were much more protective of the debtor. In Illinois, at the time of the study, debtors earning $45 or less per week were exempt from garnishment and 85 percent of the wages of those earning up to $200 were also exempt. If the debtor earned more than $200, he could claim only a $170 exemption, everything in excess of that being subject to attachment. In the following year the initial exemption in Illinois was raised from $45 for everybody to $60 for a family head and $50 for a single person, a rule that is still in effect. In New York the rule was that debtors earning $30 or less were exempt from garnishment and that 90 percent of the wages of those earning more was also exempt. Thus the worker earning $100 per week could lose $50 of his wages because of garnishment in Michigan, $15 in Illinois, and only $10 in New York. (By 1970, the initial exemption in New York had been raised to $85, New York's minimum wage level.)

A second consideration is the time period covered by a single garnishment order. Here the three states differ markedly. In New York, since 1958, a garnishment order remains in effect until the debt is settled. In Chicago, since 1960, the garnishment order covers a period of 30 days, which for the weekly earner amounts to four pay periods. If the debt is not settled by these four deductions, the creditor–plaintiff in Chicago

---

[3]The inadequacy of the Michigan partial payment plan has been noted in earlier research. Thus in a note on wage garnishment in the 50 states, 53 Cal. L. Rev. 1214 at 1226, ftn. 76, "This procedure [partial payments in Michigan] is not widely used except in Wayne County. Even there it is not very successful; in 1957, more than 70% of partial payment orders were vacated because of non-payment." See Fusfeld, "Don't Get Garnisheed!" Michigan State University, Labor and Industrial Relations Center, 17, undated.

must then apply for an additional garnishment order.[4] In contrast to New York and Illinois, the garnishment order in Michigan (as in Wisconsin and a number of other states) applies to only a single pay period. If the creditor–plaintiff is not satisfied after the first garnishment, he must apply for another, with the costs again being passed on to the debtor. Thus the Michigan law in one respect is most favorable to the creditor in that he can realize the most return in any given pay period, but from another perspective it is the least favorable because of the short duration of any garnishment order.

In both Michigan and Illinois, garnishment proceedings are carried out by salaried court officials (sheriffs and bailiffs), with the result that the courts in those states keep garnishment records. In New York, however, executing court judgments, including the task of garnishment, is turned over to quasi-public officials, city marshals, who work on a fee for service basis. City marshals are appointed by the Mayor and there are about 70 of them in New York City. Their earnings depend solely on the volume of their business, and some of them are reputed to make considerable sums of money.[5] They are regulated not by the court but by the city's Department of Investigations, and it is extremely difficult to find out just how many garnishments take place each year in New York.

Finally, the costs of garnishment, which are almost invariably passed on to the debtor, vary significantly. In Illinois, the cost of filing the garnishment is $1.00 for a debt up to $1,000, and $2.00 for a debt up to $5,000, and the cost of the service of the garnishment order upon the employer is $6.00 plus mileage. For the typical Chicago debtor, the cost of a garnishment proceeding ranges from $8.00 to $10.00. In Michigan, garnishment costs at least $8.50, often somewhat more. In New York garnishment involves multiple costs, one of which, the initial one, is not passed on to the debtor. By statute, the debtor in New York must be given a 20-day notice of the garnishment action against him. The purpose of this law is to provide the debtor with an opportunity to work out a settlement before his employer is contacted. Although a fine idea in principle, our interviews disclosed that a substantial proportion of New York debtors who were garnisheed never received a notice. In any case, the plaintiff is charged a fee of $5.00 by the marshal for sending out this notice.

---

[4]Before 1960 garnishment in Illinois covered but a single pay period. The law was changed in that year as the result of the highly publicized suicide of a Spanish-speaking debtor who found himself getting deeper in debt each week as the cost of the garnishment proceeding which he had to pay exceeded the amount of his wages withheld for the creditor. This episode resulted in the Illinois legislature extending a garnishment order to 30 days.

[5]The sheriff's office is also empowered to carry out executions, including garnishment, but the sheriff is rarely used by plaintiffs in actions under $10,000. In actions above $10,000 the law requires that the execution be carried out by the sheriff's office.

Should the debtor fail to pay up in the 20-day period, the marshal then charges a $3.00 fee for executing the garnishment order on the employer. This fee is added to the amount to be collected. Finally, as an entrepreneur operating on a fee for service basis, the marshal is entitled by law to charge 5 percent of the judgment for his efforts, which is also passed on to the debtor. Thus, if the initial judgment against the debtor is for $1,000, the marshal attaches $1,053 of the debtor's wages, a figure that includes the cost of notifying the employer and the marshal's 5 percent charge.

On balance the Michigan garnishment law is much harsher than that of Illinois or New York, but it must be judged in the light of the employer's one-, two-, or three-garnishment rule.[6] Any Michigan creditor who relies solely on garnishment to collect a large debt is apt to find that his multiple garnishments are self-defeating, for they result in the debtor's dismissal from his job. On the basis of these marked variations in garnishment laws, it would seem that a garnishment execution is less efficacious in Michigan than in the other states. By the same token, the severity of the Michigan law should make it more effective than the laws in the other states as a *threat* to force debtors to reach settlements or resume payments.

In view of these statutory differences, how does the rate of garnishment vary from city to city? The question of garnishment frequency, like the factual questions confronted in chapter 11, cannot be answered precisely. Some debtors may not have known that they were garnisheed, having worked out a settlement after they were informed of the judgment against them. Others may not have been garnisheed until after the interview, perhaps because they were unemployed at the time. And some of the people interviewed may not have known that some other party connected with the debt, perhaps a cosigner or missing spouse, had been garnisheed. In short, the reported rates of garnishment in each city (based on the interviews with respondents) are no doubt well below the true garnishment rates. In Chicago it was possible to determine what might be thought of as the true rate, for three years after the survey the court records in that city were checked for notices of garnishments. As noted, such records do not appear in the New York City files because in that city garnishment notices are sent out by marshals. For practical reasons it was not possible to check the Detroit files for garnishment orders, and so our knowledge of the true rate compared with the reported rate is based only on the Chicago sample. According to the court records, 79 percent of the Chicago cases had garnishment orders in their files three years after the survey, but at the time of the interviews (conducted between four and six months after the initiation of the legal action), only 51 percent of the Chicago debtors were aware that they had been gar-

[6]Because of the harshness of the Michigan law, the Wayne County court clerk, Herbert Levitt, has prohibited garnishment proceedings during December in order for debtors to have enough earnings for their Christmas shopping.

nisheed. On the basis of the data for Chicago it would seem that the true rate is at least half again as great as the reported rate.

On the assumption that the Chicago discrepancy is applicable to the other cities, we present "estimated" as well as "reported" garnishment rates for all three cities. There is one further consideration in assessing the amount of garnishment. As noted, some debtors were unemployed both at the time of their default and at the time of our interview and therefore could not be garnisheed. To this group must be added the few debtors in each city who were self-employed. Thus we must consider not only a reported rate of garnishment based on all debtors, but a corrected "reported" rate based on those who could have been garnisheed. Table 12.1 presents four versions of the garnishment rate for each city.

Table 12.1 / Garnishment Rate by City (percent)

type of rate	Chicago		Detroit		New York		total	
Reported rate based on:								
Total sample	51	(312)	30	(396)[a]	37	(332)	40	(1,040)
Those employed	60	(273)	38	(337)	47	(265)	48	(875)
Estimated true rates based on:								
Total sample	79	(312)	46	(396)	57	(332)	58	(1,040)
Those employed	93	(270)	59	(337)	73	(265)	73	(875)

[a] Omitted from the Detroit sample are the 38 replevin cases and the four debtors who were never served with summons.

Both the reported rates and the estimated true rates show that garnishment is most common in Chicago and least so in Detroit. Even when the reported rate is computed on all debtors, including those not in the labor force (first row), at least half of the Chicago respondents were garnisheed, compared with almost two out of five New York debtors but less than one out of three in Detroit. When the reported rates are based on those who could have been garnisheed, the pattern becomes more evident as the discrepany between Detroit and New York increases. That Chicago is a garnishment city is more readily seen from the true rates based on inspection of the files three years after the interviews. Seventy-nine percent of all Chicago debtors and almost all of those who held jobs in this period were in fact garnisheed. If the Chicago discrepancy is applicable to the other cities, then almost half of all Detroit debtors were eventually garnisheed, as were more than half of those in the labor force. In New York these estimates come to more than half of all debtors and almost three-fourths of those who were employed.

The data of Table 12.1 thus support the prediction that the very harshness of the Michigan garnishment law coupled with the rule that a garnishment order applies to a single pay period would result in this remedy being used less often in Detroit than in Chicago or New York. One additional finding supports this interpretation of the relative infrequency of garnishment in Detroit. If the need to file a new order each pay period discourages creditors from using this remedy, then Detroit creditors who are suing for large amounts of money should rely on garnish-ment less often than those suing for small amounts. For the creditor who is owed a small amount, say $100, a single garnishment can go a long way toward settling the debt, given the rule that no more than $50 of the debtor's weekly wages are exempt. But for the creditor who is suing for over $1,000, a single garnishment makes little dent in the debt. In such instances the *threat* of repeated garnishments with the specter of job loss is perhaps more effective than actual garnishment. Whether there is any validity to this line of reasoning can be seen from Table 12.2, which shows garnishment by amount of debt in each city. (In this and all subsequent tables the garnishment rate is calculated on the basis of those employed, the second row of Table 12.1.)

Table 12.2 / Frequency of Garnishment by Size of Debt and City (of Those Who Could Have Been Garnisheed) (percent)

size of debt	Chicago		New York		Detroit		total	
Under $100	61	(36)	54	(46)	50	(46)	55	(128)
$100–$199	52	(46)	53	(51)	48	(80)	50	(177)
$200–$499	63	(86)	51	(79)	32	(84)	49	(249)
$500–$999	60	(57)	36	(45)	36	(72)	44	(174)
$1,000 and over	63	(41)	48	(27)	22	(41)	44	(109)

The hypothesis is borne out by the patterns shown in the table. In neither Chicago nor New York is there any relationship between gar-nishment and the size of the debt. The aggregate pattern shown in the last column is due entirely to the strong *negative* relationship in Detroit. When the debt is small (under $100), half of the Detroit debtors report garnishment. As the debt increases, the proportion of Detroit debtors who are garnisheed steadily declines, dropping to 22 percent among those who were sued for more than $1,000.

It is evident from Table 12.1 that garnishment is frequently used by plaintiffs in consumer actions. Several questions now arise. Is garnish-ment more likely to be used against certain types of debtor–defendants than other types? Are certain types of creditor–plaintiffs more likely than others to resort to garnishment? How effective is garnishment as a collec-tion device?[7] These questions are discussed in the remainder of the chapter.

[7]Although this chapter focuses exclusively on the creditor's remedy of garnishment, it should be noted that the laws in these states did permit property executions as well. But in almost all instances the debtors in Chicago, Detroit, and New York did not suffer property executions, except for repossession of the goods bought in the transaction that broke down. Real property collateral is apt to be involved in home repair contracts. It may be recalled that one Detroit debtor pointed out that he had lost his home because of a home repair contract which had preceded the debt currently in dispute.

CORRELATES OF GARNISHMENT

In previous chapters whenever some aspect of the defective credit transaction was examined, be it reasons for not paying, the degree of deception in the original transaction, harassment, or service of process, the roles of the two parties to the credit relationship, the debtor and the creditor, were always considered. The issue of garnishment introduces a third figure, the debtor's employer. What little information is available on the employer will be examined. Characteristics of debtors as they relate to garnishment are considered first, followed by characteristics of plaintiffs, and then those of employers.

Garnishment and Characteristics of the Debtor

Among those who are not excluded by fiat[8] or by law from garnishment, there are no obvious reasons for assuming that one type of default-debtor will be subjected to this sanction more often than another. But the data suggest that some types of debtors are indeed more likely than others to be garnisheed. For example, the higher white collar workers escape garnishment more often than those below them in the occupational scale, 37 percent as compared with 46 percent among the lower white collar, and 52 and 48 percent, respectively, among the higher and lower blue collar workers. Perhaps those of higher occupational status avoid garnishment more often because they earn more and are better able than those of lower income to settle the debt. There may be some merit to this reasoning, for income is negatively associated with garnishment, as those earning over $8,000 were more likely to avoid garnishment than those earning less.

We know that income and occupation are related to ethnicity, the blacks being poorer and of lower occupational status than the whites. In light of the previous findings, it is perhaps not too surprising that ethnicity is strongly related to garnishment. For the three cities combined, only 36 percent of the whites were garnisheed compared with 50 percent of the blacks and 59 percent of the Puerto Ricans. The white–black differential is smallest in Chicago (55 percent compared with 62 percent) and greatest in New York (27 percent compared with 50 percent).

Since income is negatively related to garnishment and blacks and Puerto Ricans earn less on the average than whites, perhaps income

[8]Debtors who could not be garnisheed because they were not in the labor force, or unemployed or self-employed at the time of the survey are excluded from this analysis of garnishment.

is the cause of the ethnic difference. But these differences persist even when income is taken into account. Among the poor, the white–Puerto Rican differential is 13 percentage points; in the middle-income group, 30 points; and in the high-income group, 12 points.

We saw in chapter 11 that whites were somewhat more likely than blacks to seek legal help with their debt problem, and the debtor with a lawyer, we might suppose, is more likely to have his case settled out of court. The flaw in this argument is the assumption that the debtor turned to a lawyer at the initiation of the legal process, when in fact many debtors seek legal help only when they learn that they have been garnisheed. Thus instead of a lawyer helping the debtor avoid a garnishment, it may well be that the garnishment led the debtor to retain a lawyer. The latter process might well explain why poor people in particular seek legal help. Neighborhood legal service offices report that they typically receive consumer cases only *after* garnishment proceedings have been initiated. The data on hand indicate that both processes are at work, for in the aggregate there is little relationship between having a lawyer and garnishment. In fact, those who did have lawyers were slightly *more* likely to have been garnisheed, 50 percent compared with 47 percent, indicating the tendency of debtors to contact lawyers *because* of a garnishment problem. That this motive applies particularly to the poor is shown by the patterns in Table 12.3, which presents the garnishment rate according to the debtor's income and obtaining legal assistance.

Table 12.3 / Percentage Garnisheed by Debtor Income and Legal Assistance

had legal help	under $4,000		$4,000–$7,999		$8,000 and over	
Yes	67	(27)	53	(107)	35	(51)
No	49	(144)	49	(360)	41	(147)

Among the poor, those who had lawyers were much more likely to be garnisheed than those who did not, indicating that in this group the garnishment stimulated the search for legal help. Among those in the middle-income group, this pattern virtually disappears, and it reverses in the highest income group, where those without lawyers were somewhat more likely to be garnisheed. This would suggest that the more well-to-do are more likely than the poor to approach lawyers *before* garnishment and are able to avoid garnishment for this reason. This inference is amply supported by the pattern in the top row of Table 12.3. Thus two thirds of the poor who had lawyers were garnisheed, a figure that drops to 53 percent in the middle income group and 35 percent in the highest income category. This finding fills out the picture of the correlates of legal assistance presented in the previous chapter. Default-debtors seek lawyers not only when there are large sums at stake and when they feel that they have been wronged, but also when they have been the victim of a harsh collection practice such as garnishment.

Garnishment and Types of Creditor–Plaintiffs

We have seen that some types of plaintiffs are more likely than others to rely on harassment. Will a similar pattern occur with respect to the collection practice of garnishment? The plaintiffs that were least prone to harass their default-debtors were the credit unions and general retailers. Not surprisingly, they were also least likely to resort to garnishment. In the three-city aggregate, only 29 percent of the debtors sued by general retailers were garnisheed, as were an equally small proportion of the debtors sued by credit unions. At the other extreme we find that 60 percent of the debtors sued by direct sellers and 57 percent of those sued by low-income retailers were garnisheed. In between these extremes are the finance companies (50 percent), small loan companies (46 percent), automobile dealers (46 percent), and banks (43 percent).

Since blacks and Puerto Ricans were more likely than whites to have dealt with the type of creditor quick to garnishee wages, it is possible that the greater likelihood of minority group debtors to be garnisheed is explained by the type of creditor with whom they dealt. To test this possibility we have grouped plaintiffs into three categories, according to their propensity to garnishee default-debtors. The high-garnishment category consists of direct sellers, low-income retailers, and finance companies; the medium-garnishment category comprises small loan companies, banks, and auto dealers; and the low-garnishment group consists of general retailers and credit unions. Whether type of plaintiff explains why blacks are more likely than whites to be garnisheed can be seen from Table 12.4.

Table 12.4 / Percentage Garnisheed by Ethnicity and Type of Plaintiff

ethnicity	high-garnishment plaintiffs (low-income retailers, direct sellers, and finance companies)		medium-garnishment plaintiffs (small loan companies, banks, and auto dealers)		low-garnishment plaintiffs (general retailers and credit unions)	
Whites	45	(155)	40	(119)	19	(48)
Blacks	55	(289)	47	(179)	35	(62)

The rows of Table 12.4 show that type of plaintiff is related to garnishment within each ethnic group, and the columns show that the ethnic difference persists even when type of plaintiff is held constant. Whether the plaintiffs resort to garnishment frequently or occasionally, they still exact this retribution more frequently from their black than from their white debtors.

The plaintiffs who resort to garnishment most frequently are the very ones who also rely on harassment and whose business practices leave much to be desired. Thus 60 percent of the debtors subjected to a great deal of harassment were garnisheed; among those who experienced a moderate amount of harassment, 49 percent were garnisheed and the comparable figure among those who received little or no harassment is 38 percent. A similar pattern emerges when the index of deceptive sales practices is related to garnishment. Even though the deception index refers to the original seller, who may not be the plaintiff who institutes garnishment proceedings—a fact that can only attenuate the relationship between these properties—such a relationship is found. Where there is little or no deception at the outset, 43 percent of the default-debtors were subsequently garnisheed, a figure that rises to 49 percent of those in the medium-deception category, and 52 percent of those in the high-deception group.

The findings linking harassment and deception to garnishment would indicate that creditor–plaintiffs tend to be grouped into at least two strata. One class consists of those who use high-pressure tactics to sell their goods and resort to strong measures to collect their debts. The other class consists of creditor–plaintiffs who are more ethical in their business dealings and less prone to resort to harsh collection measures, perhaps because they are concerned with the goodwill of their customers and/or do not view default-debtors as a source of profit. The picture that emerges from these findings is that garnishment is more often relied on by the less ethical creditor–plaintiffs. If this analysis is correct, its implications are profound. It would seem that the law places a powerful collection weapon in the hands of those who least deserve it, those firms likely to engage in deception at the time of the sale and undue harassment when the debtor, perhaps because he feels that he has been cheated, stops making payments.[9]

Garnishment and the Debtor's Employer

As noted, the issue of garnishment ushers yet another party onto the consumer credit stage—the debtor's employer. Whether the creditor–plaintiff uses garnishment may well be related to the type of employer the debtor has. This is certainly true in one respect. By law, federal

[9]The Federal Trade Commission's study of low-income and general retailers in Washington, D.C., supports this conclusion. That study found that the less scrupulous low-income retailers were much more likely to rely on repossession and garnishment than the general retailers. See Federal Trade Commission, *Economic Report on Installment Credit and Retail Sales Practices of District of Columbia Retailers,* 1968. A case in point in our study is provided by the unscrupulous New York jewelry firm, Trademark Jeweler, which garnisheed 76 percent of its default debtors, a figure far higher than that for any other plaintiff in the city.

employees cannot be garnisheed. Thus the country's largest employer is sufficiently powerful to exact legislation that protects it from the nuisance of garnishment. Some states, including Michigan and Illinois, but not New York, have laws exempting state employees from garnishment. But in all three states, city employees were subject to garnishment.

Employees of local government would seem to be ideal targets for garnishment. They are apt to be civil servants with assured job security. Moreover, public employers are probably less concerned than private employers about the costs of garnihsment.[10] However plausible this reasoning, the data show that debtors employed by local government were *less* likely to be garnisheed than those employed in the private sector, 32 percent compared with 48 percent. This aggregate difference holds within each city, especially Chicago, where garnishments in the private sector far exceed those in the public sector. In fact, only 2 percent of the Chicago debtors were employed by the city (5 of the 270 employed debtors in the sample). In contrast, 9 percent of the Detroit debtors with jobs were employed by local government, as were fully 16 percent in New York.[11]

One might suppose that creditors would hesitate to garnishee workers whose employers had little tolerance for garnishment, for such efforts to tap the debtor's wages might well be self-defeating. Of the debtors in the three garnishment cities, 54 percent reported that their employer did have garnishment rules, 34 percent were of the opinion that he did not, and 13 percent were uncertain. The data on hand lend some support to the notion that creditors are sensitive to garnishment rules, as 44 percent of those employed by firms with harsh rules (dismissal for one or two garnishments) were garnisheed compared with 55 percent of those employed by firms with more lenient rules (three or four garnishments before dismissal). But, although in the expected direction, this difference is not large. A substantial minority of debtors who work for firms with harsh garnishment rules were garnisheed, and, as we see below, a number of debtors did lose their jobs because of garnishment.

JOB LOSS AS A RESULT OF GARNISHMENT

Although the data are meager on the types of firms for which the garnisheed debtors worked, we do know whether the employer dismissed the worker

---

[10]The cost of garnishment to the employer is fairly substantial. In a separate survey of 1,500 manufacturing establishments, we learned that the average cost of processing and carrying out a garnishment order is $22.24. In firms employing many workers, garnishments can cost thousands of dollars a year.

[11]This finding may well be a testimonial to the old-style political machine still in effect in Chicago. In its heyday, the political machine served the important function of adjudicating disputes in an extralegal fashion. Perhaps public employees in Chicago who have debt problems can count on the informal mechanisms of the machine to settle their debt problems without their being confronted with a law suit.

rather than submit to the garnishment and whether the worker quit his job rather than risk dismissal because of garnishment. We now confront the self-defeating aspect of garnishment, its contribution to job loss rather than debt collection. In chapter 14 the costs of the debt problem to the debtor, including its impact on his employment status, will be examined in more detail. For the moment our concern is with the frequency of job loss due to garnishment, the types of employers who dismiss their workers, and the types of debtors who experience this debilitating consequence of their debt problem.

Among all debtors in the three cities recognizing garnishment, 8 percent were dismissed or had quit because of garnishment proceedings by the time of the interview.[12] This figure, which amounts to about twice the unemployment rate in the year of the study, 1967, is almost certainly an underestimate of the true figure. For one thing, many debtors were not garnisheed until after the interview, and for another, even at the time of the interview, many were worried that they would lose their jobs and a number had been issued ultimatums by their employers to settle or lose their jobs. The 8 percent job-loss rate must be qualified in other respects. It is based on all debtors, including those who could not be garnisheed either because they had no job or were self-employed. Eliminating these "ineligibles" raises the rate to 10 percent. More relevant to the self-defeating aspects of garnishment is the proportion of garnisheed workers who lost their jobs. Among the garnisheed, how many were dismissed or quit for fear of dismissal? It turns out that in all three cities combined, 19 percent of the garnisheed lost their jobs because of this action. The rate of job loss was highest among the Chicago debtors and lowest among those in New York. Fully 16 percent of all Chicago debtors (compared with the aggregate figure of 8 percent) lost their jobs, a figure rising to 28 percent of all those garnisheed in that city. In contrast, the comparable figures in New York are 4 and 11 percent. The 19 percent overall rate of job loss among the garnisheed is more than five times the unemployment rate for 1967. Clearly, garnishment contributes to unemployment; depending on the number of workers who are garnisheed each year, its effect may be large or small. One thing is certain: garnishment contributes considerable risk to the debtor's job, and the ruling of the Consumer Protection Act of 1968 prohibiting dismissal for a single garnishment notwithstanding, this practice continues to threaten workers' jobs. Dismissal occurs because in many states the same debt may involve multiple garnishments, to say nothing of multiple garnishments for different debts, and because it is very difficult to prove that the dismissal stemmed from the garnishment order rather than some other cause.

[12]The great majority of these cases were dismissals rather than voluntary resignations. "Quitting" must be understood in terms of the debtor's eagerness to retain a good job history.

Type of Employer and Job Loss

We have seen that debtors employed in the private sector were more likely to have been garnisheed than those in the public sector. The former also had much more to fear from garnishment, as some 21 percent of the garnisheed in the private sector lost their jobs compared with only 4 percent in the public sector. The latter figure refers to but one of the 25 civil servants in these cities who were garnisheed, and this man was not fired but quit his job. A Detroit debtor, this man was a mechanic employed by Wayne County and earning over $10,000 a year. As he told the interviewer:

> The sheriff's department was calling all the time. They made it hot for me . . . they never stopped bothering me at work.

Executing a garnishment order in Michigan is the responsibility of the sheriff's office, and as noted, these garnishment orders apply to a single pay period. The sheriff's office might well have resorted to harassment as the less harmful alternative to repeated garnishments.

Although federal employees are protected from garnishment, they are not protected from hounding by creditors who contact their employers. The federal government views failure to pay debts as a sign of character weakness among its employees. When contacted repeatedly by creditors, federal agencies are apt to put some pressure on their delinquent employees and even issue job-dismissal warnings. Of the 16 debtors in our sample that we know for certain were employed by the federal government, two quit their jobs because of pressure applied by the creditors on their employers. Both debtors were New York post office employees. One gave this strange explanation:

> I worked for the post office and they couldn't garnish my pay and that is why I lost my job.

This debtor explains his job loss on the grounds that his wages could not be attached, but he does not tell us how this could come about. The testimony of the other New York postal worker who lost her job helps to clarify the situation. When asked whether her employer told her she would lose her job if she did not settle the debt, this 30-year-old black woman replied:

> Well not in those exact words, but it all amounted to the same thing. See I worked for the federal government and they would cause you to resign if you didn't pay your personal bills and meet your responsibilities.

As this woman's statement indicates, the federal government has evolved its own code of character and fitness, and high on such a list is whether the employee pays his bills. The fact that federal employees cannot be garnisheed is thus not the great debtor panacea that it appears to be. On the contrary, the policy of the government is to treat the creditor's dunning phone calls most seriously and to pressure their employees to either settle their debts or resign from their jobs.

One might suppose that size of firm would have some bearing on whether debtors were dismissed because of garnishment. Smaller firms might be less equipped to handle garnishments than large ones. (Many large firms have special garnishment departments.) But size of firm, a question limited to debtors employed in the private sector, turns out not to be related to garnishment-induced job loss in any consistent way. Below 1,000 workers, job loss rates vary from 21 to 29 percent, with no clear pattern; but above 1,000 workers the dismissal rate drops to 15 percent. If size is a deterrent to dismissal, its effect shows up only among the very large firms.

One characteristic of the private firm that might well be related to garnishment-induced dismissals is the nature of its garnishment rule. The data show that this does indeed affect dismissal, as the more stringent the rule, the more likely the debtor was to lose his job. Among those whose employers would not tolerate even a single garnishment, almost one half of the garnisheed—48 percent—lost their jobs. (Those who did not might well have been coerced by their employer's policy to work out settlements with their creditors.) Among employers who tolerate a single garnishment but fire workers who have had two garnishments, the discharge rate declines sharply to 30 percent and continues to decline as the employer's rule becomes progressively more lenient until among employers with no rule at all, only 12 percent of the garnisheed lost their jobs. This finding is a striking reminder that rules do make a difference and if legislative bodies want to eliminate job loss due to garnishment they might well insist on employers accepting three garnishments before dismissal rather than none, a difference in discharge rates of 48 percent compared with 19 percent.

Types of Debtors Who Suffer Job Loss because of Garnishment

The analysis of debtors who lost their jobs because of garnishments is somewhat of a digression from the main theme of this chapter, the assessment of the efficacy of garnishment as a collection device. Nonetheless, we pursue the digression one step further by pointing out the types of debtors most likely to suffer job loss because of garnishment. The first characteristic to be considered is one that reflects type of employment and employer as well as debtor—whether the debtor belonged to a union.

Union membership is apt to increase with the size of the work force, and yet we saw that size of firm is not related to job loss because of garnishment. However, union membership does protect workers from dismissal, as garnisheed union members were much less likely than garnisheed nonunion members to lose their jobs, 13 percent compared with 33 percent.

Turning to the ethnicity of the debtors, we find results not at all in keeping with the patterns developed in previous analyses. In many respects blacks and Puerto Ricans have been found to suffer more than whites because of the debt problem. But job loss because of garnishment is more often a problem for whites than for blacks or Puerto Ricans. Thirty percent of the whites who were garnisheed compared with 19 percent of the blacks and only 9 percent of the Puerto Ricans lost their jobs. Although whites are much more likely than blacks to escape garnishment, they pay a higher price when confronted with this collection device. The poor, vulnerable in every other respect, are also more likely than the well-to-do to lose their jobs once they are garnisheed. Among garnisheed debtors earning under $4,000, only 35 percent lost their jobs; among those earning between $4,000 and $8,000, this figure drops to 16 percent; and among those earning over $8,000, job loss among the garnisheed is 15 percent.

When income and ethnicity are considered jointly, we find that the ethnic pattern persists in that whites on every level of income except the highest suffer more from garnishment than do the blacks and Puerto Ricans. The differential is most pronounced in the low-income group, where only a few of the whites are located. Only 29 percent of the 14 whites in this category who were garnisheed kept their jobs compared with 66 percent of the blacks. In the middle-income group the gap narrows as the comparable figures are 75 and 86 percent, and in the highest income group the ethnic difference disappears (83 percent of the whites and 84 percent of the blacks kept their jobs).

Although income sheds little light on the ethnicity pattern regarding job loss, the other factor related to job retention or loss, union membership, does largely explain the ethnic pattern. Among the garnisheed, blacks and Puerto Ricans belong to labor unions more often than do whites (68 and 70 percent compared with 50 percent). As Table 12.5 shows, in every ethnic group union membership serves to protect the garnisheed worker from loss of his job.

Table 12.5 / Percentage Retaining Job among the Garnisheed by Ethnicity and Union Membership

union membership	whites		blacks		Puerto Ricans	
Union member	79	(47)	87	(206)	97	(32)
Nonunion member	62	(48)	65	(95)	79	(14)

Although garnisheed blacks are more likely than their white counter-parts to keep their jobs, taking union membership into account reduces the ethnic difference. In short, one reason why blacks more often keep their jobs than whites is that they are more likely to be union members.

Garnishment and Notification of Law Suit

Garnishment has been analyzed in light of characteristics of the debtor, plaintiff, and debtor's employer, and its contribution to job loss. But there is still another perspective from which garnishment must be viewed, the constitutional doctrine of due process. In the previous chapter we saw that a substantial minority of debtors, especially those in New York, did not receive notice of the law suit against them. To what extent were these debtors deprived of their wages (or at least experienced an *attempt* to deprive them of wages) in violation of the Fourteenth Amendment? If their creditors did not execute the judgments against them, these debtors could not easily argue that their constitutional rights had been violated. But if their creditors did try to attach their salaries and assets, then clearly their rights were violated, for they would have been deprived of property without due process of law.

Table 12.6 shows how service of process is related to garnishment in each city and in the aggregate. From the last column we learn that in the aggregate the debtor who was not notified of the suit was more likely to be garnisheed than the debtor who was. This aggregate pattern holds in Detroit and New York, but in Chicago there is a reversal in that those who were served were slightly more likely to be garnisheed than those who were not. The aggregate pattern undoubtedly reflects the fact that minority-group members and the poor were both less likely to be served and more likely to be garnisheed. But it also indicates that notification may in itself lessen the likelihood of garnishment, for debtors who know that they are being sued are apt to contact the creditor's attorney and work out a payment arrangement. This model would seem to apply to New York and Detroit, and the apparent deviant case, Chicago, is not too different in that the garnishment rates are quite high both among those who were and were not notified.

Table 12.6 / Percentage Garnisheed by Receipt of Summons and City

receipt of summons	Chicago		Detroit		New York		total	
Yes	62	(189)	36	(290)	41	(142)	45	(621)
No	56	(80)	52	(46)	54	(123)	54	(249)

The failure of the judicial system is dramatized by these results. A substantial minority of debtors, especially in New York, did not receive notice of the law suit against them; yet a majority of these noninformed debtors were subjected to garnishments. The attention of Americans today is focused on the issue of "law and order" as many citizens register anger at the rising crime rate. The import of Table 12.6 is that there is much more deviation from law—deviations that affect a broad spectrum of the citizenry—than the current discussion of law and order would indicate. Apart from crime in the streets, there is crime in the marketplace; that society should view the former harshly and the latter benevolently, if at all, is perhaps a reflection of national hypocrisy rather than a rational response to society's greatest dangers. Crimes of violence, for all their publicity, are much less frequent than white collar crime, their monetary cost is much less, and the perpetrators of such crimes are more likely to be apprehended. The final irony, perhaps, is that over the past decade, a sensitive and liberal judiciary in the name of due process has been most solicitous of the rights of those accused of criminal offenses, but a comparable concern for constitutional rights has not been extended to those accused of not paying their bills.

OUTCOME OF THE DEBT IN
THE GARNISHMENT CITIES: SETTLEMENT

Various facets of garnishment have been examined, but still to be considered is perhaps the most critical question: How efficacious is garnishment as a collection device? How often did the threat of garnishment and actual garnishment result in resumption of payments and how often did debtors avoid payments in spite of the garnishment threat? In short, we now confront the ultimate outcome of the case by examining the extent to which plaintiffs in the three garnishment states achieved satisfaction in their suits against default-debtors. We shall approach this issue by examining two questions asked of the debtors that bear on the resolution of the case: (1) whether they settled "out of court" once they learned of the law suit against them, and (2) how the matter stood at the time of the interview, that is, whether the debtor had paid off the debt, had resumed payments, or had made no payments. The questions overlap in that debtors who settled their debt out of court were likely to have paid it in full or to have resumed payments. The overlap is not complete insofar as some debtors who viewed their debt problem as settled had declared bankruptcy or had somehow been exonerated of the obligation as a result of the legal proceeding. In spite of the overlap, the issue of settling out of court is of interest because of the possible role of the threat of garnishment in coercing debtors to work out settlements.

"Settling out of court" means that the parties to a dispute reach an agreement without having their case go to trial or to judgment. Although few of these cases resulted in a trial, most led to judgments against the defendant. Thus settlement out of court refers in this instance to debtors who contacted the plaintiff's attorney after they learned of the suit or of the judgment in order to work out some kind of payment arrangement.[13] But, as noted, this category also includes a few who took steps to ensure that they did not have to pay. Almost half of the debtors (48 percent) in these three cities were sufficiently alarmed by the legal actions taken against them that they contacted the plaintiff's attorney and tried to settle the case. Not all those who tried to settle succeeded. In all, 29 percent did manage some kind of settlement, 19 percent tried but apparently failed to work out an arrangement, and 52 percent did not try to work out a settlement. These figures varied little from city to city, with the exception that among those who tried to settle their case, Chicago debtors were most often successful (34 percent) and New York debtors least often (26 percent).

Not surprisingly, those of high income were more likely to work out settlements than those of low income (40 percent of those earning over $8,000 contacted the creditor and settled the debt compared with 21 percent of those earning under $4,000). But although whites in the sample earned substantially more than blacks, there was little difference between the two groups on the matter of settling the debt (31 percent of the whites and 29 percent of the blacks worked out settlements; among Puerto Ricans this figure drops to 20 percent).

An important issue is whether garnishment induces debtors to work out settlements that they might otherwise have avoided. Testing this empirically is a difficult matter, for it is impossible to separate the power of the *threat* of garnishment from the garnishment itself in bringing about such settlements. Just as the threat of garnishment may force debtors to settle with their creditors even when they may not want to, so the garnishment order, which often evokes a warning from the employer, "you had better settle or else . . .," may have the same result. Nonetheless, those who do respond to the threat of garnishment by working out a settlement must be included among the nongarnisheed. If they are substantial in number, then garnishment and settlement should be negatively related. In the aggregate this is true, as 37 percent of those who were not garnisheed worked out settlements, compared with 26 percent of the garnisheed. This pattern was particularly pronounced in New York, moderately strong in Detroit, but nonexistent in Chicago, where both groups had identical rates of settlement. Moreover, the greater likeli-

---

[13]The question read, "Did you or someone on your behalf contact the company or its lawyer to try to settle this matter out of court?" If yes, "Did you succeed in settling it?"

hood of the nongarnisheed to settle may reflect factors other than the power of the threat of garnishment. For example, debtors may refuse to settle because of the merits of their case, thereby unwittingly inviting the creditor to garnishee. Just as the threat of garnishment may coerce some debtors into settling, so the refusal of some debtors to settle because they believe they do not owe the money may trigger the garnishment. No doubt both processes are at work, but their relative importance cannot be determined with the data on hand.

Default-debtors were asked not only whether they had settled out of court, but, if so, whether they considered the settlement fair. This information is important, for it tells us something about the power of harsh collection practices, such as garnishment, in exacting settlements that debtors do *not* consider fair. Of the 314 debtors who did succeed in settling their debt out of court, only 53 percent considered the settlement to be fair. This is a most revealing statistic, for it suggests that many of the settlements represent unhappy compromises on the part of debtors seeking to avoid harsh collection practices. If garnishment is the instrument that makes debtors settle on less than satisfactory terms, we should find a negative relationship between garnishment and satisfaction with out-of-court settlements. These data are shown separately for each city in Table 12.7.

Table 12.7 / Percentage Satisfied with Settlement by Garnishment and City

whether debtor garnisheed	Chicago		Detroit		New York		total	
Yes, was garnisheed	28	(57)	61	(28)	37	(19)	38	(104)
No, was not garnisheed	57	(37)	57	(70)	71	(59)	62	(166)

One might suppose that debtors who worked out settlements only after garnishment proceedings had been instituted were negotiating with guns to their heads and consequently were not likely to view the settlement as fair. In the aggregate, this view finds much support in that only 38 percent of the garnisheed debtors who settled thought that the settlement was fair, compared with 62 percent of the nongarnisheed who settled. But this aggregate pattern must be qualified. It holds in Chicago and New York, but not in Detroit, where garnishment was an extremely harsh remedy. In that city satisfaction with the settlement was slightly more prevalent among the garnisheed than the nongarnisheed. Perhaps the harshness of the Michigan garnishment law made the threat of garnishment as powerful as garnishment itself in forcing debtors into settlements that they did not consider fair.

OUTCOME OF THE DEBT:
THE SUCCESS OF THE COLLECTION PROCESS

Apart from whether settlements were obtained, there is the ultimate question of the outcome of the case. To what extent did the creditor receive satisfaction insofar as this could be determined some four to six months after the initiation of the law suit? This qualification is most important, for in a number of cases the creditor–plaintiff does not collect until several years after the initiation of the law suit, often not until the debtor can be found and his new employer served with a garnishment notice. All we know is the state of the case as reported by the debtor–defendant at the time of the interview. Relying on the testimony of the debtors themselves, we find that in the three garnishment cities combined, 22 percent reported paying in full, 38 percent claimed they had resumed payments, and 40 percent said they had made no payments. Based on the connection between garnishment and resumption of payments, these figures appear to underestimate creditor satisfaction. In all, 414 debtors in Chicago, Detroit, and New York reported that their employers had been served with garnishment notices. Seventy percent of this group said they had resumed payments; the remaining 30 percent (126 debtors) claimed they had made no payments. In a majority of these 126 cases the debtor's claim was accurate: in spite of the garnishment no payment was made. Fifty percent of these debtors were fired, quit their jobs, or went bankrupt. Another 25 percent claimed that in spite of the garnishment order their employer did not make deductions from their pay. No doubt some of these debtors (31 in all) were mistaken, but we shall give them the benefit of the doubt and treat them as nonpayers. (In some of these cases, the employer may have challenged the legitimacy of the garnishment or claimed that he did not owe the debtor any wages at the time the garnishment order arrived.) But there still remain 25 percent (of 126) who claimed they had not resumed payments even though they had been garnisheed, and, according to their own testimony, their employer had made deductions from their pay. These debtors clearly were differentiating between voluntary and forced payments when they answered the queries about resumption of payments. In the subsequent analysis we shall treat them as members of the group that resumed payments, since our focus in this section is on the success of the creditor's suit, independent of the debtor's readiness to pay.

When the debtors' reports are revised in light of the garnishment outcomes, we find that in the aggregate, 63 percent of the debtors had made at least some payments on their obligation by the time of the interview and 22 percent had paid in full. There is little intercity variation. In New York and Chicago about one fourth of the debtors had paid in full, with full payments lagging somewhat in Detroit. But in all three cities, creditors met with relatively equal success in getting debtors at least to resume payments (slightly more so in Detroit—66 percent; and slightly less so in Chicago—60 percent). Had we information on a much longer time period than one third to one half a year after the initiation of the suit, the proportion of debtors forced to resume payments would no doubt be much higher. (We have already seen that the garnishment rate increased substantially in Chicago when a longer time span was taken into account.) Creditors who bring suits against defaulting debtors thus do quite well in getting additional payments, for in the majority of cases the debtors resumed payments, although many of them probably had valid defenses.

The debtors who said they had not made payments were asked to explain their reasons, which are presented in Table 12.8. (Included here are the 31 debtors who by their own testimony were nonpayers even though they have been counted as payers based on their answers to the garnishment questions.)

Table 12.8 / Reasons for Not Paying by City (percent)

reason category	Chicago	Detroit	New York	total
Never heard from firm—assumes debt is settled	2	4	6	4
Court action pending, or currently negotiating	16	11	5	11
Cannot pay—will pay when able	41	56	63	54
Declared bankruptcy	20	12	4	12
Refuses to pay (cheated)	21	17	22	20
Total percent	100	100	100	101
N	(135)	(184)	(131)	(450)

Although the table shows five categories of reasons, they tend to reduce to three: uncertain outcome (failure to hear from creditor or action pending), inability to pay, and refusal to pay. In the aggregate, about one in five had not paid because they refused to honor a debt that they did not consider fair. These are the debtors who felt cheated and would not be intimidated into resuming payments. (Others who also felt cheated were coerced into resuming payments.) In each city a few of the debtors who had not paid claimed they had not heard from the company, and as far as they knew the debt was somehow settled. Somewhat more, especially in Chicago, reported that the issue was still being negotiated or that a court action was pending. All told, 15 percent of those who had not paid gave such reasons (the first two groups combined). By far the most common reason offered by default-debtors in each city was their inability to pay. Although this reason would appear to be much more frequent in New York than in Chicago, the next category, "bankruptcy," undoubtedly also reflects inability to pay, and bankruptcies were much more likely to occur in Chicago than in New York. These two categories together—"cannot pay" and "bankruptcy"—account for about two thirds of the nonpayers, both within each city and in the aggregate.

Characteristics of Debtors and Outcome

Whether debtors are black or white, poor or not so poor, has influenced a number of the phenomena examined. Will these characteristics also be related to the success of the collection effort? Ethnicity is related to collection but in a way different from that suggested by the results on settlement. Although whites were more likely than blacks to report their cases settled, they were less likely than blacks or Puerto Ricans to have resumed payments. Forty-five percent of the whites had not made any payments, compared with 34 percent of the blacks and 32 percent of the Puerto Ricans. This finding is all the more puzzling because income is related to the resumption of payments, and, as we have noted time and again, blacks and Puerto Ricans earn less than whites. Among those earning under $4,000 only 48 percent had at least resumed payments by the time of the interview; in the $4,000–$7,999 group this proportion rises to 68 percent, and among those earning over $8,000, it increases to 73 percent. Minority-group debtors were thus more likely than whites to resume payments even though they earned less than whites. How these contradictory forces of ethnicity and income jointly affect collection can be seen from Table 12.9.

Table 12.9 / Collection by Ethnicity and Income
(Percentage Who Resumed Payments)

income	whites		blacks		Puerto Ricans	
Under $4,000	31	(39)	47	(171)	66	(41)
$4,000–$7,999	56	(149)	73	(336)	69	(32)
$8,000 and over	69	(91)	79	(116)	69	(13)

These figures report the percentage in each ethnic and income group who had resumed payments or paid in full after being sued. From the columns we learn that the income pattern is particularly strong for whites and blacks but is virtually absent among Puerto Ricans, and from the rows we see that even when income is taken in account, whites pay less frequently than blacks and, on two income levels, less often than Puerto Ricans as well. In fact, the ethnic pattern is now more pronounced when the masking effect of income is removed. Why is it that whites, who are more likely than blacks to settle out of court, are least likely of the three ethnic groups to resume payments? Whites were less likely than blacks to feel cheated, and hence this reason for not paying cannot explain the patterns of Table 12.9. But another "reason" category shown earlier might be relevent—"bankruptcy." Debtors who declared bankruptcy were presumably exonerated of their debts and were likely to have reported their debt problem as settled. Apart from the volunteered reason of "bankrupt," we have independent information on the number of debtors who declared bankruptcy at the time of this debt problem. All debtors were asked if and when they had ever gone into bankruptcy. On the basis of these questions, some 85 debtors in the three garnishment cities, 8 percent of the entire sample, filed for bankruptcy during the period of this debt problem. Bankruptcies were most common in Chicago (12 percent) and least so in New York (3 percent) with Detroit in between (10 percent). In the aggregate, whites were more likely than blacks and Puerto Ricans to declare bankruptcy, 13 percent compared with 7 and 6 percent, respectively. Given the greater likelihood of whites to enter bankruptcy, does this in any way explain why whites were less likely than the other ethnic groups to make payments on their debts? Table 12.10 shows that bankruptcy does help explain the ethnic difference.

Table 12.10 / Collection by Ethnicity and Bankruptcy (Percentage Who Resumed Payments)

declared bankruptcy	whites		blacks		Puerto Ricans	
Yes	22	(36)	25	(44)	[40]	(5)
No	60	(252)	69	(612)	69	(85)

Among the bankrupts (top row) the difference between whites and blacks virtually disappears. Among nonbankrupts, whites are somewhat more likely than blacks or Puerto Ricans to avoid payments, but these differences are much smaller than those recorded in Table 12.9. Bankruptcy, then, explains in large part the ethnic differences regarding resumption of payments.

There is one by-product of Table 12.10 that deserves comment. One might suppose that all bankrupts were freed of their debts and did not have to make payments on the debt in question. But the top row shows that even among the bankrupts, approximately one fourth did resume payments. This finding reflects less on the accuracy of our data than on abuses of the bankruptcy law. Many creditors whose claims against debtors should be erased by bankruptcy nonetheless continue to press their claims, taking advantage of loopholes in the bankruptcy law. One provision of the law requires that the debtor disclose to the creditor all his other debts at the time of the transaction. Creditors who can demonstrate that they never learned of the debtor's other obligations can claim an exemption to the bankruptcy proceeding, and, as Table 12.10 makes clear, some creditors continue to press their claims against bankrupts and even manage to collect.[14]

The Role of Garnishment in Collection

A central concern of this chapter is the efficacy of garnishment as a collection device. As noted, it is of value to the creditor not only as a means of recovering his loss, but also as a threat to coerce those not officially garnisheed into resuming payment. The power of this collection remedy cannot be deduced simply by comparing the outcomes in cases where the debtor was or was not garnisheed. We have already seen that in a number of instances, garnishment is not successful, for it either leads to job loss or encourages the debtor to file for bankruptcy. Nonetheless, there is some value in comparing collection among those who were and those were not garnisheed. Among those who could be garnisheed (the employed), some 77 percent of those who were in fact garnisheed resumed payments or paid in full, compared with 63 percent of the nongarnisheed. Of perhaps more significance than the 14-percentage-point difference is the similarity between the two groups. Whether garnisheed or not, a majority of the debtors resumed payments. Of course those who were not garnisheed might well have been responding to the threat of garnishment, but it is also conceivable that many of them are men of goodwill who are ready to make payments on their debts when they can.[15]

The Debtor's Sense of Fairness and Outcome

Earlier we saw that garnishment induces settlements that debtors do not consider fair. Does garnishment have a similar effect among those who did not settle? More precisely, are debtors who did not think they should have to pay the court judgment more likely to resume payments if they were garnisheed? Presumably debtors who do not consider the debt fair, other things being equal, would be less likely to pay than those who did not question the legitimacy of their obligation. And the data show this to be so. Among those who did not settle (the question was asked

[14]For an excellent critique of this loophole, see Philip Shuchman, *The Fraud Exception in Consumer Bankruptcy,* 23 Stanford L. Rev. 735 (Apr. 1971).

[15]Vivid proof of the fundamental honesty of debtors is provided by events in the state of Nebraska. In 1969 the Supreme Court of Nebraska declared that the interest rates on time sales contracts violated the state's usury laws and therefore were unconstitutional. The court decision meant that installment debtors in Nebraska were not obligated to continue payments on their debts. Nonetheless, to the surprise of the credit industry, most debtors continued to make payments even though they were not legally required to do so.

only of this majority group) 47 percent of those who felt they should not have to pay did resume payments, whereas 60 percent of those who accepted the obligation resumed payments. (It will be noted that the average of these figures is lower than that reported in previous tables. This is because the substantial minority who "settled" are excluded.) Although the difference is in the expected direction, one might well ask why any of those who considered the judgment unfair resumed payments, much less 47 percent of them. Can these "unwilling" payers be explained by the creditor's use of garnishment? That garnishment may be a factor is suggested by its relationship to the debtor's sense of fairness. Of those who questioned the judgment, 55 percent were garnisheed compared with 48 percent who accepted their obligation. Presumably those who consider the burden unfair are more likely to need coercion. The joint roles played in collection by garnishment and the debtor's sense of fair play are shown in Table 12.11.

Table 12.11 / Collection by Garnishment and Whether There Was a Good Reason for Not Paying (Percentage Resuming Payments)

	garnishment among employed	
good reason for not paying	yes	no
No	82 (143)	58 (152)
Yes	63 (155)	38 (128)

The efficacy of garnishment can be seen from the rows of the table. Regardless of whether the debtor considered the debt legitimate, he was much more likely to resume payments if he had been garnisheed. Debtors most likely to resume payments were those who were both garnisheed and accepting of the obligation; their opposite numbers were least likely to pay. Where these forces were working at cross pressures, more than one half of the debtors resumed payment (63 percent of the garnisheed who objected to the debt and 58 percent of the nongarnisheed who had no objection). In sum, the difference shown in the first row testifies to the effectiveness of garnishment in overcoming the debtor's resistance to pay on what he considers an illegitimate debt, whereas the difference in the first column measures the impact of the debtor's attitude toward the debt, for even when garnisheed, those who felt the debt unfair paid less often than those who did not question it.

Collection and Reasons for Default

The reasons for the breakdown in the credit transaction were examined in chapters 4 through 8. We now consider whether any relationship exists between reasons for the breakdown and the likelihood that the creditor will receive some satisfaction. This matter is most central to the collection business. If certain reasons for the breakdown are less productive than others, then creditors would clearly stand to gain by screening such cases and concentrating on those leading to retribution. On the other hand, if the art of collection rests on wearing down debtors in default and using against them whatever sanctions are at hand, then reasons for default should not be related to collection. To examine this issue, we shall deal with only the *primary* reason for default.[16] Although 12 major categories of reasons were identified, some appeared as primary reasons too infrequently to be included. In all, 9 categories of primary reasons are considered as they relate to the resumption of payments. These categories contain from 18 to 426 cases and account for 90 percent of the Chicago, Detroit, and New York debtors. Table 12.12 shows how collection is related to these 9 primary reasons for default.

Table 12.12 / Primary Reason for Default by Outcome of Collection (Three Garnishment Cities Combined)

reason for default	percentage resuming payments	No. cases
Debtor leaves town	79	(19)
Payment misunderstanding	77	(78)
Voluntary overextension	73	(145)
Victim of own third party	68	(82)
Involuntary overextension	67	(49)
Debtor irresponsibility	61	(18)
Loss of income	60	(426)
Allegation of fraud	54	(143)
Marital instability	45	(51)

The categories have been ordered according to the frequency with which debtors resumed payments. It is of considerable significance that the two categories heading the list stand for error rather than incapacity, malice, or resentment. The group most likely to resume payments consists of debtors who simply forgot to pay while they were out of town. Virtually four of every five debtors in this group resumed payments. Close behind are those debtors who appear to be victims of the creditor's error, that is, the cases of payment misunderstanding. Once such a misunderstanding is straightened out, a great majority of such debtors resume payment

[16]The reader will remember that we recorded, where appropriate, primary, secondary, and tertiary reasons for the default, but to simplify the analysis on hand, the focus will be on what seemed to be the most important reason.

(77 percent). It is quite significant that presumably satisfactory resolutions result in those cases in which the default can be traced to error on the part of either the debtor or his creditor. Were there sufficient communication between debtors and their creditors, cases such as these would not have to go to court. Somewhat surprisingly, not far behind in third place are the voluntarily overextended debtors. In fourth place are the debtors who got into trouble through no fault of their own (other than volunteering to be cosigners or lending their credit cards to people they thought they could trust). More than two thirds of these innocent third parties had made at least some payments by the time of the interview.

Still another group of debtors that prove "trustworthy" from the creditor's point of view are those who found themselves overextended because of an unexpected demand on their income, such as illness or death in their family. About two thirds of these debtors had resumed payments. There are only 18 debtors in the group that comes closest to the creditor's stereotype of the "deadbeat," debtors who had little intention of paying or simply forgot about their payments, and, 61 percent of this group had made at least some payments. By far the largest category of default-debtors consists of those who lost income either because of illness or unemployment, and 60 percent of these debtors had resumed payments. This would suggest that most people who experience temporary setbacks are well aware of their debt obligations and will resume payment without legal action being brought against them.

Of particular interest is the group of debtors ranking next to last in resumption of payments, those who felt they were victims of fraud. Even in this category, 54 percent resumed payments. These debtors perhaps more than any others serve as a testimonial to the power of creditor's remedies, for even when debtors are convinced that they have been victims of fraud, they are likely to resume payment. But whereas the slight majority who do pay testifies to the strength of collection practices, the large minority who do not pay when they think they have been wronged (a finding in keeping with the pattern in Table 12.11) points to the need for channels of communication between creditors and debtors which might well reduce the costs of collection and increase the satisfaction of both parties.

Of all the reasons for default, only marital instability results in less than a majority resuming payments. But since communication between the spouses was apt to have broken down, the respondents' reports in this category are highly suspect. It is quite possible that in a number of cases, the missing spouse was forced to resume payments, even though the spouse we interviewed was adamant that he or she was not making payments on the debt. In short, were we to know the full story for the last category in Table 12.12, we might find that the rate of repayment was at least as high as for some of the other categories.

Remaining to be seen is the role of garnishment in producing payments when reason for default is taken into account. Two categories drop out of this more refined analysis because of their small numbers, "debtor irresponsibility" and "debtor leaves town." The categories of Table 12.13 have been ordered according to the difference in repayment rates between garnisheed and nongarnisheed debtors in the labor force, a difference that might be taken as a measure of the efficacy of garnishment.

Table 12.13 / Percentage Resuming Payments by Primary Reason for Default and Garnishment (among Those in Labor Force)

primary reason for default	garnishment among the employed				percentage difference (columns 1 and 2)
	yes		no		
Involuntary overextension	86	(22)	64	(22)	+22
Loss of income	80	(164)	58	(183)	+22
Allegations of fraud	68	(56)	48	(60)	+20
Marital instability	67	(15)	52	(21)	+15
Payment misunderstanding	87	(31)	75	(33)	+12
Voluntary overextension	76	(68)	74	(65)	+02
Victim of own third party	66	(35)	79	(38)	−13

With one exception, garnisheed debtors in all categories were more likely to resume payments than the nongarnisheed. The inexplicable oddity consists of the category comprised largely of cosigners, those who were victims of their own third parties. Another strange result is supplied by the group of voluntarily overextended debtors. One might assume that these debtors, many of whom behaved irresponsibly, would need considerable prodding to pay their creditors. But this turns out not to be the case at all. The overextended who were not garnisheed were almost as likely to resume payments as those who were. The three categories of reasons in which garnishment is most effective from the creditor's point of view are involuntary overextension, loss of income, and fraud. In each of these instances the garnisheed workers were much more likely than the nongarnisheed to resume payments. One might expect such a result in the fraud group, for the inclination of these debtors is not to pay unless forced to do so. But it is also true of the debtors who were confronted with unexpected expenses and loss of income. Garnishment is also a factor, although less influential, in the "marital instability" and "payment misunderstanding" categories.

On the basis of these and earlier findings, it is obvious that garnishment is a powerful collection device. In fact, it is probably more important than these differences indicate, for, as noted, the threat of garnishment coerces the nongarnisheed to resume payments. But it is perhaps more significant that regardless of garnishment and the reason for default among those still in the labor force, a majority in all but one instance (the nongarnisheed who defaulted because of fraud, who missed being a majority by 3 percentage points) did resume payments. It may well be that debtors who default are ready to resume payments more often than the credit industry realizes. In short, it would seem that creditors need not depend solely on their coercive collection devices. Many debtors in default are aware of their obligation to pay and will do so when they can, even if not garnisheed. These findings strongly suggest that creditors unduly rely on their harsh collection devices and have much to gain from developing channels of communication with their debtors which in turn would make law suits and enforced collections less necessary.

EXECUTION

UPON JUDGMENT:

THE PHILADELPHIA

STORY

How do creditors collect from default-debtors in a state that prohibits garnishment? The answer, at least in Pennsylvania, is that they attach assets other than income: personal and real property.[1] The former refers generally to household furnishings and appliances and the latter to real estate. Such property executions are greatly facilitated by Pennsylvania's recognition of the confession-of-judgment doctrine, which is frequently incorporated in installment-sales contracts. Under this law the debtor waives all defenses against the seller in advance, and thereby forfeits

[1] In the other state that prohibits garnishment, Texas, creditors are much less prone to attach real property and rely instead on harassment and unusually high interest rates, which make losses easier to bear. Behind this discrepancy in collection practices in the two states prohibiting garnishment are sharp differences in their Homestead Act exemptions. In Pennsylvania, only $300 of the debtor's property is exempt from execution. In Texas, until 1970, $5,000 of the debtor's property, plus additional exemptions for automobiles and other personal property, was exempt from execution by law. After 1970, the limit was raised to $10,000. Undoubtedly these variations in Homestead Acts account for much of the difference in collection practices between Pennsylvania and Texas. Creditors in garnishment states can also attach the debtor's real and personal property but rarely do so except in home improvement transactions. Apparently creditors routinely take a lien on the house as security for a home improvement loan.

his right to a day in court.[2] The creditor's reliance on real and personal property executions in the Philadelphia sample is, of course, not problematic, for these default-debtors could be located only by sampling the sheriff's real and personal property execution books.

The analysis in this chapter focuses on four sets of questions. How frequent are confession of judgment contracts and how do they differ from open suits? How do the plaintiffs and defendants in real property executions differ from those in personal property executions? How often do property executions actually occur? To what extent do Philadelphia plaintiffs collect on their bad debts, and how does collection in Philadelphia compare with collection in the garnishment cities?

OPEN SUITS VERSUS
CONFESSION-OF-JUDGMENT CONTRACTS

Although Pennsylvania recognizes confession of judgment, not all creditors use such contracts. Of the 249 default-debtors in the Philadelphia sample, 41 debtors, 17 percent, had not signed confession-of-judgment contracts. Their creditors had sued them and won judgments against them before turning to the sheriff for execution. Since the type of contract used is the decision of the creditor, we should find that it is related to type of creditor. The data show this to be so. General retailers, in sharp contrast with other types of creditors, tend to shun the confession-of-judgment contract. Only 29 percent of their cases employed confession contracts, whereas the substantial majority of cases of all other types of creditors involved this form. Confession of judgment contracts are typically used by creditors who plan to sell their contracts, for such a clause makes the contract more negotiable. In contrast, creditors who keep their own contracts, such as general retailers, may be less inclined to rely on confession of judgment for fear of generating ill will among their customers. After all, to deprive a person of his property without giving him his day in court is certainly one way to lose goodwill. But why the heavy reliance on confession-of-judgment contracts by the lenders—the banks and small loan companies—since they almost always keep their own paper? Most likely these institutions use such contracts on the assumption in the loan business that defaults invariably stem from errors and failures on the part of the debtor. Given this assumption of debtor guilt, the debtor presumably is done a good turn by being found automatically guilty, for he is saved the added expense of court costs.

---

[2] As noted, this doctrine was modified in 1970 as a result of a law suit brought by the OEO legal services program in Philadelphia. Confessions of judgment are no longer binding on debtors who earn under $10,000 a year.

TYPE OF EXECUTION

Although personal property executions were filed much more frequently than real property executions, the latter were oversampled, with the result that 34 percent of the Philadelphia sample involved real property executions, and 66 percent, personal property executions.[3]

What circumstances result in creditor–plaintiffs seeking real rather than personal property executions? Type of contract turns out to be strongly related to type of execution. Of the minority of open suits, only 3 percent resulted in real property executions, but of the confession-of-judgment cases, 40 percent led to executions against real property. Clearly, the harsher contract is associated with the harsher collection device.

The type of execution sought is a decision that rests with the plaintiff, who is often a third party rather than the original seller. Of course, there are constraints operating on the plaintiff; he can execute against real property only if the debtor has such property, but a large proportion of Philadelphians are home owners. In our sample, property owners constituted a majority of the debtors—some 64 percent—or almost twice as many as the number of real property executions sought by the plaintiffs. The plaintiffs in Philadelphia did then exercise discretion on this issue. The question that now confronts us is whether real rather than personal property executions were sought by certain types of plaintiffs more often than by others. The shift from original creditor to plaintiff results in two dramatis personae leaving the stage and being replaced by two others. Very few automobile dealers and low-income retailers appeared as plaintiffs, but finance companies and collection agencies showed up in large numbers. Table 13.1 shows that certain types of plaintiffs were indeed more likely than others to execute against real property.

Table 13.1 / Type of Property Attachment by Plaintiff (percent)

type of execution	collection agency	small loan company	finance company	bank	direct seller	general retailer
Real property	90	37	25	15	8	—
Personal property	10	63	75	85	92	100
Total percent	100	100	100	100	100	100
N	(31)	(63)	(102)	(13)	(12)	(11)

None of the relatively few general retailers who kept their own paper and sued in their own name sought real property executions, and hardly

[3]The true proportion of real property cases is about one in six rather than one in three.

any of the direct sellers who brought suits against delinquent debtors went after real property. Sellers of merchandise would seem to avoid attachment of real property. But the same cannot be said of lenders and the various third parties who were brought into these cases. Banks and small loan companies are most likely to be original lenders rather than holders-in-due-course, whereas finance companies by definition are third parties to the transaction. Substantial minorities of these plaintiffs pursue real property executions ranging from 15 percent of the bank plaintiffs to 37 percent of the small loan companies, with finance companies falling in between at 25 percent. It should be noted that all these creditor–plaintiffs entered the picture before the debt went bad. The one plaintiff who appears after the debtor has defaulted is the collection agency, a business that thrives in Philadelphia. Collection agencies, the table shows, almost always attack the debtor's most valuable asset, his real property. This finding is in keeping with a number of exposés of sheriff's sales of homes in Philadelphia that have appeared in the newspaper of the Consumer Education and Protection Association, *Consumer's Voice*. [4] These articles identify several collection agencies, including those that appear in our sample, as conspiring with unscrupulous real estate firms which buy the homes at these auctions for a fraction of their value. It must be kept in mind that the suits brought by these collection agencies represent transactions between debtors and such presumably reputable firms as banks and general retailers. Such creditors prefer to turn their bad accounts over to collection agencies rather than risk injury to their goodwill. Debtors dealing with the most reputable firms can nevertheless suffer the most severe sanctions as the collection work is turned over to hard-nosed professionals. A cautionary note must be sounded, however. So far we have identified only the proportion of property executions sought by various types of plaintiffs, not the proportion actually carried out. As we shall see, most of these executions are not carried out.

One might suppose that creditors will seek the more valuable collateral of real property when the amount of money at stake is large, and the data show this to be the case. Among debts under $200, only 10 percent involved real property as distinct from personal property threats. This figure steadily rises with amount of debt, reaching 64 percent for debts over $1,000. Will amount of debt negate the earlier pattern linking real property executions to type of plaintiff? The answer is provided by Table 13.2.

The differences between plaintiffs in their attachment of real property is not explained by the amount of the debt. Whether the debt is above or below $500, collection agencies, followed by small loan companies, are most likely to execute against real property, whereas banks, direct sellers, and general retailers are least likely to do so.

[4] See *Consumer's Voice* (Feb. 1970), V. 5, No. 2, V. 6, No. 1 (Jan. 1971).

Table 13.2 / Percentage of Real Property Executions
by Amount of Debt and Type of Plaintiff

| | amount of debt | |
type of plaintiff	under $500	$500 and over
Collection agency	81 (16)	100 (15)
Small loan company	14 (29)	56 (34)
Finance company	2 (46)	42 (57)
Bank	a (3)	20 (10)
Direct seller	— (9)	a (3)
General retailer	— (4)	— (7)

^a Base too small to percentage.

As might be expected, the more well-to-do Philadelphia debtor was especially likely to be a home owner, although in each income group a majority did own their own homes at the time of the debt problem. Home ownership ranged from 56 percent of those earning under $4,000 to 63 percent of those in the middle-income group, to 80 percent of those earning over $8,000. But real property executions do not follow this income pattern. Real property executions were sought against 36 percent of the poor, 27 percent of the middle-income group, and 43 percent of the high-income group. When the rate of executions is compared with home owner-ship within each income group, it is evident that creditors sought real property executions from the poor much more often than from those financially better off. The Philadelphia white debtors were more likely than the blacks to experience real property executions, 43 percent compared with 30 percent, a finding reflecting, no doubt, their greater likelihood of being home owners.

THE OUTCOME OF THE PROPERTY EXECUTION

The Philadelphia debtors were asked whether they knew that their property was being threatened, and whether they had, in fact, lost their real or personal property because of the debt problem. Table 13.3 shows these results separately for real and personal property executions. In most cases, the execution, whether against real or personal property, was not carried out.[5] These collection devices apparently serve mainly to coerce debtors to resume payments rather than to satisfy the debts directly. This general pattern notwithstanding, some debtors did lose their property by the time of the interview and, when they did, it was usually real

[5] Of course many debtors were having their property threatened at the time of the interview, and some no doubt have since lost their property. As in the case of garnishment rates, these figures no doubt underestimate the true rate of property loss.

Table 13.3 / Outcome of Execution according to Type (percent)

outcome	real property	personal property
Property seized	24	5
Property not seized but debtor aware of threat	66	68
Debtor not award of threat	10	26
Total percent	100	99
N	(79) [a]	(165)

[a] Real property executions were obtained against 84 debtors according to the execution books. Five respondents claimed that they did not own their home at the time of the debt problem and these cases are excluded from the table. This anomaly may reflect errors on the part of either the plaintiff or the respondent. It is conceivable that in some cases, the plaintiff was mistaken in assuming that the debtor owned property and conversely a few respondents, especially those who were not themselves the debtor, may have misinterpreted the question as applying to them rather than the debtor or they may have been unaware that the debtor owned real property.

property that they lost. The 24 percent in the first column who lost their homes represents 19 cases, 8 percent of the Philadelphia sample. (The 5 percent who lost personal property amounts to only nine debtors.) In chapter 12 we saw that at least 8 percent of the debtors in the garnishment cities (including the unemployed and those who were never garnisheed) lost their jobs because of garnishment proceedings. We now see that an equal proportion in Philadelphia suffered perhaps as serious a consequence—the loss of their home.

The 19 debtors who lost their homes tended to have larger than average debts. They were apt to have gotten into trouble because of fairly large personal loans or home repair transactions of some magnitude. But a few lost their homes as a result of fairly trivial transactions. For example, a 67-year-old black woman lost her home because she cosigned for her granddaughter who had bought a $150 wig from a door-to-door salesman. A 43-year-old black lost his home because a door-to-door salesman had talked him into buying a cemetery lot on time. And in chapter 6 we presented the case of a black woman whose home was being threatened because she had been tricked by a door-to-door salesman into buying a garbage disposal unit. (Neither she nor the other Philadelphians whose homes were in danger are counted among the 19 who lost their homes by the time of the interview.)

Among the nine debtors who experienced personal property executions are several who had horrifying experiences. A black woman, now separated from her husband, explained how her husband had responded to an advertisement about consolidation loans. He borrowed $1,500 from a small loan company and over a period of five years had repaid almost $4,000 on this loan. Eventually he defaulted and the plaintiff seized all their furniture, including a TV set, living room furniture, a freezer, and a $350 dining room set that had been purchased shortly before the seizure. These goods realized a grand total of $25 in the "public" auction, and it was this paltry sum that was deducted from her debt. It is dubious whether debtors who default receive fair value in the initial transaction, but it is obvious that those who experience repossessions and the resale of their goods do not.[6]

Type of Plaintiff and Outcome of Execution

We have seen that most of the executions actually carried out involved real rather than personal property, and that where property was not seized, debtors were more likely to be aware of the threat to their real rather than their personal property. Table 13.4 shows how type of plaintiff is related to property execution when real and personal property cases are combined.

Table 13.4 / Outcome of Property Executions by Type of Plaintiff (percent)

outcome	direct seller	general retailer	finance company	collection agency	bank	small loan company
Property taken	—	8	11	12	15	16
Debtor aware of threat	85	50	69	76	69	66
Debtor not aware of threat to property	15	42	20	12	15	19
Total percent	100	100	100	100	99	101
N	(13)	(12)	(103)	(34)	(13)	(64)

The plaintiffs are ordered in Table 13.4 according to the likelihood of their carrying out the property execution (the top row). Direct sellers who sue in their own name cause less harm to debtors than collection agencies, banks, and small loan companies. The pattern in the second row indicates that plaintiffs do not generally seize the property of their default-debtor but rather use the execution as a threat. From the last row we learn that only one type of plaintiff deviates from this pattern, the general retailer. In more than two of five cases, the debtor who has dealt with a general retailer does not even know that his property has been threatened. This may well be a testimonial to the milder collection techniques employed by general retailers.

[6]Philip Shuchman, *Profit on Default: An Archival Study of Automobile Repossession and Resale,* 22 Stanford L. Rev. 20 (Nov. 1969).

Type of Debtor and Outcome of Execution

Although whites were more likely than blacks to be the targets of real property executions, they were more successful than blacks in avoiding actual executions. Among the real property cases, only 14 percent of the whites lost their homes compared with 26 percent of the blacks, and for personal property cases the comparable figures are 2 and 6 percent. Although actual property executions were uncommon, they were much more likely to affect blacks than whites.

One might suppose that income serves as a deterrent to property executions, since those of higher income would be better equipped to resume payments and thus stave off the execution. In the aggregate this is true, as only 7 percent of Philadelphians earning above $8,000 lost property, compared with 22 percent of those earning under $4,000. Since whites earn more than blacks, income might possibly explain why blacks were more likely than whites to lose their property. That there is much merit to this view can be seen from Table 13.5. Within each income group the difference between whites and blacks narrows sharply, indicating that blacks experience more property loss in the aggregate than whites because they tend to have lower income.

Table 13.5 / Percentage Losing Property (Real or Personal) by Income and Ethnicity

ethnicity	under $4,000	$4,000–7,999	$8,000 and over
Whites	27 (11)	6 (35)	5 (19)
Blacks	22 (60)	6 (81)	9 (21)

Amount of Debt and Outcome of Execution

We have seen that size of debt was associated with the creditor's seeking real rather than personal property executions. By the same token, we might expect that the actual seizure of the debtor's property, whether real or personal and especially the former, is also related to the amount of money at stake. This expectation does hold for real property executions. In this group the rate of seizures steadily increased with size of debt, reaching 28 percent in cases where the debt exceeded $1,000. Among personal property executions, there is no relationship; personal property is rarely seized, no matter what size the debt is.

Legal Assistance and Property Executions

The conditions under which debtor-defendants in the three garnishment cities obtain legal assistance were considered in chapters 11 and 12. Note was taken of the fundamental irony of consumer law suits: the cost of an attorney for the debtor is frequently greater than the amount of money in dispute. On this basis it was found that the seeking of legal help by debtors tended to follow economic considerations. Those being sued for large sums of money were more likely to hire lawyers than those sued for small sums, and debtors whose jobs were threatened by garnishment were more prone to hire lawyers than their nongarnisheed fellow debtors. A similar pattern of rationality underlies the use of lawyers by Philadelphia debtors. All told, some 28 percent of the Philadelphia debtors turned to lawyers, a figure somewhat higher than those in the other cities. Those who experienced a property loss were most likely to turn to lawyers (52 percent), and those not even aware of the threat to their property were least likely to do so (13 percent). (Among those aware of the threat to their property, 25 percent hired lawyers.) Debtors are thus more likely to use lawyers when they stand to lose a great deal than when they have valid defenses. Financial considerations tend to override the legal system's assumption that matters in dispute will be decided on their merits.

COLLECTION IN PHILADELPHIA

From chapter 12 we learned that at least 63 percent of the default-debtors in the three garnishment cities had either paid in full or resumed payments (an estimate that takes account of those who had been garnisheed even though not admitting to resuming payments). How does this figure compare with the rate of collection in Philadelphia, a nongarnishment city? Just as we found some debtors in Chicago, Detroit, and New York who admitted to being ganisheed but insisted they had not resumed payments, so we find some Philadelphia debtors who experienced property execu- tions but insisted they had made no payments. Of the 29 debtors in the Philadelphia sample who lost either real or personal property because of the debt, 16 claimed that they had not made payments. They will be counted as payers, as were their garnisheed counterparts in the other cities. Table 13.6 shows the comparative outcomes of the debt problem in all four sample cities. These data allow comparison of two very different systems of collection of consumer debts. The Philadelphia system, which rests upon property executions rather than wage garnishments, turns out

Table 13.6 / State of Collection at Time of Interview by City (percent)

outcome	Philadelphia	Chicago	Detroit	New York
Debt paid off	20	26	18	24
Resumed payments	49	34	48	40
No payments made	31	40	34	37
Total percent	100	100	100	101
N	(245)	(312)	(396)	(328)

to be, if anything, more effective than the collection system in the three garnishment cities. Sixty-nine percent of the Philadelphia default-debtors had at least resumed payments, compared with 66 percent in Detroit, 64 percent in New York, and 60 percent in Chicago. But these differences are not large. In fact, Chicago, the city with the lowest overall rate of resumed payments, is nonetheless first in terms of debts paid in full by the time of the interview. Had we a different measure of the efficacy of collection, such as the *proportion* of the total outstanding debt actually collected, Chicago might well lead the other cities. Perhaps the safest conclusion to be drawn from Table 13.6 is that in spite of sharp variations in the laws governing collection in the four cities, the outcomes are remarkably similar. Presumably, giving the creditor the right to attach the debtor's real and personal property is as powerful a weapon as allowing him to attach the debtor's wages. But underlying the relative efficacy of these coercive remedies may well be the fundamental goodwill of most debtors, their readiness to pay, when they can, debts they consider legitimate.

Type of Execution and Collection

Which type of execution, attachment of real or of personal property, is more likely to lead to collection? What is the efficacy of the *threat* of these types of executions? We have seen that real property threats are carried out more often than personal property ones, and on this basis alone we might expect executions against real property to be more productive for the creditor. Real property executions are indeed more likely than personal property executions to result in payments, 82 percent compared with 62 percent. This difference is much greater than that based on executions actually *carried out* (which we count as payments). In fact, when the minority who lost their property are eliminated, we find that 77 percent of those who faced a real property execution resumed payments, compared with 60 percent of those confronted with a personal property execution. This difference is further reinforced when those who paid in full are examined. Among those faced with a real property threat and who did not lose their homes, 41 percent had paid in full by the time of the interview, compared with only 10 percent of those threatened with a personal property execution. The more severe weapon of execution against real property is clearly more productive for the creditor, even though it is used less frequently than the personal property execution.

As noted, not all Philadelphia debtors were aware of the threat to their personal or real property. To what extent did their awareness influence payments? (It could be of course that debtors were not aware of the threat because they had resumed payments, but it is also possible that they did not pay because they did not know their creditor had filed papers for a property execution.) It turns out that awareness has an impact on payment only among those confronted with a real property execution. In this group, 79 percent resumed payment compared with 63 percent of the handful who did not know their homes were threatened. Among the personal property cases, awareness made little difference, as 61 percent of the aware and 58 percent of the unaware resumed payment. These findings further confirm the greater efficacy of real property executions as a collection device in Philadelphia, but the critical point, as noted, is that most Philadelphia debtors resumed payments even, as we now learn, when they were not aware of a threat to their real or personal property. This again speaks well for the integrity and good intentions of most default-debtors.

Characteristics of Debtors and Collection

We saw that in the garnishment cities blacks and Puerto Ricans were more likely than whites to resume payments and that the more well-to-do were more prone to pay than the poor. In Philadelphia only the income pattern is supported. Philadelphia whites were much more likely than blacks to have paid in full (35 percent compared with 14 percent) and were slightly more likely to have at least resumed payments (72 percent compared with 69 percent). In contrast, income was much more decisive. Some 36 percent of those earning over $8,000 had paid in full, and 72 percent in this income bracket had at least resumed payments, compared with 11 percent and 63 percent in the lowest income group, with the middle-income group falling in between.

When income and ethnicity are considered simultaneously, we find that the income pattern holds mainly for the whites. Among whites, the rate of repayment increases from 54 percent to 84 percent as income rises from less than $4,000 to more than $8,000. But this pattern does not pertain among blacks. Blacks earning over $8,000 were no more likely than those earning less than $4,000 to resume payments (62 and 64 percent, respectively).

Outcome of the Debt Problem and the
Debtor's Sense of Justice

About one half the debtors in the three garnishment cities felt that there was a good reason for not paying the court judgment, an attitude that influenced their resumption of payments. In Philadelphia, an even larger proportion, 54 percent, felt they should not have to pay. By their own testimony, substantially fewer of the debtors who questioned the legitimacy of their obligation resumed payments (53 percent) as compared with debtors who accepted their liability (73 percent). But this pattern must be qualified in light of those who lost their property and yet refused to admit that they had made payments. When these reluctant payers are taken into account, the gap narrows to 65 percent versus 75 percent. Those who questioned the fairness of their obligation were much more likely to experience property executions (16 percent) than those who did not (6 percent). This finding is in keeping with those presented earlier regarding garnishment. The picture that emerges strengthens the previous indictment of the legal process. Apparently the debtors most likely to have valid defenses are the very ones who are apt to experience the harsher collection practices, presumably because of their reluctance to pay.

Reasons for the Default and Resumption of Payments

In chapter 12 we saw that with one exception a majority of debtors resumed payments regardless of the reason for their default, but that reasons still had some influence on resumption of payments. Breakdowns that could be attributed to errors were most likely to result in future payment, whereas breakdowns stemming from fraud and marital instability had a much lower probability of resulting in subsequent payment. But these are not the findings in Philadelphia. Whatever the pressures on Philadelphia debtors to resume payment, they are sufficiently powerful to force most to resume payment regardless of their reason for defaulting. Moreover, the little variation that does occur does not correspond closely to the pattern shown in the other cities. As can be seen from Table 13.7, the category of "payment misunderstandings" is associated with a relatively poor repayment rate, and the "marital instability" category is now toward the middle rather than the bottom. But there are some similarities. "Voluntary overextension" and "debtor's third parties" are associated with high rates of resumption of payments, as in the garnishment cities.

Table 13.7 / Percentage of Philadelphia Debtors Resuming Payments by Primary Reason for Default

Voluntary overextension	75	(20)
Victims of own third party	71	(14)
Loss of income	70	(107)
Marital instability	68	(25)
Allegations of fraud	68	(37)
Payment misunderstandings	64	(11)
Involuntary overextension	63	(16)

Two categories drop out of the Philadelphia sample for lack of cases. Only one Philadelphian defaulted because he had left town, and all told only six were placed in the category "debtor irresponsibility." It may be noted that all but one of the latter did resume payments, a finding not too surprising when it is recalled that debtor irresponsibility includes cases of forgetfulness. Table 13.7 shows very little spread in payment rates over the range of reasons, as only 12 percentage points separate the highest and lowest categories. In contrast, in the three garnishment cities this overall difference came to 34 percentage points (Table 12.12).

We have seen that the threat of a real property execution was more effective than a personal property execution in getting the Philadelphia default-debtors to resume payments. Whether it is equally effective for all categories of reasons for the initial default can be seen from Table 13.8. In this more refined analysis two additional categories of reasons drop out because of insufficient cases: voluntary overextension (there were only four real property executions among these cases), and payment misunderstandings (only 2 of these 11 cases involved real property threats).

Table 13.8 / Percentage of Philadelphia Debtors Resuming Payments by Primary Reason for Default and Type of Property Execution

reason for default	real property execution		personal property execution		percentage difference
Marital instability	91	(11)	50	(14)	+41
Victim of own third party	[86]	(7)	[50]	(6)	+33
Involuntary overextension	[83]	(6)	50	(10)	+33
Allegations of fraud	85	(13)	56	(23)	+29
Loss of income	76	(33)	66	(71)	+10

The results for the first four categories of reasons are remarkably similar. Threatening the real property of debtors who defaulted for reasons of marital instability, betrayal by their third parties, involuntary overextension, and even fraud is remarkably productive for the creditor as the great majority of such debtors resumed payment. The threat to personal property is not nearly so effective in these reason groups. But the picture is quite different for the one category of reasons for default that deals most clearly with the debtor's ability to pay, loss of income. Executing against real rather than personal property is least effective in this group, as both fewer who experience such executions resume payments and more of those who find only their personal property threatened do resume payment, in contrast with the other reason categories. This finding is most plausible. In the other reason categories (with the possible exception of involuntary overextension) the default–debtors might well believe that they should not have to pay and thus are likely to do so only when threatened with severe sanctions. But the loss of income category touches upon ability rather than willingness to pay, and hence severity of threat makes relatively little difference. These debtors pay when they can, regardless of the threats made by their creditors. Perhaps the most impressive finding of Table 13.8 is that substantial numbers of debtors resume payments regardless of the reason for their default and the type of creditor threat. We have repeatedly made this observation in order to question the basic premise of the credit industry—that harsh collection devices are needed to control the credit system.

CONSEQUENCES

OF

THE DEBT

PROBLEM

14

IMPACT OF THE
DEBT PROBLEM
ON THE
DEBTOR'S LIFE

Previously, this book viewed the respondents from several perspectives: as consumers entering a variety of credit transactions, as default-debtors, and as defendants in a law suit. We now view them from yet another perspective: as persons whose lives have been burdened by a debt problem. We shall examine the extent to which this debt problem has intruded upon various sectors of their lives.

When listing the things of greatest value to them, most people would include their health, job, and marriage, although not necessarily in that order. The data permit us to explore the impact of the debt on each of these critical aspects of the debtor's life. Two additional ramifications will be considered: the pressure upon the debtor to seek relief through bankruptcy, and the constraints that the problem of indebtedness has placed on the debtor's normal standard of living and life style. In sum, we now explore a range of negative consequences of indebtedness: bankruptcy, job instability, ill health, marital instability, and curtailment of family expenditures.

BANKRUPTCY

In previous chapters the legal remedies available to creditors in their actions against default-debtors were examined. Under the general theme of the *costs* of the debt problem to the debtor, we consider what at first glance appears to be a benefit rather than a cost—the debtor's legal remedy of bankruptcy. To be sure, bankruptcy is a remedy for the debtor in that it can free him from his obligations to his creditors. But bankruptcy is frowned upon by society, and the person ready to admit to bankruptcy is at the same time admitting to his incompetence and is thus stigmatized. Since shame is attached to bankruptcy, many who are eligible for this relief do not seek it, and those who do are likely to pay immeasurable psychological costs.

Bankruptcy was introduced in chapter 12 in an effort to explain why whites were less likely than blacks to resume payments in the garnishment states. At that time we learned that whites were more likely than blacks to resort to this remedy, but the fundamental facts of the bankruptcy remedy were not made clear. Although many of these default-debtors were no doubt eligible for bankruptcy, only 7 percent of the 1,261 debtors who answered this question filed for bankruptcy. This figure is far below the proportion of those who did not pay because they were overextended. This disparity is symptomatic of the stigma attached to bankruptcy but may also reflect differing degrees of information about bankruptcy.

That variations in knowledge of bankruptcy affect its use is suggested by the intercity differences in bankruptcy rates. If the sole obstacle to bankruptcy among those eligible were the stigma associated with it, we would expect debtors to be similarly affected in the four cities represented in our sample. Bankruptcy, it must be remembered, is a federally regulated relief from indebtedness and hence should have much the same force in the different states. But in fact there are sharp differences among the four cities. Bankruptcy is most popular in Chicago, where 12 percent of the debtors had entered bankruptcy proceedings. Detroit was close behind with 10 percent of the sample declaring bankruptcy. The figures drop off sharply in the two Eastern cities, as only 3 percent of the New York debtors (10 in all) and 2 percent of Philadelphia debtors (a mere four persons) declared bankruptcy. These city differences strongly suggest that knowledge of the bankruptcy remedy varied sharply. In keeping with this interpretation, during the 1960s several Chicago lawyers advertised their skills in assisting debtors to declare bankruptcy. Presumably such publicity was absent in New York and Philadelphia.

Garnishment and Bankruptcy

We have noted one self-defeating aspect of garnishment, dismissal of the employee. Conceivably another would be the pressure that garnishment places on the debtor to declare bankruptcy. George Brunn has tried to document a connection between harsh garnishment laws and bankruptcy, arguing that the harsher the garnishment rule, the more likely debtors are to declare bankruptcy. He was able to establish some connection between state bankruptcy rates and harsh garnishment laws, noting that California had both a harsh law and a high bankruptcy rate, whereas states like New York, with more lenient garnishment laws, had low rates.[1]

The data of our study, however, provide little evidence of a connection between garnishment and bankruptcy. As noted, the state in our sample with the harshest garnishment law is Michigan, and yet the bankruptcy rate in Detroit was slightly below that in Chicago. Relating garnishment to bankruptcy in the three garnishment cities fails to uncover any significant differences, as 9 percent of the garnisheed debtors compared with 8 percent of the nongarnisheed filed for personal bankruptcy. Within each city, the garnisheed and nongarnisheed had virtually identical rates of bankruptcy. (In Chicago the figures are 14 and 12 percent; in Detroit, 10 percent in each group; and in New York, 3 percent in each group.)

In chapter 12 we noted that whites were more likely than blacks to file for bankruptcy. This finding is in no way explained by garnishment, as the ethnic pattern holds among both the garnisheed and nongarnisheed. (Among the garnisheed, 14 percent of the whites compared with 9 percent of the blacks filed for bankruptcy; among the nongarnisheed, the rates are 12 percent for the whites and 7 percent for the blacks.)

In sum, bankruptcy seems to be affected much more by the amount of indebtedness and by ethnicity than by garnishment. Our sample, of course, is too narrow to provide an adequate test of the Brunn thesis, but the limited data that we have lend it no support. Although the aggregate data fail to show a relationship between garnishment and bankruptcy, this does not mean that in individual cases garnishment did not contribute to bankruptcy. For one Chicago debtor, a 41-year-old black, it was the direct cause. He had stopped paying on a car because he had been laid off.

> Finally I went back to work and they found out I was working, so they started to send wage assignments on my job and that is when I filed for bankruptcy.

IMPACT OF THE DEBT PROBLEM
ON THE DEBTOR'S JOB

Part of the story of the impact of the debt on the debtor's job has been told in chapter 12. It was seen that 8 percent of the debtors in the garnishment cities lost their jobs because of garnishment orders, a figure that

---

[1]George Brunn, *Wage Garnishment in California: A Study and Recommendations* 53 Cal. L. Rev. 1214 (1965).

came to 19 percent of those who were garnisheed. But these data seriously underestimate the impact of the debt on the debtor's job security. As noted, many debtors were garnisheed after the interview. Also, the garnisheed debtors who had not yet lost their jobs were asked whether their employer had threatened to fire them if they did not settle the debt. Thirty-five percent reported that they had indeed received such warnings. These debtors amount to 10 percent of the entire Chicago, Detroit, and New York samples.[2] When added to the 8 percent who had already lost their jobs because of garnishment, we find that 18 percent of all the debtors in the three garnishment cities had either lost their jobs or were threatened with imminent loss of job if they did not settle the debt. This finding further highlights the damaging effects that garnishment has on debtors. Not only did 19 percent of the garnisheed lose their jobs by the time of the interview, but fully 43 percent of the garnisheed had either lost their jobs or were threatened with job loss by their employer. Presumably some if not most of these debtors were unable to come to terms with their creditors and hence did lose their jobs.

Information was obtained on a third dimension of job security. All debtors who held jobs at the time of the interview (a criterion omitting 14 percent) were asked if they were worried about losing their jobs because of the debt problem. Some 25 percent answered in the affirmative, a group that includes almost all the garnisheed who had received warnings from their employers and many more. If the fears of only one third or even one fourth of these debtors were warranted, the rate of job loss due to the debt problem would be substantially higher.

Apart from the ultimate penalty of job loss, the debt problem interferes with the debtor's livelihood in other ways. Although we do not know its impact on his productivity, we do know if it caused him to lose time from work. In the three garnishment cities (where job-related questions were asked), 20 percent of the employed lost at least one day of work because of the debt problem. (In Chicago, 27 percent of the debtors lost at least one day of work compared with 20 percent in Detroit and 14 percent in New York.) The loss of manpower in the economy due to illness, alcoholism, accidents, and sundry other disabilities has been widely documented and publicized. We now encounter a heretofore unpublicized cost to the economy—days lost from work because of debt problems. A crude estimate suggests that the 1,082 Chicago, Detroit, and New York debtors who were asked the question collectively lost 800 days of work, or almost one day of work per debtor. The number of default-debtors sued in any year is not known, but in New York City alone, suits are brought against 200,000 or more debtors each year. If New York were typical of the rest of the country, then debtors subjected

[2]The Philadelphia debtors are excluded from this section and in all subsequent analyses involving the variable of job impact.

to legal actions might amount to as many as 5 million persons. But New York is not likely to be typical and the nationwide figure for default-debtors subjected to legal actions may be only 3 million. But whether 3 or 5 million, it is clear from our data that absenteeism due to debt problems is a major source of inefficiency in our economy.

Correlates of Debt-Induced Job Problems

Not surprisingly, debtors who were already garnisheed were much more prone than those who had not been garnisheed to worry about losing their jobs. Thus 35 percent of the garnisheed in Chicago, Detroit, and New York expressed fear that they would lose their jobs, compared with only 19 percent of those who had not (yet) been garnisheed. Garnishment clearly contributes to job insecurity in large part because many of those who are garnisheed are warned by their employers that they will be fired if they do not settle the debt.

Whether the debt problem has an impact on the debtor's employment is partly related to occupational rank. Among the higher white collar workers, 21 percent reported either job loss or worry about job loss; in the lower white collar group, 24 percent reported such impacts; this rate climbs to 31 percent for the skilled blue collar workers and 33 percent among the unskilled blue collar group. We learned in chapter 12 that whites were as likely as blacks (if not more so) to lose their jobs because of the debt problem. Similarly, there is virtually no difference between whites and blacks with respect to worry about job loss, as 20 percent of the whites and 19 percent of the blacks expressed such worry. Even though blacks were more likely than whites to be unskilled workers, they did not feel their jobs were more vulnerable than did the whites, probably because, as seen in chapter 12, they were more likely than whites to belong to unions.

In light of the connection between occupational status and job insecurity induced by the debt, it is perhaps not surprising that those of low income were more likely than those of higher income to report that the debt problem intruded upon their work life. Among those earning under $4,000, 36 percent had either lost their jobs or were worried that they would; in the middle-income category, this rate comes to 30 percent; and in the highest income group, those earning over $8,000, the job impairment rate declines to 25 percent.

Not only are attributes of debtors, such as their job classification and income, related to the debt problem's impact upon their work life, but at least one characteristic of the creditor also contributes to the debtor's job insecurity—harassment. As can be seen from Table 14.1, the more harassment the debtor experienced, the more likely he was to experience job insecurity.

Table 14.1 / Impact of the Debt Problem on the
Debtor's Employment by Harassment
from Creditors (percent)

impact of debt on debtor's job	high	harassment index medium	low
Lost job	17	8	5
Worried will lose job	25	22	18
No impact on job	58	70	77
Total percent	100	100	100
N	(234)	(323)	(392)

Underlying the strong relationship shown in Table 14.1 is the fact
that harassment includes contacting the debtor's employer in the hope
that he will put pressure on the debtor to settle. The table shows the
success of such harassment, as the debtors whose employers were presumably contacted were most insecure about their jobs.[3]

Fate of Those Who Experienced Job Loss

As noted in chapter 12, 8 percent of the Chicago, Detroit, and New
York debtors, 90 persons in all, lost their jobs because of the debt problem.
(For reasons cited above, this is a minimum figure.) Job loss stemming
from a debt problem may be, like bankruptcy, a stigma to the debtor.
Employers rely increasingly upon credit bureaus for reports on prospective
employees. Persons with garnishment records are apt to be shunned by
employers because they may still be vulnerable to garnishments and
because the existence of a debt problem is treated as a sign of character
weakness. A great deal has been written about the "hard-core" unemployed, and they are generally viewed as persons with no occupational
skills and/or with criminal records. We can now identify still a third group
among the hard-core unemployed, those with garnishment records or
court judgments against them stemming from their debt problems. The
relevant data may now be cited. If loss of job due to debt problems
is an obstacle to subsequent employment, then we should find that the
90 debtors who did lose their jobs were much more likely than the other
default-debtors to be unemployed at the time of the interview. The data
on hand support this view. Some 37 percent of those who lost their jobs
were still unemployed, a figure far exceeding that in both the general

[3]The Department of Consumer Affairs of the City of New York passed a regulation
in 1971 prohibiting prejudgment communications between creditors and debtors' employers.
The city's collection lawyers sued the DCA in an effort to have this regulation revoked,
but a State Supreme Court judge upheld the regulation by dismissing the suit.

population and in our sample of default-debtors. Those who lose their jobs because of their debt problems clearly have a more difficult time in the job market.

The debtors who lost their jobs because of the debt problem were asked whether they applied for unemployment insurance during the time they were out of the labor market. Some 28 of the 90 who lost their jobs (31 percent) applied for unemployment insurance and almost all of those who applied—25 of the 28—received such insurance. That relatively few applied for unemployment insurance might be somewhat disconcerting, but that almost all of those who did apply received this coverage is reassuring, for it has been rumored that in many states unemployment insurance bureaus exclude those who lost their jobs because of garnishments on the grounds that they were fired for cause. Our figures suggest that such an abuse of the debtor's rights is not prevalent in the three garnishment states we sampled.

But only a minority of the debtors who lost their jobs applied for unemployment insurance and many, as we have seen, were unable to find new jobs. Apart from unemployment insurance, there is another institutionalized source of support for the destitute—welfare. The debtors who lost their jobs were asked whether they had applied for welfare and 14 of the 90 had (15 percent). The rate of welfare applicants in this sample is substantially above that in the population at large, a finding that indicates that credit problems contribute to the "welfare crisis" in America today. Those who applied for welfare were less successful than those who applied for unemployment insurance in that only 9 of the 14 applicants obtained it. These 9 persons amount to 10 percent of those who lost their jobs. Debt problems not only lead to job loss but also contribute to the burgeoning welfare rolls. A particularly dramatic instance of how a debt problem can undermine a debtor's employment potential and force him to turn to welfare is provided by a 32-year-old white Detroit man who, at the time of his debt problem, had been earning over $12,000 a year. The father of six children, this man had bought a stereo hi-fi for $600 and fell into arrears when, because of a gun accident, he was unemployed for seven months. When he recovered his health, he found a new job, only to be dismissed because of a garnishment order stemming from the debt for the hi-fi set:

> After that, every time I found a job, they would garnishee me and I would be fired. So finally I had to apply for welfare to feed my children and I'm on welfare today.

Of course, most debtors did not experience such extreme misfortune, but the very fact that some did is a reminder that debt problems can be a cause of impoverishment and not merely a consequence of it.

IMPACT OF THE DEBT PROBLEM
ON THE DEBTOR'S HEALTH

Debt problems, as NORC's studies of happiness[4] have shown, are a major source of unhappiness in America. It would not be surprising to learn therefore that debt problems contribute to poor health. To test this possibility, the debtors in our sample were asked two sets of questions. The first consisted of a battery of questions tapping such psychosomatic ailments as insomnia, stomach upsets, headaches, nervousness, and loss of appetite.[5] Those who answered these questions affirmatively were then asked if the symptom was a habitual problem or one of recent origin. The proportion answering in the affirmative to having these anxiety symptoms ranged from 30 to 57 percent, and in every instance the great majority identified the condition as being of recent origin. These results are shown in Table 14.2

Table 14.2 / Frequency of Psychosomatic Symptoms among Default-Debtors and the Proportion Whose Symptoms Are of Recent Origin

symptom	percentage with symptoms	of those with problem percentage of recent origin
Tension	57	74
Headaches	44	66
Insomnia	38	75
Upset stomach	31	73
Loss of appetite	30	70

The presence of one symptom might well be a sign of anxiety induced by the debt problem, but we shall use the more conservative criterion of at least two symptoms as the definition of stress induced by the debt problem. On this basis, 53 percent of all debtors admit to having at least two of these symptoms in the past month and 38 percent identify two or more symptoms as being of recent origin. Thus a conservative estimate of the proportion who suffered psychosomatic symptoms as a result of the debt problem ranges from 38 to 53 percent.

[4]Norman Bradburn and David Caplovitz, *Reports on Happiness* (Chicago: Aldine-Atherton, Inc., 1965) and Bradburn, *The Structure of Psychological Well-Being* (Chicago: Aldine-Atherton, Inc., 1969).

[5]Such questions for tapping anxiety and psychoneurosis were first used in the surveys of American soldiers in World War II as reported in S. Stouffer *et al.*, *The American Soldier* (Princeton, N.J.: Princeton University Press, 1949). The same battery of symptoms appeared in the Michigan survey: G. Gurin *et al.*, *Americans View Their Mental Health* (New York: Basic Books, Inc., 1960), and in somewhat abbreviated form in the NORC surveys of happiness, *ibid.*

In addition to this indirect measure of the impact of the debt problem on the debtor's health a more direct question was asked:

> In general, do you think your debt troubles have had any effect on your health?

Forty-nine percent of the debtors in the total sample answered this question affirmatively. These persons were then asked whether their health problem required them to visit a doctor, and 48 percent responded affirmatively. Combining these questions, we find that about one half the debtors felt that their health was impaired by their debt problems, and almost one half of this group felt sufficiently ill to consult a physician (23 percent of the entire sample). Debt problems thus contribute not only to unemployment and lowered work productivity but also to poor health. It may not be too facetious to suggest that installment contracts be required to carry the following warning: "Caution. Signing your name to this contract may be hazardous to your health."

The two measures of health impairment due to the debt problem, the index of psychosomatic symptoms and the direct question about the impact of the debt on the debtor's health, are highly related. Among those who claimed that the debt had impaired their health, 82 percent experienced at least two psychosomatic symptoms, whereas among those whose health was not impaired by the debt, only 25 percent experienced two or more symptoms in the past month.

The accounts of a New York and Detroit debtor provide some flavor for debt-induced health problems. The New York debtor was a black woman typist who was being sued for having defaulted on a loan from a large bank. Besides answering affirmatively to all the questions bearing on psychomatic symptoms, she offered the following description of the impact of the debt upon her health:

> You know I live alone and I've been separated from my husband for 20 years and it's lonely so you buy something here or there on credit. You have to brighten up your life a bit. There was one point there when all the bills and debts seemed to be closing in on me. I had no one to turn to, and I had a nervous breakdown.

This debtor was under the care of a psychiatrist.

The testimony of the Detroit debtor demonstrates how the additional worries presented by a debt problem can exacerbate a health problem. The respondent is the wife of a machine operator who was sued when he became ill and could not maintain payments on a car purchase:

> He had been sick for two or three years but he never would go to the doctor. I guess with him worrying it got worse but he was afraid

> if he not work [sic] what we going to do. He just be sick worrying about it. He try to sleep and can't. The doctor said he must be very worried about something. When they got ready to operate on him his blood pressure went up so much they couldn't operate then. He's so worried he not getting well the way he should.

At the time of the interview the husband was in the hospital.

Correlates of Health Impairment
Caused by the Debt Problem

In this review of correlates the focus is on the direct question that indicated that almost one half of the debtors felt that their health had been affected, with 23 percent feeling sufficiently ill to require consultation with a doctor.[6]

Somewhat surprisingly, there were rather substantial variations between the cities with regard to the impact of the debt problem on health. In Philadelphia, fully 56 percent of the debtors answered affirmatively, compared with 51 percent in Detroit, 48 percent in New York, and 40 percent in Chicago. This may reflect the psychic cost of the threat of loss of home to the Philadelphia debtors, but it is also true that the Philadelphia debtors were being sued for larger amounts of money on the average than those in the other cities. The data show that health impairment is related to the amount of the debt; 58 percent of those with debts over $500 compared with 44 percent of those with debts under $500 reported that the debt problem had affected their health.

In addition to the amount of debt, health impairment is related to threats to the debtor's employment. Among debtors who had lost their job, 65 percent reported a health problem; among those who were worried that they might lose their job, almost as many, 63 percent, said their health had suffered. In contrast, only 39 percent of those whose jobs were not affected reported that the debt problem had some impact on their health.[7]

So far we have seen that the health of the debtor is likely to be impaired to the extent that the debt problem undermines his economic well-being, that is, his solvency as represented by the extent of his indebtedness and the threat to his income. But other factors also contribute to the undermining of the debtor's health, including harassment. As can be seen from Table 14.3, harassment is closely related to health impairment.

Debtors who experienced considerable harassment were much more likely to suffer poor health than debtors who were not harassed by their

---

[6]Since this measure was highly correlated with the index of psychosomatic symptoms, whatever findings emerge in this section would no doubt hold if the other measure had been used.

[7]This finding, like all the others dealing with job impact, is limited to the three garnishment cities.

Table 14.3 / Debt-Induced Health Problem by
Harassment (percent)

impact on debtor's health	index of harassment		
	low	medium	high
No effect	61	49	38
Some effect—no physician	23	28	29
Debtor consults physician	16	23	33
Total percent	100	100	100
N	(548)	(450)	(335)

creditors. This relationship is supported by the testimony of the debtors. For example, a Detroit carpenter was sued by his creditor when he missed two payments because he and his wife had been out of town. The bank that had purchased his contract refused to make arrangements for late payments. The wife reported that the creditor used harsh and abusive language, with the following effect:

> I almost had a nervous breakdown after talking to the man from the bank. I was so upset I had to go to the doctor that night. I had nervous spasms around the heart. I nearly died of this last year and it's all because of the debt problem. My husband had to be hospitalized for a nervous stomach. They had thought it was ulcers.

We saw in chapter 8 that a few debtors mentioned harassment as an additional reason for not paying their debt. Table 14.3 demonstrates another way in which harassment can be self-defeating. By undermining the debtor's health, harassment places additional strain on the family budget at the same time that it interferes with income, factors that prevent rather than induce the resumption of payments. Laws in Texas and some other states make it possible for debtors to sue employers who use unreasonable harassment on the grounds that such harassment is injurious to the debtor's well-being. The close connection we have cited between harassment and health indicates the need for harassment laws in these northern cities as well.

IMPACT OF THE DEBT
ON THE DEBTOR'S MARRIAGE

Just as debt troubles affect the debtor's employment and health, so, too, do they have an impact on his marriage. It is difficult to separate the impact on the marriage of a particular debt problem from that of cumulative debt troubles. For example, a Detroit steel worker linked his marital difficulty to a series of debts:

> I got in bad shape with the bills. I wasn't making enough money.
> I didn't have any money in the clear to buy clothes for the kids.
> We started fighting and separated.

And a Chicago waitress who was being sued for a loan which her husband incurred was relieved to be separated from him:

> I've had debt problems with him ever since I married him. He never wanted to pay his bills. We fought like cats and dogs, day and night. I'd have to call him at work to tell him the lights were turned off. I'm so glad he's gone.

Her husband fits the description of a deadbeat and it would seem from her comment that their marriage was undermined by a history of debt problems. More so than in the previous sections, we are probably describing the impact of *cumulative* debt troubles when we examine debt-induced marital difficulties. We can rule out one source of ambiguity, the instances in which marital problems preceded the debt trouble and even contributed to it. (As we saw earlier, marital instability was a cause of the debt problem in many instances.) The questions that we now examine elucidate the time sequence. The first asked:

> Did this debt trouble lead to your getting divorced or separated?

The second question reads:

> Did your debt troubles lead to any quarrels with your wife/husband?

Of the 1,331 debtors in the sample, 985, or 74 percent, were married at the time of the default. Of this number, 87, or 9 percent, were subsequently divorced or separated because of the debt problem.[8] (Whether the current debt problem was the only one or simply the "last straw" is not known.) Of those marriages which survived, many had strains because of the debt trouble. In addition to the 9 percent whose marriages terminated, 34 percent answered the question about quarrels affirmatively. A total of 43 percent of the married respondents reported that the debt trouble had some negative impact on their marriage. Upon reading these findings dealing with the strains that debts place on marriages, the inimitable Philip Schrag has suggested that the marriage vow be changed to pledge fidelity " 'til debt do us part."

---

[8]One of the questions inserted in the NORC national survey in 1967 asked whether the respondent knew of anyone whose marriage had split up because of debt problems. Twenty-three percent, well above the rate in our sample, answered affirmatively.

Correlates of Marital Strain Caused by a Debt Problem

Many of the correlates of debt-induced health problems apply to marital strains stemming from the debt as well, although some relationships are stronger than others. The amount of indebtedness had a strong impact on health and one might presume, in the light of the anecdotes cited above, that it has a similarly strong impact on the debtor's marriage. But although in the expected direction, the relationship is not strong. Among those who were being sued for under $200, 37 percent reported marital strain, and among those being sued for over $500, this figure rises to 47 percent.

The debtor's marriage was much more likely to be affected when the debt problem undermined his job security. Sixty-three percent of those who actually lost their jobs because of the debt problem experienced marital strain and 58 percent of those who were worried that they might lose their jobs did compared with 40 percent of those whose jobs were not threatened.

We have seen that harassment contributed to the debtor's developing a health problem. The dynamics of such a relationship are not hard to imagine. Threats and persecution are conducive to strain and anxiety, which in turn become translated into physical symptoms. But the connection, if any, between harassment and marital strain is not so obvious. Does harassment, which might well be directed at both spouses, by upsetting the debtor's routine, including his health, exacerbate or create marital tensions? There is considerable merit to this logic, for as harassment increases so, too, does marital strain. The separation–divorce rate increases from 6 to 12 percent across the low- to high-harassment categories and quarrels increase from 30 to 42 percent. In short, the percentages whose marriages were not affected range from a high of 64 percent in the low-harassment group to a low of 46 percent in the high-harassment category.

Not surprisingly, the debt's impact on the debtor's health is related to its impact on his marriage. Among those reporting no debt-induced health problems, only 5 percent experienced marital breakups and an additional 25 percent quarrels with their spouse for a total debt impact on marriage of 30 percent. But among those whose health did suffer because of the debt, 13 percent had their marriages break up and 46 percent quarreled with their spouses for a total marital impact of 59 percent. Of course, the causal direction is not clear. The health problem may undermine the marriage or the marital problem may undermine health, but it is clear that the debt trouble contributes to both and these two problems may well interact.

IMPACT OF THE DEBT PROBLEM
ON THE DEBTOR'S BUDGET AND EXPENDITURES

Most debtors in default experienced a financial squeeze. We have seen that many of them ended in default because of unexpected financial troubles. Some found themselves in financial difficulty because they had been misled about the cost of their credit obligation. Recall those who were saddled with two debt obligations when they went to buy a car, with the combined payments far exceeding their financial capabilities. Others were confronted with late payment fees or by their creditor's demand for full payment. In these various ways the debt problems that we have been examining symbolize for many debtors a financial bind—a condition that in many instances caused the default and in some instances was created by the debt obligation. Many persons thus entangled in debt find themselves forced to make dramatic curtailments in their standard of living and patterns of expenditure. The extent to which the debt problems forced debtors to change their patterns of consumption is the issue now at hand. Even more than in the case of the marital impact, we are now examining the cumulative impact of the debtor's debt troubles rather than the particular debt that was the focus of the study.

The debtors were asked four questions concerning the impact of the debt problem on their budget: whether they had to cut down on food expenditures, on social activities, medical care, and dental care. The proportion who answered "yes" to each of these queries is shown in Table 14.4.

Table 14.4 / Impact of the Debt Problems on the Family Budget

	percentage delaying or reducing expenditures for:			
	social activities	food	dental care	medical care
Percent	57	53	43	35
N	(1,323)	(1,321)	(1,326)	(1,325)

As these figures show, debt entanglement has a substantial impact on the debtor's standard of living. A majority of debtors cut back on their social activities and food expenditures; almost one half put off necessary dental care; and more than one third put off necessary medical care. This ordering of the four budgetary items may signify the relative ease of cutting back such expenditures, social activities being easiest to curtail and medical care least so. But it may also indicate the relative frequency of such expenditures, food purchases and expenditures on leisure being more regular than expenditures on dental and medical care. In any case, the debt problem required most debtors to curtail their pattern of expenditure in at least one respect. These four budgetary items are empirically related in that those who made cutbacks in one category were apt to cut back in others as well. Because of these relationships, we can combine the four items into a measure of the impact of the debt problem on the debtor's budget or standard of living. It turns out that 39 percent of the debtors responded affirmatively to three or four of these questions. This group constitutes the high-impact group. Another 31 percent responded affirmatively to one or two of the items, consitituting the medium-impact group; and 30 percent—the low-impact category—did not make cutbacks in any of these categories. That the debt problem had a heavy impact on the standard of living of many debtors and relatively little impact on that of many others is a reminder of the different processes through which debtors ended in default. As we saw, not all were in this predicament because they were overextended or unable to pay. The differential impact of the debt problem on standard of living is also indicative of the differences in financial resources. As we have seen, not all debtors were equally in debt, and we shall soon see that some had more financial assets than others.

Correlates of Impact of Debt Problem
on Standard of Living

Income, as we have repeatedly seen, is a financial resource that affects in many ways the debtor's ability to cope with his debt problem. Somewhat surprisingly, income modifies only slightly the impact of the debt problem on the debtor's standard of living. Among those earning under $4,000, 42 percent experienced a high impact; in the middle-income group the extent of impact is virtually the same, 41 percent; and in the highest income group (over $8,000), those who experienced a severe impact declines to only 34 percent.

Information was obtained on another aspect of the debtor's financial situation, one not yet introduced in the analysis—his savings. All debtors were asked whether they had savings and, if so, whether they exceeded $500. Not surprisingly, the great majority of these default-debtors—65 percent—had no savings at all, and of those who did, most had relatively small savings. Twenty-four percent of the debtors had savings under $500 and only 11 percent had savings amounting to more than $500. Yet this measure of financial solvency is more strongly related than income to the impact of the debt on standard of living. Among those who had no savings, 41 percent were in the "high-impact" category concerning budgetary restrictions; for those with savings under $500, virtually an identical proportion—42 percent—experienced a "high-impact"; but among the minority with savings over $500, the "high-impact" group drops to 20 percent. Having relatively substantial savings thus mitigates the burden that the debt problem places on the standard of living.

We have seen that the impact of the debt on other facets of the debtors' lives, such as work, health, and marriage, were interrelated. The same is true of curtailment of standard of living. Those who found the debt problem interfering with their work were much more likely to report that the debt problem caused them to curtail their standard of living. Among those who lost their job because of the debt problem, 54 percent registered high on the index of impact on budget; among those worried that they might lose their job, this figure is even higher, 59 percent; but among those who felt that their jobs were secure, it declines to 33 percent.

Although it would seem that impact upon job is more likely to cause an impact on standard of living than the reverse, the issue is not so clear when the debt's impact on standard of living is related to its impact on health or marriage. Among the classics of sociological literature is the study of suicide by Emil Durkheim.[9] Durkheim identifies several types of stress that contribute to suicide. Among them are those social conditions that break down the conventional rules regulating behavior, thus leaving the individual in a state of normlessness. Without rules to regulate their behavior, persons in such situations experience considerable stress to the point where some are moved to suicide. The conditions that Durkheim identifies as provoking a state of anomie are sudden changes in social status, generally provoked by rapid shifts in the economy. Thus Durkheim was able to show that it was not the traditionally poor who were inclined to suicide but rather those who moved suddenly from affluence to poverty. Conversely, those who moved rapidly from relative poverty to relative affluence also experienced a disjointedness between ends and means and were also prone to suicide. For those in the latter group, activities and desires that were sharply limited suddenly knew no bounds in the state of affluence, and this condition produced as much strain on the individual as its opposite. We cite this theory of anomie by Durkheim as a basis for assuming that the debt problem's impact on the debtor's standard of living might well cause strain on the debtor's health and marriage. In short, we assume that curtailment of standard of living is symptomatic of a sudden decline in one's fortunes and hence represents a state of anomie caused by the sudden disruption of means and ends. Whether this is, in fact, a correct hypothesis can be seen from the results of Table 14.5. This table shows the connection between curtailment of expenditures and each of two stress symptoms, health impairment and marital strain.

Curtailment of standard of living because of the debt problem is strongly related to impairment of health and to marital strain, findings in keeping with the Durkheimian anomie thesis. It may well be, judging

[9]Emil Durkheim, *Suicide,* trans. by John Spaulding and George Simpson (New York: The Free Press, 1951).

Table 14.5 / Impact of the Debt Problem on Health and Marriage
by Its Impact on the Family Budget[a]

| | impact of debt on family budget | | |
	low	medium	high
Percentage experiencing health problem because of debt	18	48	74
N[b]	(406)	(411)	(516)
Percentage experiencing some marital strain because of debt	20	41	62
N[b]	(266)	(291)	(427)

[a]Although at first glance this would appear to be a three-variable table, it actually consists of two separate two-variable relationships. The top row shows the connection between family budget and health, and the second row shows the connection between family budget and marital strain.

[b]Substantially more debtors appear in the first part of the table, dealing with health, than in the second part, dealing with marriage, because the single as well as the married are counted.

from these findings, that the debt problem undermines health and marriage, particularly when it causes a sharp reversal in the debtor's standard of living. The strain thus provoked might well find expression in psychosomatic health problems and marital tensions. But as we have seen, other factors are involved, such as the impact of the debt on the debtor's job and the harassment tactics of the creditor.

In sum, debt problems can be extremely costly and debilitating. Law suits against default-debtors can result in job loss, undoubtedly in magnitudes greater than our data, collected so soon after the debt problem, indicate. They can undermine health in at least two ways: by producing the psychosomatic symptoms often associated with anxiety and worry, and by forcing the debtor to so skimp on his budget that he neglects health needs. They can interfere with the debtor's marriage as debt problems become a source of contention between spouses; and finally they force the debtor to lower his standard of living, a process that might well further undermine his health and marriage. These findings would suggest that the current system of resolving disputes between creditors and debtors is far too costly both to the debtors and to society at large.

CONCLUSIONS

This book represents an effort to describe the system of consumer credit as it existed in 1967. It is a portrait of the system taken from a specific vantage point, that of the system under stress when the assumptions of the system have broken down and the creditor and consumer–debtor are in confllict. The focus was on this extreme view in order to lay bare the legal machinery underlying consumer credit and to assess the relative responsibility of debtors and creditors in these breakdowns. Although by limiting the study to defaults, we have dealt with no more than 2 percent or so of all consumer credit transactions, we believe that these breakdowns, however infrequent, provide a strategic site for assessing the fairness of the system of credit as it has evolved in America.

As this study has indicated, the institution of consumer credit, as of 1967, is found wanting in a number of respects. The credit system has been heavily biased in favor of the creditor. But as indicated in the opening chapter, much has happened since 1967. Many of the legal bases for the bias have come under sharp attack in the interim, and the consumer credit reform movement, stimulated in large part by the enormous growth of consumer credit, has begun in some states to strike down the laws that favored the creditor and contributed unwittingly to consumer fraud. But on balance, in spite of the growing attention given to consumer problems, relatively little has been done in the years since this study was made and the system is pretty much the same today as it was then. In short, the relevance of this study has by no means been undermined by intervening events.

THE CONSUMER CREDIT REFORM MOVEMENT

Holder-in-Due-Course

As noted in various chapters, the doctrine of holder-in-due-course, which evolved in commercial transactions and became incorporated into consumer transactions, has been a great stimulus to consumer fraud. There is no better way to illustrate this assertion than to examine the magical nature of consumer credit. Before the advent of consumer credit, purchases depended on cash and in the typical transaction a seller exchanged goods for the buyer's cash. But the emergence of consumer credit permitted duplicity on both sides of the transaction. For the first time a person who had no money could become a consumer at the same time that a person who had nothing to sell could become a seller. The transaction no longer represented an exchange of money for goods and services but rather consisted of signatures on a contract promising payment for the future delivery of goods and services. It is easy to imagine a fraudulent consumer taking advantage of a seller by agreeing to make future payments for some merchandise when he lacks the funds to pay for it. But what is meant by a fraudulent seller, one who has nothing to sell? Such a person has been created by consumer credit, for example a door-to-door salesman selling food freezer plans or television sets on the basis of catalogues rather than on the demonstration of his goods, or the used-car dealer whose lot is filled with metallic objects in the shape of automobiles. If these "automobiles" do not run, then they are not automobiles, for a defective car is a violation of the implied warranty of merchantability, a valid consumer defense. We have quoted debtors whose cars broke down minutes after they were driven off the lot. According to the law, the goods that these debtors bought were misrepresented as automobiles since they did not perform the basic function of an automobile, that of transporting a person from one place to another. One might suppose that a transaction carried out between a fraudulent consumer (one lacking the ability to pay) and a fraudulent seller (one with nothing to sell) would end in a standoff, with neither party at a disadvantage. But the doctrine of holder-in-due-course undermines this logic by giving a decided advantage to the fraudulent seller who is able to sell his contract to a third party and thus realize immediate cash. Meanwhile, the law permits the third party to sue the "irresponsible" default-debtor and attach his personal and real property and future income. In this fashion, the dishonest dealer does much better than the dishonest consumer. The inequity of the doctrine of holder-in-due-course, as shown in this account of the magic of consumer credit, has come to the attention of even moderate forces in the past few years, and a concerted attack on this doctrine has developed on both the state and federal levels. Five years ago, Massachusetts, which has pioneered various consumer reforms, abolished the doctrine of holder-in-due-course in all consumer credit transactions. Contrary to the dire predictions of the credit industry, credit for low-income people in Massachusetts has not dried up nor has the cost of extending credit increased, even though banks and other financing institutions must now exercise more caution before buying consumer paper lest they be stuck with paper obtained under fraudulent circumstances.[1] A number of years ago, Pennsylvania abolished the holder-in-due-course provision in automobile transactions and in 1968 Connecticut abolished holder-in-due-course in home improvement transactions. In 1970 New York's legislature, bowing to consumer pressures, passed a law abolishing holder-in-due-course in all but two types of transactions, automobile paper and home improvement transactions. Clearly these state differences reflect less the reality of the transactions than the power of the lobbies of various vested interests.[2]

The doctrine of holder-in-due-course has come under a more muted attack in the Uniform Consumer Credit Code, which has now (the fall of 1973) been adopted by six states. The drafters of this code could not decide whether the holder-in-due-course doctrine should be abolished outright or whether it should be retained, with the debtors having a sufficient period of time in which to exert their defenses against the seller—as long as six months from the time of transaction. If such defenses are not raised within six months, the third party is entitled to immunity from the debtors' defenses. The efforts of the UCCC drafters to compromise on this issue may well be for nought in light of the more aggressive posture of the consumer's newly found friend, the awakened "old lady" of Massachusetts Avenue, the Federal Trade Commission. The Federal Trade Commission announced in 1971 that it was contemplating outlawing the holder-in-due-course doctrine from all credit transactions, an announcement that may well exceed its authority. The FTC is determined to hold hearings on this issue and pursue its plan of abolishing holder-in-due-course. Although this administrative ploy may not succeed, it is possible that Congress will eventually pass legislation abolishing holder-in-due-course in consumer transactions.

The complexity of the world of consumer credit is indicated by the various ways in which creditors may circumvent this reform and create a situation that is even worse for the consumer. For example, instead of trying to sell their contracts to finance companies which would no longer be protected from the original creditor's excesses, creditors may

---

[1]These investigative costs are probably more than offset by the reduction in collection costs that results from screening out the paper of unscrupulous dealers.

[2]By now almost one half the states have reformed holder-in-due-course laws, although Massachusetts is the only state so far to have abolished it entirely.

take their prospective customers to a small loan company to borrow money for a cash purchase. The small loan company in such a transaction will treat the debtor's salary rather than the merchandise purchased as the collateral for the loan. The consumer will be hurt because the interest rate on a small loan is substantially higher than that on an installment sale. Moreover, the firm making the loan would argue that it had nothing to do with the use of the money it had lent and thus should be free of any liabilities against the firm that sold the debtor merchandise. To combat collusion between lenders and retailers, consumer advocates have sought to establish rules to define such collusion on the basis of which the lender would be treated as a "holder" instead of an innocent bystander. Such rules are probably not too difficult to promulgate, but the very notion of the dealer-arranged loan casts a pall upon the presumed benefits of abolishing holder-in-due-course.

Still another loophole in the proposal to abolish holder-in-due-course is presented by the explosive growth of credit cards. If a debtor should use his Master Charge card to buy furniture from a ghetto merchant and if the furniture delivered should be defective or different from that which the debtor ordered, is he entitled to exert his defenses against the bank that issued him the card and gave its decal to the ghetto merchant? The resolution of this issue is still unclear in most parts of the country, although Massachusetts has again pioneered by passing legislation that holds the credit card company, like the finance agency, responsible for the debtor's defenses against the original seller. As other states catch up with Massachusetts, it is likely that this loophole, too, will eventually be plugged and that consumers will finally benefit from the abolition of the holder-in-due-course doctrine. The consumer advocates argue with considerable persuasiveness that this doctrine has encouraged fly-by-night outfits with "nothing to sell' to bilk consumers and simultaneously sell their paper to respectable banks and finance companies. Whether abolishing holder-in-due-course will wipe out the fraudulent entrepreneurs remains to be seen, but it is obvious that they will have more difficulty operating in the absence of this law.

Confession of Judgment and Cognovit Notes

The confession-of-judgment doctrine, under which the debtor waives all defenses and his right to a day in court, exists at this writing in several states. As noted, the constitutionality of this doctrine was attacked by the legal services program in Philadelphia and a partial victory was won in that state. But the Supreme Court failed to abolish the doctrine, and it remains for the consumer movement to attack it in the states that still recognize this doctrine, such as Ohio.

Repossession and Deficiency Judgments

In the past several years major inroads have been made on the creditor's right to repossess merchandise and seek deficiency judgments, that is, judgments for the amount of the debt owed after the value of the resale of the repossessed merchandise has been subtracted. In chapter 1 we noted that a major victory for the consumer was established by the Supreme Court's decision in the Snaidach case, which declared prejudgment garnishments unconstitutional because of violation of due process provisions. The logic of the Snaidach decision has been extended by aggressive lawyers for the poor to include attacks not only on the confession of judgment doctrine but also on repossession, which typically consists of the creditor engaging in "self-help" tactics to reclaim the merchandise bought on time to which he, the seller, retains title. A number of recent court decisions are contributing to a new theory, that the creditor cannot repossess without due process. In chapters 6 through 8 we encountered a number of instances of automobile repossessions in which the dealer or finance company reclaimed the car in the middle of the night and the debtor had the mistaken notion that his car was stolen. The reform now afoot would make such actions by dealers illegal. The Supreme Court recently declared that advance notice must be given in replevin actions, and a number of suits now in progress are seeking to extend this decision to cover the more prevalent "self-help" repossessions.

More sinister from the consumer's perspective than repossession is the deficiency judgment, under which the debtor not only loses the merchandise but also finds himself liable for the balance of the debt, after the money realized on the resale of the merchandise is subtracted. For a number of years consumer advocates have considered the deficiency judgment a scandal, for the simple reason that the sale of repossessed goods never realized the amount of the outstanding debt or even the value of the goods as determined by independent assessors, such as the authors of the blue books for used automobiles. It was generally suspected, although until recently proof was lacking, that the resales were rigged and that the consumers who were victims of repossessions were also victims of subsequent fraud in the resale of their merchandise. Considerable hostility developed during the 1960s against the deficiency judgment doctrine, and the National Commission on Uniform State Laws, when drafting the UCCC, felt obliged to take some cognizance of this sentiment. The UCCC rule on this matter also represents a great compromise. The model code now before most state legislatures advocates abolishment of deficiency judgments on all transactions under $1,000 but permits the practice on transactions over that amount. This means that the seller of merchandise sold for less than $1,000 must decide whether he wants to repossess or sue the debtor for the balance owed him, whereas the seller of merchandise over $1,000 can both repossess and sue for the balance of the debt.

This rule of the UCCC must be evaluated in the light of the empirical finding that almost all repossessed merchandise consists of automobiles, the one commodity that has some resale value. Most automobiles sold in America, new or used, are priced in excess of $1,000; the probable effect of the UCCC ruling will be to raise both the cost and the trade-in allowance on used cars. Where the dealer was ready to sell a car for $700 in conjunction with a trade-in of $200, he would now be apt to raise the price to $1,000 and credit the buyer with a $500 trade-in. Under this arrangement he makes the same amount of profit on the car and is ensured of his right to a deficiency judgment under the logic of the UCCC. But there is good reason to assume that the UCCC is outdated on this issue and that another reform benefiting the consumer will soon be passed on the state and national level—that creditors will be allowed to either repossess or sue for the balance but not do both. Contributing to this reform is the classic study by Professor Philip Shuchman that showed how fraudulent the resale of repossessed automobiles is.[3] The Shuchman study has since been replicated by the National Commission on Consumer Finances, a body created by the 1968 Federal Consumer Protection Act. The Commission's study, conducted in Washington, D.C., confirmed Shuchman's Connecticut findings, that repossessed automobiles are sold far below their value as a result of intrigue between the original dealer and the finance company. Although there will undoubtedly be a great outcry from the spokesmen of the credit industry, it is likely that in the next few years the doctrine of the deficiency judgment will also be eliminated either on the federal level or in most states.

Given these pending reforms, what more needs to be done to make the system of consumer credit more equitable? For one thing, none of the proposed reforms has gone so far as to advocate the abolishment of garnishment, although, as the data of his study have shown, a good case can be made for such a reform. We have noted that the reforms on this issue are of two kinds: (1) to increase the exemptions from garnishment as advocated in the 1968 Consumer Protection Act, and (2) to prohibit employers from firing an employee because of garnishment, at least for the first garnishment, a principle that the federal Consumer Protection Act borrowed from New York. But our study has shown that garnishment is a threat against the debtor out of all proportion to the amount of his liability. Debtors, as we have seen, are so frightened of garnishment that they will settle debts with their creditors even though they believe their own defenses to be valid; and some debtors when confronted with

[3]Philip Shuchman, *Profit on Default: An Archival Study of Automobile Repossession and Resale,* 22 Stanford L. Rev. 20 (Nov. 1969).

a garnishment will even quit their jobs to avoid a garnishment stigma on their record.

Availability of Legal Services
for Consumers in Trouble

The issues of holder-in-due course, confession of judgment, and deficiency judgment represent not only major armaments in the creditor's arsenal, but also complicated legal issues that take the talents of a lawyer to challenge. A major flaw of the consumer credit system is the inequality between creditor and debtor regarding access to courts and more generally to legal counsel. As we have noted time and again, the default-debtor who has valid defenses may well find that he has to pay more in the way of legal expenses than the amount in dispute. This condition is endemic to disputes involving relatively small sums of money (that is, $500 or so). A reform intended to deal with this issue is the consumer class action, a type of law suit in which a large number of consumers who have been similarly aggrieved by a seller can join forces and bring a collective law suit against the seller. Massachusetts has such a consumer class action law, and California has an old law that has recently been interpreted as applying to classes of consumers. Several versions of consumer class actions are now before Congress. One that is relatively conservative has been presented by the Nixon administration. This bill would make class actions dependent upon successful actions brought against sellers by the Department of Justice. The more liberal Democratic bill, first identified with Senator Tydings of Maryland but since his defeat in 1970 known as the Eckardt Bill, does not require a Justice Department "trigger" before consumers can institute class actions. If consumer class action legislation is ever passed by Congress (the opposition is quite strong and the outcome is very much in doubt), debtors' chances of having a day in court will be improved. But most debtors with valid defenses probably do not belong to a class, and these persons will still have difficulty being heard in court.

Our study has documented the thesis that the courts do not administer justice in consumer disputes but rather act as the collection agents of the creditors, a situation that was found to be particularly true in New York. Many debtors never know they are being sued and almost all these suits result in default judgments against the debtors, even though many of them have valid defenses. In large part because of the findings of this study, efforts are now under way in New York City to cope with the problems of sewer service and default judgments. A committee of all the governmental agencies dealing with consumer fraud has recently been formed in that city, a committee consisting of representatives of the FTC, the City's Department of Consumer Affairs, the Attorney General's Office, the U.S. Attorney's Office, and the New York County District Attorney's Office. The Committee is now considering new forms of summonses, including one that has the address of Legal Aid offices on it, and tightening the venue rules, issues that were reported on in chapter 11. A proposal that has come before the New York City Bar Association's Committee on Consumer Affairs is to have a tear-off answer attached to the summons and complaint—a post card on which the debtor could enter his defense and request a trial. Such a procedure would certainly overcome the various obstacles that now prevent debtors from appearing in court by the answer date. But the question still remains whether even these reforms if enacted will be adequate to give the debtor a day in court.

The Neighborhood Court Proposal

A number of consumer advocates have come to the conclusion that the current court machinery for handling consumer problems is totally inadequate and should be replaced by a highly decentralized neighborhood court or arbitration system. The proponents of this view note that the 9-to-5 hours of the central courts that now handle consumer complaints are suitable to parties represented by lawyers but are of little value to the consumer, who must be at work during those hours and who does not have a lawyer. They would like to see the model of the small claims court, which is a night court, extended to all consumer disputes. Most small claims courts have a rather low monetary ceiling on eligible cases and prohibit a corporation from being a plaintiff. But they do permit arbitrators who are volunteer lawyers to decide cases. The advocates of the neighborhood court idea for consumer disputes would like to see the model of the small claims court extended to cover all consumer disputes by raising the ceiling from $300 (as it is now in New York) to, say, $10,000. They would also permit corporations as well as individuals to institute actions. Such a court would be established in each neighborhood and venue rules would be changed to require the creditor to bring action in the neighborhood in which the debtor lives.[4]

Underlying the idea of the neighborhood court or arbitration center for consumer disputes is the recognition by scholars of fundamental differences between commercial transactions and consumer transactions. The research of one law professor, Stewart Macaulay, shows that conformity with contracts entered into by businessmen tends to rest not on the legal

[4]The Special Committee on Consumer Affairs of the New York City Bar Association developed a plan for such neighborhood arbitration centers. See "Toward the Informal Resolution of Consumer Disputes," Vol. 27, *Record of the Association* of the Bar of the City of New York, June 1972, p. 419.

terms of the contracts but on the personal relationship between the contracting parties. Macaulay found that most firms did not have legally binding contracts with their suppliers, as each party to the contract would have his own standard form that he would sign and send to the other party, and each party's form would have significantly different conditions specified on the back. The rare instances in which such contracts result in disputes have been characterized by the legal profession as battles of the forms. The point of Macaulay's study is that business contracts rest not on the legal language embodied in them but on the personal relationship between the partners and their ability to reward and sanction each other.[5] Arthur Leff of Yale Law School has carried the Macaulay observation still further by contrasting the situation that holds in business relationships with that in relations between creditors and debtors. Leff notes that in the garment industry, where some 35,000 firms engage in untold thousands of contractual relations with each other every year and where arbitration machinery has been set up to handle disputes, no more than 200 cases come to arbitration each year.[6] Like Macaulay, Leff attributes this exceedingly low rate of disputes to the fact that the parties to these business relationships know each other and work out accommodations in personal communications. In short, the personal relationship between the two parties ensures an exchange of information whereby one party explains why he has not lived up to the terms of the contract ("Artie, I know, the widgets are not up to snuff; we had trouble with the machinery that day. So I'll give them to you at half price, O.K.?") and the other party is ready to make an appropriate adjustment.[7] But as Leff points out, the situation is quite different in the transaction between a creditor and a consumer–debtor. These parties are not likely to know each other, especially, as we noted in the opening chapter, as society becomes more and more urbanized. The reasons the debtor is unable to pay are not known to the creditor, nor are the reasons the creditor may be unable to live up to his half of the bargain known to the debtor. In the absence of face-to-face communication, the creditor has no recourse but to rely on the formal structure, the terms embodied in the contract and the collection procedures sanctioned by law. The creditor's wholesale employment of formal collection procedures is, as we have seen, often self-defeating. Debtors sometimes lose their jobs because of garnishment proceedings or are prevented from finding new jobs because of the garnishment threat. Similarly, the legitimate complaints of consumers often go unheard by creditors who assume that they need not listen to complaints when they have powerful sanctions at their disposal. The severity of

[5]See Stewart Macaulay, "Non-contractual Relations in Business," *Amer. Sociolog. Rev.*, *28* (1963), 55.

[6]Arthur Leff, *Injury, Ignorance and Spite–The Dynamics of Coercive Collection* 80 Yale L.J. 1 (Nov. 1970).

[7]This is one of several such scenarios supplied by Leff, *ibid.*

the dispute between creditor and debtor, the fact that it often ends up in court with harsh sanctions imposed on the debtor, is in no small part due to the absence of communication between the two parties, their failure to know each other in the same way that business firms that have dealt with each other for long periods of time come to know and depend on each other.[8]

It is in this context that the idea of neighborhood arbitration systems for consumer disputes is proposed. The advocates of such a plan hope that the neighborhood setting and the forced confrontation between the parties to the dispute would result in information exchanges that would lead to accommodations. This neighborhood model might be criticized for assuming that the parties to the dispute are motivated by good faith, when some debtors and creditors are not. Also the neighborhood model may not be equipped to handle the hundreds of thousands of consumer law suits that arise each year in our major cities. But the feasibility of this model should not detract from the theory underlying it—the need to build bridges for communication between sellers and buyers, creditors and debtors so that information can be exchanged and accommodations worked out.[9] One thing is clear: the present system of resolving consumer disputes does not work, at least in the way in which it was intended, and some alternative method of resolving disputes is needed if justice is to be served.

The imbalances in the consumer credit system that have existed these many years are so blatant—the package of holder-in-due-course, deficiency judgments, confession of judgment, and garnishment—that one might well ask why society has taken so long to recognize these injustices and to try to correct them. A facile answer is that the institution of consumer credit is so new that an understandable cultural lag is involved in the reform process. But a more significant explanation for the slowness to reform the system might stem from the nature of the people who are most likely to suffer from these inequities. As we saw in chapter 2, default-debtors are overwhelmingly persons of marginal if not poverty-level income, persons of low occupational status, and persons disproportionately recruited from minority groups—blacks and Spanish-speaking citizens. The persons who fit these descriptions do not have powerful voices in our society. On the contrary, they tend to be exploited and have little power to correct the injustices practiced upon them. The pressures recently developed to reform consumer credit can probably be

[8] As Leff points out, business firms have some control over their contractual partners because they can influence the partner's reputation in the industry, presumably by spreading the word throughout the industry about the other firm's failings. Consumers typically lack such power to harm the reputations of merchants. The picket lines of CEPA in Philadelphia are a notable exception to the consumer's powerlessness, but to form such picket lines takes an incredible amount of organization.

[9] To some extent something like this does occur when the creditor's lawyer invites the debtor to his office to discuss the problem.

attributed partially to the civil rights movement of the 1960s and the government's war on poverty, especially its sponsoring of legal services for the poor.[10]

ALTERNATIVE SYSTEMS OF CONSUMER CREDIT

Reforming the present system of consumer credit is not the only solution to the problems posed in this book. Entirely different systems, if enacted, might prove to be even more just than reforms of the old system. As background for considering such alternative systems, it is necessary to note the peculiarities that now surround the money market in our free enterprise economy. Although merchants of automobiles, TV sets, clothing, food, and a thousand other products and services are expected to respond to the laws of supply and demand and compete with other companies in their industry for their share of the market, the institutions that symbolize the essence of capitalism, the financial institutions (whether they be banks, small loan companies, finance companies, or merchants extending credit) are not required to live by these principles of free enterprise. On the contrary, laws protect lending institutions from competition and permit even inefficient lenders to remain in business. These laws state who may enter the business of lending money and the amount that they can charge for their product. We are accustomed to thinking that price fixing in a capitalistic society is an extreme measure that is reasonable only in times of total mobilization for a war effort, as in World War II. But such government regulation is the norm of the money market. Ceilings are imposed on interest rates for loans and for sales made on the installment plan as part of an old tradition of usury laws. Moreover, not everyone with money to lend is allowed to enter this business. Government has established criteria of fitness and need that sharply curtail entry into the lending business. If a community has a lending institution, then another potentially rival lender may be denied the right to set up business in that community. These constraints stem from well-intentioned efforts to protect the public interest against bank failures and usury, but they have had the consequence of creating a banking and lending industry that has many of the attributes of public utilities rather than an industry responding to the dynamics of free enterprise.

The Free Market Model

The most critical features of the UCCC are those designed to make the lending industry conform to the principles of the free market economy.

---

[10]For further documentation of the flaws and horrors of the current system of consumer credit and for recommendations to correct the abuses, see Philip Schrag, *Counsel for the Deceived* (New York: Pantheon Books, Inc., 1972).

The UCCC would do this in two ways. First, it proposes a sharp increase in the legal ceilings on consumer loans, including goods bought on time. Second, the UCCC advocates free entry to the business of selling money. Thus, if a department store wants to make loans as well as sell merchandise, it would be able to do so, and no restrictions would be placed on the number of lenders who could be located in a given territory. Through these devices, the drafters of the UCCC envision a system in which the price of loans will be regulated by the free market. By raising the ceilings and allowing all to enter the industry, the drafters assume that competition alone will keep interest rates at a reasonable level and that efficient lenders will drive inefficient (that is, more costly lenders) out of business. Many consumer advocates argue that raising interest ceilings means only that the ceiling will become the floor, as all lenders will charge the highest possible rate and will not compete with each other in terms of rate. There is little evidence to support either position. The consumer advocates note that loans have always been made at the ceiling, no matter what the ceiling has been. The advocates of the free market model counter by pointing out that the ceilings have always been too low and, besides, the constraints on free entry restricted competition.

Unfortunately, the drafters of the UCCC who wish to regulate the money market by the dynamics of free competition nonetheless hedge their position by relying on the state ultimately to regulate the system by sanctioning breaches of contract through the devices of repossession, deficiency judgments, garnishment, and executions against real and personal property. What would happen if the credit industry gave up these harsh remedies, which amount to the big stick method of control, and instead shifted to the "carrot" of rewarding prompt payers with low rates, "punishing" poor risks with high rates, and ultimately controlling the system by banishing the deadbeats from the credit market? What is being suggested is a model in which would-be debtors are charged interest according to the risk they represent, and that the ultimate weapon at the disposal of the creditor would be to prevent debtors with a history of defaults from again becoming borrowers. This latter element in the model places a great burden on the systems of information exchange that the credit industry has developed—credit bureaus. Were creditors forced to relinquish their clubs, they may well spend more time investigating the would-be debtor and exercising greater caution in their extension of credit. Moreover, by charging different rates of interest on the basis of the debtor's past performance, creditors would be using the carrot to motivate prompt payments by their debtors. This might be illustrated by imagining a hypothetical world in which persons who reach a certain age, say, eighteen, are allowed to become debtors at a maximum rate of interest, say, 100 percent, irrespective of their income. Should these new debtors prove to be prompt and reliable payers, they would become eligible for a reduced interest rate on their next loan, say 50 percent, and so forth, until they earn the right to pay the low rate of say 6 or

7 percent. Those who perform poorly or default would be punished by having to pay higher rates of interest or by being excluded entirely from the credit game. The latter punishment should not be treated lightly. The economy of America is predicated on consumer credit, and the use of consumer credit is so pervasive that one can truly identify America in the latter third of the twentieth century as a credit society. In such a world, the individual's life chances, his ability to buy an automobile, a home, to finance his vacations, to pay for his education, to marry and start a family early rather than late, all depend on his credit rating. A person's credit rating thus emerges as a new dimension of social stratification and as a new form of what Charles Reich has called the "new property."[11] To have one's credit rating drop can be a severe blow to one's happiness, and this alone might serve as sufficient control of the credit system. But to view a credit rating as "new property" raises further difficulties. Credit bureaus would have to be regulated to ensure that their information is correct. The notion of credit rating as property conjures up the doctrine of "due process." The radical proposal of self-regulation and the free market model for the credit industry thus comes up against the thorny issues of "due process" and "invasion of privacy" (the open credit file). But these potential problems aside, there is some merit to thinking the unthinkable and forcing debate on such a radical proposal as the carrot rather than the big stick approach to consumer credit. Consumer advocates might well be unhappy with such a proposal, for they would consider it unconscionable for the poor to pay extraordinarily high rates of interest, say 100 percent. But this criticism loses much force in light of the fact that the poor already pay extraordinarily high hidden interest rates, as merchants in low-income areas circumvent the ceilings by having exorbitant markups on their goods. Bound by law not to charge more than 18 percent interest on a credit sale, the ghetto merchant does not hesitate to mark up his goods by one, two, or even three numbers, each number, in this quaint jargon of the trade, representing a 100 percent increase of the wholesale price. Given these evasions of ceilings in the form of unconscionable markups, the imposition by government of ceilings on interest is a rather ephemeral and pointless exercise. On the other hand, the credit industry is bound to object to this proposal, for it is convinced that most debtors are would-be deadbeats who would not pay unless forced to do so by the threat of the big stick. In taking this position, the credit industry strongly underestimates the basic goodwill of most debtors, the forces, for example, that led most Nebraska debtors to continue paying their creditors even when the State Supreme Court declared that they had no legal obligation to make such payments. Moreover, such a view does not take full cognizance of the importance of one's credit rating in this credit society and of the reluctance of most people to injure this "property."

[11]Charles A Reich, *The New Property,* 73 Yale L.J. 733 (Apr. 1964).

One advantage of eliminating creditor's remedies, especially garnishment, is that it would further discourage the unscrupulous creditor, the firm that fails to carry out a credit check before extending credit because it knows that it can garnishee the debtor's wages. All too often, the last firm that piles on, and in so doing, pushes the debtor over the brink, is the first to attach his wages, with the result that the more conservative creditors who behaved more responsibly are forced to wait in line before they can exert their claim against the debtor's income.

Credit Insurance Plans

One flaw in the free market model presented above is that it tacitly assumes that debtors default only because they are unwilling to pay, that is, because they are deadbeats. But we have seen that the great majority of debtors default because they are unable to pay, and most in this position were unable to pay because they suffered sudden reversals in income due to illness or unemployment (rather than by imprudently taking on more obligations than they could manage). These victims of the vicissitudes of life who constitute the bulk of default-debtors would suffer blows to their credit rating for reasons beyond their control. To protect these debtors and their creditors, it has been suggested that insurance systems, either public or private, be established to guarantee consumer loans. It should be noted that there are now several types of private insurance that debtors are often forced to buy as part of the transaction, insurance ranging from credit life to credit health insurance. These private insurance arrangements have been heavily criticized as having exorbitant charges and multiple escape clauses that result in debtors continuing to be liable even though they purchased the policy. In this study we encountered several debtors who thought that they had bought health insurance policies in connection with their debt obligation but who found themselves being sued even though their default stemmed from illness. The advocates of private insurance have in mind a quite different system. One proposal well exemplifies the possibilities of private credit insurance.[12] Each debtor would be issued a "credit limit card," which, in this world of computers, would be presented to the creditor at the time of a would-be credit transaction. The creditor would plug the card into his remote terminal and would learn instantly from the computer the debtor's credit limit and whether he has approached or overextended it. In short, the computer would instruct the creditor on the probability that the debtor would be able to repay the loan. Creditors who extend credit only to those who have not exceeded their credit limit would be insured against loss. This insurance would be paid by the creditors rather than the debtors. For example, suppose that a major department store now loses $5 million dollars a

[12]See Cary Temple, "A Proposal for a Credit Insurance System," 1968, unpublished.

year on bad debts. It would pay for this department store to cut its losses by subscribing to the credit limit plan at a cost of say $3 million a year. This model of private insurance not only assumes a high level of computer technology, but it also assumes that creditors want to extend credit only to those who will repay them. Should such a plan be institutionalized, the unscrupulous merchant eager to extend credit regardless of the debtor's ability to pay would be driven out of business since his customers would not qualify for further credit. In this model, the merchant's only redress would be the insurance policy rather than the current mechanisms of law suits, judgments, and garnishments, and he would be eligible for the insurance claim only if he respected the debtor's credit limit. Obviously this somewhat pie-in-the-sky model also places a heavy burden on systems of information exchange about debt obligations. Like the free market model, it assumes that all creditors will feed information on their credit transactions into the local credit bureau, which may be nothing more than the local computer.

The plan of having government provide the insurance for consumer loans also involves the idea of regulating creditors and debtors. The government certainly would hesitate to extend insurance to unscrupulous creditors or debtors. Thus any insurance scheme involves some control over the credit industry as the insuring party moves to eliminate dishonest participants in the credit game. For this reason alone, insurance systems should probably be encouraged.

ALTERING THE MARKETING STRUCTURE

We have speculated about alternative systems for extending credit to consumers, systems based on a free market model for the sale of money and insurance systems to protect the lenders from unexpected hardships to the borrowers. Apart from these radical proposals, much can be done to improve the plight of debtors and remove blatant injustices in the current credit marketplace by regulating the conditions under which consumer credit transactions occur. For example, in chapter 3 we saw that a disproportionate number of these transactions that went awry involved door-to-door sales of expensive merchandise on credit. It is virtually impossible for these sales not to involve high-pressure tactics, deception, and exorbitant markups. For one thing, the salesman's effort, especially his readiness to enter ghetto communities, places a heavy tax on the sales price in the form of the salesman's commission. Merchants accused of unconscionable markups on such items as burglar alarm systems, watches, and deep freezers that are sold door to door at many times the wholesale price or even the retail store price defend their pricing policies by pointing out the extraordinary premium they must pay the salesmen. In addition, the salesmen in these transactions are prepared to tell falsehoods to get the customer's signature on the contract. The various constraints based on repeated sales, familiarity between debtor and seller, the creditor's concern for his reputation, and even the debtor's readiness to shop around are completely absent in these "con-man" transactions. To call door-to-door salesmen "con men" might seem at first a harsh indictment, but an examination of their techniques (for example, "bait and switch," "referral sales," "free gifts," and out-and-out misrepresentation such as telling the customer that the freezer comes free with the food plan or that the burglar alarm system is plugged into the police station when it is not) shows that these salesmen are indeed con men and that the border between the illegitimate con man and the legitimate one is extremely thin.[13] Even if the carrot model of consumer credit cannot be instituted, a great deal can be done to reform the present system by simply abolishing door-to-door sales of expensive merchandise on credit. In view of the abuses associated with this method of selling, why cannot Congress further the public good by making it illegal to sell outside the merchant's place of business any item on credit that costs, say, $50 or more? (The $50 cutting point would probably eliminate all these sales, since the salesman would not be able to realize a commission that would make the transaction worthwhile.)

Eliminating door-to-door sales is perhaps the most dramatic example of regulating the transaction. Others include prohibiting small loan companies from making loans outside their places of business, one of several criteria for eliminating dealer-arranged loans, or regulations that would eliminate the practice of referral sales and bait-and-switch selling practices. No doubt other controls over the initial transaction might prove fruitful. The key point is that an alternative to reforming the system at the end point when the transaction has broken down and the creditor invokes harsh collection practices is to regulate it at the outset so that shady transactions conducive to default do not occur.

This study has documented the history and outcomes of consumer credit transactions that failed. It has uncovered many imperfections in the present system that are costly to creditors and debtors alike. We hope that this study has presented the case for radical reforms of the system of consumer credit. Whether the types of reforms suggested are desirable is a matter of public debate and empirical inquiry. It is our hope that this research will stimulate such debate and inquiry.

[13] Arthur Leff has noted that all retailing in America involves elements of the con game. This discovery stimulated him to read the literature on confidence games and he learned that confidence men make a distinction between the "little con" and the "big con." In the "little con," the confidence man and his confederates seek to relieve the victim (the "mark") of all the money in his pocket. In the "big" con, the confidence man sends the mark home to withdraw his life savings from the bank and contribute them to the scheme. Leff makes the interesting observation that as long as retailing depended on cash it was strictly a "little con" game. But with the invention of installment credit, retailing suddenly entered the world of "big con," as the creditor not only had his hands on the debtor's savings but on his future income also.

APPENDIXES

GLOSSARY

OF TERMS

Add-on Contract
An "add-on contract" is an agreement between a buyer and a seller whereby each purchase by the buyer is one of a series of credit sales and the deferred payment price of the most recent purchase is added on to the buyer's existing balance. The monthly payments are pro-rated against each of the items on the contract, with the result that even though the payments far exceed the cost of the initial items on the contract, the seller's records show that the initial items are not yet paid for. Should the debtor default under such a contract, the seller is entitled by law to repossess all the merchandise purchased under the contract.

Affidavit of Nonmilitary Service
The Soldier's and Sailor's Relief Act prohibits military personnel who are on duty from being served with legal papers, for they may be unable to return and defend themselves. In order for substituted service and even personal service to be valid the process server is required to file an "affidavit of nonmilitary service." On this affidavit he must list the names and addresses of the people whom he asked about the defendant's status with regard to the military.

Answer
An "answer" is what the word connotes: it is the defendant's opportunity to tell his side of the story or "answer" the questions raised by the

This glossary was prepared with the assistance of Howard Rubin, now an attorney with the New York City Department of Consumer Affairs.

plaintiff. In this pleading, the defendant sets out the facts as he sees them. He can deny what the plaintiff has said or he can bring in additional facts that will explain away the complaint and convince the court that the plaintiff is not entitled to the remedy demanded. If the defendant fails to put in an answer to the complaint, he subjects himself to a judgment in default.

Assumpsit

"Assumpsit" is a legal action to recover money owed to another due to a contract between them. It is an action that can be brought to recover damages any time one individual has promised, explicity or implicitly, to do an act or pay something to another. Although the term "assumpsit" applies to all the consumer actions dealt with in this book, it appears in court records only in Detroit.

Balloon Payments

In most installment sales, the contract specifies payments of the same amount at regular intervals. But this is not always the case, and the timing as well as the amount of the payments may vary. Any payment that is more than the regularly scheduled equal payments is called a "balloon payment." The purposes of "balloon payments" have been several. First, where legislation restricted the length of time of an installment purchase as in the case of automobile sales in certain periods, the balloon payment was a device for enticing buyers to buy with the inducement of easy payments except for the last, which was a stiff payment. The second function of balloon payments was to encourage the buyer or borrower to refinance the purchase or loan because of his inability to meet the last payment and thus remain in continued debt to the creditor.

Class Action

A "class action" is an action brought on behalf of numerous persons similarly situated. A "class" is a group of individuals who have similar legal claims and factual situations with regard to a common defendant. A class can be as small as the tenants on one floor of a building or as large as all the customers of the telephone company. Class actions are usually brought against a defendant when the remedy that can be gained by any individual plaintiff would not be great enough for him to undertake the risk or expense of bringing a suit. The class action spreads the costs of the suit more widely and makes the cumulative rewards much greater.

Complaint

The "complaint" is the first pleading on the part of the plaintiff in a civil action. The summons issued to a defendant informs him that a complaint has been made against him. Although there are legal technicalities and requirements for a complaint, it is more or less what one would expect it to be. It tells the defendant all the important facts on which the plaintiff is making his demand, for example, in a consumer action, the amount that is owed and the conditional sales contract underlying this demand. In many jurisdictions the complaint is attached to the summons.

Conditional Sales Contract
Unlike an "absolute sale," in which ownership of the property passes to the buyer upon completion of the bargain, a "conditional sale" is one in which the transfer of title is made to depend on the performance of some condition by the buyer, usually the final payment of the price. The buyer does not own the merchandise until he has completed the payments. The seller can repossess the property, which he still owns, in the event of a default in payment by the buyer.

Confession of Judgment
A "Confession of judgment" is the act of a debtor in permitting judgment to be entered against him by his creditor, for an agreed-upon sum, by a written statement to that effect, without the insititution of legal proceedings of any kind. Most consumers would confront a confession of judgment on a conditional sales contract. The contract would have a provision, called a cognovit note, by which the buyer confesses that he is at fault in whatever action later arises between himself and the seller. This provision would say that the seller has the power to enter this confession into court and secure a judgment against the buyer without telling the buyer he was doing so. On the basis of this judgment, court-ordered procedures for collecting the debt can be instituted.

Cognovit Note
A "cognovit note" is a part of the confession of judgment. It is the contract provision or agreement which the debtor signs permitting the creditor to enter a confession of judgment against him.

Default Judgment
A "default judgment" is a decision of a court entered against the defendant when he does not appear to defend himself or does not submit an answer to the complaint. It has the same effect as if the defendant had appeared and the court had decided the case against him. The critical point is that the default judgment has nothing to do with the merits of the case. The defendant is judged the loser simply because he has not appeared.

Deficiency Judgment
Although many consumers believe they have no further obligation once the creditor repossesses the merchandise bought under an installment con-

tract, in fact they may be subjected to a "deficiency judgment." This refers to the creditor's right to sue the debtor for the balance of the debt when the amount realized from the sale of the repossessed merchandise is subtracted from the original balance. Repossessed merchandise is hardly ever sold for an amount that covers the balance of the debt, so a deficiency almost invariably exists and the creditor is entitled to sue the debtor for a deficiency judgment.

Garnishment

A "garnishment" is a form of property execution which is used to get property of debtors that is in the keeping of a third party (for example, an employer or a bank) in order to pay off a debt. Most often, garnishment refers to attachment of the debtor's wages and is called an "income execution" in New York and "wage deduction" in Chicago. Pursuant to a court order, the creditor notifies the third party that he must pay some portion (set by state law, for example, in New York 10 percent of incomes more than $85.00 per week) of the debtor's property to the creditor.

Holder-in-Due-Course

"Holder-in-due-course" is a complex legal doctrine which immunizes the finance company, the company that buys the installment contract from the seller, from any defenses that the buyer might have against the seller. The theory underlying this doctrine is that the finance company bought the contract in good faith and was unaware of any shenanigans the seller may have committed. Although of some value in commercial transactions, in the consumer field this doctrine has been a stimulus to consumer fraud as fly-by-night companies (many of which would go bankrupt) would sell shoddy merchandise and get their money from the finance company, which in turn had the legal right to enforce the buyer to maintain payments. Few consumers understand this doctrine and feel justified in withholding payments until the merchandise is repaired. But the holder-in-due-course is not legally responsible for the merchandise and when the consumer stops payments, he is apt to sue the consumer for the balance of the debt. The unfairness of this doctrine in consumer transactions is gradually being recognized, and in a number of states the holder-in-due-course doctrine has been abolished or has been limited to only certain types of transactions.

Judgment

A "judgment" is the official decision of a court of law about the rights and claims of those who have submitted their dispute for determination. Essentially, the judgment is the outcome of the suit, the court order that tells who owes what to whom. An appropriate public official (for example, a sheriff, U.S. Marshal, or city marshal) can be ordered to "execute" the judgment. The expression "to have a judgment outstanding against you" means that the other party is waiting for you to act according to the terms of the judgment or he will have the judgment enforced by an appropriate official.

Personal Service

"Personal service" refers to a type of delivery of a summons to the defendant in a legal action. Personal service means that the summons has been handed directly to the defendant himself. Leaving the summons with some other member of the defendant's family is not personal service.

Property Execution

The term "execution" applies to the process used to carry out the final judgment of the court. Any writ or order that authorizes a public officer to seize debtor's property as a means of putting into effect the judgment of the court is a "property execution." It authorizes a public officer to seize and hold enough of the debtor's property to satisfy the judgment against him. The property seized will be sold at public auction and the proceeds, up to the amount of the debt, given to the creditor. A certain percentage is also given to the public officer for his labors. Property execution differs from repossession in that the public officer may seize any goods the debtor owns (with some specified exceptions), not merely the object of the contract on which the debtor is in default.

Replevin

Technically, "replevin" means "redelivery to the owner of things taken in distress." It is a legal action taken to recover possession of goods unlawfully taken. An action in replevin is brought when the owner wants to recover the actual property taken from him rather than damages. In consumer actions the creditor seeks a replevin order when the goods he wants to repossess are located in the debtor's home; the order protects him from charges of breaking and entering. A recent Supreme court decision has declared that the debtor must be given advance notice of a replevin action so that he can contest its validity. This decision has not yet been extended to "self-help" repossessions (for example, when an automobile on the street is repossessed).

Repossession

The word "repossession" has become such a common part of the language that its commonly understood meaning is close to its legal definition. When one buys something under a conditional sales contract, the seller retains title to the merchandise until the buyer has made the last of his payments. Should the buyer default, the seller has the right to reclaim, or repossess the merchandise. Should the merchandise be located outside the debtor's home (for example, an automobile), the seller can reclaim it without a court order. This is known as self-help repossession.

Revolving Credit

"Revolving credit" is one kind of "open-end credit." It is a system of borrowing or installment buying under which the buyer makes purchases up to his "credit limit" and makes monthly payments that include a finance charge on the unpaid balance. The finance charge in most states is 1½ percent a month, 18 percent a year. Unlike purchases made under a conditional sales contract, those made under a revolving credit system belong to the buyer at the outset. The seller in such a system forfeits his right to repossess merchandise bought on credit since he does not retain title to the goods.

Sewer Service

The term "sewer service" refers to the failure of the process server to deliver the summons. Instead he destroys it or throws it "down the sewer" and then fills out an affidavit in which he falsely swears that he delivered the papers to the defendant. This happens quite often in consumer cases in which the defendants tend to be poor and poorly educated. Sewer service is especially common in New York City, where process serving is a private industry. As a result of sewer service, the defendant does not know of the legal action against him and because he fails to make an appearance to file an answer, he becomes the victim of a default judgment. Sewer service is difficult to prove and relatively few people have been caught at it, although in recent years the U.S. Attorney's office in the Southern District of New York has successfully prosecuted some process servers for sewer service and recently won a civil judgment against a firm on the grounds that all its judgments against debtors were based on "sewer service."

Substituted Service

The law does not always require that legal papers be delivered to the defendant personally. Any form of service other than personal service is known as "substituted service." Most typically the process server will leave the summons with a person over 21 years of age at the defendant's dwelling unit. In such cases the law requires that he mail a copy of the summons to the defendant as well.

Summons

A summons is a notice to an individual that an action is being taken against him in a court of law and instructs him to appear in court and answer the complaint against him. In most jurisdictions, summonses are served by court officials (for example, sheriffs, bailiffs), but in some states,

New York being one, process serving (process referring to all kinds of legal papers, including a summons) is a private industry and anyone over eighteen can be a process server.

Wage Assignment
An "assignment" is an expression of intention by an individual that his rights in some property shall pass and be owned by another under certain conditions. On the basis of such an assignment a third party would be authorized to pay the assignor's property interest to the assignee. A "wage assignment" is an agreement in which one person (the debtor) gives another (the creditor) his right to his own future wages in the event of a default. The wage assignment circumvents the need for a court judgment. Wage assignments are built into consumer contracts in a number of states. This was the pattern in New York until 1968, when wage assignments were prohibited in instances of conditional sales. But wage assignments are still legal in New York regarding consumer loans. Suits are now under way challenging the constitutionality of wage assignments.

THE ISSUE OF

BIAS

As noted in chapter 1, this study of breakdowns in the system of consumer credit is based entirely on interviews with debtors in default. At no point were interviews conducted with the creditors. An attempt has been made to analyze a social system and, more specifically, a social conflict by consulting only one member of the system and only one party to the dispute. Our image of the system of consumer credit and the causes and consequences of its breakdowns have been based primarily on the materials gathered in our interviews with the debtors. This study design is thus contrary to the method that has evolved in law as the most appropriate tool for ascertaining the truth—the adversary system. For this reason, the findings might well be considered suspect, especially by the members of one of the more important audiences of this report—the legal profession. Lawyers have learned, often from bitter experience, not to trust the testimony of any given party to a dispute without checking and cross checking its substance. The question of the truthfulness of our respondents, the issue of "validity" as it is called in social research, takes on added significance in this study, given the prima facie suspicion that the respondents will be inclined to distort the critical events so as to present themselves in the most favorable light. On what bases, then, might such a one-sided view of the system of consumer credit be defended? The burden of this appendix is to present some arguments in such a defense.

PROBABILISTIC VERSUS DETERMINISTIC MODELS

The differing reactions of the lawyer and the survey researcher to the issue of the respondent's truthfulness—the skepticism of the former and the optimism of the latter—can be traced largely to the lawyer's concern with the individual case and the survey researcher's concern with the aggregate pattern. In the language of science this refers to the distinction between determinism, the ability to predict the behavior of the individual case, and probability, the ability to assess the likelihood that certain types of cases will act one way rather than another. Two types of error can creep into the survey researcher's method, one rather harmless, the other quite serious. These are known as random error and systematic error, or bias.

Random Error

Many errors of measurement in social science have no apparent order; they are, in other words, "random." For example, because of the respondent's misunderstanding of the question or because of a key-punching mistake, a college graduate might be misclassified as someone who has not graduated from college. Comparable errors might creep into the classification of the respondents in terms of age, religion, political affiliation, or any other attribute. Social scientists have long accepted as inevitable the occurrence of such random errors, and their efforts are devoted to keeping them at a minimum. But they do not worry about random error because, in the aggregate, they tend to cancel each other out. The unfortunate cost of random error is that it reduces correlations between variables. (It is for this reason that social scientists are apt to give credence to small correlations on the grounds that the removal of the random error would make the observed differences more significant.)

The Problem of Systematic Error or Bias

Clearly it is not random error that critics have in mind when they argue that our respondents might have distorted the truth to present themselves in a more favorable light. Such motivation would give rise to systematic error or bias, and biased error is a serious flaw in any research project. The respondents in this study were provided with a number of occasions for less than truthful, self-serving answers. For example, irrespective of the facts, they could have blamed the default on the creditor. (In point of fact, most blamed themselves or their circumstances and not the creditor, a point in favor of their credibility.) Or they could have replied that they never received a summons, when in fact they did, as a way of explaining why they did not appear in court. On what grounds can their answers to such questions be believed?

SOLUTIONS TO THE BIAS PROBLEM

Intercity Comparisons

The fact that the study was done in four cities in which consumer laws and procedures differ provides an important basis for checking the validity of the debtors' responses. The matter of service of summons is a good example of this type of check. It is widely assumed that the system in New York is not nearly as efficient as the system in other cities ("sewer service" is a New York term). Granted that the absolute proportions who say they were not served may be inflated because of the self-serving principle, the intercity differences, especially if they show that service in New York is much worse than in Chicago and Detroit, are nonetheless a valid finding and tell us something about the inadequacies of the New York system. (It will be recalled that 54 percent of the default-debtors said they were served in New York, compared with 71 percent in Chicago and 84 percent in Detroit.) The only alternative is to assume that New York debtors are more prone to lying than those in Chicago and Detroit, clearly a less plausible hypothesis.

In a similar fashion we were able to "catch" the New York process servers "fibbing" about personal service by comparing the difference in the rate of such service based on the process server's testimony and that of the respondents in each city. The huge gap in New York and the fact that the process servers in that city were much more prone to claim personal service than those in the other cities gave credence to the debtors' reports of how service was made and challenged the veracity of the New York process servers.

The Plausible Pattern

What we call the "plausible pattern" solution to the problem of bias is very similar to the one based on previous research or widely held beliefs. For example, it is known that the more well-to-do are more likely than the poor to turn to lawyers for help when they encounter legal problems. This pattern was confirmed in our study, giving credence to the responses to the questions about seeking legal help. Similarly, it is known that legal fees often outweigh the gains in consumer suits and hence those being sued for large amounts might be expected to be more likely to turn to lawyers than those sued for small amounts, an expectation again confirmed by the data. In chapter 3 we developed a measure of deception in the initial transaction, based on responses to questions about when the contract was received and disclosure of costs at the time of the transaction. The respondents' answers to such questions, especially because they involve recall of events that occurred at least a year ago, might well be viewed with suspicion. And yet the resulting measure turned out to be strongly related to the traditional reputations of the various types of sellers. Thus the direct sellers and automobile dealers (mostly used-car firms) scored high on this measure of deception, whereas general retailers—the large downtown stores—scored low. These plausible patterns thus lend validity to the data, for if the respondents were prone to lie in self-serving ways, they presumably would have done so regardless of type of seller.

The Testimony of Multiple Witnesses

Although we did not have any witnesses for the plaintiffs in these disputes, there were occasionally *multiple* witnesses for the defense. Moreover, our multiple witnesses, unlike those in a trial, are totally free of the suspicion of collusion, for they did not know each other. This phenomenon of multiple witnesses arose in chapters 6, 7, and 8, where the debtors' accounts of why they defaulted were presented. We sometimes found one debtor corroborating the story of another by reporting his experience with the same seller or finance company. For example, when several Detroit debtors reported that used-car dealers arranged loans for down payments late at night from the same finance company, the chances are that this small loan company did indeed stay open late at night and had some arrangement with used-car dealers. When a number of New York debtors who bought watches from direct sellers employed by the same firm reported that they never got their copy of the contract and sometimes never received a payment book, it is quite likely that this firm is derelict in these ways. And when a number of Detroit debtors report being sold $125 suits by door-to-door salesmen for the same firm who promised them $25 discounts for each customer they referred, it is reasonably safe to assume that this firm does employ the chain-referral scheme as one of its sales gimmicks.

Of course, most of the episodes dealt with in the study were *not* verified by multiple witnesses, but the very fact that some were is highly significant and lends much weight to the stories told by others. For example, when a woman tells us that she was tricked into signing an installment contract under the ruse that she was signing a paper acknowledging delivery of the goods, it would seem wiser to assume that other debtors who did not fall into our sample were similarly tricked, rather than to assume that she is either lying or represents a unique case.

THE ROLE OF COURT RECORDS

The assertion that we have no information from the creditor–plaintiffs must be qualified in one major respect. We did learn some extremely important things about the case from the court records. Thus we know the amount of the judgment sought (and it was this figure taken from the records rather than the comparable information supplied by the debtor in the interview that was used in the analysis); we know whether the case resulted in a default judgment and, if not, what its final determination was; we know whether the case ever went to trial and, if so, its outcome; and we know from the affidavit filed by the process server how he claimed service was made. Such information taken from the court records proved of great value in the analysis carried out in chapters 11, 12, and 13.

For the reasons enumerated above, the apparent one-sidedness of this study of breakdowns in the system of consumer credit is not the obstacle that it seemed at first.

C

THE SAMPLE

This appendix describes decisions affecting the sampling and interviewing of default-debtors. The basis for selecting the four cities, the methods of sampling cases within each city, and the difficulties encountered in contacting sampled debtors are described.

The Selection of Cities

Each state has the right to regulate consumer credit transactions. Although there is much overlap in state laws, there is also some variation. Most states require the creditor to obtain a court judgment before acting against the real and personal property of debtors, but some states recognize contracts containing confession-of-judgment clauses, which deny the debtor his right to a day in court. Philadelphia was included in the sample to represent such a state. Philadelphia actually served a dual purpose. Not only did it recognize confession-of-judgment contracts, but it denied the creditor's most powerful remedy, garnishment of wages and bank accounts. Thus Philadelphia was also intended to provide a picture of the collection process in the absence of the garnishment remedy. New York was chosen because the author knew a good deal about consumer credit law in that state (the site of the research reported in *The Poor Pay More*) and because in New York, unlike most other states, the all-important matter of service of process is left to private industry. One objective of the research was to assess the adequacy of the notification process in New York relative to that in states that rely on court officials to serve process. Detroit was chosen because of Michigan's harsh garnishment law and because of its large working class population, the occupational group that we suspected would be most vulnerable to credit problems. Chicago was selected because of its closeness to the interviewing agency, the National Opinion Research Center of the University of Chicago. In addition, Illinois was, or so we thought, another state that permitted confession of judgment, although allowing garnishment. In fact, confession of judgment in Illinois involves a notification procedure known as the "confirmation of judgment" that makes it equivalent to the open suits brought in Detroit and New York. (Although Illinois retains the *language* of confession of judgment, it has so emasculated this doctrine as to reduce it to the procedures in states that forbid confession of judgment.)

Docket Books and the Types of Cases Sampled

Creditors in Chicago can bring suits either under the confession-of-judgment rules or through open suits that follow procedures much like those in New York and Detroit. On the advice of several Legal Aid attorneys in Chicago, we decided to limit the study in that city to confession-of-judgment contracts recorded in the confirmation-of-judgment book. Apparently, almost all the small loan companies and installment sellers in Chicago use the confession-of-judgment contract, the open-suit procedure being preferred by department stores that offer charge accounts and revolving credit. Thus the Chicago sample obtained a purity that was lacking in the other cities. It consists exclusively of conditional sales and small loans whereas in the other cities, revolving credit accounts and perhaps even charge accounts are represented, although we tried to eliminate the latter.

Whereas the relevant docket book in Chicago was the confirmation-of-judgment book, in Detroit and New York it was the docket book for open suits in the relevant courts, the Court of Common Pleas in Detroit and the Manhattan branch of the Civil Court of New York, each of which has jurisdiction over monetary disputes under $10,000. The confession-of-judgment contracts in Philadelphia required sampling default-debtors from a later stage in the collection process than in the other cities. In Philadelphia, information about breakdowns in credit transactions can only be obtained from the sheriff's execution books against real and personal property. The entries in these books result from creditor's requesting the sheriff to carry out an execution against a default-debtor. The sheriff's office maintains separate books for personal property executions and real property executions. Since there were many more of the former (in a ratio of about 6:1), we oversampled real property executions in order to have a sufficient number represented in the Philadelphia sample.

The Eligible Cases

The study was limited to consumers who defaulted on either installment loans or installment purchases of merchandise. This eliminated a large number of debtors who were being sued for failure to pay for services, mainly health services, but also a wide range of dubious and exploitative services such as correspondence schools, judo lessons, dance lessons, reducing programs, and so on. The screening of ineligible cases took place in two stages. First, all cases in which the plaintiff was an individual rather than a firm and the defendant was a firm rather than an individual were eliminated. Among other things, this eliminated contractual disputes between commercial firms. The second stage of screening took place when the files of the initially sampled cases were examined. The files contained the summons and complaint and in Detroit and Chicago, but not in New York, copies of the contract as well. This further information permitted screening ineligible cases.

A special problem was posed by the numerous large department stores that showed up as plaintiffs, mainly in New York and Detroit. Did these cases refer to installment purchases of single items, to revolving credit accounts, or to charge accounts? We were primarily interested in the first, only secondarily in revolving credit, and not at all concerned with charge accounts. No reliable distinctions could be made prior to the interview. We assumed that the more elite stores among the plaintiffs, such as Abercrombie and Fitch, Brooks Bros., Lord and Taylor, and Saks Fifth Avenue, were suing their charge account customers and thus we eliminated all such plaintiffs from the study. Department stores such as Macy's and Gimbel's in New York were not excluded, since they offer revolving credit to their customers. But since we were less interested in revolving credit, we undersampled the nonelite department store cases by eliminating half of them.

The Time Period Sampled

The objectives of the study required sampling cases that were neither too old (a year or more) nor too new. If we chose relatively old cases, we would have had more difficulty finding the debtors, and they would likely have forgotten many of the details of the case. Very recent cases were not desirable because the legal action and its consequences would not have unfolded. Since the interviewing in New York, Detroit, and Chicago was scheduled to begin in May 1967, cases in these cities were selected that had been filed with the court four to six months previously.

The Philadelphia survey required a questionnaire that omitted questions about garnishment and inquired instead about real and personal property executions. The need for a somewhat different questionnaire led us to put off the interviewing in Philadelphia until August and September 1967.[1] As noted, the Philadelphia cases were sampled from the sheriff's docket books and the period was March, April, and May 1967.

The Response Rate

In most surveys the researcher is interested in a class of persons, such as eligible voters, college students, or family heads. The techniques of probability sampling are employed in most modern surveys, and these usually involve multistage area sampling and the random selection of respondents from the units (households, colleges, factories, and so on) that fall within the sample. The critical point is that the eligible members of the sample are those who *currently* reside at the location sampled. The sampling design for this study was of a different nature, one considerably more difficult to realize. Instead of interviewers approaching respondents because of their membership in a broad class at the time of the interview, our interviewers were seeking particular persons on the basis of residence data that were at least six months old and, in some unknown number of instances, much older than that.[2] Our one-shot survey had built into it the problem that arises in longitudinal studies in which a panel of respondents is reinterviewed at different points in time: "panel mortality." This refers to the disappearance of respondents by the time of the reinterview at a later point in time.

The normal amount of panel mortality for a six-month interval is compounded by the unusual character of the population that we were trying to sample. People who have defaulted on installment debts are likely to be very mobile, for if they have trouble paying their debts they may also have trouble paying their rent. They may also decide to move to avoid being hounded by their creditors. "Second wave" interviewing in a one-shot survey raises questions about computing the response rate. Should we use as the base all those whom we tried to locate or only those known to live at the address at the time that the interviewer called? We shall come back to this question after describing our method for anticipating the high loss rate and compensating for it.

Our initial plan was to interview approximately 325 to 350 default-debtors in each city. The court records were heavily oversampled to

---

[1]One purpose for this delay was to permit us to improve the Philadelphia questionnaire on the basis of the experience in the other cities.

[2]For the most part, the address that appeared on the summons was also the address entered on the contract at the time of the transaction, which occurred months or even years before the initiation of the court action. In instances of improper service, the process server might claim to have delivered a summons to a particular address even though the building had been torn down. In short, we cannot be certain in all these cases that the person did reside at the given address at the time that the summons was served, and in some cases it was obvious that he did not.

ensure sufficient cases to meet the intended quota of interviews. In Chicago, New York, and Detroit, between 900 and 1,000 cases were sampled in each city. In Philadelphia, where samples were taken from property execution books, we reasoned that the creditors were pretty certain that the debtor resided at the address in question (since the filing fees were quite high), and hence in Philadelphia we sampled only twice rather than three times as many cases as we wanted to interview—about 550.[3] In each city these initial samples were divided arbitrarily into two subsamples, a primary sample and a back-up sample to be used if the primary sample did not yield sufficient cases. The interviewing agency (NORC) was instructed to concentrate on the primary sample (making the usual three or four call-backs where the respondent was known to live at the address) and to turn to the secondary sample only when the primary sample was exhausted. As a result, the response rates were better for the primary sample than for the secondary sample. Many in the back-up sample were never contacted, and, in general, the number of call-backs for respondents not at home was smaller in the secondary sample, for the interviewing ceased once the requisite quota was met. This description of the response rates for the primary and secondary samples applies to New York, Chicago, and Detroit, but in Philadelphia, where we initially sampled many fewer cases, it was necessary to work equally hard on the cases in the secondary sample as in the primary one, with the result that the response rates are much the same for these samples in Philadelphia.

In presenting data on response rates, we used as our base (at least initially) all those whom the interviewing agency made some effort to contact, including those who had long since moved away. In short, the base figures in Table C.1 are equivalent to a first-wave set of respondents in a panel study. Calculated in this fashion, it should come as no surprise that the response rates were rather low—47 percent for the primary sample in all four cities, and 35 percent for the secondary one—an average of 43 percent overall.

Table C.1 / Response Rate in Each Sample by City Calculated on the Basis of Cases Where Some Attempt Was Made To Contact the Respondent (percent)

	New York	Chicago	Detroit	Phila-delphia	total
Primary sample	41 (555)	43 (491)	53 (575)	53 (365)	47 (1,986)
Secondary sample	30 (349)	31 (338)	39 (357)	53 (109)	35 (1,153)
Total	37 (904)	38 (829)	48 (932)	53 (474)	43 (3,139)

[3]As we shall soon see, this turned out to be an incorrect assumption. Philadelphia debtors were almost as hard to find as those in the other cities.

As can be seen from the top row, the response rate in the primary sample ranged from 41 percent in New York to 53 percent in Detroit and Philadelphia, and it was still lower in the secondary sample, ranging from 30 percent in New York to 53 percent in Philadelphia. In all, the response rate (based on the addresses provided in the court records) was lowest in New York, 37 percent, and highest in Philadelphia, 53 percent.

As noted, these response rates are based on cases where some attempt was made to contact the default-debtor regardless of where he lived at the time. It is instructive to review the outcomes of these attempts. Letters were sent to all prospective respondents in the primary sample explaining the purpose of the study. A substantial number of these were returned "address unknown." The address unknown rate was highest in New York, 21 percent, and probably reflects the inaccuracies in the service of process in that city. In Chicago 12 percent of the letters came back, and in Detroit, only 4 percent. (In Philadelphia, so few letters came back that the interviewers were instructed to check those addresses as well.) When the interviewers went into the field they discovered that the records of the post office were incomplete. Even though letters had not come back, they found that many debtors had either moved from the address or according to neighbors and building superintendents had never lived at the given address. In some of these unlocatable cases, the building at the given address had disappeared. The total of missing persons based on the returned letters and the interviewers' subsequent discoveries constituted 35 percent of the cases sampled in New York, 39 percent of the Chicago cases, 23 percent of the Detroit cases, and only 18 percent of the Philadelphia cases. These "missing persons" do not exhaust the list of unreachable respondents. The interviewers discovered that in 10 cases the default-debtor had died and that an additional 33 cases involved instances of mistaken identity in which the person at the address was not the default-debtor that the plaintiff had in mind even though he might have had a similar name. When the missing persons, the cases of mistaken identity, and the few deaths are removed from the sample, the response rates rise precipitously. When the rate is based on those debtors who presumably still lived at the given address (and could have been interviewed if they were at home or were willing to cooperate), it increases to 56 percent in New York, 61 percent in Chicago, 62 percent in Detroit, and 66 percent in Philadelphia. For all cities the adjusted response rate is 61 percent, a figure that is far below that achieved by the census in its surveys based on area sampling, but one that is not too far below that achieved in many sociological studies.

The reader may judge for himself how "generalizable" the findings reported in this survey are. Perhaps they do not reflect all default-debtors who are sued but only the more stable segment of that population, the segment still residing at the same address six months after the law suit. In chapter 2 we examined a number of the social characteristics of the debtors that were interviewed, and if they are the more stable segment of the default-debtor population, a more representative sample would show this group to be even more disorganized and marginal, thereby raising the question of how they qualified for credit in the first place.

We conclude this account of the sample by noting that the 1,331 interviews are distributed rather unevenly among the four cities. Only in New York and Chicago did the number of interviews approximate the intended quota; 332 debtors were interviewed in New York and 312 in Chicago. In Philadelphia, where the initial sample was much smaller, only 249 interviews were obtained, whereas in Detroit, 438 default-debtors were interviewed, far exceeding the intended quota.[4]

[4] The high Detroit figure was the result of an overzealous field staff somewhat out of touch with NORC's main office in Chicago. These figures on the number of interviews exclude a few cases in each city that were discarded after the interview because the transaction was an ineligible one.

THE QUESTIONNAIRE

First I want to talk with you about the legal problem you're having with *(plaintiff)*.

1. Did this trouble start because of a particular item that was bought on credit, because of money that was borrowed, or because you missed payments on a revolving charge account?

Credit purchase *(go to Q. 2)*	1	10/0
Money borrowed *(go to Q. 2)*	2	
Revolving charge *(go to Q. 2)*	3	
None of these *(ask A)*	4	

    A. *If none of these:* How did you get involved in this problem?

Cosigner with immediate family member *(go back and ask Q. 1)*	6	11/5
Cosigner with other	7	
Mistaken identity *(go to instruction below B)*	8	
Other *(specify)* *(go to Q. 2)*	9	

    B. *If cosigner with other:* Was the person you signed for a relative, friend, coworker?

Relative *(skip to Q. 40)*	1	12/0
Friend *(skip to Q. 40)*	2	
Coworker *(skip to Q. 40)*	3	
Other *(specify)* *(skip to Q. 40)*	4	

If mistaken identity: Record circumstances on noninterview report form (NIR), then terminate interview.

This Appendix includes only those questions that were used in the analysis. Anyone interested in the complete questionnaire may contact the author or the Bureau of Applied Social Research of Columbia University for a copy.

2. How long ago did you (make the purchase) (borrow the money)?

Within the past 6 months	1	13/0
6 months to a year	2	
1 or 2 years	3	
3 or 4 years	4	
5 years or more	5	

If credit purchase or revolving charge, go to Q. 3.

If money borrowed, skip to Q. 24.

3. What did you (last) buy that led to this problem?

   _____

   (name of item)   14-15/00

5. Did you go to a store *(dealer)* to buy the *(merchandise)*, did you buy it from a salesman who came to your door, did you buy it through the mail, or did you buy it some other way?

Store (dealer) *(go to Q. 6)*	1	19/0
Door-to-door salesman *(ask A)*	2	
Through the mail *(go to Q. 6)*	3	
Other *(specify, then go to Q. 6)*	4	

   A. *If door-to-door salesman:* Did the salesman tell you that he wanted to sell you something or did he say he had come to see you for some other reason?

Wanted to sell something *(go to Q. 8)*	6	20/5
Other reason *(ask B, then skip to Q. 8)*	7	

   B. *If other reason:* What did he say?

      (go to Q. 8)   21/0

8. What was the name of the company you bought it from?

   _____   24/0

   (Name)

9. What was the name of the company you were supposed to make payment to?

   _____   25/0

   (Name)

   A. Any other company?

   _____   26/0

   (Name)

11. Was it sold to you as a new or used *(merchandise)*?

New	8	28/7
Used	9	

13. Were you misinformed about the *(merchandise)* in any way at the time of the purchase or did they withhold any information which you think they should have told you, or did they deliver the wrong merchandise?

        Yes *(ask A)*   4 32/3
        No   (go to Q. 14)   5

   A. *If yes:* Did this concern price, quality, wrong merchandise, or something else?

        Price   *(go to C)*   1 33/0
        Quality   *(go to C)*   2
        Wrong merchandise *(go to C)*   3
        Something else *(ask B and C)*   4

   B. *If something else:* What?   34/0

14. About how often do you use the *(merchandise)?*

        Everyday   5
        Few times a week   6
        Once a week   7
        Less   8
        Never   9

15. In general, would you say you are satisfied or dissatisfied with the *(merchandise)?*

        Satisfied   1 38/0
        Dissatisfied   2

16. At the time you bought it, what did they tell you it would cost altogether—including carrying charges and insurance.

        $ _____   39-42/RRRR
        Did not say   ×

17. What did it actually cost altogether, including carrying charges and insurance?

        $ _____   43-46/RRRR
        Do not know   ×

18. Do you happen to know what the *cash* price would have been?

        Yes *(ask A and B)*   1 47/0
        No   *(go to Q. 19)*   2

   A. *If yes:* What?   48-51/RRRR

        $ _____

B. Were you told this price at the time you bought it?

Yes *(go to Q. 19)*   4 52/3
No *(ask C)*   5

C. *If no to B:* What did they say the cash price was?

$ _____   53-56/RRRR
Did not say   ×

19. Did you sign a contract when you bought the *(merchandise)*?

Yes *(ask A)*   1 57/0
No *(go to Q. 20)*   2

20. Did you receive a copy of the contract at the time you made the purchase, or in a few days, or a week or two later?

Time of purchase   5 60/4
Few days   6
Week or two later   7
Never received   8

22. Did you have to make a down payment?

Yes *(ask A)*   4 64/3
No *(go to Q. 23)*   5

A. *If yes:* How much?

% _____ or $ _____   65-66/RR

(Begin Deck 02)

For borrowers, ask Q's. 24–29; otherwise go to Q. 30.

24. What is the name of the company that you borrowed the money from?

_____ (Name) _____

25. Is that a bank, a loan company, a credit union, or what?

Bank   1 10/0
Loan company   2
Credit union   3
Other *(specify)*   4

27. Since you first borrowed money on this contract, have you ever gone back and borrowed more money under the same contract (refinance the loan)?

Yes *(ask A and B)*   4 12/3
No *(ask C)*   5

A. *If yes:* How many times have you refinanced this loan?

—————
(number) 13/0

B. How much did you borrow the last (most recent) time?

$ ———— 14-18/RRRRR

C. *If no:* How much money did you borrow?

$ ———— 14-18/RRRRR

28. What was your reason for borrowing the money (the last time)?

19/0

Ask everyone

30. At the time you (made the purchase/borrowed the money) did they ask you whether you had any other debts?

Yes 1 52/0
No 2

31. How many months did you have to pay off the *(merchandise) (loan)?*

———— 26-27/RRRR

32. How much were the payments supposed to be?

$ ———— per ———— 28-31/RRRR

In case of freezers, do not include payments for food.

33. Before you stopped paying altogether, were you ever behind on payments?

Yes 1 32/0
No 2
Never made payments *(skip to Q. 35)* 3

34. About how many payments did you make before you stopped paying?

———— 33-34/RR

35. About how much did you owe at the time you stopped paying?

$———— 35-39/RRRRR
Do not know ×

36. At the time you were paying this company, were you supposed to be making payments to anyone else?

Yes *(ask A and B)* 1 40/0
No *(go to Q. 37)* 2

A. *If yes:* What were you making payments on? *Enter below—ask B for each*

_____	41/0
_____	42/0
_____	43/0
_____	44/0

B. How much were these payments on the (item)?

$ _____ per _____
$ _____ per _____
$ _____ per _____
$ _____ per _____   45-48/RRRR

37. What were the main reasons why you stopped making payments on the (merchandise/loan)? *Record verbatim and field code (circle only one)*

Could not pay—no money	1	49/0
Would not pay—fraud, deception, etc.	2	
All other	3	

50-51/00

If credit purchase, ask Q. 38

If borrowers, skip to Q. 40

38. Do you still have the *(merchandise)*?

Yes *(skip to Q. 40)*	1
No *(go to Q. 39)*	2.

39. Has it been repossessed by the company?

Yes *(ask A–E)*	4 53/3
No *(ask G)*	5
Do not know *(ask G)*	6

A. *If yes:* When did they repossess the *(merchandise)*?

_____
(month) (year)   54-56/RRR

G. *If no or do not know to Q. 39:* What happened to the *(merchandise)*?

65/0

Now I'd like to find out what the company did to you when you fell behind on payments.

                                        do not
                            yes no *know*

40. Did they send you insulting letters?   1   2   -   66/0

41. Did anyone from the company call
you names or use bad language in
talking with you?   4   5   -   67/3

42. Did they call or threaten to call any
of your friends or relatives about this
debt?   7   8   9   68/6

43. Did they threaten to call (either) your
(or your husband's) employer about
this debt?   1   2   -   69/0

44. Did they *actually* call your (your
husband's) employer *before* they
sued you?   4   5   6   70/3

(Begin Deck 03)

45. How did you *first* find out that you were being *sued* because of this
debt?

        From summons   1   10/0
        Learned from employer   2
        Other   *(specify)*   3
        Not aware of suit   *(skip to Q. 47)*   4

46. When did you find out that you were being sued?

     _____
     (month) (year)   11-13/RRR

47. Did you get a summons telling you that you were being sued and to
go to court?

        (Show summons forms A and B in Chicago)
        (Show summons from B in New York)
        (Show summons from A and B in Detroit)

        Yes   1   14/0
        No   2

   A. *If yes:* Did you get this summons at your home or at your (your
husband's) place of work?

        Home   4   15/3
        Work   5

   B. Did someone give you the summons, did you get it in the mail,
did they leave it with someone else in your building, did they
slip it under your door, or what?

Personally served	1 16/0
Mail	2
Gave to someone else	3
Slipped under door	4
Other *(specify)*	5

C. When did you get this summons?

_____
(month) (year)   17-19/RRR

D. Did you or someone representing you go to court when you got the summons?

Yes *(go to Q. 48)*	1 20/0
No *(ask E)*	2

E. *If no to D:* Why didn't you go to court?

21/0

22-24/RRR

48. Did you or somebody on your behalf ever file any papers with the court telling your story about why you shouldn't have to pay?

Yes	1 25/0
No	2

49. Did your case ever go to trial before a judge?

Yes *(ask A)*	4 26/3
No *(go to Q. 50)*	5
Do not know *(go to Q. 50)*	6

A. *If yes:* What was the result of the trial? Did the company win the case, did you win the case, or was something worked out?

Company won *(skip to Q. 51)*	1 27/0
Respondent won *(skip to Q. 57)*	2
Something worked out *(ask B)*	3

B. *If something worked out:* How much did you have to pay?

$ _____   28-32/RRRRR

(Now skip to Q. 51)

50. Did you or someone on your behalf contact the company or its lawyer to try to settle this matter out of court?

Yes *(ask A)*	1 33/0
No *(go to Q. 51)*	2
Do not know *(go to Q. 51)*	3

A. *If yes:* Were you able to settle the matter?

Yes   *(ask B and C)*   4 34/3
No   *(go to Q. 51)*   5
Do not know   *(go to Q. 51)*   6

C.   *If yes to A:* Do you think the settlement was fair?

Yes   *(go to Q. 57)*   1 40/0
No   *(ask D)*   2

D.   *If no to C:* Why not?

(Now skip to Q. 57)   41-42/00

51. Do you think there was a *good* reason why you should not have had to pay this debt?

Yes   *(ask A)*   1 43/0
No   *(go to Q. 52)*   2

A.   *If yes:* What was that?   44-45/00

52. Because of this problem, did you have to go to court and answer questions about your financial situation and where you work?

Yes
No   *(go to instruction above Q. 53)*   1 46/0
                                                              2

Ask in New York and Detroit only. For Chicago go to Q. 54.

53. Did you get a notice from the court (that looked like this) telling you how much you would have to pay?

(In New York show Default Judgment, form C)
(In Detroit show Levitt Letter, form C)

Yes   1 48/0
No   2

54. About how much did the court papers say you would have to pay to clear up this debt?

$_____   49-53/RRRRR

57. Did the sheriff, a bailiff, or a city marshal take away any of your belongings because of this debt?

Yes   *(ask A)*   1 61/0
No   *(go to Q. 58)*   2

A.   *If yes:* What did he take?   62/0

58. Did you get a lawyer to help you with this debt problem?

Yes   *(ask A–G)*   1 63/0
No   *(ask H)*   2

A. *If yes:* Did you go to the lawyer before you got the summons, after you got the summons, or when?

    Before summons   4 64/3
    After summons   5
    Other *(specify)*   6

B. Was this lawyer in private practice or did he work for an organization?

    Private practice *(ask C)*   1 65/0
    Organization *(ask D and E)*   2

C. *If private practice in B:* How did you find the lawyer?

                                         66/0

D. *If organization in B:* Which organization?

    Legal Aid   1 67/0
    Other *(specify)*   2

(Begin Deck 04)

59. Who was the chief wage earner in this family at the time this trouble started?

    Respondent who is male   1 10/0
    Respondent who is female   2
    Husband of respondent   3
    Wife of respondent   4
    Other *(specify)*   5

Ask questions 60–69 about chief wage earner circled above.

60. Did you (Did the chief wage earner) have a job at the time you stopped paying?

    Yes *(go to Q. 61)*   7 11/6
    No *(ask A)*   8

A. *If no:* Have you had any jobs since then?

    Yes *(go to Q. 61)*   1 12/0
    No *(ask B)*   2

B. *If no to A:* Has this debt problem interfered in any way with your finding work?

    Yes *(skip to Q. 70)*   4 13/3
    No *(skip to Q. 70)*   5

61. Did you (Did the chief wage earner) ever lose or quit a job because of this particular debt problem?

Yes *(go to Q. 62)*	1 14/0
No *(skip to Q. 65)*	2

If lost or quit job, ask Q.'s 62–64; otherwise go to Q. 65.

62. Did you (Did the chief wage earner) lose or quit the job because your boss received a garnishment order telling him to make deductions from your pay, or did you lose it because the company contacted your boss about your debt problem, or for some other reason?

Garnishment order *(ask A—in New York only)*	4 15/3
Contact from the company *(go to Q. 63)*	5
Other reason *(specify and go to Q. 63)*	6

If garnishment circled above, ask A in New York only.

A. Did you (Did the chief wage earner) get a notice that looked like this *before* your employer was contacted telling you that if you didn't pay in 20 days your wages would be attached?
(Show income execution, form D)

Yes	1 16/0
No	2

Ask Q.'s 63 and 64 if chief wage earner lost or quit job.

63. A. During the time you were out of work, did you apply for unemployment insurance?

Yes *(ask B)*	4 17/3
No *(go to C)*	5

B. *If yes to A:* Did you receive unemployment benefits?

Yes *(ask C)*	1 18/0
No *(ask C)*	2

C. During the time you were out of work, did you apply for welfare?

Yes *(ask D)*	4 19/3
No *(go to Q. 64)*	5

D. *If yes to C:* Did you receive welfare?

Yes	1 20/0
No	2

64. Are you (Is the chief wage earner) employed now?

Yes *(ask A–D)*	4 21/3
No *(skip to Q. 69A)*	5

For those who did not lose job because of debt problem, ask Q.'s 65–68; otherwise skip to Q. 69.

65. Are you (Is the chief wage earner) employed now?

        Yes *(go to Q. 66)*   1   28/0
        No   *(skip to Q. 70)*   2

66. Has your employer ever received a garnishment order telling him to make deductions from your pay because of this order?

        Yes   4   29/3
        No   *(ask E)*   5

C. Has your employer made any deductions from your pay?

        Yes   1   33/0
        No   2˙

D. Did your employer tell you that you would lose your job if you didn't settle this debt?

        Yes *(go to Q. 67)*   4   34/3
        No   *(ask E)*   5

E. *If no:* Has the company contacted your boss in connection with this debt?

        Yes   1   35/0
        No   2
        Do not know   3

67. Have you lost any days of work because of this debt problem?

        Yes *(ask A)*   4   36/3
        No   *(go to Q. 68)*   5

A. *If yes:* How many?   37-38/RR

    ———————

68. Are you worried that you might lose your job because of this debt problem?

        Yes *(ask 69B)*   1   39/0
        No   *(ask 69B)*   2

69. A. *If lost or quit job:* Was the job that you lost or quit a government job, or was it a job in private industry?

    B. *If did not lose or quit job:* Is your job a government job, or do you work for private industry?

        Government job *(go to Q. 70)*   1   40/0
        Private industry *(ask C–F)*   2

    C. *If private industry:* How many people usually work for that firm?

Under 10	4	41/3
10–25	5	
26–100	6	
101–500	7	
500–1,000	8	
Over 1,000	9	

D. Does (Did) the company have a rule about the number of garnishments a worker could have before he (is/was) fired?

Yes *(ask E)*	1	42/0
No *(go to F)*	2	

E. *If yes:* What is the rule?

_____

43/R

Questions re wife's job: (If respondent is a woman not currently married and has already answered Q.'s 59–69—skip to Q. 75.)

70. Did your wife (you) have a job at the time you stopped paying?

Yes *(go to Q. 71)*	1	44/0
No *(ask A)*	2	
Not married then *(skip to Q. 75)*	3	

A. *If no:* Has she had any jobs since then?

Yes *(go to Q. 71)*	5	45/4
No *(skip to Q. 75)*	6	

71. Did your wife (you) lose a job because of this debt problem?

Yes *(skip to Q. 74)*	1	46/0
No *(go to Q. 72)*	2	

72. Was there ever an attempt made to attach or garnishee your wife's salary because of this debt problem?

(New York, ask A)	4	47/3
Yes *(Detroit and Chicago, ask B–D)*	5	
No *(go to Q. 73)*	6	

Now, just to finish up the technicalities regarding this problem, I want to review how it stands at this time.

75. (You may have already told me this, but . . .) Have you paid off the debt?

Yes *(ask A)*	8	56/7
No *(ask B)*	9	

A. *If yes:* Where did you get the money to do this? *(Field Code)*

New commercial loan	1 57/0
Friends or relatives	2
Extra job	3
Sold something (What? _____)	4
Wage assignments, garnishments	5
Bankruptcy	6
Other *(specify)*	7
(go to Q. 76)	

B. *If no:* Are you now making regular payments on the debt?

Yes	1 58/0
No *(ask E)*	2

E. *If no to B:* How does the matter stand now? *(Probe, if necessary: How do you think it will work out?)*

77. Were you or your wife (husband) ever told by an employer that you would lose your job if you didn't pay off the debt?

Yes	1 66/0
No	2

If you don't mind, I'd like to ask you some questions about your health.

(Begin Deck 05)

78. In the last month or so . . .

		yes [ask (1)]	no (go to next item)	*(1) if yes:* Do you usually have this problem or is it a recent one? usual recent	
A.	Have you had any difficulty sleeping?	1	2 10/0	4 5	11/3
B.	Have you been feeling tense and nervous?	7	8 12/6	1 2	13/0
C.	Have you had upset stomach?	4	5 14/3	7 8	15/6
D.	Have you had headaches?	1	2 16/0	4 5	17/3
E.	Have you had any loss of appetite?	7	8 18/6	1 2	19/0
		7	8 18/6	1 2	19/0

79. In general, do you think your debt troubles have had any effect on your health?

> Yes *(ask A and B)* — 1 20/0
> No *(go to Q. 80)* — 2

B. *If yes:* Have you gone to a doctor about this problem?

> Yes — 1 22/0
> No — 2

80. Did your debt troubles lead to any quarrels with your wife (husband)?

> Yes — 4 23/3
> No — 5
> Never married *(skip to Q. 84)* — 6

81. Did this debt trouble lead to your getting separated or divorced?

> Yes, separated or divorced *(skip to Q. 83)* — 1 24/0
> No, no change in marital status *(go to Q. 82)* — 2

		yes	no	
84.	Have you had to cut down on what you spend for food since your debt troubles began?	1	2	31/0
85.	Have you had to put off any medical care that you or your family need since your debt troubles started?	4	5	32/3
86.	Have you had to put off any dental care that you or your family otherwise would have gotten since your debt troubles started?	1	2	33/0
87.	Have you cut down on your social activities since your debt trouble started?	4	5	34/3

90. Have you ever gone into bankruptcy?

> Yes *(ask A)* — 1 39/0
> No *(ask B)* — 2

A. *If yes:* When did you go into bankruptcy?

> _____
> (month) (year) — 40-41/RR

B. *If no:* Are you now thinking about bankruptcy?

> Yes *(ask C)* — 4 42/3
> No — 5

C. *If yes to B:* What have you done about it?

> 43/0

92. When you consider all the money that you now owe to different places and people, such as stores, loan companies, and doctors—how much money would you need to pay off all your debts (not including mortgages)?

$ _____   45-49/RRRRR

130. Do you or your wife (husband) have a savings account at a bank or at a credit union?

Yes   1 48/0
No   2

131. Does your family now have $500 or more in savings (in any form)?

Yes *(go to Q. 132)*   4 49/3
No *(ask A)*   5

A. *If no:* Do you have $100 or more in savings?

Yes   7 50/6
No   8
                                                            7

139. Do you or your wife (husband) belong to a labor union?   8

Yes   1 58/0
No   2

Now, just a few more questions and we'll be through.

(Begin Deck 08)

146. How many people are living in this household now?   8-9/RR

_____

(1) *Composition of Family*

Single-person household   1 10/0
Married couple, no children   2
Married couple, children   3
Broken family, female head   4
Broken family, male head   5

(2) *Other Adults*

Yes   7 11/6
No   8

148. Does your family income right now come from earnings, welfare, social security, or what? *(Code all that apply.)*

Earnings *(go to Q. 149)*   1 12/0
Unemployment benefits *(go to Q. 149)*   2
Welfare *(ask A)*   3
Social Security *(skip to Q. 153)*   4
Other *(specify)* *(go to Q. 149)*   5

A. *If welfare:* How long have you been on welfare?   13/0

_____

(Now skip to Q. 154)

If only welfare, skip to Q. 154.

If only social security, skip to Q. 153.

If both welfare *and* social security, *skip to Q. 154.*

149. What kind of work (do you/does the chief wage earner) (usually) do? *(Use "usually" if currently unemployed.)*

      Occupation: _____   14-16/RRR
      [*Probe, if vague:* What do you (does
      he) actually do in that job?]

If employed, continue with Q. 150; if unemployed, skip to instruction before Q. 152.

150. How many different jobs do you (does the chief wage earner) now have?

      One   1 20/0
      Two   2
      Three   3

If not married, go to Q. 153.

152. Does you wife (Do you) now have a job?

      Yes   *(ask A–B)*   1 23/0
      No   *(go to Q. 153)*   2

153. Have you or your family ever been on welfare?

      Yes   *(ask A)*   1 32/0
      No   *(go to Q. 154)*   2

A. *If yes:* When was that?

155. What was your age at your last birthday?
    Your wife (husband)?   36-37/RR

_____

156. What was the last grade of school that you completed? What about your wife (husband)?

      Elementary school or less   1 50/0
      Some high school   2
      High school graduate   3
      Some college   4
      College graduate   5

164. *(Hand respondent income card.)* In which category was your total family income in 1966 before taxes?

INDEX